Caribbean Currents

Caribbean Currents

Caribbean Music from Rumba to Reggae

REVISED AND EXPANDED EDITION

PETER MANUEL

with

KENNETH BILBY *and* MICHAEL LARGEY

TEMPLE UNIVERSITY PRESS
Philadelphia

OCM60796276

Temple University Press
1601 North Broad Street
Philadelphia PA 19122
www.temple.edu/tempress

⊗ The paper used in this publication meets the requirements of the
American National Standard for Information Sciences—Permanence of Paper
for Printed Library Materials, ANSI Z39.48-1992

Library of Congress Cataloging-in-Publication Data

Manuel, Peter Lamarche.
Caribbean currents : Caribbean music from rumba to reggae / Peter Manuel
with Kenneth Bilby and Michael Largey. — Rev. and expanded ed.
p. cm.
Includes bibliographical references (p.) and index.
Contents: Introduction : The Caribbean crucible—Cuba—Puerto Rico—Salsa and
beyond—The Dominican Republic—Haiti and the French
Caribbean—Jamaica—Trinidad, calypso, and carnival—East Indian music and big
sounds from the "small islands"—Five themes in the study of Caribbean music.
ISBN 1-59213-462-9 (cloth : alk. paper)—ISBN 1-59213-463-7 (pbk. : alk. paper)
1. Music—West Indies—History and criticism.   2. Music—Caribbean
Area—History and criticism.   I. Bilby, Kenneth M., 1953–.   II. Largey, Michael
D., 1959–.   III. Title.

ML3565.M36   2006
780′.9729—dc22   2005050676

2 4 6 8 9 7 5 3 1

Contents

Preface to the Second Edition

This book arose originally out of a simple necessity that two of the authors encountered in trying to assemble readings for their overflowing Caribbean music classes. The amount of English-language academic literature on Caribbean music is growing, but most of it is, in one way or another, unsuitable for the general reader or for college students. Journalistic articles and websites on the region's pop music also abound, but they are scattered in a thousand sources and represent nearly as many perspectives and topics. Clearly, a need has existed for a readable guide to Caribbean music oriented toward a broad audience.

A more fundamental need, of course, is for greater knowledge of Caribbean music and culture in general, both in the United States and in the Caribbean itself. Caribbean immigrant communities now constitute significant and dynamic parts of North American society, making up, for example, well over a third of the population of New York City. Urban neighborhoods throb to the pulse of Caribbean music, and Caribbean stores and products have become familiar and colorful parts of urban America's cosmopolitan landscape. As the U.S. government and economy continue to dominate the Caribbean, the two regions have become more closely intertwined than ever.

This book is oriented toward a few distinct yet overlapping sets of readers. One group includes the music lover who has taken a fancy to some kind of Caribbean music and wants to know more about the background of that style and about the region's music as a whole. Another set includes the student of Caribbean society, or of pan-American society in general, who seeks an introduction to this most dynamic aspect of our hemisphere's culture. Last, but not least, are readers of Caribbean descent, increasing numbers of whom now populate college classes. Many such students love their own culture's music and are proud of their ethnic identity but know woefully little of their musical heritage beyond the current hit parade. Ignorance of other local Caribbean cultures is even greater, inhibiting the formation of pan-regional alliances and contributing to the perseverance of rivalries and stereotypes. North American universities are only beginning to rectify this situation. Even in a Caribbean cauldron like New York City, very few colleges have made any effort to recognize the musical cultures of their immigrant populations, whether out of a Euro-American ethnocentric disdain or because of a lack of qualified teachers and suitable course materials.

Caribbean Currents attempts to address this need, providing a readable and informative overview of Caribbean music for the student and general reader. This book does not pretend to be an original scholarly monograph, although it does contain much new information, especially on recent developments that are only beginning to be documented in print. Similarly, it does not attempt to be a comprehensive reference book for Caribbean music, for such a volume would have to be several times the size of this one. Instead, we have chosen to circumscribe the book's scope. For one thing, we have adopted the relatively narrow rather than the broad conception of the "Caribbean Basin," excluding, for example, the musics of coastal Venezuela, Central America, and Mexico, however interesting they may be. Further, even within such limits, we have tried to highlight the most important and representative aspects of each musical culture rather than attempted to include all possible genres and subcategories. As a result, the range of subjects not adequately covered is considerable, from Cuban *criolla* to Jamaican *benta* music. But, as our title promises, rumba and reggae are definitely present, as are many other genres, and they are given more thorough treatment than could be provided in a sketchy survey that tried to mention everything. To the Cubanophile interested in *abakuá* chants or the Tortola immigrant wishing to learn more about her island's *funji* music, we offer our apologies—and a set of recommended readings.

As for the authorship of this book, Ken Bilby wrote the first sections of chapter 7 (up to pp. 191–93), and Michael Largey wrote chapter 6. Peter Manuel wrote and takes sole responsibility for the remainder.

Production of a second edition of this book has seemed appropriate for several reasons. The first edition, printed in 1995, clearly served some purpose, as it sold well among both college students and lay readers and received the Annual Best Book Prize from the Caribbean Studies Association. However, that edition was clearly in need of updating if it were not to be consigned to the dustbin. In the decade that has elapsed since 1995, there have been a number of dramatic developments in Caribbean music, from the flowering of reggaetón and timba to the mainstreaming of Dominican bachata, not to mention the emergence of an entire new generation of performers. The sheer amount of accessible information on Caribbean music has also increased phenomenally, both on the Internet and in publications of Gage Averill, Robin Moore, Norman Stolzoff, Ned Sublette, Chris Washburne, and others.

This new edition also embodies some editorial changes. The Jamaica chapter has been substantially rewritten, with Ken Bilby's treatment of Afro-Jamaican traditions and ska supplemented by a greatly expanded discussion of the reggae and dancehall scenes (written mostly by myself). The Cuba chapter has also been much revised, especially to draw on recent developments and new literature regarding the Revolutionary period. In place of Bilby's ground-breaking but geographically peripheral section on Suriname, a new subchapter on the music of smaller islands has been added. The text is also adorned with several new illustrations. However, due to permissions issues, some illustrations in the first edition (along with some extended song lyrics) have had to be deleted. Similarly, the inclusion of some charcoal adaptations of photos, drawn by myself, is intended less to highlight my artistic talent, which is in any case unimpressive, than to avoid copyright complications. Finally, I have corrected various minor errors of fact that reviewers of the first edition were kind enough, as it were, to point out—as well as a few they did not spot. In fact, the entire new edition is laden with miscellaneous new material and reworkings of the old, reflecting my ongoing education in the field.

Given the rapidity with which Caribbean music evolves and new information on it appears, it may be inevitable that yet another edition of this book will be needed in ten years. In the meantime, however, the authors believe that the need for a book of this nature is stronger than ever and that this edition will prove even more useful and satisfactory than the first.

In writing this book I have drawn heavily from the earlier work of such writers as Leonardo Acosta, Alejo Carpentier, Juan Flores, Donald Hill, Argeliers León, Gordon Lewis, Fernando Ortiz, John Storm Roberts, Gordon Rohlehr, and, among the younger generations of writers, Paul Austerlitz, Hal Barton, David Garcia, Frank Korom, Ben Lapidus, Robin Moore, Deborah Pacini, Roberta Singer, Ned Sublette, Steven Steumpfle, Sue Steward, Chris Washburne, and Lise Waxer, to name but a few. Journalistic articles by Daisane McClaine, Enrique Fernandez, Gene Scaramuzzo, and others have also been useful, and I am indebted to them not only for their information content but for more than one felicitous turn of phrase that I have borrowed.

More specific thanks are due to the many individuals and institutions that have assisted me in completing this volume. Delfín Pérez and Chris Washburne have been invaluable Latin music gurus in this project, as in previous ones. Edgardo Díaz Díaz provided helpful comments on chapter 3. With regard to the researching of Indo-Caribbean music, I must mention Jeevan Chowtie, who guided me through Guyana, and such informants as Moean

Mohammad, Mangal Patasar, Kries Ramkhelawan, and Rudy Sasenarine. I have also been fortunate to have another set of excellent informants in my many Caribbean students at John Jay College, who have been of great help in keeping me in touch with current developments and in providing their own perspectives on music. I have also learned much from my students at the City University of New York Graduate Center, especially Ejima Baker, Lázaro Pujol, Angelina Tallaj, and others already mentioned. In collecting photographs for the volume, thanks are due to the Ethnic Folk Arts Center, Roberta Singer of City Lore, Chantal Regnault, Lois Wilcken, John Amira, Sydney Hutchinson, and Sandra Levinson of the Center for Cuban Studies. Don Hill was of particular assistance in guiding me through the treacherous world of copyright permissions. Gratitude is also due to Sophia Manuel for trying to teach me how to draw with charcoal, to Liliana for keeping me up on the latest reggaetón and R&B hits, and to Beth for letting me neglect domestic duties to undertake Caribbean research trips (which mostly consisted of various sorts of "liming"). Thanks are also extended on behalf of Michael Largey to Gage Averill, Lolo Beaubrun, and Allison Berg, and on behalf of Ken Bilby to Jake Homink, Dermott Hussey, and George Eaton Simpson. Finally, I thank Susan Deeks for her fine copy editing.

—*Peter Manuel*

The Caribbean at a Glance
(Country, Capital, 2004 Country Population)

THE DUTCH CARIBBEAN

Netherlands Antilles (Aruba, Bonaire, Curaçao, Saba, St. Eustatius, St. Maarten) (Neth.): Willemstad; pop. 218,126.
Suriname: Paramaribo; pop. 436,935 (31 percent African, 37 percent East Indian, 15 percent Javanese).

THE ENGLISH-SPEAKING CARIBBEAN

Anguilla (U.K.): The Valley; pop. 13,000.
Antigua and Barbuda: St. John; pop. 68,320.
Bahamas: Nassau; pop. 299,697.
Barbados: Bridgetown; pop. 278,289.
British Virgin Islands (U.K.): Road Town; pop. 22,187.
Cayman Islands: George Town; pop. 43,103.
Dominica: Roseau; pop. 69,278. English and French creole spoken.
Grenada: St. George; pop. 89,357.
Guyana: Georgetown; pop. 705,803 (30 percent African, 51 percent East Indian, 14 percent mixed).
Jamaica: Kingston; pop. 2,713,130.
Montserrat (U.K.); pop. 9245.
St. Kitts-Nevis: Basseterre; pop. 38,836.
St. Lucia: Castries; pop. 164,213. English and French creole spoken.
St. Vincent and the Grenadines: Kingstown; pop. 117,193.
Trinidad and Tobago: Port of Spain; pop. 1,096,585 (43 percent African, 40 percent East Indian, 14 percent mixed).
Turks and Caicos Islands (U.K.): Grand Turk; pop. 19,956.

Map by the Center for Cartographic Research and Spatial Analysis,
Michigan State University

U.S. Virgin Islands (St. Croix, St. John, St. Thomas) (U.S.): Charlotte
  Amalie; pop. 108,775.

THE FRENCH CARIBBEAN

Guadeloupe (France): Basse-Terre; pop. 444,515.
Haiti: Port-au-Prince; pop. 7,656,165.
Martinique (France): Fort-de-France; pop. 429,510.

THE SPANISH CARIBBEAN

Cuba: Havana; pop. 11,308,764.
The Dominican Republic: Santo Domingo; pop. 8,833,634.
Puerto Rico (U.S.): San Juan; pop. 3,897,960

1

Introduction: The Caribbean Crucible

The global impact of Caribbean music constitutes something of an enigma in world culture. How could music styles of such transnational popularity and influence be fashioned by a population numbering well under 1 percent of the world's peoples, scattered in an archipelago, and quite lacking in economic and political power? How is it that reggae, emanating from small and impoverished Jamaica, can resound and be actively cultivated everywhere from Hawaii to Malawi? Why should it be Cuba that produces the style that comes to dominate much of African urban music in the mid-twentieth century? Or, to go farther back in time, what made the Caribbean Basin so dynamic that its Afro-Latin music and dance forms like the *sarabanda* and *chacona* could take Spain by storm in the decades around 1600 and go on to enliven Baroque music and dance in Western Europe?

This book, alas, does not propose to answer these questions, although a few tentative hypotheses might be suggested. On a metaphorical level, the Caribbean has been likened to a fuse that connects the Old Worlds—Europe and perhaps especially Africa—to the New World, and with so much energy and intensity passing through it, that fuse gets very, very hot, with a heat that generates music of extraordinary expressivity. Perhaps somewhat more tangibly, the Caribbean, like certain other parts of the New World, constituted a site where those two dynamic Old World music cultures met and interacted in ways that would otherwise not have happened. Much of the richness of these original music cultures was lost in crossing the Atlantic, but much was retained. And in the crucible of the Caribbean—with its particular combination of white political power and black demographic power, and of insular isolation and maritime cross-fertilizations—these musical elements simmered, effervesced, and eventually bubbled over, enriching the world around with the unique vitality of the mambo and the merengue.

1

There are other senses in which Caribbean vernacular musics evolved as quintessentially suited to modernity and global appeal. Some have argued that the cultural encounter enabled African-derived musics to replenish the warm sensuality that centuries of Christianity had repressed in Europe, making Caribbean and Afro-American musics ideally suited to a distinctively *modern* aesthetic and social worldview at last liberated from such inhibitions. Others, as we suggest later, have contended that the uniquely modern and expressive power of Caribbean musics has derived from their inherently creole nature, as the product of people at once liberated from Old World traditions but able to draw on them, and having a heightened self-consciousness as being part of mainstream Western culture and, at the same time, on its margins.

Some of the vitality of Caribbean music seems to derive from its importance within Caribbean society and the sheer amount of attention and creative energy it commands. Caribbeans are well aware of the international prominence of their music, and they accord it a preeminent symbolic status at home. It is not merely that in Cuba a timba singer can earn thousands of dollars a month while a doctor earns only $20, or that legions of young Jamaican men dream of being a dancehall deejay, with a Benz, a gold chain, and a "truckload of girls." Jamaicans are well aware that artists like Bob Marley and Buju Banton are famous throughout much of the world—certainly more so than their political leaders. We can also well imagine the incommensurate renown that a Kevin Little enjoys in little St. Vincent when he produces a platinum-selling hit such as "Turn Me On." Likewise, in Trinidad calypso not only spreads news; it *is* the news, with politicians, journalists, and other public figures endlessly debating and denouncing the latest songs. Indeed, when Muslim militant Abu Bakr attempted to seize power in a 1990 coup, one of his first acts was to set up an all-calypso radio station. Music, in a word, is the most visible, popular, and dynamic aspect of Caribbean expressive culture.

As styles like reggae and Cuban dance music achieve international popularity, they become part of world cultural history as well as that of the Caribbean. Ultimately, Caribbean music can scarcely be compartmentalized as a local, regional entity when some 5 million people of Caribbean descent populate the cities of North America and Great Britain, and when the world is united as never before by the mass media and international capital. In a global village where Sri Lankan schoolboys sing Bob Marley tunes, Hawaiian cowboys sing Puerto Rican *aguinaldos*, Congolese bands play mambos, and Vietnamese urbanites dance the bolero, Caribbean music has truly become world music and, in its own way, world history, as well.

THE INDIAN HERITAGE

The prehistory of Caribbean music begins with the culture of the region's first inhabitants, the Amerindians, whose fifteenth-century population historians have estimated, not very helpfully, at somewhere between 250,000 and 6 million. The currently favored guess is about half a million, with the largest concentration on the island now called Hispaniola. The Ciboneys of Cuba had been in the region the longest but became outnumbered by other groups, especially the more advanced Taino Arawaks and, in the Lesser Antilles, the supposedly warlike Caribs. Because of the presence of these Indians, it may be better to speak not of a "discovery" of the region by Europeans but of the encounter of two cultures, although the actual period of cultural interaction lasted little more than a century, by which time most Indians had perished. Nevertheless, any historical account of Caribbean music and culture must commence with the practices of the Amerindians, as described by the Spanish.

Indigenous Caribbean music centered on a socioreligious ceremony called *areito*, in which as many as 1,000 participants danced in concentric circles around a group of musicians. The musicians sang mythological chants in call-and-response style, playing rattles (later called maracas), gourd scrapers (*güiros*), and slit drums called *mayohuacán*. These last were hollowed logs with H-shaped tongues cut into them. Although most scholars think the Indians of the Caribbean originally came from what is now Venezuela, the use of slit drums suggests some affinity with Aztecs and other Mexican Indian groups, who played similar instruments called *teponaztli*. The absence of mammals bigger than rodents prevented the making of drums with skin heads.

The Spaniards, far from bringing progress and civilization to their Caribbean subjects, enslaved and effectively exterminated them. The Indians were forced to work in mines, while Spanish pigs overran their crops. Those who did not perish from starvation, disease, or forced labor were killed outright or committed mass suicide. Christopher Columbus himself set the tenor, presiding over the death of a third of the population of Hispaniola during his sixteen-month governorship (1496–97). By 1600, the Caribbean Indians had on the whole passed into history, taking their music with them. Today they and their language survive only in a few villages in Dominica and in the form of the African-intermixed "Black Caribs," or Garifuna, of St. Vincent, later exiled to Honduras and Belize. To fill the need for labor, the colonists had to turn to slaves from Africa; as Trinidad's Prime Minister Eric Williams put it, the Europeans used negroes they stole from Africa to work the land they stole from the Indians.

Taino dancers in Hispaniola, as portrayed by the seventeenth-century artist R. P. Labat

To a certain extent, early colonial-era culture emerged as a mixture of European, African, and Amerindian traditions. The still popular Cuban cult of the Virgen de la Caridad del Cobre, for instance, mixes elements of the worship of the Taino god Atabey, the Yoruba deity Oshún, and the European Virgin of Illescas. On the whole, however, little remains of Indian culture except for place names, foods, and words like "hammock," "manatee," "yucca," "hurricane," and "tobacco"—the last surviving as the Indians' parting gift (or retributive curse) to the world. But if Indian culture and music are largely lost, the Indian past has continued to be invoked as a symbol for various purposes. Still celebrated in Cuba are the names of the Arawak princess Anacaona and the chieftain Hatuey for their valiant struggle against the Spaniards. Puerto Ricans still use the Taino name for their island, Borikén, as a symbol of independence, which lives on as a memory and a goal. In other contexts, a mythical Indian heritage has often been asserted as a way to deny the reality of the region's African heritage. Thus, obscurantist folklorists such as Cuba's Eduardo Sánchez de Fuentes have tried to argue—in a musical equivalent of the flat-earth theory–that their country's music derived mostly from an

Taino dancers as imagined, perhaps more accurately, by a modern artist (adapted by Peter Manuel from O. J. Cardoso and M. García, *Los Indocubanas* [Havana, 1982])

admixture of Hispanic elements with those of the Tainos, rather than of the Yorubas and Bantus. Even some blacks and mulattos have tried to deny their own ancestry—for instance, in the Dominican Republic, where a negrophobic ideology has led many to refer to themselves euphemistically as *indios* or *indios oscuros* (dark-skinned Indians).

If the Amerindian heritage has played little role in post-Columbian music, then we must look elsewhere for the roots of most Caribbean music—specifically, in the musical cultures of Europe and Africa.

THE AFRICAN HERITAGE

The Caribbean is host to a variety of ethnic groups, including East Indians, Chinese, Syrians, and Caucasian Europeans. However, throughout the region, descendants of the 4 million or 5 million enslaved Africans brought by the colonists are a common denominator. In islands such as Haiti, they constitute nearly the entire population, while even in the more Caucasian Puerto Rico, black communities have exerted a musical influence quite incommensurate with their size. Moreover, just as Afro-American musics and their derivatives, like rock, came to pervade world culture in the twentieth century, so have the African-derived elements in Caribbean music provided much of what has distinguished it and made it internationally famous. Afro-Caribbeans, like Caribbean people as a whole, have traditionally been divided not only by insular geography but also by language and the political fragmentation of colonialism. At the same time, however, they have shared the general experiences of slavery, the cultural uprooting it entailed, and the direct roles of creating a set of new, creolized cultures.

For the past two centuries, scholars (and pseudo-scholars) have argued about the degree to which black communities in the Caribbean and the United States have been able to retain elements of their traditional African cultural roots. A traditional white view had been that Africa had little particular culture to begin with, and that the slaves had lost touch with that, as well. Anthropologist Melville Herskovits challenged this conception in *The Myth of the Negro Past* (1941), and in his wake scholars have devoted many volumes to documenting or claiming the existence of African-derived elements in modern Afro-American and Afro-Caribbean cultures. Such writing has also criticized the tendency to regard slaves as passive victims of circumstance, instead stressing the ways in which slaves and free blacks fashioned their own culture—"the world the slaves made," as the subtitle reads in the historian Eugene Genovese's influential *Roll, Jordan, Roll* (1974). In recent decades, the scholarly pendulum may have swung a bit too far in the direction of emphasizing the ability of slaves to retain and construct their own cultures. Further, within the Caribbean itself, the degree to which diverse black communities were able to retain African traditions has varied considerably from place to place.

Regional variation notwithstanding, there are many specific features of Caribbean music that can be traced directly to Africa. Such correlations are particularly evident in religious musics, which tend throughout the world to be more conservative than secular musics, preserving archaic features. Thus, in music associated with Afro-Caribbean religions like Cuban Santería and Haitian Vodou, one finds song texts in West African languages and a few actual songs that are still sung in Africa. Some music traditions can be regarded as "neo-African" in the sense that they reflect little Euro-American influence, although they may have changed and evolved in the Caribbean in ways that make them different from anything in Africa. Much research remains to be done in tracing the direct music correlations between Africa and the Caribbean, and the links are increasingly obscured as traditions die out or change on both sides of the Atlantic. In particular, Christianity in Africa—whether imposed by European colonial rulers or by modern evangelists—has eroded many of the local religious practices that in the colonial period provided the sources for New World entities such as Santería.

Perhaps the most conspicuous sorts of Africanisms evident in Caribbean music consist more of general principles than specific elements. Slave communities usually combined people from different African regions and ethnic groups, whose musical traditions tended to blend accordingly. Interaction with European musics further diluted the original African practices, as did the relative cessation of contact with Africa after the slave trade stopped. Moreover, Afro-Caribbean musicians have always applied their own creativity to their art, so that the music has tended to take on its own life, departing from its original, transplanted forms. Given these conditions and the diversity of sub-Saharan music itself, it is often better to speak of general than of particular elements of African music that survived the infamous Middle Passage and the cultural repression of the slave period.

During the colonial era, as now, sub-Saharan Africa was home to hundreds of ethnic groups with different languages and social structures, ranging from simple hunter-gatherer Pygmy clans to more elaborate societies like the Yoruba, with substantial towns, trade networks, and specialized occupation groups. Although African music is similarly diverse, it is possible to speak of a set of general features that are common throughout most of the continent (excluding the culturally Arab and Berber north) and that continue to pervade Afro-Caribbean and Afro-American musics.

One sociomusical characteristic of much African music is *collective participation*, a feature typical of many classless societies lacking occupational distinctions between performers and consumers. Soloists and specialists do play roles in Africa, but it is extremely common for all or most members of a rural community to participate actively in musical events, whether by singing, clapping, dancing, or playing instruments. This convention accompanies a conception of musical talent as something innate, albeit in different degrees, in everyone, rather than being the property only of specialists. Likewise, collective participation, starting as early as the baby bound to its dancing mother's back, tends to promote the cultivation and development of musical talent to a greater degree than in more stratified societies. The persistence of communal music-making in the New World has naturally been dependent on social structure as a whole, but it has been perpetuated by the fact that most Afro-Caribbeans have tended to occupy the same social classes—that is, the lower ones.

In the realm of more distinctly musical features, the most often noted feature of African music is its *emphasis on rhythm*. African music is rich in melody, timbral variety, and even two- and three-part harmony, but rhythm is often the most important aesthetic parameter, distinguishing songs and genres and commanding the focus of the performers' and listeners' attention. Accordingly, the rhythms of African and Afro-Caribbean traditional music are often formidably complex in ways that lack any counterparts in Western folk or common-practice classical music. Much of the rhythmic interest and complexity derives from the interaction of regular pulses (whether silent or audible) and offbeat accents. This feature is often described as "syncopation," but that term is vague and problematic, as is, indeed, the notion of a single, regular pulse in the multiple, distinct layers of much African ensemble music.

When two or more regular pulse patterns are combined, the result is what musicologists call polyrhythm or polymeter, which is a common kind of West and Central African rhythmic organization. Polyrhythm is most typically performed by an ensemble, in which a "cell" consisting of twelve beats is divided by different instrumental patterns into groups of twos and threes (a division not so possible with the four- or eight-beat meters that pervade most contemporary North American and Caribbean pop music). Often a "time line" played on an iron bell provides a referential pattern.

Playing a Polyrhythm

The schematic example in Musical Example 1 shows a simplified polyrhythm, using the so-called standard time line, that is common throughout West and Central Africa as well as in neo-African religious musics in Cuba, Haiti, and Brazil. For those who do not read Western notation, the equivalents are given both in staff and in what is called TUBS (time-unit boxes) notation, in which each box represents a regular pulse unit (of which there are twelve, in this case).

You can try tapping twelve regular beats with your left hand and tapping the time line with your right, repeating the pattern without pause. The next step is to add the subsidiary parts, one of which divides the twelve beats into groups of twos and the other into groups of threes. Once you get the feel of the time line, try tapping that with one hand and tapping the twos with the other. (This can be challenging for musicians as well as non-musicians.) Then try combining the time line with the threes (which is even harder for most people). We do not yet have a polyrhythm. But if you get a

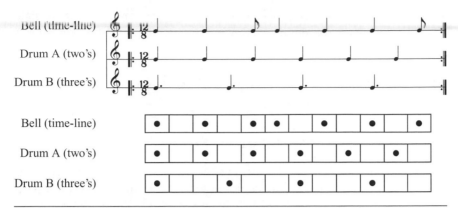

Musical Example 1. A basic polyrhythm

friend to help out, you can put together the time line, the twos, and the threes, and the result is a polyrhythm, in which duple and triple pulses, or meters, are combined with the time line.

In a typical West African or similar Afro-Caribbean ensemble, the accompanying drum parts would be more interesting than simple reiterations of two- or three-beat pulses. For example, in the Ghanaian *agbadza* rhythm, which uses the standard time-line, the *kidi* drum establishes the duple pulse with the following rhythm, alternating muted ("x") with open ("X") strokes:

x X X X x x x X X X x x

A few more distinct, interlocking accompanying parts—played on drums and shakers—complete the composite *agbadza* rhythm, which would then be supplemented by singing and dancing. The dancing itself might stress either the duple or the triple pulse, or in some cases, one's feet are moving to one pulse and one's shoulders to the other. The result is uniquely expressive and rewarding for listeners and performers. From the aesthetic point of view, the individual polyrhythmic cell is interesting enough that one does not mind hearing it repeated again and again, especially when combined with a varying vocal part or with improvisation by a master drummer.

Another widespread feature of African music is vocal *call and response*, which is well suited to communal performance in general. It is also found in many types of Afro-Caribbean music. A related characteristic is the technique of building a piece on *repetition*, especially of a short musical cell, or *ostinato*. Variety can be provided by altering the pattern or by combining it with another feature, such as a narrative text, responsorial singing, or a drum solo. This way of structuring pieces pervades Afro-American as well as Afro-Caribbean music, including countless rock, R&B, and rap songs based on a repeated riff, especially in the accompaniment parts. Pieces using this format are open-ended, additive entities, loosely expandable or compressible in accordance with the desires of the performers, the audience, or the occasion. This sort of structure contrasts with that of most European-derived music—from sonatas to Frank Sinatra ballads—in which a song or piece has a finite, symmetrical structure, such as the thirty-two-bar AABA form typical of American popular song.

PATTERNS OF MUSICAL RETENTION

The sort of classic polyrhythm shown in Musical Example 1, although common in Afro-Cuban and Haitian religious music, is unusual in most Caribbean creole and popular music forms. These generally use simpler rhythms, although they are often animated by syncopations and cross-rhythms influenced, however indirectly, by older polyrhythmic forms. The degree to which neo-African traits like polyrhythms are retained in contemporary musics depends on various factors and raises broad questions about the relative ability of Afro-Caribbean communities in different regions to maintain cultural autonomy over the generations. Why, for example, are polyrhythms and neo-African musics common in Haiti, with its population of only 6 million, when such features have long since disappeared from the music of the much larger Afro-American population of the United States, which now numbers some 30 million? Why are such musics so strong in Cuba, with its large white population, and far less common in overwhelmingly black Jamaica? Why do we find certain African-derived features in one part of the Caribbean and other features elsewhere?

Many factors are involved in answering such questions, which have engaged the interest of scholars for decades. We can start with the last question, which is in some respects the simplest. Although most slave communities combined people of diverse ethnic origins, in certain regions slaves from one distinct area of Africa predominated. For example, in the early 1800s, the collapse of the great Yoruba kingdom led to that people's subjugation by the Dahomey and other rival groups, who sold many Yoruba as slaves to the Europeans. The British, however, had withdrawn from the slave trade by this time; as a result, the tens of thousands of captured Yoruba went primarily to Iberian-ruled Cuba and Brazil, whose imports continued through the 1860s. Accordingly, Yoruba-derived music and religion are much more prominent in these countries than in the former British colonies or in Haiti, whose own slave imports ended with the Haitian Revolution in the 1790s. In this way also, the cultural heritages of Akan and Congolese slaves, from the Gold Coast and Central Africa, respectively, are more influential in Jamaica.

A more problematic issue is whether the different policies and attitudes of individual colonial powers allowed for different degrees of African cultural retention. This question overlaps with a hypothesis, first argued in the 1940s by historian Frank Tannenbaum, that slavery in the Roman Catholic colonies—especially those of Spain and Portugal—was milder than in the British and Dutch colonies. This "Tannenbaum thesis" has been rehashed and re-bashed by subsequent scholars. Critics have pointed out that there are several criteria by which the severity of slavery should be measured. In terms of diet, longevity, and reproduction rates, for example, the North American slaves seem to have fared considerably better than Caribbean and Brazilian ones. In other respects, however, practices and attitudes in the Iberian and, to some extent, the French colonies may have favored greater degrees of cultural autonomy for blacks. For one thing, it was much easier for slaves in Spanish and French colonies to buy their own freedom (manumission) than it was in North America, and slaveowners were much more likely to free their mulatto children. The large communities of free blacks in Cuba and elsewhere were able to form socioreligious clubs (*cabildos*) and maintain considerable cultural independence, including traditional musical practices.

Of greater relevance to the study of music than matters of diet and the like is the argument that the Iberian and French colonists may have been culturally more tolerant of neo-African practices than were the northern European slaveowners. Counter-Reformation Iberian Catholicism, with its elements of saint worship, ritual, and folk beliefs, blended more easily with African religions than did Enlightenment-oriented, spiritual, and inflexible Protestantism. The early Spanish and Portuguese colonists, unlike the bourgeois, more economically advanced English, were in some ways premodern, precapitalist peoples who, however racist in their own way, seem to have recognized Africans as human beings with their own culture. Unlike the inbred, blue-eyed, ethnically isolated English, the olive-complected southern Europeans had a certain Mediterranean cosmopolitan nature bred from centuries of contact with diverse Arabs, Jews, gypsies, and Africans—according to this hypothesis.[1]

Such arguments might partially explain, for instance, why in the United States neo-African drumming was effectively outlawed everywhere except in New Orleans, where, because of the city's distinctively French Caribbean cultural orientation, it was tolerated until 1845. This thesis might also help explain why neo-African music and religion are so widespread in Cuba and so marginal in the British Caribbean, and why some Protestant missionaries in Haiti today, unlike local Catholic priests, demand that their congregations abandon all their traditional, African-influenced musical practices.

However, there are other factors that may better explain the different degrees of African retentions in the New World. One of these concerns the time that has elapsed in the various areas of the Caribbean since the end of slave imports. In the British colonies, importation of slaves ended in 1807, and by the 1870s, there were few African-born slaves in the United States. Hence it was natural for neo-African practices in British colonial areas to weaken during the subsequent long period of isolation from Africa. Cuba, by contrast, continued to receive slaves—and fresh infusions of African culture—as late as 1873. Most Cuban blacks are descendants of slaves brought in the 1800s, and quite a few know the specific ethnic ancestry of some of their great-grandparents. Similarly, the only neo-African religion in Trinidad, Shango or Orisha worship, survives as the legacy not of the slave period but of Yoruba indentured servants who arrived in the mid-1800s. (Haitian slave imports also ended early, in the 1790s, but at the time of the Haitian Revolution, most slaves were African-born, and the subsequent absence of Europeans allowed neo-African culture to flourish unimpeded.)

Perhaps the most important factor involved in the different degrees of African retentions is the difference between plantation colonies like Jamaica, whose populations consisted primarily of slaves, and settler colonies like Cuba, which had a more diverse balance of whites, free blacks and mulattos, and slaves. In Jamaica, slaves, who constituted about 90 percent of the population in 1800, were subject to rigid cultural repression and could exert little cultural influence on local whites. In contrast, sugar plantations came relatively late to Cuba and had to adapt themselves to the already well-formed and more lenient creole culture with its substantial free black population (20 percent in 1774). The communities of free Afro-Cubans played important roles in preserving neo-African culture, including musical practices based in the *cabildos*. Santería, for example, derives less from the assorted African traditions that managed to survive in rural plantations than from the formalized practices that coalesced in the *cabildos* of Havana and Matanzas in the late 1800s. Thus, the cultural attitudes of the colonists, although not insignificant, were only one among many factors influencing the nature and degree of African retentions in the New World.

THE EUROPEAN HERITAGE

The other primary ingredient in the formation of Caribbean music consists of the diverse forms of music introduced by the European colonists—primarily the Spanish, British, and French. These forms included not only the well-documented classical music of the era but, more important, the various folk and popular songs and dances of contemporary Europe. Thus, more influential than the rarefied music of Bach and Beethoven were the innumerable sailors' chanteys, church hymns, military marches, and, especially, social dances like the quadrille and contredanse. The contredanse—brought from England to the Caribbean by the French—spawned all manner of local incarnations, from the rowdy, thunderous neo-African *tumba francesa* of eastern Cuba to the elegant, Chopinesque piano pieces of Puerto Rican composer Manuel Tavárez. The related quadrille and other "set" (i.e., suite) dances were popular throughout the Caribbean as played on ad hoc ensembles of fiddles, guitars, fifes, and whatever else was around. As in Europe, most were round or line dances led by a caller, although ballroom-style couple dancing gradually became popular. As performed over the generations by Afro-Caribbeans, the dances eventually became creolized and came to incorporate typical syncopations and other distinctly local features.

Several of these European musical genres shared some of the aforementioned features associated with African music. Indeed, scholars have commented on the considerable degree of compatibility between African and European musics (not to mention the African practice of dancing in lines, as in a contredanse). Two- and three-part vocal harmony occurs in African as well as in European traditional music, while Protestant hymns used call-and-response "lining out" compatible with African practices. The French and Spanish, like many African communities, had traditions of seasonal carnivals with festive music. Further, most European folk musics, like African music, were orally transmitted traditions rather than written ones. Perhaps as a result of such precedents, oral poetry—especially as sung—has long played a much more prominent role in Caribbean culture than in more "developed" countries like the United States, where poetry is cultivated only by college English majors and a few literati. Caribbean people still take great interest in amateur versification, whether in the form of calypso, Jamaican dancehall, or Spanish *décimas.* Indeed, Caribbean popular culture in general is primarily oral rather than written. For that matter, the same can be said of Caribbean politics, with its prominence of brilliant orators, from Eric Williams to Fidel Castro.

The nature and extent of European influence have varied in accordance with several factors, some of which we have already mentioned—for example, the distinction between culturally repressive plantation colonies, where large slave populations were managed by a handful of white entrepreneurs, and settler colonies, which attracted substantial numbers of European immigrants. In the settler category, with some qualifications, would fall Cuba and Puerto Rico, which received hundreds of thousands of European immigrants. These settlers (primarily but not only Spanish) brought a rich spectrum of

European musics with them and, over the generations, played crucial roles in developing distinctive creole cultures in their new homelands. The British colonies, in contrast, attracted relatively few settlers. Most of those who came were what historian Gordon Lewis pithily described as "scum"—that is, social derelicts and mountebanks out to make a quick killing in the tropics. For their part, the British upper-class owners and managers generally came for limited periods, remaining attached to England, where they invested their earnings and sent their children to be educated. The contrast between the two sorts of colonies could be seen in their cities: Colonial Havana was an opulent and beautiful metropolis with fine cathedrals, mansions, and promenades, whereas the British Caribbean ports consisted of dreary warehouses surrounded by shantytowns, with a few bleak barns passing as the "great houses" of the rich. Similarly, because the British colonial elites made little attempt to develop their own art forms, it may be said that the musical heritages transmitted by the Spanish to Cuba and Puerto Rico were considerably richer than whatever the British bequeathed to their colonies.

In general, the European heritage brought to the Caribbean included instruments, chordal harmony, sectional formal structures (rather than the reliance on cellular ostinatos), concepts of ensemble orchestration and arrangement, the practice of notating music, and a vast repertoire of written and orally transmitted musics. New World Africans, while retaining many types of African drums, generally adopted the stringed and wind instruments played by Europeans. The Spanish musical heritage was particularly distinctive and influential. One might expect this heritage to include flamenco, the most famous kind of Spanish music, but flamenco, a product primarily of urban Andalusian gypsies, did not emerge until the latter 1800s, and there is no evidence that it was transmitted to the Caribbean in the colonial period. More influential were verse forms like the ten-line *décima* and the narrative *romance*, the fondness for triple meter, which persists in some Hispanic-derived folk forms, and chord progressions like the familiar Andalusian Am–G–F–E. The trajectory of the *décima* is especially curious: A minor verse form in sixteenth- and seventeenth-century Spain, it came to be widely cultivated as a song text in diverse forms in Latin America but essentially fizzled out in peninsular Spain itself.

CREOLIZATION

A Haitian Vodou chant that presumably dates from the slavery period runs, "Se Kreyòl no ye, pa genyen Ginen ankò" (We are creoles, who no longer have Africa). The transition from being an African—or a European—to being a Caribbean is a key concept in the formation of Caribbean culture and

music, embodied in the term "creolization," which connotes the development of a distinctive new culture out of the prolonged encounter of two or
more other cultures. The process is also described as "syncretism," although
"creolization" is particularly appropriate in the Americas, and especially in the
Caribbean, due to the long usage of the term "creole" there and its ability to
suggest some of the complex sociocultural issues also involved in the process.[2]
In linguistic terms, a pidgin language is one evolved through the blending of
two or more prior languages, especially of peoples who meet on territory that
is the original homeland of neither. This language subsequently becomes a
creole when it becomes a native tongue to later generations, who may forget
or lose contact with the original languages. This process is more than, say,
the mixing of blue and yellow to make green, since people are active, creative
agents, not inert chemicals, and the new human product, whether a language
or a musical style, takes on a life of its own.

Creolization—as extended more broadly to musical and cultural processes
rather than just language—also tends to involve a certain self-consciousness,
well evident in the Haitian verse cited earlier. More subtly, Caribbean creole
cultures, rather than being backwaters of the Western world, are in some
ways quintessentially modern, with their self-conscious hybridity and their
often dramatic sense of rupture with the inherited, unquestioned traditions
from the past. Further, the Caribbean people's traditional consciousness of
being at once part of and separate from the Euro-American mainstream, and
their ability to combine premodern African and New World features, have
accounted for much of the extraordinary expressive power of Caribbean arts,
especially music.

Caribbean creolization has primarily involved the encounter between
Africans (mostly from West Africa) and Europeans (mostly Spanish, British,
and French). Other groups, like the East Indians, the Chinese, and the Dutch,
have also played roles, some of which we consider later. There have been
various stages and subsidiary developments in the creolization process. One
can speak of an initial stage in which new forms of both neo-African and
European-derived musics began to develop in the Caribbean. Cuban rumba
can be regarded as such a genre, evolving partly through the interaction of
slaves from different African regions. European influence is obvious in many
melodies and the use of the Spanish language, but in other respects the rumba
is essentially neo-African. However, whereas Santería music is to some extent a
transplanted and recombined Yoruba entity, the rumba is not a transplant but
a distinctly Cuban creation. Likewise, the nineteenth-century Puerto Rican
piano danzas of Manuel Tavárez reflect only the most subtle, rarefied sort of
Afro-Caribbean influence, and in terms of style the danza can be regarded

as essentially European-derived. It is not, however, a European genre but a Puerto Rican one and has been celebrated as a symbol of Puerto Rican nationalism. Both the danza and the rumba are, in a preliminary sort of way, creole entities.

A more definitive sort of creolization occurs when African- and European-derived musical styles and elements combine in more overt ways. In many cases, this creative mixing started among the Afro-Caribbean lower classes, whose products, such as the early calypso or Cuban *son*, were generally denounced by Eurocentric elites (whether black, white, or mulatto). In the typical pattern, these lower-class, syncretic forms gradually percolate upward, acquiring more musical sophistication and eventually coming to be enjoyed by the upper classes. When all classes and races of a given population come to embrace local syncretic genres—whether merengue, reggae, calypso, the *son*, or the Puerto Rican plena—as nationalistic symbols, then one can truly speak of a creole national musical culture.

The evolution and acceptance of creole musics in the Caribbean have thus been closely bound up with nationalism and elite recognition of the Afro-Caribbean heritage. Cuban nationalists, for example, prized the habanera partly because it was a local creole invention rather than an archaic product of despised Spain; part of what distinguished the habanera was the use, however diluted, of Afro-Caribbean syncopations. With the emergence of the Cuban danzón in the late 1800s, the Afro-Caribbean element became more overt and, accordingly, more controversial. The danzón, with its felicitous combination of genteel melodies, sophisticated ensemble writing, and jaunty rhythms, quickly gained popularity in elite and petty bourgeois circles. To the modern ear, the genre may sound quite tame and quaint, but many negrophobic purists, because of the music's bouncy Afro-Caribbean rhythm, denounced it as barbaric, grotesque, and somehow foreign. Other obscurantists tried to legitimize it by falsely attributing its distinctive rhythm to Taino influence.

In the Spanish and French Caribbean, the *negritud* movement of the 1930s and '40s did much to discredit such foolishness and to force Eurocentric elites to acknowledge and accept the African heritage in their national cultures. The later scholarship of Cuban ethnologist Fernando Ortiz, the writings of Puerto Rican essayist Tomás Blanco, and the poetry of Aimé Cesaire, Nicolás Guillén, and Luis Palés Matos played important roles in this movement and in many cases explicitly celebrated the role of Afro-Caribbean music in national culture. In subsequent years, the attainment of political power by black and mulatto leaders further legitimized Afro-Caribbean culture. For that matter, the Cuban Revolution, although dominated by whites, has made particular progress in integrating the nation's black underclass into the economic and cultural mainstream of society.

Historically, creolization depends on an attitude of cultural openness and flexibility. Late-nineteenth-century Cuba would constitute one fertile petri dish of creole creation, with its lively urban interactions of free black and mulatto professional musicians and white patrons. A receptivity to new musical ideas can also be instilled from above, as when colonial policies dictate a rupture with the past, whether through prohibitions or persuasion. The British were especially effective at getting the slaves to adopt a colonial mentality that regarded everything African as backward. Hence, an 1823 visitor to Jamaica, after describing the African-style dancing to the goombay drum, remarked, "In a few years it is probable that the rude music here described will be altogether exploded among the creole [local-born] negroes, who show a decided preference of European music."[3] While such a rejection or repression of a musical tradition can cause a kind of deculturation or cultural impoverishment, it can also stimulate new creation, typically in a creolized form. The St. Lucian poet and Nobel Prize–winner Derek Walcott has written eloquently both of the tragedy of such cultural loss and of the brilliant creativity that it subsequently inspired: "In time the slave surrendered to amnesia. That amnesia is the true history of the New World."[4] Hence, as one Trinidadian told me, "I'm *glad* that the British banned our traditional drumming, because it inspired us to invent the steel drum."

In the twentieth century, urbanization, emigration, the mass media, and the internationalization of capital have brought new dimensions to musical syncretism in the Caribbean. Gone are the days of isolated peasant communities cultivating their traditional creole songs in ignorance of the wider musical world. Flipping the radio dial anywhere in the Lesser Antilles, one can pick up everything from salsa, soca, zouk, and reggae to East Indian film songs—not to mention rap and R&B. As such radio signals crisscross the sea and satellites transmit MTV International, musical trends spread and proliferate in weeks, not decades, and geographic, linguistic, and international boundaries seem to melt into the airwaves. In metropolitan hubs like New York, Toronto, and Birmingham, immigrants mingle with one another and with longtime locals, developing intricate multiple senses of identity reflected in the most eclectic musical tastes. Meanwhile, musical styles and influences cross-pollinate and multiply, spawning every conceivable sort of fusion, from Spanish-language reggae to merengues in Hindi. As creolization reaches a new level and the internal and external musical borders of the region dissolve, any book attempting to take stock of the contemporary music scene is doomed to rapid obsolescence. But snapshots have their own utility, and the authors of this book have done their best to cover the present as well as the past, starting with the largest and most influential island of all.

BIBLIOGRAPHY

For general reading on the Caribbean, see Gordon Lewis, *The Growth of the Modern West Indies* (New York: Monthly Review, 1968); and Franklin Knight, *The Caribbean* (New York: Oxford University Press, 1990). A good study of creolization is Richard Burton's *Afro-Creole: Power, Opposition, and Play in the Caribbean* (Ithaca, N.Y.: Cornell University Press, 1997).

2

Cuba

A DAY IN HAVANA, 1986

It is a sultry Saturday in Cuba's capital, a few years before the collapse of the Soviet Union and the economic problems it caused. At this point, the economy is running relatively smoothly, in its generally inefficient way, and most Cubans are more concerned with how to enjoy their weekend than with the size of the sugar harvest. My friends and I—Latin music fans visiting from the United States—are also trying to decide how to spend the day. The problem is that there is too much to choose from. The options are dizzying: For the afternoon, they include the *Sábado de la rumba* (Rumba Saturday), performed weekly by the national folkloric group; a set of free concerts in the old city; some touristy facsimile of a campesino (white peasant) festival out of town; and, for the less energetic hotel guests, the poolside band. As for the evening, there are salsa-style dance clubs, joyously kitsch cabarets at the Tropicana and the Havana Libre Hotel, some Soviet-bloc pop-ballad bands at the Karl Marx Theater, and more hotel folkloric shows featuring Afro-Cuban music and dance. Or we could rent a car and find our way to a real campesino music festival, which I see advertised in the newspaper. All of this is either cheap or free. Eventually, I opt for the old-city concerts, not knowing what to expect, and we decide to regroup in the early evening.

I head off by bus for old Havana, the waterfront area dominated by elegant colonial-era buildings, including the cathedral and the National Museum, where free concerts often take place. It's Saturday, and no one is in a particular hurry—certainly not the bus driver, who at one point stops the bus, full of people, calmly steps out, and walks into a drugstore to make a purchase. This gives me some time to savor the atmosphere of this part of the old city. Havana, like other Cuban cities, has a timeless charm that is hard to find in more modernized Caribbean countries. Most of the buildings are either colonial or early-twentieth-century edifices, many with majestic and ornate

19

facades. They are rather run down, to be sure, but they retain their faded elegance. There are few billboards, few neon lights, and no Burger Kings. The cars enhance the sensation that one is in a sort of time warp, for most of them date from the 1950s, before the U.S. government cut off trade with Cuba. So one sees DeSotos, Thunderbirds, and even the occasional Edsel chugging along, miraculously kept running by Cuban ingenuity and a local cottage industry producing spare parts for otherwise extinct vehicles. I notice that in an open-air tavern at the corner, among the patrons seated in front of the long mahogany bar and an immense rusted mirror, a man is strumming a guitar and crooning to the woman next to him.

Soon enough, our driver is again at the wheel, honking at passing girls and hailing friends as we proceed. As we near the museum, I hop out, noting that I have forgotten my umbrella; the morning has been clear and sunny, but in the Caribbean, one never knows. I arrive in time to hear the last pieces by a large wind orchestra playing in front of the museum to a relatively elderly audience. The ensemble is performing a mixture of European light classics and Cuban nineteenth-century salon-dance pieces—habaneras and danzones. The latter have a marked Afro-Caribbean rhythmic flavor, provided especially by the prominent timpani. The tubas are as battered as the T-Birds, but the playing is sweet and professional.

As soon as they stop, I hear another band starting up in the courtyard, playing a 1950s-style mambo. As I enter the courtyard, I am amazed to see that the performers consist of eight or nine rather ancient, matronly women. Several of them are wizened, stooped, and bespectacled, but the music is hot, and a few couples are already dancing: "What the Fidel is going on here?" I wonder. I ask someone who the performers are, and it turns out that they are Orquesta Anacaona, an all-woman dance band formed in 1939, which is still going strong, with the addition of a few new members. Eventually, they are followed by another cultural institution, the Sexteto Habanero, which has been performing, with similarly replenished membership, since 1925. They play old-style *son* with the traditional format of guitar, *tres* (like a guitar), bass, trumpet, and percussion. Their style and repertoire date mostly from the 1920s and 1930s, and they preface each piece with a sort of "name that *son*" contest, whose winners get little prizes. The audience members, as could be expected, are mostly middle-aged and older, but they are dancing in the most suave and supple style. I am just starting to wish that I were a sixty-year-old Cuban skilled in Latin dancing when a torrential downpour puts an abrupt end to the concert, sending musicians and listeners scurrying for cover under balustrades.

Donning a newspaper in place of my forgotten umbrella, I make my way back to the hotel, to learn that my friends and I have been invited to attend a *bembé*—a sort of dance party connected to the Afro-Cuban religion Santería (or *Regla de Ocha*). These are semiprivate affairs, so this invitation is not to be passed up. Our Cuban friend soon arrives to take us in his car to Matanzas, a nearby town famous for its Afro-Cuban traditions. It is dark when we reach our destination, a nondescript, one-story private home in a black neighborhood. We enter the house, in which one room is dominated by a majestic Santería altar; blood and feathers scattered in front of the altar suggest that either a chicken sacrifice or a violent pillow fight has recently taken place. We pass through to the backyard where the *bembé* is already in progress. About a hundred people are crowded into the yard, and the atmosphere is festive. About half of those present, mostly women, are either singing a refrain in call and response with a lead vocalist or dancing in a roughly circular fashion. Drowning out their voices are the instruments—three drums that look like oversized congas, two cowbells, and a tambourine.

I soon deduce that the person to watch is the lead drummer, who is improvising, beating the drum with a stick in his right hand and the palm of his left. Being so accustomed to music that relies heavily on melody and harmony, I have never imagined how drumming could be so expressive. I am mesmerized by his playing, in which he repeatedly starts a basic pattern, twists it around in different syncopations, and then abandons it for another, while different duple and triple pulses in the polyrhythmic accompaniment come in and out of focus. Finally, his playing reaches a crescendo as he works up to a frenetic acrobatic passage. It seems as if electricity sweeps through the yard as people whoop and cheer, and two women dancing in front of me stiffen and collapse into the arms of their neighbors, their eyes glazing over. They are acting as if possessed—and indeed, they have been possessed by Elegba, the Santería god of crossroads. Their friends, laughing, carry them into the house, where they pass the next few hours in a trance, awakening later to remember nothing.

THE CUBAN CRUCIBLE

The array of musical events happening on any given weekend in Havana is representative of the extraordinary richness and diversity of Cuban musical culture. In the nineteenth century, the Cuban habanera charmed European audiences and worked its way into operas like *Carmen*. In the mid-twentieth century, Cuban dance music dominated urban Africa, and it has continued to flourish in all of the Spanish-speaking countries of the Caribbean Basin, providing the backbone for salsa. Within the Caribbean itself Cuba's influence is perhaps not surprising, as it is by far the largest and most populous island. But its remarkable musical richness seems to derive from other factors, as well, including the way that both African and European musics have been able to mix and enrich each other.

Since the mid-nineteenth century, Cuba's population has consisted of relatively even proportions of whites, blacks, and mulattos (with smaller groups of Chinese, Lebanese, and others). By the 1600s, the native Taino and Ciboney Indians had effectively perished along with their language, culture, and music, including the massive *areito* dances. Over the subsequent centuries of Spanish rule, Cuba, unlike most of the British West Indies, received large numbers of European settlers (mostly from Spain, including the Canary Islands). These colonists brought with them a wealth of European music, from opera and classical music to Spanish folksongs.

At the same time, conditions favored the dynamic flourishing of neo-African music in Cuba. For one thing, since the Spanish often allowed Cuban slaves to buy their own freedom and tended to free the mulatto offspring of the children they sired with slaves, by the early eighteenth century Cuban towns hosted large communities of free blacks and mulattos. These, together with urban slaves, were allowed to celebrate various sorts of musical and religious festivities, especially in the *cabildos* (mutual-aid societies). The Spanish authorities and Catholic church generally tolerated the *cabildos*, partly because they tended to divide the blacks along ethnic and religious lines, thereby lessening the chance of unified slave revolts. Most rural slaves, despite brutal work schedules, were also allowed to sing, drum, and dance as they wished on their days off, and many were even permitted to leave their plantations to attend fiestas. Moreover, while the import of slaves to the United States and the British colonies had dwindled by 1800, most Cuban slaves (especially the Yoruba) were brought in the subsequent sixty years, so that neo-African musical traditions continued to be invigorated by fresh infusions of hapless captives.

Under such conditions, both traditional African and European musics were able to flourish in Cuba, at the same time being creatively combined and reworked by musicians into a variety of syncretic styles in a process dubbed "transculturation" by ethnologist Fernando Ortiz.

AFRICAN-DERIVED MUSICS

The enslaved Africans brought to Cuba came from a variety of regions and ethnic groups. The larger of these were able to maintain many of their musical and religious traditions, especially in the realm of musics associated with religious ceremonies. One of the two largest ethnic groups among the slaves was the

Yoruba, most of whom were brought in the nineteenth century to central and western Cuba from what is now Nigeria. In Africa, the Yoruba (as they came to be called in the late nineteenth century) had a highly developed culture, with large towns, social classes, trade networks, and sophisticated and formalized musical and religious traditions. While much of Yoruba culture—including language, kinship systems, and social structure in general—was lost in slavery, the Cuban Yoruba (traditionally called *lucumí*) were able to maintain or reinvent a considerable amount of their traditional music and religion—especially in the *cabildos* of Havana and nearby Matanzas.

The Yoruba-derived religion in Cuba is called Santería, or *regla de Ocha*. Santería is a syncretic religion in the sense that traditional regional Yoruba elements have not only fused with each other, but have also acquired a thin veneer of Roman Catholicism to form a new, coherent set of beliefs and practices. The West African set of local and regional deities were consolidated into an Afro-Cuban pantheon and became further identified with Catholic saints—for example, Changó, the thunder god, with Saint Barbara, and Ogún, the god of iron, with Saint Peter. Each god, or orisha, is associated with particular colors, myths, herbs, dances, and songs—beliefs that blended easily with Counter-Reformation Spanish folk Catholicism, with its emphasis on medieval rituals, idols, and relics. Santería devotees, most of whom are black or mulatto, believe that the orishas are powerful presences who can be of great assistance if they are regularly honored. Worship, which is oriented toward worldly aid rather than spiritual salvation in the afterlife, centers in ceremonies in which participants sing, dance, and in some cases undergo possession trance, as in the *bembé* described earlier.

The *bembé* is one kind of Santería event, with its own kind of musical ensemble, repertoire, and rather festive character. Cubans describe it as a sort of "party for the orishas." The more typical Santería function is a *toque de santo*, which uses different music and has a somewhat more serious character. A *toque* usually takes place at a devotee's home, or perhaps in the basement of an apartment building. The occasion may be the anniversary of someone's initiation, an orisha's sacred day, or an honoring of the spirits in thanks for or anticipation of a boon. The first part of the ceremony (called *oru del igbodú*, or "ceremony in the orisha's room") starts in the afternoon, when the musicians, with a few guests watching, play a sequence of drum invocations before the altar. The musical ensemble consists of three hourglass-shaped *batá* drums, resembling traditional Yoruba drums of the same name. In *batá* music, there is little improvised jamming as in *bembé* drumming; instead, the drummers play a set of largely pre-composed rhythmic patterns consisting of a complex series of composite ostinatos, interlocking "conversations" between drums,

Batá drum trio marching in Carnival procession, Santiago de Cuba (Peter Manuel)

and transition passages. Several drum patterns are associated with particular orishas, and parts of the patterns, in West African "talking-drum" tradition, imitate the speech inflections of old Yoruba praise poems, which themselves are now largely forgotten.

After the *oru del igbodú*, guests start to arrive, and the musicians honor each initiate by briefly playing rhythms associated with his or her patron orisha. From then on, the main singer (who, like the drummers, is a paid professional) leads the ensemble and participants in performing various songs invoking the orishas. Men and women dance collectively in the styles associated with the orisha being addressed—whether the coquettish Ochún, the macho Changó, or the dignified Yemayá—adapting their movements to the lyrics and rhythms of the songs. The songs are mostly in Yoruba, praising or even insulting the deities to encourage them to "descend" and possess the appropriate participants. The lead vocalist's job is to get people to sing and dance and, ultimately, to help induce spirit possession. When possession does occur, the possessed individual—now regarded as the orisha—is treated with reverence and may be dressed in appropriate garments (e.g., a crown and red vest for Changó) and is often asked for advice or blessings. Some possessions are certainly faked, but the prevailing academic opinion is that they constitute, at the least, some sort of altered state of consciousness, in some ways akin to hypnosis.

While most North Americans have never heard of Santería, they have heard something of Haitian Vodou (voodoo), which is in many respects quite similar. Due in part to racist stereotypes of Haiti, Vodou has a negative image abroad, and one can find references even in academic literature to "wild and drunken voodoo orgies." But there is nothing wild about either Santería or Vodou ceremonies. Actually, *batá* music and the dancing it accompanies have a rather stately and restrained character. Drunkenness and lewd behavior are generally inappropriate at such functions, and there is no erotic couple dancing. Instead, the dancers execute their traditional steps in a loosely collective fashion. Santería, of course, is not everyone's cup of tea, and most educated Cubans (especially whites) tend to regard it as backward and part of the lumpen underworld. Nevertheless, Santería remains extremely widespread among lower-class Cubans, and the Revolutionary government has given up trying to discourage it. Furthermore, the important role of Afro-Cuban culture in national identity in general has long been widely acknowledged, especially in the wake of the intellectual *negritud* movement of the 1930s, led in Cuba by ethnologist Fernando Ortiz, poet Nicolás Guillén, and others.

Meanwhile, since the mid-twentieth century, Santería has flourished in Latino communities in the United States, especially in New York City and the Miami area, each of which hosts thousands of adherents. Many of the practitioners are from Puerto Rican or other Latino backgrounds; some are African Americans trying to get in touch with their African heritage. In New York and other North American cities, there are dozens of stores called *botánicas* that sell herbal medicines, statuettes, booklets, talismans, and other articles related to Santería and folk Catholicism. In 1993, the U.S. Supreme Court legalized animal sacrifices practiced by a Santería temple in Florida, and the religion is now in a position to emerge from underground. With the influx of several skilled Cuban musicians, Santería music is also flourishing in the United States.

Santería is not the only Afro-Cuban religion. A group of slaves roughly equal in number to the Yoruba were brought earlier from the Congo River region southeast of Nigeria. The Congolese were Bantu-speaking hunter-gatherers and agriculturalists whose society and culture were in some ways less formalized than those of the Yoruba. Nevertheless, the Congolese contribution to Afro-Cuban culture is probably as substantial as that of the Yoruba, although it is more influential in the realm of secular music. The Congolese-derived religion in Cuba is generically called *Palo* (or *palo monte*,

**Tropical religion in the barrio:
One of New York City's many
botánicas (Peter Manuel)**

palo mayombé) and its practicioners, *paleros. Palo* centers on worship of ancestors and anthropomorphic spirits, who are honored in ceremonies with music
and dance. The *Palo* drums, songs, and rhythms are distinct from those of
Santería. Instead of *batá* drums, *paleros* generally use single-headed *ngoma*
drums, which developed into the familiar conga drum, whose name reflects
its ethnic origin. Unlike Santería songs in Yoruba, *Palo* songs are mostly in
Spanish, reflecting the fact that most Congolese slaves arrived earlier in Cuba
than did the Yoruba. The *Palo* rhythms are simpler and fewer than those of
Santería, and the dances are more vigorous. *Palo* is also more secretive and
has a stronger component of what could be called black magic. Like Santería,
Palo flourishes in New York City and elsewhere.

Another distinctive Afro-Cuban music and dance tradition is that associated
with the *abakuá* brotherhoods, whose founders came from the West African
Calabar region of coastal islands and swamps, where secret societies traditionally took the place of centralized government. In Cuba, their descendants
and others formed all-male societies, based mostly in and around Havana
and Matanzas, especially among dockworkers. *Abakuá* is an ethnic and

religious brotherhood rather than a religion per se, but in ceremonies, *abakuá* members (called *ñañigos*) perform music and dance that reenact events from their mythological history. *Abakuá* societies still flourish, and their remarkable dances, like those of *Palo* and Santería, are often performed in folkloric contexts. The most characteristic figure in *abakuá* dance is the *ireme* or *diablito* (little devil), who nervously darts about with a whisk broom, dressed in a hooded costume, which closely resembles those still used by dancers in the parallel secret societies in Calabar today. As with Santería and *Palo*, several words derived from Calabari culture have entered Cuban and Caribbean Spanish—especially the common term "chévere," which means "cool" or "great." Two other African-derived sects are the Dahomeyan *arará* and the Yoruba sub-group *iyesá*. The distinctive ceremonies and musical traditions of these groups still survive in *cabildos* in the city of Matanzas—and some of the same songs and rhythms of the *arará* tradition can be heard today in Benin, West Africa.

Scholars have yet to connect many of the historical dots linking Afro-Cuban traditions with counterparts and sources in Africa. Such connections are naturally obscured by the changes that have taken place both in Cuba and in Africa. For example, Santería music represents a sort of consolidation and reassembling of different African traditions. Thus, if one goes to Yorubaland today and looks for Yemayá rhythms played on the *batá* drums, one won't find them, since the *batá* is not used to worship Yemayá in Nigeria. Other traditions have survived more in Cuba than in Africa, where evangelical Christianity has obliterated many of them. Hence, interested Nigerians have traveled to Cuba to study Santería, especially to learn more about their ancestral Babalú-Ayé cult, which the British had effectively repressed. Another remarkable reunification occurred recently when some Calabari immigrants in the United States noticed an article on *abakuá* by the American scholar Ivor Miller. They then invited him to Nigeria, where he traced the roots of Afro-Cuban songs and organized a historic encounter between Cuban *ñañigo* performers and their Ekpe counterparts in Nigeria.

RUMBA

By far the most famous and influential Afro-Cuban secular music and dance genre is rumba. The word "rumba" has long been used rather loosely in the realm of commercial dance music and salsa. Properly speaking, however, rumba denotes a traditional genre in which one or two dancers are accompanied by an ensemble consisting of three congas, two pairs of tapped sticks, and a lead singer and chorus. In the absence of any European melodic or chordal

Abakuá diablito dancer

instruments, rumba sounds very African, and it appears to derive from secular dances cultivated by the Congolese slaves in Cuba. But unlike Santería music, rumba is a distinctly Cuban creation, not a retention or re-creation of an old African genre.

Rumba seems to have emerged in the late 1800s as an entertainment genre performed at parties, mostly in urban, lower-class black neighborhoods. While several different kinds of rumba once flourished, since the mid-twentieth century only three have persisted. Of these, the most popular is the *guaguancó*, which is distinguished by its particular rhythm and dance styles.[1] (The basic *guaguancó* pattern is shown in Musical Example 2.) In the *guaguancó*, an ostinato (recurrent pattern) is played by either one or two drummers on two differently tuned congas (better referred to as *tumbadoras*); another player taps an interlocking pattern with hard sticks (*palitos*) on the side of one drum.

Musical Example 2. Rumba *guaguancó*

The lead singer strikes two short hardwood sticks together to provide another pattern; these sticks and the standardized pattern played on them are both called *clave*, the importance of which as an underlying rhythmic concept we discuss later. Meanwhile, another conga player (playing the higher-pitched *quinto* drum) improvises throughout. Over this intricate composite rhythm, the lead vocalist, after singing a few introductory nonsense syllables, performs an extended text, perhaps loosely improvising melodies and lyrics. The rumba lyrics can be about anything—love, politics, cockfights, or neighborhood events and people. This section of the rumba, the *canto*, can last a few minutes; sooner or later, the lead vocalist cues the other singers to commence singing a short refrain, and they then proceed in call-and-response fashion. This part is called the *montuno* (a word we will encounter again later).

As soon as the *montuno* starts, a couple begins to dance in a pantomime game of coy evasion on the woman's part and playful conquest on the man's. While the female dancer undulates gracefully about, the man, without touching her, performs a variety of improvised, constantly changing steps and gestures around her, alternately importuning her, pretending to ignore her, mimetically cajoling her, and then, when he senses an opportunity, performing a *vacunao*, which consists of a pelvic thrust or even a graceful kick or swat in the direction of the woman's groin. A sense of fun and humor prevails throughout, and the sophistication, variety, and suppleness of the dance save it from being vulgar. Indeed, rumba dance is a difficult art and is only attempted by Cubans who have really cultivated an interest in it. There are many colonial-era descriptions, from Cuba and elsewhere in the Caribbean, of dances like rumba, which European onlookers generally regarded as lewd and vulgar. Accounts suggest that many contemporary Africans felt the same way about European couple dances, as in traditional African dancing men and women would rarely touch each other.

Of the two other types of rumba still performed, the *yambú* is like a slower, more restrained *guaguancó*, while the *columbia* is a solo male dance, stressing the dancer's acrobatic grace and virtuosity. The *yambú* is often traditionally played on wooden boxes (*cajones*) instead of congas.

As an informal fiesta dance, rumba is no longer very common. It is, however, often performed in prisons, and in folkloric contexts, which should not be regarded as "artificial." Any group of amateur *rumberos* can form a folkloric group to perform in various competitions or variety shows held throughout the island. Winning groups could even try to get regular gigs at a tourist venue. Meanwhile, in New York barrios, rumba caught on in its own fashion in the 1950s, and on summer weekends Spanish Harlem and Central Park have since resounded to the intricate pounding of conga drums. From there the rumba spread to Puerto Rico and elsewhere, and it continues to flourish among Latino communities outside Cuba, although the emphasis tends to be more on flashy conga playing than on the dance and singing.

A MUSIC FESTIVAL IN SANTIAGO DE CUBA

For another look at Afro-Cuban music, I'll describe an evening I spent in Santiago de Cuba in the 1980s. Santiago is the largest city in the eastern part of the island (traditionally called Oriente) and has quite a different flavor from Havana. There are no skyscrapers there, and the atmosphere is more provincial and laid back. However, the region is renowned for its rich cultural heritage and for its proud, independent populace, who were leaders in the anticolonial wars. Oriente was traditionally a region of small coffee and tobacco farms, whose largely mulatto population had, over the centuries, generated a music culture that is distinctively creole. By contrast, western Cuba, with its legacy of large sugar plantations worked by slave labor, and the influx of Spanish and Canary Island immigrants in the later colonial period, has been the main center both of the more strictly Afro-Cuban traditions like Santería as well as overwhelmingly Hispanic-derived forms like *punto*, discussed later. Yet Oriente also has its own Afro-Cuban music traditions.

When I visited Santiago de Cuba, a music festival was in progress. Various groups from other Caribbean countries were performing, along with some European acts. The one country conspicuously absent was the United States, which would never have sent a cultural delegation to communist Cuba, its sworn enemy that supposedly threatens the United States' soft underbelly. The Cubans, of course, would have welcomed a troupe from the United States, and Michael Jackson's song "Thriller" was then a big hit on the island.

But there was no shortage of performances to choose from. I ended up at a sort of Afro-Cuban variety show in a courtyard.

The first act represented a tradition unique to eastern Cuba, called *tumba francesa*. The *tumba francesa* societies were social clubs formed by the more than 30,000 Haitians who fled to eastern Cuba around 1800 during the Haitian Revolution; several thousand more Haitians immigrated in the early 1900s. The main *tumba francesa* activities are nightlong social dances in which call-and-response singing is accompanied on a set of three large *tumba* drums, a hollowed log (*catá*) struck with sticks, and metal rattles (*chachas*). At present, only two dances survive. One of these, the *masón* (from *maison*, "house"—or from the egalitarian "Masons"?) derives from the French contredanse (itself from the English "country-dance") as cultivated by Afro-Haitians in the early 1800s. As in Europe of the time, and in related dances like the Virginia reel, men and women line up opposite each other and perform a series of "figures," advancing and retreating, and dancing together and then splitting up. *Tumba francesa* music, however, consists not of dainty minuets but of vigorous Afro-Haitian-style drumming with call-and-response singing. In the other surviving dance, the *yuba*, a solo male dancer improvises acrobatic steps in a sort of a duel with a drummer, who plays straddling the largest *tumba* drum, which is laid lengthwise on the floor.

Nowadays, the *tumba francesa* societies no longer fulfill important functions, although the government encourages their art by hiring them to play at events like this one. The *tumba francesa* may have become "folkloric" in that sense, but for these musicians and dancers, it was just another party that happened to be on a stage, as they were clearly having a wild time. I noted that several of the performers were young, and many audience members were singing along with the songs, which are in Haitian creole, not Spanish. Others standing near me were conversing in creole, as well. In fact, the Franco-Haitian immigrants have contributed a special flavor to Oriente's culture.

The next act was an amateur rumba group, consisting mostly of black teenagers. Their performance was loosely structured in the form of a skit set in the pre-Revolutionary days, when rumba parties and Santería ceremonies were often harassed by the police. In the skit, they reconstructed a rumba fiesta, which came to an abrupt halt when a lanky black "policeman," played by a tall black youth, appeared and broke up the festivities. The dancers pleaded with him and then offered him a few pesos, which he furtively accepted. The dancing resumed with a lively solo rumba *columbia*. After a few minutes, however, the "policeman," who had been watching from the side, looked around to make sure his superiors were not watching and then, pushing the dancer aside, stepped into the ring and proceeded to perform his own virtuoso *columbia*. The audience roared with delighted applause and laughter.

After the rumba group came another set of Afro-Cuban teenagers, doing congas. Conga, as mentioned earlier, is the Congolese-derived drum used in dance bands, but it is also a kind of Afro-Cuban processional dance and music (and the group that performs it), somewhat like rumba but less complex. Congas are usually performed in connection with Carnival processions called *comparsas*, and the dancing generally consists of simple steps accompanying percussive music provided on slender conga drums, iron bells, and a marching-band-type bass drum (called *bombo* or *galleta*). This group, shunning the low stage, started performing fast congas in the middle of the courtyard, and the drummers were playing as if possessed—but of course they were not, because conga, like rumba, is a secular entertainment form and has no particular connection with Afro-Cuban religion. However, a problem soon arose, as within minutes a few hundred people had pressed into the small space, laughing, dancing, and shouting (and flattening our correspondent against a wall). There was clearly only one solution—and so the crowd, performers and all, burst out into the street, where more revelers joined in a wild, wriggling procession that gyrated around energetically for another hour.

This conga event turned into a sort of miniature version of Carnival (Carnaval), which until recently was celebrated on a vast scale in Cuba. Carnival originated as a Christmastime fiesta held, elsewhere in Cuba, on Three Kings Day (*el Día de Reyes*, 6 January), during which the Afro-Cuban *cabildos* were allowed to form street processions, with drumming and dancing (and, often, fighting). In 1900, the negrophobic government banned the processions, except in the context of political campaigns, but after being legalized in 1937 they rebounded on an unprecedented scale. Groups of white revelers also joined the fun, and eventually the processions came to be organized by competitive clubs with traditional titles and themes, from established Afro-Cuban barrio *comparsas* like Los Alacranes (the Scorpions) to bourgeois white groups like Los Dandys. The clubs, after months of practice and preparation of elaborate costumes, floats, conga-style theme songs, and dance routines to be performed in the street, would form processions, parading through the central avenues lined with onlookers and, at one locale, a panel of judges. Congas also came to flourish in the cabaret shows, including as performed by Desi Arnaz prior to his *I Love Lucy* fame. The Santiago Carnival had always been held in July, and Fidel Castro timed his initial revolutionary escapade—the 1953 attack on the Moncada barracks—to coincide with the festivities and prevailing inebriation. The attack was a fiasco, but after the eventual triumph of the Revolution in 1959, Carnival throughout the island was shifted to

Street festivities on el Día de Reyes (Three Kings' Day), from a painting by Landaluze (Museo Nacional de Bellas Artes de La Habana)

July to commemorate the event and to coincide with the end of the summer harvest. With a combination of state funding and avid grassroots participation, the event soon grew to be more extravagant and lavish than ever. Unfortunately, the economic exigencies of the "special period" led it to be cancelled in the early '90s, although it has since reappeared in an irregular and greatly diminished capacity.

EUROPEAN-DERIVED MUSICS

The various kinds of Afro-Cuban music were generally confined to a social underground until the mid-twentieth century, by which time they had come to pervade commercial dance music and had been celebrated by scholars like Fernando Ortiz. They have since come to be recognized as among the most

Conga drummers in Carnival procession, Santiago de Cuba (Peter Manuel)

dynamic parts of Cuban popular culture. But they represent only half the story of Cuban music, as the best-known forms of Cuban music—especially the country's dance-band music—have been formed as much by European influences as by African ones.

As we mentioned, Cuba's population has consisted of relatively equal proportions of whites, blacks, and mulattos since the early 1800s. Mainland Spanish and Canary Island settlers continued to come even through the early 1900s. The Spaniards brought their own musical traditions with them, from rustic peasant songs to genteel aristocratic dances. In Cuba, all these musics gradually acquired a distinctively national flavor, in some cases due to a clear Afro-Cuban influence. With the advent of Cuban nationalism in the late 1800s, these creole forms became symbols of Cuban patriotism, as opposed to the perceivedly *gallego* (stiff and stuffy) Spanish forms of music and dance.

The music of white Cuban farmers, who are called *guajiros*, derives primarily from peninsular Spanish and Canary Island origins, especially as reflected in its reliance on guitars and mandolin-like instruments. A popular colonial-era *guajiro* pastime was the *zapateo*, a lively couple dance featuring fancy footwork accompanied by a guitar or similar instrument, playing melodies full of *hemiola* syncopations (along the lines of "I like to live in Ame-ri-ca," or one-two-three-one-two-three-one-and-two-and-three-and). Still popular are songs based on the *décima*, an old Spanish-derived verse form consisting of ten-line stanzas usually in the *espinela* rhyme scheme *abbaaccddc*. Although its use largely died out in peninsular Spain after the 1600s, it is widely cultivated in various parts of Latin America. In Cuba and Puerto Rico, the *décima* is as familiar as limericks are in the United States, and students and literati have long learned to recite and compose them. Cuban peasants developed various styles of singing *décimas* (under the label *punto*) and would hold frequent contests at rural fiestas, especially in the western, white-populated tobacco-growing regions of the island. Singers would often be expected to compose impromptu *décimas*, perhaps using a fixed last line (*pie forzado*; literally, "forced foot") given to them on the spot. Such informal performances often take the form of a duel (*controversia*) between two singer-poets, who trade off *décimas*, attempting to outdo each other in their clever rhymes and witty insults (which are more important than ability to sing well). Here is a famous *décima* from around 1900; it expresses the ambivalence of Cubans toward the United States, which had invaded Cuba in 1898, finishing off the already collapsing Spanish rule and establishing its own pattern of intervention in the island.

	(rhyme)
La tierra del Siboney	a
que da el tabaco y la caña	b
de la tutela de España	b
nos liberó McKinley.	a
Dále vivas, que es del ley	a
a nuestros buenos hermanos	c
¡Vivan los americanos!	c
sin cesar repiteremos,	d
pero también les diremos:	d
¡Cuba para los cubanos!	c

[U.S. President] McKinley has liberated the land of Siboney,
with its tobacco and sugarcane, from Spanish rule;
Let's sing the praises of our good brothers.
"Long live the Americans!" we'll ceaselessly repeat.
But we'll also tell them,
"Cuba is for the Cubans!"[2]

The *Punto Cubano*

The Cuban *punto* is sung in a variety of styles throughout the island. The predominant style in the western part of the island is the so-called *punto libre*, in which the verses are rendered in free rhythm in a stock melody, or personal variants of it. In between the

Colonial-era *zapateo*

sung lines, the guitar (with perhaps a *clave*) plays a simple chordal ostinato, with flashy improvisations on the mandolin-like *laúd*. The *décima* given above would be sung roughly as in the transcription shown in Musical Example 3. To non-Hispanic ears, it may sound as if the tonic were C major, but, in accordance with Spanish-derived harmonic conventions, there is an equal polar repose on G major, which is stressed in all cadences.

To perform or read this *décima* (which is a bit hard to transcribe clearly): the first four lines (*abba*), notated in the example as (1) proceed to the end, leading to (2) (lines *ac*), which, after the ensemble interlude (second staff), segues to (3) ("vivan ... repetiremos"), which goes directly to the last two lines ("pero ...") without an ensemble interlude.

In the 1800s, while the Cuban *punto* styles were evolving in the countryside, the white and mulatto populations of the island's towns and cities were cultivating their own lively musical culture. In the early 1800s, the favored dance genres in urban white society consisted of European styles like the waltz, minuet, gavotte, and *pasodoble*. Over the course of the century, however, these styles gradually came to be replaced by distinctively Cuban forms, which thus became nationalistic symbols in a time of growing resentment—and, eventually, outright rebellion—against Spanish colonial rule.

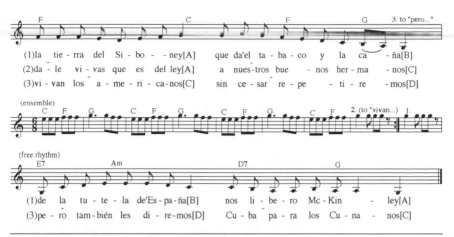

Musical Example 3. Punto

Many Cubans were growing increasingly frustrated by the economic restrictions and corrupt and inefficient government Spain imposed on Cuba. Both culturally and politically, the Cuban middle classes became attracted less to backward, feudal, and repressive Spain than to the liberal bourgeois cultures flourishing in other European countries. The Franco-Haitian immigration from Haiti around 1800 brought cosmopolitan French culture to eastern Cuba. At the same time, the melodramatic Italian style of vibrato-laden bel canto singing, popularized by the operas of Donizetti and Bellini, became widely popular in Cuba and elsewhere in Latin America and was eventually adopted in patriotic *canciones*. Alongside Italian operas and European concert music, particularly popular in Cuba from the latter 1800s were Spanish-language light operas, called zarzuelas, and the less formal *tonadilla* and *teatro bufo*, many of which were locally composed. Cuba's urban cultural scene became one of the liveliest in the hemisphere, and indeed, by 1800, Havana was the third largest city in the Americas (following Mexico City and Lima and well ahead of provincial Boston and New York). As Cuban author Alejo Carpentier observed, both the refinement of this bourgeois culture and the cruelty of its economic base could be seen in such newspaper classified advertisements as one in 1794 that offered for sale a spinet piano, a colt, and a seven-year-old negro boy.[3]

Musically, the most important genre in the emergence of nineteenth-century Cuban creole music culture was the *contradanza habanera* (Havana-style contradance), which in Cuba was generally referred to simply as "contradanza" (or, confusingly, as *danza*). In the late 1700s and early 1800s, various kinds of related dances–especially the aforementioned English country dance and French contredanse–had been popular among the European middle classes. These traditionally featured group-style dancing directed by a caller, in a fashion similar to a square dance. Over the course of the nineteenth century, the Cubans came to regard this style as stuffy and archaic, and they adopted the contemporary French and British trends, gradually dispensing with the dance's collective character and turning it into a dance of independent couples (in that sense like the contemporary and "revolutionary" waltz). At the same time, the Cubans gave it a bit of Afro-Caribbean spice, in the form of synco-pated rhythms—especially the pattern: x–xx-x-, or one-and-two-and-three-and-four-and, which also distinguished the early Argentine tango. Indeed, just as many upper-class Cuban white men liked to indulge themselves with black women, so did Afro-Cuban syncopations enter—albeit via the servants' door—into dainty contradanzas, many of which bore appropriately "colorful" titles like "Tu madre es conga" (Your Mother Is Congolese). Accordingly, although most contradanza patrons were white or mulatto, most professional musicians in this period were black or mulatto, prompting one writer to pro-claim with alarm in 1832, "The arts are in the hands of people of color!"

The contradanza was cultivated in different forms (aside from relatives like *tumba francesa*). Animated versions of it were performed by various ad hoc ensembles (e.g., guitar, flute, and fiddle) at all manner of bourgeois and lower-class fiestas. While this tradition has died out, we still have the notated scores of the light-classical salon contradanzas, which were written either for dance or for listening, to be played by pianists or chamber groups in aristo-cratic parlors and ballrooms. The most gifted composers of such pieces were Manuel Saumell (1817–70) and Ignacio Cervantes (1847–1905), who wrote his elegant and tuneful contradanzas as trivial gifts for friends. Although the contradanzas were parlor pieces rather than political protests, they became at least indirectly associated with the independence movement insofar as they were celebrated as distinctly creole Cuban entities. And, of course, what gave them that creole character was precisely the Afro-Cuban syncopation, how-ever diluted and camouflaged. Thus commenced the complex and ambivalent relationship between Afro-Cuban culture and bourgeois white Cuban nation-alism, which could be as racist as it was patriotic.

By the 1830s, the *contradanza habanera* had become popular in Europe, where, especially when enhanced with a vocal text, it was known as "habanera" (or, incorrectly, as "habañera"). Georges Bizet used a contemporary habanera melody in his 1875 opera *Carmen*, and another habanera, "La Paloma," became one of the most popular songs in Latin America. Both songs use the basic ostinato shown in the previous paragraph.

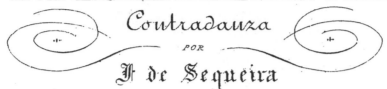

A typical nineteenth-century contradanza for piano

Musical Example 4. Cinquillo

In the 1850s–60s, Cuban urban musical life was enlivened by the presence of Louis Moreau Gottschalk, a flamboyant composer and virtuoso pianist from New Orleans. In his extended visits to Cuba, Puerto Rico, and elsewhere, Gottschalk inspired local composers and audiences with his flashy compositions using contemporary Caribbean melodies and rhythms.

By the 1880s, especially through the influence of composer and bandleader Miguel Faílde, the contradanza was eclipsed by a new form, the danzón, which reigned as the national dance of Cuba until the 1930s. The danzón retained a European light-classical orientation in its use of rondo-like sectional structure (often ABABACAC), written scores, sophisticated harmonies, and instrumentation. But if Afro-Cuban rhythmic flavor was hinted at in the contradanza, it was unmistakable in the danzón (much to the horror of negrophobic stuffed shirts), especially in the persistence of the *cinquillo* ostinato (Musical Example 4, or one-and-two-and-three-and-four-and). This ostinato, of evident Afro-Haitian derivation, is found in a variety of Afro-Caribbean musics, including Haitian Vodou drumming, *batá* music, and West Indian folksongs like "Yellow Bird."

Through about 1910, for outdoor occasions the danzón was generally played on a horn-dominated *orquesta típica* ensemble, sounding a bit like early New Orleans jazz, with which it had some ties. By 1920, however, this tropical ragtime ensemble had been largely replaced by a sweeter, indoor-type ensemble called *charanga* (or *charanga francesa*), in which a wooden flute and two violins were backed by piano, string bass, güiro scraper, and timbales (small, metal-framed drums with a crisper sound than the timpani). The *charangas* and their favored idiom, the danzón, retained a certain bourgeois character, but their suave mixture of guts and grace ensured their vitality through the 1940s.

While the danzón was a popular dance idiom, it was also a sophisticated salon genre whose composition and performance required training in European art music. Since the mid-nineteenth century, Cuba had been producing many skilled classical performers—both white and black—and in the early twentieth century some of its composers achieved international renown. Amadeo Roldan (1900–39) and Alejandro García Caturla (1906–40) were two remarkable modernists who, inspired by Parisian avant-garde primitivism, synthesized

Afro Cuban rhythms with bold, Stravinsky-like sonorities. If Stravinsky, in a work like the *Rite of Spring*, had to turn to a fantasized Africa or an imaginary pagan Russia for inspiration, Caturla and Roldán found inspiration in the actual Afro-Cuban music of their own homeland. Particularly outstanding are works like Roldan's percussion-dominated *Rítmicas*, where *clave* and *cinquillo* patterns and other syncopations weave in and out of each other, and Caturla's *Tres Danzas Cubanas,* which succeed in being both avant-garde and catchy. Tragically, both composers perished in their thirties. Roldán died of cancer, and Caturla–a social rebel who had a black common-law wife and as a magistrate was a heroic crusader for social justice–was murdered by a thug. Both collaborated extensively with Alejo Carpentier (1904–80), a brilliant and progressive music critic, librettist, musicologist, and novelist. Musical themes recur in Carpentier's fiction, especially in *Concierto Barroco*, a playful postmodern novel showing Afro-Latin music invigorating the European Baroque, in the form of a Mexican gentleman and his black factotum jamming with Vivaldi and Scarlatti.

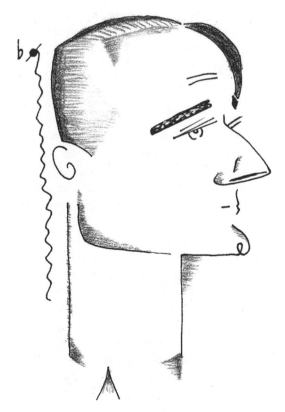

**Alejandro García Caturla
(adapted by Peter Manuel
from a cartoon by Maribona)**

Meanwhile, white composers and performers had been highlighting Afro-Cuban culture in a different, and more equivocal, manner in the context of the *teatro bufo*. This was kind of local minstrelsy, with skits and songs featuring stock characters—especially the gregarious and musical *negrito*, the sexy *mulata* (mulatto woman), and the petty bourgeois and untalented white *gallego* (literally, Spaniard from Galicia). Such shows foregrounded saucy verse-and-refrain songs called *guarachas* and corny stage versions of Afro-Cuban rumbas and congas, performed by whites in blackface, at a time when the authentic street versions of these dances were outlawed. But despite the reliance on cartoonish racial stereotypes, the prominence of black and mulatto characters represented a kind of musical nationalism and indirectly helped legitimize Afro-Cuban culture.

In the 1930s, a more elaborate and sophisticated music theater came to flourish in the form of the zarzuelas of Ernesto Lecuona (1895–1963), Gonzalo Roig, and Ernesto Prats. These works, such as *El Cafetal, María la O*, and *Cecilia Valdés*, typically involved love triangles among a male slave, a *mulata*, and a white man. They portrayed the plight of the slave sympathetically but set the whole drama in the comfortable distance of the colonial past rather than the present, with its still unresolved racial tensions. Due to the advent of cinema, the expense of their production, and the lack of tourist interest, these zarzuelas are seldom performed today, but tunes like Lecuona's "Siboney" and "María la O" remain familiar evergreens in Cuba. The composer and pianist Lecuona is also remembered for his impressionistic piano pieces, such as the still popular "Malagueña."

Finally, in discussing the more European-oriented Cuban musics, we should also mention the bolero, which evolved in Cuba around the turn of the twentieth century as a popular, guitar-based, slow-dance song, especially as cultivated by singer-composers like Sindo Garay (1867–1968) and Pepe Sánchez (1856–1918). The bolero's lyrics, sung in European bel canto style, are unabashedly sentimental and romantic, celebrating eternal love, basking in the sweet pangs of unrequited longing, or lamenting the fickleness of faithless women. The bolero became widely popular as a voice-and-guitar idiom throughout much of Latin America by the 1920s. While the original Cuban style was sung solo or duet in medium tempo, often with a prominent *cinquillo* syncopation, Mexican groups like the Trío Calaveras popularized the practice of singing it in suave, smooth, three-part harmony, accompanied by sophisticated guitar playing and light percussion, with a languid rhythm akin to that of a greatly decelerated *son*. This style then became the norm in Cuba, Puerto Rico, and elsewhere. The most famous of all bolero groups was the New York-based Trio Los Panchos, which flourished in the 1950s and '60s, and generally consisted of two Mexicans and a Puerto Rican. In Cuba, guitar-based boleros and romantic *canciones* (not intended for dance)—which are often referred to collectively as *trova* (as in *trovador*/troubador)—are performed today by groups at restaurants and at state-run *Casas de la Trova* for tourists and elders. Outside Cuba, the bolero is mostly enjoyed by elders, although modernized boleros by the likes of Charlie Zaa and Marc Anthony may occasionally enjoy hit status in the international Latin music scene.

THE *SON* AND MODERN CUBAN DANCE MUSIC

The twentieth century constituted a new chapter in Cuban history. With Spain out of the picture, Cuba developed closer economic, political, and cultural ties with the United States. At the same time, many Cubans, fiercely nationalistic as always, resented the growing Yankee domination of the island and especially the humiliating occupations by the U.S. Marines in 1906–09, 1912, 1917–20, and 1933–34. Meanwhile, Cuban society was modernizing and transforming. Slavery was over, although most black people continued to face dire poverty and overt discrimination until the Revolutionary reforms of the 1960s. One important challenge for the country was the need to develop a national cultural identity that would unite the entire population—white, black, and mulatto. Insofar as this goal has been achieved, music has played an important role in the formation of such an identity. From the 1920s on, hostility to Yankee imperialism and to corrupt dictators like Gerardo Machado fueled the growth of a vibrant cultural nationalism. Despite the persistence of racism, the 1930s saw the belated legalization of drumming and *comparsa* processions, the increasing penetration of Afro-Cuban features in popular music, and a dynamic *afrocubanismo* intellectual movement spearheaded by the music of Caturla and Roldán, the ethnographic studies of Fernando Ortiz, and the poetry of Nicolás Guillén. Perhaps most important for our purposes was the emergence of dance-music genres that synthesized European and Afro-Cuban elements.

We have suggested how the contradanza and danzón became symbols of creole national identity by departing from Spanish traditions and acquiring a distinctively Cuban flavor. Much of this flavor came from the incorporation, whether subtle or overt, of Afro-Cuban syncopations. But the medium-tempo danzón, for all its once controversial rhythmic "oomph," was still a rather genteel and restrained form, far removed from the rumba loved by lower-class blacks. The genre that was to succeed in creatively fusing equal amounts of white- and black-derived musical features was the *son*, which subsequently came to dominate musical culture not only in Cuba but in much of the Spanish-speaking Caribbean.

The *son* originated in eastern Cuba in the first decades of the century, related to similar Oriente genres like *changüí* and *nengón*. From the start it represented a mixture of Spanish-derived and Afro-Cuban elements. In the early *son*, the European features were somewhat more prominent, as is reflected in the predominance of string instruments (guitars and the guitar-like *tres*), the rather moderate tempo, and a "song"-like first section (the *largo*) that had an extended harmonic progression and narrative verses often sung in suave bel canto style. When the *son* took root in Havana, it incorporated pronounced Afro-Cuban features from rumba, notably the *clave* pattern and the extended *montuno* section (following the *largo*), in which vocal call-and-response patterns were sung over a simple harmonic ostinato. These supplemented the use of Afro-Cuban bongo drums and the *marimbula*, a bass instrument derived from African "thumb-pianos" like the mbira. Further, the repeated riffs (*guajeos*) played on the *tres* echoed patterns played on the mbira in Africa. Finally, most *soneros* themselves were black or mulatto, and their song texts were rooted in Afro-Cuban street life and slang.

By 1920, the *son* had become popular in Havana, where most ensembles added a trumpet and replaced the *marimbula* with a stand-up bass, making the standard format a septet. Recordings by the Sexteto Habanero and Ignacio Piñeiro's Septeto Nacional became popular throughout the island and outside Cuba (where their music was often confusingly labeled "rhumba"). The *son* managed to achieve commercial appeal without losing its barrio flavor, reflected in its song texts dealing, like rumba lyrics, with all manner of topics, from romance to neighborhood events.

A spin-off of the *son* was the *guajira* or *guajira-son*, which, as flourishing from the 1930s, fused a medium-tempo *son* rhythm with guitar-based backing and lyrics that praise the beauty of the Cuban countryside and the simple, happy life of the Cuban peasant, as imagined and romanticized by urban songwriters. In that sense, many early *guajiras* represented a kind of fake country music, sort of like North American commercial cowboy music. But, as with cowboy music, rural people grew quite fond of these songs, which thus acquired their own sort of authenticity. The most famous *guajira* is "Guantanamera," which uses a patriotic text by Cuban nationalist José Martí (d. 1895).

The subsequent evolution of the *son* was marked by increasing sophistication featuring, on the one hand, the inclusion of more complex, jazz-influenced harmonies and European instruments (horns and piano) and, on the other hand, the gradual adoption of faster tempos and a more percussive, rhythmic sound. In that sense, the mature *son* was as much an heir to the proletarian rumba as to the suave and genteel danzón.

The most dramatic change came in the 1940s, especially in the music of the Conjunto Casino and of bandleader Arsenio Rodríguez (d. 1970), an Afro-Cuban *tres* player, composer, and arranger. Arsenio, who had lost his sight in childhood after being kicked by a horse, became the most influential bandleader of the decade. In Cuba, however, he was largely shut out of the white-dominated ballrooms and, like other black performers in Cuba's virtual apartheid system, his band was relegated to lower-class and often dangerous black clubs. (Unlike in 1832, white musicians now occupied the good jobs.) Although blind, he could certainly learn from such discrimination what it meant to be black, and many of his songs defiantly asserted the pride he took in his Afro-Cuban heritage, some of which was allegedly transmitted to him by his grandfather, who was born in Calabar. Arsenio's direct contact with his African ancestry gave him both a sense of the continuity of his African ancestry and an acute awareness of the cultural rupture slavery had wrought. As he sang,

> I was born of Africa
> Maybe I'm from the Congo, or maybe from Ampanga...
> I'm not a Rodríguez, I'm not a Fernández...
> Maybe I'm an Amoto, maybe I'm a Momomba.[4]

Together with the Conjunto Casino, Arsenio popularized an enlarged *son* ensemble, adding a conga, a piano, and second or third trumpets (a format called *conjunto*). Most important, all the instruments were to play regulated parts: The horn players played precomposed sectional arrangements while the rhythm section (piano, bass, and percussion) played standardized accompaniment patterns strictly, if subtly, aligned with the *clave* pattern (see Musical Examples 5a and 5b later in this chapter). This modernized *son* gave up some of the informal, collective looseness of the traditional *son*. But it provided a tight, composite rhythm that had a unique drive and an electrifying appeal to dancers. In the early 1950s Arsenio moved to New York, where he laid the foundations for salsa, which was taking the Latin music scene by storm at the same time as Arsenio was dying in relative poverty.

Better able to adapt to the New York salsa scene were mambo bandleader Machito (Frank Grillo) and vocalist Celia Cruz (1924–2003), who achieved fame in the 1950s as the singer with the Sonora Matancera, a conjunto with a somewhat cleaner, less syncopated, and "whiter" sound than Arsenio's (Celia being the *café* in the band's *leche*, or milk). A colorful contemporary of Celia's was the flamboyant, transgressive singer La Lupe, whose wild temperament

**Arsenio Rodríguez (adapted
by Peter Manuel)**

at once animated and unhinged her career in New York; her collaboration
with bandleader Tito Puente ended when she threw one of her high-heeled
shoes at him, hitting him in the head. (Note to aspiring musicians: Don't do
this to your boss.)

The basic two-part formal structure of the *son* has remained the same from
the 1920s to the present, and almost all salsa songs (which many Cubans
would call *son*) also follow this pattern. The first part (the *tema, guía,* or verse
section) is like a closed "song" in itself, usually lasting less than two minutes. Often it uses the thirty-two-bar AABA format typical of Euro-American
popular songs, in which the B section is a modulating bridge. The *montuno*
is usually much longer than the "song" section. It can include extended instrumental solos as well as short horn-based interludes (in salsa terminology,
mambo or moña), which punctuate the call-and-response vocals.

One of the most distinctive features of the composite rhythm of the *son*
(including most salsa songs) is the bass pattern. In most North American and
Afro-American popular musics, from rock and rap to disco and doo-wop,
the bass emphasizes the downbeat, falling strongly on the "one" beat of the
four-beat measure. In the *son*, by contrast, the bass usually omits the downbeat

entirely, in a pattern known as the "anticipated bass." You can get the feel of this rhythm by repeatedly counting "one-two-three-<u>one</u>-two-three-<u>one</u> two" and tapping on the underlined "ones" (not the first "one"!). The pattern is called "anticipated" because the note of the last "one" indicates the chord of the following measure. The resulting effect is quite different from the steady "thump-thump-thump" of such musics as disco, merengue, and most rock. Instead, the rhythm seems to glide along in a fluid manner reflected in the dance style. At fast tempos, it is not too hard for gringos and the uninitiated to get lost (if that happens, listen to the bell part—or seek private therapy from a *salsero*). Jazz trumpeter Dizzy Gillespie used to relate with amusement and awe how he once became completely disoriented in a jam session with Cuban musicians, shouting helplessly, "Where's beat one?" The anticipated bass pattern is found, with some variation, in most salsa songs; together with the characteristically syncopated piano and percussion parts, it forms an essential cog in the intricate machinery of Latin rhythm (and is illustrated in Musical Example 13 (chapter 4).

Another important development of the 1940s was the emergence of the mambo. This term (which originally denoted a kind of *Palo* devotional song) was first popularized by *charanga* performers Orestes López and Antonio Arcaño in the late 1930s to denote their version of the funky, ostinato-based vamp section that had been tagged onto the end of the danzón since José Urfé's "El bombín de Barreto" of 1910. But the better-known mambo consisted of a sped-up, big-band version of this section. Essentially, the mambo was a fusion of Afro-Cuban rhythms with the big-band format adopted from swing jazz. The key to big-band music—aside from its ability to fill a dance hall with sound—was the concept of sectional writing for contrasting instruments, in which distinct trumpet, trombone, and saxophone sections would play interlocking, often responsorial lines. Typically, the saxes might play *guajeo*-type ostinatos adapted from *tres* patterns of the *son* (or the violin vamps of Arcaño's coda), while the other sections would toss melodic fragments back and forth, occasionally all joining in for climactic bursts. Mambos were primarily instrumental dance music, with vocal parts, if present, generally restricted to short nonsense phrases.

Although bands in Cuba like Orquesta Riverside were already playing mambo-style arrangements in the 1940s, the invention of the big-band mambo is usually credited to innovative Cuban bandleader Pérez Prado, who spent most of his years touring in Mexico and elsewhere outside the island. The advent of microphones enabled bandleaders like Beny Moré to combine mambo format with the *son*. The mambo reached its real peak in New York City in the 1950s, where bands led by Machito (with his brother-in-law

Benny Moré (adapted by Peter Manuel)

Mario Bauzá) and the Puerto Rican American Tito Puente incorporated jazz-influenced instrumental solos and more sophisticated arrangements. These bands, together with that of Puerto Rico's Tito Rodríguez, aside from regular gigs at the Palladium, played variously for Latino, Anglo-American, and Afro-American audiences, as well as the Jewish "borscht belt" resorts in the Catskills–outshining corny crossover orchestras like Xavier Cugat's and setting the stage for the salsa boom of the 1970s. As Latin music savant Max Salazar noted, Manhattan's mambo Mecca, the Palladium, was "the laboratory":

> The catalyst that brought Afro-Americans, Irish, Italians, Jews. God, they danced that mambo. And because of the mambo, race relations started to improve in that era. What social scientists couldn't do on purpose, the mambo was able to accomplish by error.[5]

The Palladium was also the site of the evolution of flashy, exhibition-style mambo dancing, which supplemented the basic moves of the Cuban *son* style with figures taken from ballroom, swing, and other styles. With Prado based chiefly in Mexico and the New York mambo bands developing their own styles, Cuban-derived music—now more inclusively called "Latin music"—had already taken on a life of its own outside the island.

Machito and vocalist Graciela at the Savoy Ballroom (Photographs and Prints Division, Schomburg Center for Research in Black Culture, New York Public Library, Astor, Lenox and Tilden Foundation)

A Word about *Clave*

We have mentioned that *clave* (originally meaning "key" and the wooden pegs used in ships) refers to the pair of hardwood sticks used in rumba and *son*, as well as the pattern played on them. *Clave* is actually a rhythmic concept that underlies most forms of Latin (i.e., Afro-Cuban) dance music, from rumba to salsa; for musicians and, on an intuitive level, dancers and listeners, *clave* really is a "key" that makes the music fit together. Musicians swear by the importance of *clave*, and it is worth describing here, even if it is a somewhat technical matter.

In Latin dance music, there are basically two *clave* patterns, the "three–two" *clave* and the more common "two–three" *clave*. Those familiar with early rock 'n' roll will recognize the three–two *clave* from its use in Bo Diddley songs like "Not Fade Away" (Musical Example 5a). The two–three *clave* is the same, but reversed (Musical Example 5b). A given song will be set in one or the other of these patterns (as is generally indicated on the sheet music chart). The *clave* rhythm has been common in

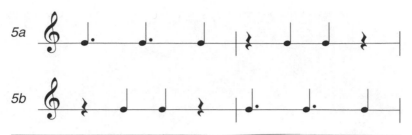

Musical Examples 5a–b. 5a: Three–two *clave*; **5b: Two–three** *clave*

Afro-Cuban music since at least the 1850s, but it may not have been until the music of Arsenio Rodríguez in the 1950s that its use in popular music was consciously codified and standardized.

In the traditional rumba and *son*, these patterns are clearly played on the *clave* sticks (although the rumba pattern, as shown earlier in Musical Example 2, is slightly different). In *conjunto*, mambo, and salsa bands, the *clave* sticks are often absent, so the basic pattern is not sounded. However, in all of these forms, the *clave* pattern is always present in the minds of the musicians and, in a composite, subtle manner, in most of what they play or sing. Thus, the arranger composing the horn parts, the trumpeter or pianist improvising solos, the lead vocalist singing lines in the call-and-response *montuno*—in short, everyone—must have the *clave* pattern going in his head and be following it, however subtly, in his music. (I say "his" because there are precious few women in Latin music.) The idea is not to be slavishly and mechanically beating out the *clave* pattern—that would be obtuse. Instead, for example, if a piece (or a section of a piece) is in two–three *clave*, the musicians will try to suggest that pattern and, above all, to avoid playing or composing lines that suggest three–two *clave*.

Irregularities in *clave* can happen in different ways, aside from the case of a hopelessly amateurish band. Perhaps a guest soloist is present, in the form of some gringo jazz trumpeter who likes Latin music but doesn't really understand *clave*; or perhaps, after a long percussion solo in the middle of the song where the *clave* is especially subtle, the musical director of the band cues the horns to reenter on the wrong measure. Also, some popular songs have always been written with what hardcore musicians would regard as incorrect or *cruzao* (crossed) *clave*. An example is the 1989 hit "Cali Pachanguero," by the Colombian band Grupo Niche. Chris Washburne, a New York salsa trombonist, relates, "That's a catchy song, and audiences love it, but most musicians hate to play it, because the *clave* is all messed up." Another thing that can really screw things up is when some misguided zealot in the audience stands up and starts clapping *clave*—the wrong way—and everyone else joins in. (Rhythmically challenged singers have also been known to do this on occasion: Not to mention names, but the young Marc Anthony did it in 1994, much to the dismay of his band members.)

If, for whatever reason, a dance band starts playing out of *clave*, knowledgeable musicians will exchange despairing glances at one another as they play, and some veteran dancers on the floor may sense, however intuitively, that the sound is somehow jumbled and confused and perhaps this is a good time to take a break and have another beer.

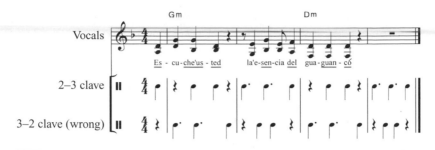

Musical Example 6. "La esencia del *guaguancó*"

Musical Example 7. "Consuélate"

You can get some idea of how *clave* is observed in the *montuno* refrains shown in "La esencia del guaguanco" (Musical Example 6), from a *son* recorded by Johnny Pacheco and Pete "El Conde" Rodríguez, and "Consuélate" (Musical Example 7), from a 1930s Cuban rumba by Tío Tom, later recorded in *son* and salsa versions by Eddie Palmieri.[6] Musical Example 6 is in two–three *clave*; Musical Example 7 is in the somewhat less common three–two. In each case, several of the *clave* beats (as shown by the underlined syllables) coincide with structural beats of the melodies. Try singing these patterns (with help, if need be) while clapping the *clave*. Then try doing the same thing over the "incorrect" three–two pattern. Ideally, you should be able to hear that the "incorrect" *clave* is clearly out of sync with the melody. However, your reaction might still be, "What's so bad about that? It sounds OK to me." But if you listen to a lot of Latin music, you will reach a point where such incongruities sound messy and inappropriate to you (and the rest of the music will sound even better).

While the mambo and conjunto bands were in full flower, the *charangas*, with their quaint yet soulful flute-and-violin sound, were surviving by changing with the times and making their music hotter and more Afro-Cuban. We have mentioned how in the 1930s and '40s, Antonio Arcaño's group codified the use of the "mambo" coda and shortened the opening, more "European" sections. Other *charanga* groups, like the famous Orquesta Aragón, started playing up-tempo *son*, effectively Afro-Cubanizing the charanga repertoire (even if many of its audiences and performers were white). Then, around 1950, *charangas* got a big boost when bandleader Enrique Jorrín popularized the chachachá, a funky, medium-tempo song form with unison vocals, a rhythm like the *charanga*-style mambo, and a catchy "one—two—chachacha" choreography. The chachachá enjoyed its own craze in the United States, but its accompanying commercialization and Arthur Murray–style dilution also guaranteed its decline, at least among Latin musicians, who seemed to be saying, "You Anglos like the chachachá, take it—we're moving on."

Commercial or not, it was through such syntheses of Euro-American and Afro-Cuban elements that these fresh forms, especially the modernized *son*, became the favorite dance music of Cubans of all ages, classes, and races. Meanwhile, the success of the synthesis was reflected internationally, as the *son* and mambo became widely popular in the United States, Africa, and Latin America and provided the basis for what later came to be known as salsa.

In the late 1940s, New York became the crucible for another dynamic Afro-Cuban spin-off when Dizzy Gillespie teamed up with Cuban conga player Chano Pozo to form a Latin big band. Although jazz influences had already come to permeate Cuban dance music, Gillespie's band was the first to present mambo-style big-band pieces like "Manteca" not as dance music but as listening music, emphasizing jazz-style solos. Thus began the subgenre known as Latin jazz, which came to denote listening-oriented, predominantly instrumental music, usually played by a combo rather than a big band and featuring sophisticated improvised solos.

Cuban dance music reached a peak of sorts in the 1950s. The *son*, mambo, and chachachá were in full flower, with New York and Havana as the twin poles of a Latin dance dynamo. Havana had also become America's bachelor entertainment center, with its glittery world of casinos, cabarets, and more than two hundred brothels. Bands led by Miguelito Cuní, Felix Chappotin, and Benny Moré were in constant local and international demand.

But the revelry and merriment of the '50s could barely mask the deep tensions in Cuban society that were in the process of exploding. More and more Cubans were growing disgusted with the prostitution and the poverty and alienation of the lower classes; the continued domination of the Cuban economy by Yankee businesses and mafiosi; and the corrupt dictatorship of Fulgencio Batista, who spent most of his waking hours playing canasta and whom the U.S. government indulgently regarded as "a son of a bitch, but *our* son of a bitch." People of various political leanings began to sympathize with the earnest urban guerrillas and with the ragtag band of bearded revolutionaries off in the Sierra Maestra led by one Fidel Castro.

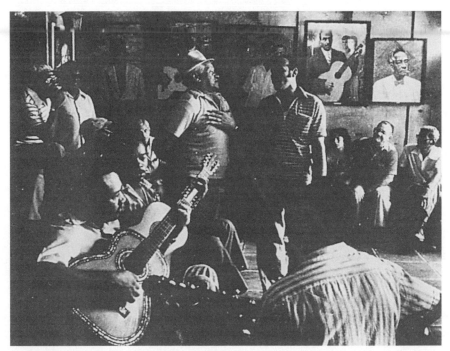

Old *trovadores* (both by María "Marucha" Haya, courtesy of Center for Cuban Studies)

"SOCIALISM WITH PACHANGA"

Regardless of whether a communist dictatorship was what most Cuban supporters of the anti-Batista struggle had in mind, that was the direction in which the Cuban Revolution was driven by events, including hostility from Washington, D.C., Soviet friendship, and Castro's personal vision. The Revolution had profound effects on every aspect of Cuban life and culture, including music. One change was that, because of the U.S. embargo of Cuba, North Americans and Puerto Ricans were cut off from musical activities on the island. Cuban groups and their records were not allowed into the United States, so a myth began to spread in this country that communism had killed Cuban music. The reality is far more complex, and whatever the merits or demerits of the Revolution as a whole, music has done presentably well in recent decades. In general, the communist government—at least, since the 1970s—has treated the arts and culture as high priorities, and music has received fairly generous support. Revolutionary leader Che Guevara envisioned Cuban communism not as a drab work regime but as a dynamic program of economic justice and lively popular culture—or, as he put it, as "socialism with *pachanga*" (referring to a popular dance rhythm of the '50s).

Guevara's vision was only partially achieved, and not without some egregious shortcomings—starting, perhaps, with the defection of pachanga inventor Eduardo Davidson and the subsequent banning of his songs. The initial decades of the Revolution were tough for dance music and musicians, as the tourist venues that had sustained them closed, and the government seemed generally indifferent to local popular music. The performance of the record industry—a nationalized bureaucracy since the early 1960s—was particularly undistinguished. The records produced were generally too few and too late, their sound was uneven, and they have had little international distribution (partly due to the U.S. embargo). Some would say that a state bureaucracy is simply incapable of running anything so complex as a music industry, not to mention a national economy, and that the Cubans who knew how to run it went to Miami. Because the mass media in Cuba do not disseminate any music by defectors, Cubans lost touch with the music of expatriates like Celia Cruz just as the bamboo curtain kept North Americans in the dark about the Cuban music scene. As Sue Steward wrote, "Musicians found themselves playing to mystified audiences in Moscow or Budapest, to grateful Cuban soldiers serving in Angola, and to factory workers' co-operatives and students at home."[7] Among the most frustrated musicians were Latin jazz superstars like trumpeter Arturo Sandoval and saxophonist Paquito D'Rivera, who were unable to tour the United States because of the American embargo; both eventually defected and now live in the United States. Critics also argue, with some legitimacy, that the extraordinary musical vitality of the 1950s has not been matched since, with the Revolution having "Castrated," as it were, the lively music culture that thrived in the colorful world of casinos, brothels, and nightclubs. Harsh times for Cuban dance music continued in the '70s, as many young people came to prefer rock and in any case had little opportunity to hear live music of any sort. For its part, during this period, the state—the nearly exclusive employer of professional musicians—did little to promote Cuban dance music, regarded rock and jazz as decadent Yankee imports, and in various inconsistent ways attempted to discourage the practice of Afro-Cuban religions and their traditional music.

By the mid-'80s the situation had improved markedly. The foreign salsa vogue—and a tour by Venezuelan *salsero* Oscar D'León—did much to rekindle youth interest in local dance music. In effect, the *son*, after stagnating in its homeland, had to get a fashionable facelift and approval stamp in New York before being revived in Cuba. Belatedly, the government began to promote it energetically while also outgrowing its hangups about rock, jazz, and Afro-Cuban religion. The two most popular groups of the era (which are still going in 2005) were Los Van Van, a sort of enlarged *charanga* ensemble that popularized the *comparsa*-influenced *songo* beat, and Irakere, a brassy supergroup that does both straight-ahead dance music and eclectic avant-garde syntheses of *son*, jazz, rock, and Afro-Cuban music. In a more straightforward *son*/salsa format was Adalberto Alvarez's Son 14, which was as hot as any New York band.

In some respects, the Revolution has had more impact on how music is produced and consumed than on the nature of the music itself. With the nationalization of all aspects of the music industry—from clubs and conservatories to the manufacture of conga drums—all forms of commercialism were removed from musical culture. Qualified students have enjoyed free music education at conservatories, which have continued to churn out impressive ranks of rigorously trained performers. By the 1980s, musicians were free to experiment, and they have not been pressured to politicize their art (although they would also be ill-advised to criticize the basic goals of the Revolution in public). In accordance with the generous state support of music, most full-time professional musicians, until the economic crisis of the 1990s, enjoyed leisurely work schedules and cradle-to-grave security. (In the United States, by contrast, most dance-band musicians have to work full-time day jobs to survive.) In the 1980s, Antonio, a pianist in a hotel dance band, told me, "I play three hours a day, and for that I get full salary, a month's vacation, and, of course, free health care. The rest of the time I practice, hang out, and watch American TV, which I pick up via my homemade antenna." (That kind of low productivity is exactly what is wrong with Cuban socialism, say some critics.) Meanwhile, the state supported all kinds of old and new music, from *punto* contests to the avant-garde experiments of guitarist Leo Brouwer and the pyrotechnics of jazz pianist Gonzalo Rubalcaba.

For people like folklorist Rogelio Martínez Furé, director of the Conjunto Nacional Folklórico, the biggest improvement resulting from the Cuban Revolution was the integration of lower-class Afro-Cubans and their culture into the mainstream of Cuban society. This reform was achieved partly by raising the lower class's standard of living and education (at the expense of the rich); by eliminating the racial discrimination that barred black people from many pre-Revolutionary clubs, beaches, hotels, and restaurants; and by providing state support—however qualified and inconsistent—of Afro-Cuban culture and music and fostering a new, integrated Cuban sense of identity. Although racism and various forms of discrimination certainly persist, in many ways Cuba and its culture have grown increasingly blacker in the Revolutionary period—partly due to the emigration of several hundred thousand whites around 1960.

In its early years, the fervent nationalism, invigorated sense of purpose, and state support fostered by the Revolution unleashed considerable creative energy, manifesting itself in several aspects of Cuban life, from music and cinema to sports and medical research. For that matter, the vitality of music in Revolutionary Cuba must also be viewed in relation to changes in society as a whole. Communist Cuba, for example, was for several decades the only country in the Americas with a music industry free of under-the-table payoffs, liquor-company and narco-dollar sponsorship, advertisements, and commercialism in general. It was also the only country in the hemisphere with no homelessness, drug addiction, and malnutrition (until the present crisis, which owes much to a crippling U.S. embargo). Insofar as these aspects of modern Cuba have influenced musicians, audiences, and cultural life in general, they have been relevant features of the Cuban musical milieu. Another relevant feature, unfortunately, has been the stultifying atmosphere of censorship, fear, and bureaucratized stagnation that has impoverished many aspects of intellectual life, artistic creativity, and civil society in general.

The most distinctive new music associated with the revolution has been *nueva trova*, the Cuban variety of Latin American *nueva canción* (new song), which is itself loosely related to North American "protest music." *Nueva trova* emerged in the early 1970s, and insofar as its performers were inspired by Yankee singers like Bob Dylan and Joan Baez, it had to struggle to overcome a profound mistrust on the part of the state bureaucracy. Nevertheless, in the

Nueva trova singer Pablo Milanés (María "Marucha" Haya, courtesy of Center for Cuban Studies)

1970s and '80s, its leading performers, Pablo Milanés and Silvio Rodríguez, became international stars, especially among educated, politically progressive Latin American youths. Some *nueva trova* songs make self-conscious use of traditional Cuban elements, but most are in the singer-songwriter vein of international balladeers.

Much *nueva trova* sounds essentially like soft-rock ballads, appreciated by listeners for its sophisticated lyrics, its often beautiful melodies, and the progressive politics of its singers. Many *nueva trova* songs are about love, but many deal with contemporary sociopolitical issues. As one singer recently related, "We are free to be controversial; we do songs about housing shortages, pollution, how vacation spots give priority to foreigners."[8] Still, most songs implicitly endorse the ideals of the Revolution; they generally avoid vulgar slogan mongering, preferring the pensive yet committed affirmation of Pablo Milanés's "I Don't Live in a Perfect Society" or Silvio Rodríguez's "Little Daytime Serenade," a subtle, poignant tribute to the martyrs of the Cuban Independence Wars and the Cuban Revolution:

> I live in a free country,
> which can only be free in this land, in this moment
> and I'm happy because I am a giant. . . .
> I'm happy, a happy man
> and I wish to beg pardon for this day
> from all those who died for my happiness.[9]

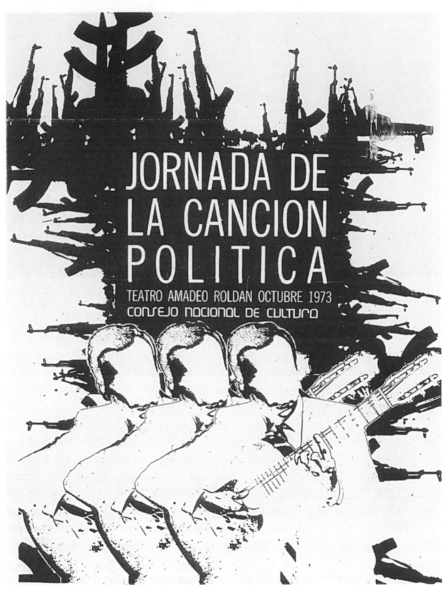

Poster for 1973 festival of political song (courtesy of Center for Cuban Studies)

THE "SPECIAL PERIOD" AND ITS SPECIAL MUSIC

In the early 1990s, the Cuban economy collapsed because of the loss of the Soviet umbilical cord, the inflexibility of hard-line Communist policies ("Castro Inconvertible"), and a tightened American embargo designed either to provoke civil war or to starve the country (children and all) into submission.[10] Life for most Cubans has since come to revolve around securing basic needs of food, clothing, and shelter. With the state-run economy more inefficient than ever, black-marketeering has become pervasive, and a spirit of cynicism and opportunism has largely replaced the Revolutionary ideals of earlier decades. As the government has belatedly turned to tourism to stay afloat, the worst aspects of 1950s urban culture have returned with a vengeance: prostitution, crime, and an opulent tourist sector that is inaccessible to Cubans. Accompanying these are a demoralizing parallel economy that separates those who have access to dollars from the other 95 percent who have to survive on pathetically small peso salaries. As of 2005, the *"periodo especial"* (special period) continues as dismally as ever, although much may change when a certain individual passes away.

The effects of the changes on music have been profound, and profoundly mixed. The biggest structural developments, as in (post-)communist China, have been a decrease in state subsidies of and controls on the arts, and tolerance, or even promotion, of any kind of music that can bring in a few dollars. Classical music and zarzuela, which have little tourist appeal, have suffered. Santería music can be said to be thriving, as the state has fully recognized Afro-Cuban religions, and from all accounts more people than ever are turning to Santería as a source of social, civic, and spiritual fulfillment. Many songs, whether in rap or salsa styles, openly celebrate Santería. For its part, the appeal of *nueva trova* has decreased along with Revolutionary idealism, although a few singers have modernized the genre in style and content. Especially notable in the "special period" has been Carlos Varela, whose most famous song, "Guillermo Tell," portrays William Tell's son asking his aging father to give him the bow and arrow and put the apple on his own head. As Cuban audiences know well how to interpret this, in recording such a song on a foreign tour Varela is clearly pushing the boundaries of the permissible, as does Pedro Luís Ferrer in "El abuelo Paco":

> Be patient with grandpa, remember how much he's done....
> Don't forget that he has a revolver and a knife
> And as long as they're not taken away, he poses a threat
> Even if you know the answer is no, say yes,
> If you contradict him, it will go badly for you.

Grave problems notwithstanding, the post–Soviet period has been a fertile time for dance music, especially in the emergence of a new sound called timba. As popularized in the 1990s by NG La Banda, Charanga Habanera, and other bands, most timba sounds like jazzed-up salsa/*son* with an aggressive, avant-garde edge, featuring multiple, often rapped or shouted *coro* refrains, virtuoso horn lines, funky slapped bass lines, and breaks in which several instruments drop out. Other timba performers, like the doctor-turned-crooner (and subsequent defector) Manolín "El Médico," offer a smoother, *salsa romántica* sound. In the tradition of calypsos like "Rum and Coca-Cola," lyrics typically comment with wry ambivalence on the world of tourists and dollar-chasing *jineteras*—a word that literally means "female jockeys" but now implies women who, one way or another, hustle dollars from tourists. Charanga Habanera's "La temba" is typical, especially in its use of contemporary slang:

> Find yourself a *temba* (an eligible middle-aged bachelor) who can keep you,
> so that you can have what you need,
> a *papirriqui* (sugar daddy) with *wanikiki* (dollars).

Dance has changed accordingly, with the standard salsa-type *casino* style being supplemented by the *despelote* in which women shake their waists freestyle with their hands raised. The dominance of women in this style, which parallels counterparts in reggae and soca dancing, seems to reflect the independence and entrepreneurial spirit of *jineteras* in the new, dollar-driven milieu. Alternately, dancers might form a collective *casino de rueda*, in which several couples do complex figures following signals given by a leader.

For their part, the poor bureaucrats weren't quite sure how to handle the whole timba scene. On the one hand, it brings in money, especially via taxes paid by the musicians, who are now allowed to tour abroad and record with foreign labels. On the other hand, the state disapproves of the flashy, consumerist lifestyle of the stars and the way that the whole genre is entrenched both in the seedy side of tourist culture and in urban, black, lumpen-proletarian street culture. In 1997, Charanga Habanera was grounded for six months after it referred to marijuana and obliquely criticized Castro in a live concert. Nevertheless, Cuban music is finally back on the Latin music map, as fancy recording studios have been built by *nueva trovadores* Pablo Milanés and Silvio Rodríguez and enterprising European indie labels are relicensing classics and signing contracts with the hottest timba groups.

A different sort of musical development came in the form of the American guitarist Ry Cooder's 1997 album trio and Wim Wenders's subsequent film *The Buena Vista Social Club*, which featured a set of octogenarian performers of 1920s-style *son* and bolero. The records and film, with their nostalgic "discovery" of this quaint and authentic-sounding music, became interna tional hits (except among the more pragmatic Latino communities), and the performers enjoyed an unprecedented international stardom in their twilight years. Cubans themselves had mixed reactions. The state was happy with the money made; some Cubans were proud of new fad of their heritage; timba musicians felt annoyed by the focus on such old-timers; and most people seemed at once indifferent to this long-out-of-vogue music and bemused by the faddish eccentricity of the international music scene.

CODA: REVISITING HAVANA—AND MIAMI, 2004

Having been unable to face the "special period" for many years, I have finally returned to Havana for a visit. Things have indeed changed, starting with the flight there, which is full of rowdy Cuban Americans ready to party and about twenty African Americans who are going to "make saint"—that is, to become formally initiated into Santería for a few thousand dollars apiece. From the fancy new airport to the spiffy dollar-based convenience stores and cafes, Havana of today is a much more manageable and pleasant place for me, for other tourists, and for the lucky Cubans who, one way or another, have dollars. It is not so nice for Carlos, a full-time car mechanic I meet on the street, whose monthly salary is the peso equivalent of about seven dollars—less than the price of the four beers I buy us. If you encounter him on the street and ask how he is, he, like many Cubans, may offer the standard response, "Luchando"—struggling! Indeed, the Revolutionary government has finally achieved its goal of erasing class distinctions: Just about everyone is poor. Meanwhile, I am amazed to see the 1950s DeSotos and T-Birds still chugging along, having outlasted the Soviet-bloc Ladas imported in the '80s. Over the next few days, I don't hear much *son* or timba, as all the hot bands are either touring abroad, as is typically the case, or, like balladeer Carlos Manuel, have split for good. In general, there are hardly any venues where ordinary Cubans can go to dance or hear music in Havana, and the provinces are even worse. The nicely renovated tourist hotels and restaurants, however, abound in the Buena Vista–type revival groups that tourists want to hear. The restaurants, like the CDs in the hotel stores, are for those who have dollars (although in late 2004 dollars were again banned). Most Cubans have access to recorded music only though the radio or through informally distributed cassettes, by which hits like the irreverent rap song "¿Quién tiró la tiza?" (Who threw the chalk?)" circulate completely independent of the state.

The main musical event is a three-day conference and concert series of Cuban rap, organized by the Agencia Cubana de Rap, or the Cuban Rap Agency. If the Cuban government scorned rock as a decadent Yankee import in the early '70s, it now embraces Cuban rap as reflecting how the island can keep up with trends despite the embargo. Or is it that, once again, the state has belatedly recognized the dynamism of grassroots Cuban musical culture and hopes to earn some "wanikiki" from it? The concerts featured various local *moneros*, or rappers, hoping to be discovered; conspicuously absent is the brilliant rap group Orishas, who reside in Paris most of the year. Nevertheless, although rap as a style may be from the Bronx, and the Orishas are seldom seen in Cuba, the group members are, as they sing, "*cien por cien cubano*" (100 percent Cuban). In the panel session I attend, speakers argued about the relationship of rap to the more party-oriented reggaetón, the role of women in rap, and the need to incorporate rappers from outside Havana. The discussion session is lively, with some complaining that the Cuban Rap Agency is a bureaucratic dinosaur that just wants to control the rap scene; an organizer angrily defends the agency, saying that in the absence of free-market institutions, it is the only entity that can organize events, promote artists, and facilitate contacts with foreign journalists and record companies. The organizer seems well-meaning and dedicated, but I have a sense that everything may change within a few years. In the meantime, rap seems to be perpetuating *nueva canción*'s tradition of social criticism, as rappers, most of whom are black, explicitly indict the police and society at large for the racist harassment they so often experience—evidence of a discrimination the Revolution claims to have eliminated. As one rapper said, the new situation "has brought back the need to talk about things that weren't talked about before, things like racism, sexism, homophobia . . . in a process that's healthy for the Revolution."[11] At least, that's the sort of "positive" wording that rappers have learned to use in treading the thin line between acceptable critique and criminal, counter-Revolutionary offense—a distinction that depends on the vagaries of the bureaucracy and, for all one knows, the state of Castro's bunions.

For its part, change may also come someday to the Miami area, which is home to about a million Cuban Americans, especially white and bourgeois exiles from the Revolution and their descendants. Despite the Miami community's size, the city's musical scene has traditionally been weakened both by shortage of talent and a ferocious banning of any musicians deemed less than rabidly anti-Castro—a category that has included not only Cuban nationals themselves but also the non-Cuban salsa stars Oscar D'León, Ruben Blades, and Andy Montañez, and even Spanish balladeer Julio Iglesias, who committed the sin of mentioning that he might like to visit Cuba. The few local venues that have dared to host occasional visiting Cuban musicians have been subjected to bombings, and their patrons have been physically assaulted. Such crimes are routinely ignored by Miami law-enforcement agencies, which are thoroughly intimidated by the right-wing Cuban mafia. The local star act has been Gloria Estefan, formerly of the Miami Sound Machine, with its crossover hits of the 1980s and '90s. Estefan's relationship to her ancestral homeland culture is complex. Her music embraces both Anglo rock and Cuban tradition, and her video of "The Rhythm's Gonna Get You" (included in the first *Beats of the Heart* film) adds a Hollywood-style installment to the embarrassing history of blackface minstrelsy. But in the new millennium, Miami seems finally to be emerging as a cosmopolitan cultural, as well as economic, hub of the Latin United States, enlivened by a new, more open-minded generation of Cubans as well as by the presence of defectors like Manolin, Arturo Sandoval, and innovative songstress Albita Rodríguez.

BIBLIOGRAPHY

Cuban writers have produced many excellent books on all varieties of Cuban music, but they are in Spanish and are generally unavailable even in Cuba, not to mention elsewhere. Spanish-language books available (with a bit of hunting) in the United States include Cristobal Díaz Ayala, *Música cubana del areyto a la nueva trova* (Hato Rey, Puerto Rico: Editorial Cubanacan, 1981); Tony Evora, *Orígenes de la música cubana: Los amores de las cuerdas y el tambor* (Madrid: Alianza Editorial, 1997); and Alejo Carpentier's dated but still peerless *La música en Cuba* (Mexico City: Fonda de Cultura Económica, 1946). Carpentier's book is now available in English as *Music in Cuba*, ed. Timothy Brennan, trans. Alan West-Duran (Minneapolis: University of Minnesota Press, 2001). The best overview of Cuban music before the 1950s is Ned Sublette's magisterial *Cuba and Its Music: From the First Drums to the Mambo* (Chicago: Chicago Review Press, 2004). Another fine study, in a more specialized vein, is Robin Moore's *Nationalizing Blackness: Afrocubanismo and Artistic Revolution in Havana, 1920–1940* (Pittsburgh: University of Pittsburgh Press, 1997). Two good portrayals of the modern scene are Vincenzo Perna's scholarly *Timba: The Sound of the Cuban Crisis* (London: Ashgate, 2005) and the entertaining, more journalistic *Last Dance in Havana*, by Eugene Robinson (New York: Free Press, 2004).

RECORDS AND FILMS

TRADITIONAL GENRES: *Cuban Counterpoint: History of the Son Montuno* (Rounder CD 1078); *Caliente = Hot: Puerto Rican and Cuban Musical Expression in New York* (New World 244); *Afro-Cuba: A Musical Anthology* (Rounder CD 1088); *Sacred Rhythms of Cuban Santería* (Smithsonian Folkways SFW40419 1995); *The Cuban Danzon: Its Ancestors and Descendants* (Smithsonian Folkways FW04066 1982).

ANTHOLOGIES: *A Carnival of Cuban Music: Routes of Rhythm, Volumes 1 & 2* (Rounder CD 5049); *Rough Guide to Cuban Son* (World Music Network); *Rough Guide to Mambo* (World Music Network); *Rough Guide to Afro-Cuba* (World Music Network); *Cuba Classics 2: Dancing with the Enemy* (Luaka Bop 9 26580–2); *Arsenio Rodríguez* (Ansonia ALP 1337); *Cuba Classics 3: Diablo al infierno* (Luaka Bop 9 45107–2).

FILM: Eugene Rosow and Howard Dratch, prod., *Routes of Rhythm, with Harry Belafonte (Volumes 1–3)* (Cultural Research and Communication, Inc., 1989).

3

Puerto Rico

Much of urban Puerto Rico looks more or less like parts of the mainland United States. After all, in its "commonwealth" status, Puerto Rico, although not a state, is politically and economically part of the United States. Its culture is also a mixed bag of the indigenous and the imported. Certainly, there is plenty of mainstream stateside culture there, from Britney Spears to Burger King. For that matter, in speaking of Puerto Rican society, it is ultimately impossible to separate the island from the mainland United States, where two-fifths of the people of Puerto Rican descent live. Likewise, New York is the largest Puerto Rican city and has been the biggest center for some kinds of Puerto Rican dance music since the 1930s. But there are many aspects of Puerto Rican culture that really flourish only on the island, especially its rich heritage of folk musics, from rural songs to the lively, percussive plena and bomba.

In my first trip to Puerto Rico, I visited an Anglo friend, Al, who had married a Puerto Rican woman and lived in San Juan.

"How do you get along with your in-laws?" I asked.

"It's been fine since I learned to dance," he replied. "That was a big problem at first. It seemed that every time I was over there, at the drop of a hat someone would put on a record, and then it's party time, and I have to dance with the mother, the grandmother, the aunts, you name it. But I didn't know how to dance Latin-style, so I felt like a real *pendejo* [not a nice word]. Then I actually took lessons for almost a year and learned to dance salsa, merengue, bolero, all that stuff. Since then it's been great. Man, these people just love to dance."

"Do you ever hear plena?"

"All the time. There's a business being picketed by striking union workers across from my apartment, and the protesters sing plena most of the day."

"Sounds more like a party than a picket line," I mused.

"Well, that's certainly how some people felt in New York, when it seemed to them that the Puerto Rican contingent in street demonstrations was turning them into fiestas. But that's how they use plena down here. No student protest is complete without it."

"What about bomba?" I asked, eager to see the island's oldest Afro-Caribbean dance form.

"That's a bit harder to find. But if we're lucky we'll see some at the *fiesta patronal* in Loíza next weekend."

And indeed we did. But before telling you about that, let's review some of the historical background of Puerto Rican music.

CUBA AND PUERTO RICO: "THE TWO WINGS OF THE SAME BIRD"

In its history and culture, Puerto Rico has much in common with Cuba, its sister colony under Spanish rule until 1898. As in Cuba, the Spanish conquistadors claiming Puerto Rico in 1493 found a local Taino Indian population, whom they enslaved and soon effectively exterminated. Taino culture also died out, but as in Cuba, many Taino words survive, especially food and place names—including the island's original name, Borinquen (Borikén). This name and the image of Taino culture in general live on as symbols of national identity and of a free and independent Puerto Rico. Like Cuba, colonial Puerto Rico became populated by substantial numbers of Europeans from Spain and elsewhere, and by slaves brought from Africa.

In the nineteenth century, as more and more Puerto Ricans grew frustrated with backward and oppressive Spanish rule, a nationalistic creole culture developed on the island in tandem with its Cuban counterpart. From the early 1800s until today, Puerto Ricans have avidly borrowed and mastered various music styles from Cuba and elsewhere, including the Cuban danzón, *son*, rumba, and bolero, and the Dominican merengue, not to mention rock, rap, and reggae(tón). Indeed, the richness of Puerto Rican musical culture derives in large part from the way it has adopted and domesticated so many imported musics while contributing its own dynamic folk and contemporary popular musics. Some of the major Puerto Rican music genres can also be seen as counterparts to Cuban ones; thus, for example, the Puerto Rican *seis* and danza, which we discuss later, can be regarded as parallels to Cuban campesino music and the danzón, respectively.

But Puerto Rico should not be regarded as simply a miniature Cuba, especially since genres like the *seis*, *bomba*, and *plena* are distinctly Puerto Rican creations, owing little to Cuban influence in their traditional forms. Beyond that, there are significant historical, cultural, and political differences between the two islands, which are reflected in their distinct musical heritages. One difference is that while Cuba's sugar-plantation economy brought about the massive importation of African slaves in the nineteenth century, Puerto Rico's main agricultural products in the Spanish period were tobacco and coffee, neither of which required large amounts of slave labor. As a result, proportionally fewer Africans were brought to Puerto Rico (never amounting to more than 12 percent of the population), and the institution of slavery as a whole was far less widespread and culturally significant than in Cuba (or in the United States, for that matter). Perhaps partly as a consequence of this, neo-African music and religion are less prominent in Puerto Rico than in Cuba.

The islands' political fortunes also diverged after 1898. While both came under the domination of the United States, in Puerto Rico this took the form of direct colonial rule. Since the institutionalization of the "commonwealth" arrangement in 1952, Puerto Rico has achieved the highest material standard of living in Latin America, but North American rule has been a mixed blessing. Most Puerto Ricans lived in dire poverty until the 1950s, when Governor Luis Muñoz Marin's combination of socialist public works, capitalist investment stimuli, and incentives to emigrate helped uplift the island economy. However, industry and agribusiness brought pollution and ended the island's former self-sufficiency, so that it has since exported most of its products to the mainland and imported most of what it consumes. Most of the rural population has been effectively dispossessed, driven to seek work in San Juan, New York City, and throughout the United States. Puerto Rican migrants developed an acute sense of marginalization and alienation, while many on the island came to resent the dominance of mainland corporations and the inundation of cheap American commercial culture.

Under such conditions, Latin music and, especially, indigenous genres took on a special role in Puerto Rican culture as symbols of an independent national identity. At the same time, most Puerto Ricans are cosmopolitans who are happy to enjoy and reinterpret music styles from abroad that suit their tastes.

EUROPEAN-DERIVED MUSICS

The Hispanic-derived musical forms that evolved in Puerto Rico reflected the class stratification of colonial society. Classical and light-classical musics flourished in the salons of the small but culturally significant elite, which consisted mostly of agricultural landowners, or *hacendados*. Most *hacendados* had natural cultural ties to Spain, but as in Cuba, autocratic and economically repressive colonial dictatorship bred increasing discontent. One colonial governor declared, "The locals can be ruled with a whip and a violin," while another banned beards because they looked subversive to him. Frustration with such misrule fed nationalistic sentiment and conditioned the development of an aristocratic creole culture.

The primary urban base for this culture was the southern town of Ponce rather than the capital, San Juan, whose own cultural and intellectual life was stifled by the colonial bureaucracy and the reactionary Catholic Church. The musical form that came to embody the spirit of emerging bourgeois nationalism was the danza, which appears to have derived, appropriately enough, not from Spain but primarily from the Cuban contradanza and, later, the danzón, while sharing general features with creole Caribbean genres like the Haitian salon *merèng*. However, as they did with other styles adopted from Cuba, Puerto Rican musicians turned the borrowed idiom into something new and distinctly local. This kind of creative appropriation is most evident in the ensemble danzas of Juan Morel Campos (d. 1896), and especially the piano danzas of Manuel Tavárez (d. 1895). These combine a Chopinesque sophistication with a tiny hint of jaunty Afro-Caribbean syncopation, in the form of the familiar creole *cinquillo* ostinato—perhaps rendered in a subdued, rubato style. Like the Cuban contradanza, the danza came to be adopted by petty bourgeois artisans and merchants and by peasants, all of whom interpreted it in their own livelier, more accessible fashion (leading the colonial governor to attempt to ban it in 1849). By the 1920s, the danza had become archaic; although no longer popular at dance halls, it is still often heard at weddings, and the unofficial Puerto Rican anthem, "La Borinqueña," is a suave danza rather than a pompous martial air.

More resilient and widespread forms of creole music were developed by the island's small farmers, the *jíbaros*. White or mixed-race peasants who accounted for the vast majority of the population until the 1930s, the *jíbaros* have been regarded as the epitome of traditional Puerto Rican identity. In literature and song, they have long been celebrated, however paternalistically and nostalgically, for their legendary hospitality, individuality, self-sufficiency, and love of the simple pleasures of nature, coffee, fiestas, and homespun music. Accordingly, *jíbaro* music has been regarded as a quintessential symbol of island culture, however diminished its actual popularity is now.

The most distinctive feature of *jíbaro* music is its typical ensemble of *cuatro* (a guitar relative with five doubled strings), guitar, and assorted percussion instruments (usually güiro and maracas). The *jíbaro* music repertoire today includes several forms of obvious European origin, such as the waltz and the mazurka, along with the Cuban-derived *guaracha* and the occasional Dominican merengue. But the backbone of the *jíbaro* repertoire consists of the purely local *seis* and *aguinaldo*. Both the *seis* and the *aguinaldo* have several subvarieties, distinguished by stock melodies and harmonic progressions. They are named variously after places of origin (*seis fajardeño*, *aguinaldo orocoveño*), musicians (*seis andino*), or formal features (*seis con décimas*). *Aguinaldos* are particularly associated with the Christmas season, when roving bands of amateur musicians (*parrandas*) stroll from house to house, singing, accepting snacks and drinks, and partying. Since a visit by such an entourage can be unexpected, it is typically referred to as an *asalto*, or assault.

Both the *seis* and the *aguinaldo* can accompany dance, especially at informal back-country fiestas, and they are often fast and lively. The Spanish origin of the instrumentation and Andalusian harmony is clear, although in the twentieth century, *jíbaro* music, especially in studio-recorded forms, has often incorporated an Afro-Caribbean flavor in the form of bongos, syncopated bass, and Cuban rhythms. While using stock harmonic-melodic forms, the *seis* and the *aguinaldo* are very rich musically in their alluring melodies, catchy rhythms, and often flashy *cuatro* playing.

The most important aspect of the *seis* and the *aguinaldo*, however, is the lyrics, which since the mid-nineteenth century have constituted a rich body of oral literature chronicling the joys and sorrows of the Puerto Rican people. It is important to remember that, as in Cuba, poetry and especially the *décima* have not been purely aristocratic forms but idioms widely cultivated by ordinary folk. Partly as a result of the low literacy prevailing until the mid-twentieth century, oral culture has been particularly vital in Puerto Rico, and it is safe to say that poetry in general has been much more widely cultivated on the island than in the United States. Particularly prized is the ability of the poet-singer (*trovador*) to improvise *décimas* on the spot, whether on a given *pie forzado* (forced foot, or the final line of a *décima*) or in response to a competitor in a *controversia*. Accordingly, the lyric content of the *seis* and the *aguinaldo* is rich, dealing with a wide variety of topics. The timeless themes of love, patriotism, maternal devotion, and religion are prominent, along with all manner of topical sociopolitical commentary. Often lyrics relate the cruel misfortune of the singer, who laments, *triste y olvidado*—sad and forgotten. Other *décimas* are humorous and satirical, particularly in the case of *controversias*, such as this one between the famed jíbaro singer Chuito (Jesús Sanchéz) and his son, Chuitín:

Chuitín:
Come with me, my friend, let's go hear Ejío's band,
it's a hot party, and they say it'll go on till dawn.
My wife is so proper, she'll stay at home.
Don't say no, let's go party,
and I'll show you that I'm the boss in my house.

Chuito:
I won't go there with you,
because it's known that your wife is fearsome and disliked by all.
If she finds out you're planning to drink,
God bless you, she won't let you go.
She won't let you move from the plaza to the corner,
because I know that she's the boss in your house.

Chuitín:
You're all wrong, you know that I'll go by car
and I'll spend the whole night dancing.
When I get a little tipsy, I even dance the *guaguancó*.
The dance has started, so let's go and boogie,
I'll show you who's the boss at my house.

Chuito:
You're a fool if you go there,
because your wife has you boxed up in a coffin.
She'll give you a black eye, listen Chuitín, you'll see.
In the morning when you return she'll be as hot as a coal,
because I know in your house she's the boss.[1]

Within the first half of the twentieth century, Puerto Rican society changed beyond recognition under the impact of U.S. rule. As American agribusiness acquired most of the arable land, most *hacendados* were bankrupted, and the *jíbaros* were dispossessed. Deprived of livelihood, they migrated en masse to cities, especially San Juan, where they congregated in slums like La Perla. The rate of urbanization was dramatic: In 1900, roughly 95 percent of the population was rural; by 1970, it was 60 percent urban. From the 1940s on, hundreds of thousands of *jíbaros* migrated to the mainland United States in search of work. As a result, *jíbaros*, along with their lifestyle, have nearly disappeared, although their music lives on.

Many *seises* and *aguinaldos* chronicle the migrant experience, which we discuss later. Some focus on the problems of adjusting to modernization:

The first shoes I got, I used to wear them on the wrong feet.
When I came to Mayagüez, *caramba*, what a spectacle I caused.[2]

Others, like this poignant *décima* sung by Ramito (Flor Morales Ramos, 1915–90), the most brilliant *jíbaro* singer of his century, nostalgically lament the passing of an entire way of life:

My Borinquen has changed so much,
and for me it's a surprise.
It causes me great pain,
that the past is so transformed.
It's become so modernized,
in a way I can't explain.

Jíbaro musician with *cuatro* (Center for Traditional Music and Dance)

Jíbaro musicians (Center for Traditional Music and Dance)

Today, while I sing, I'll tell you,
I feel an emptiness in my soul,
because they've changed my hut
for a house made of cement.

There is no one to shoe
either the mare or the stallion,
and in preparing his vegetables,
the peasant doesn't even want to do it by hand anymore.
He no longer listens intently
to the song of the rooster,
and to feel at home,
he can no longer walk about in the morning
when the river and brook
are replaced by a cement canal.[3]

While the decline of *jíbaro* culture is chronicled in such song texts, it is also clear in the reduced popularity and importance of *jíbaro* music in Puerto Rican culture. Most young Puerto Ricans regard *seis* and *aguinaldo* as "hick" music, preferring the contemporary sounds of salsa, merengue, and reggaetón. Mainland Puerto Ricans have little exposure to *jíbaro* music, except perhaps via their grandparents' record collections.

But if *jíbaro* music has declined, it is far from dead. Some *jíbaro* migrants to the cities have tried to maintain their traditional music, and there are many commercial recordings, however jazzed up with Cuban rhythms and non-traditional instrumentation. The recordings, which proliferate at Christmas season, document the range of vocalists, from amateur poet-crooners to the late Ramito and Chuito. Most Puerto Rican towns and villages hold annual festivals in honor of their patron saints, during which *controversias* might be featured, along with performances by school groups, salsa bands, and the like. There are several skilled *trovadores* and instrumentalists among the younger generations. A few salsa songs have made self-conscious use of *jíbaro*-music mannerisms, like singing the vocables "le-lo-lai," and *cuatro* player Yomo Toro has appeared on several albums. On a more general level, *jíbaro* music and culture, however deprecated by aspiring city sophisticates, remain for many Puerto Ricans symbols of a vital, self-sufficient, and independent Puerto Rican culture, rooted firmly and proudly in an ancestral homeland.

Seís and *Aguinaldo* Structure

About fifteen or twenty forms of *seís* and *aguinaldo* are in common usage today. Each has its own standardized accompaniment pattern and melody. The verses, which are sung solo, are usually in *décima* form. In between the verses, the *cuatro* player performs

Musical Example 8. *Seis mapayé*

Musical Example 9. *Seis fajardeño*

Musical Example 10. *Aguinaldo orocoveño*

Musical Example 11. *Aguinaldo jíbaro cayeyano*

improvisations, which may be quite virtuoso in style. A few of the most common and easily recognizable accompaniment patterns are *seís mapeyé* (Musical Example 8), *seis fajardeño* (Musical Example 9), *aguinaldo orocoveño* (Musical Example 10), and *aguimaldo jíbaro cayeyano* (Musical Example 11).

THE FIESTA DE SANTIAGO APÓSTOL AT LOÍZA ALDEA

For a look at Puerto Rico's African-derived musical heritage, we can visit the town of Loíza Aldea, some twenty miles east of San Juan. The district of Loíza, which consists of a few adjacent villages (notably, Medianías Alta, Medianías Baja, and Loíza Aldea), is populated mostly by black descendants of slaves who worked at nearby sugar plantations. Along with a few villages on the southern coast, Loíza is renowned as a cradle of Afro-Rican culture, especially music and dance.

For three days every August, Loíza comes alive for the festival of its patron saint, Santiago (Saint James), whose cult invigorated the Spanish war against the Moors (the *reconquista*). The core religious events are processions on three successive days, in which three statuettes of Santiago are carried between the towns. In the accompanying parade, townspeople symbolically reenact the Christian–Moor conflict by dressing either as swashbuckling mounted Spaniards (*caballeros*) or as the pagan adversaries. The latter include ghoulish *viejos* (old men), satanic *vejigantes* wearing grotesque African-derived spiked masks and bearing balloons or inflated bladders mounted on sticks, and *locas* (crazy women), who are actually men in drag, all behaving outlandishly. In addition, some participants wear various K-Mart costumes (Freddie Kruger, Batman, etc.), while others have designed their own clever outfits. After the parade, there are usually stage concerts and informal parties that may feature bomba.

It is 1991, and some friends and I have come to Loíza to enjoy the spectacle and, we hope, to see some bomba. The road between Loíza and Medianías is lined with spectators. In the early afternoon, the ragtag parade appears. The first thing I notice is that the "Spaniards" are far outnumbered by *vejigantes*, *viejos*, and ludicrous *locas*. My Puerto Rican friend comments, "Of course— it's much more fun to be a pagan. Besides, most of these people are black, and if anything, they identify with the Moors, not with the Spaniards who enslaved them."

Indeed, whatever religious significance the event may once have had or may still have for some people seems to be largely inverted. The *vejigantes* are running amuck, bopping women on the head with their balloons and extorting change from them, and the *locas* are dancing and strutting lasciviously; one, dressed in a bridal gown, walks calmly down the center of the street, flanked by attendants, smiling beatifically at admirers and looking angelic except for his thick moustache. Meanwhile, following the three Santiago figurines is a group of giggling, beer-quaffing men carrying a similar statuette, which on closer inspection turns out to be a Mickey Mouse doll mounted on a toy horse. To make the entire event quintessentially Caribbean, there are intermittent torrential downpours in which everyone is thoroughly drenched.

A few musical groups also pass by, including two or three trucks carrying small brass bands playing danzas. Following them comes an impromptu plena group consisting of a dozen or so young men, some of whom play *panderetas* (*panderos*), the jingle less tambourines that are the basic instrument in the genre. They pause in front of a house while one of them runs and fetches a trumpet. Plena, which emerged in the early 1900s, is informal music, performed at parties, street protests, and processions like this one. Its

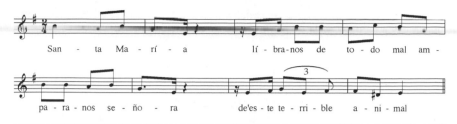

San - ta Ma - rí - a   lí - bra-nos de   to - do mal am -

pa - ra - nos se - ño - ra   de'es - te te - rri - ble   a - ni - mal

Musical Example 12. "Santa Maria"

lyrics, set to sing-songy verse-and-refrain tunes, can be about news, barrio gossip, or anything at all. Aside from the obligatory *panderos*, which play a steady four-beat pulse, a plena group could include whatever instruments are handy, whether a guitar, an accordion, or nothing at all. This group in Loíza is singing "Santa María," one plena that everybody in Puerto Rico knows (Musical Example 12).

Then they segue to other familiar plenas, some of which, like "Cortaron a Elena" (They stabbed/cut Elena), presumably originated as chronicles of barrio events but now have the same sort of historicity as "Jack and Jill."

The next day, the parade is even larger and is followed in the afternoon by a stage competition of "Afro-Antillean musics" in Loíza's central plaza. This consists of about three hours of nonstop rumba drumming on congas, with occasional vocal accompaniment and no dancing. At one point, the organizers invite audience members to come up to the stage and dance bomba; one man casually walks up and does a few indifferent steps, thereby winning a liter of beer, as he is the only contestant. I am starting to wonder if derivative rumba has overrun the local bomba scene.

In the evening, the plaza fills up with people who have come to hear the dance bands. First comes a local professional plena band, Los Pleneros de Loíza, who, like a few other groups on the island, add trumpets, keyboard, and bass to the plena format while retaining the genre's typical rhythms, melodies, and *panderos*. Then follows the real attraction, a salsa band, which is responsible for the traffic jam now ensnarling the area as people flood into town. Actually, there are relatively few salsa clubs in Puerto Rico, since many people prefer to go to free concerts at *fiestas patronales* like this one.

On the final day, the parade is bigger still, and there is another concert at Loíza. However, acting on a hunch, we decide to pass the evening at a humble barrio by the beach in Medianías. (If you visit, eat at Chicho's.) Around dusk, a small steel band sets up by the side of the dirt road and starts to play "Sopa de caracoles," a Honduran *punta*-rock ditty that became a pan-Caribbean hit.

A small crowd of schoolgirls materializes and starts doing the jerky, twist-like *punta* dance. The same tune and indefatigable dancing go on for almost an hour.

Then, just as we are contemplating leaving, two men appear, each carrying a squat bomba barrel drum (called *barril*) and, seating themselves on benches in a cafe open to the road, start to play. Another man, playing a cowbell, assumes the lead-singer role, and the women standing by energetically join in singing the responsorial choruses. But the real focus is the dancing, which is done by a solo dancer directly in front of the drummers, with the singers and onlookers forming a dense ring (a *soberao*) around them. While one drummer, along with the bell player, provides a steady ostinato, the lead drummer (on the *subidor*) mimics and follows the dancer, who performs a variety of stock, improvised movements. I can see that everyone has his or her own personal style of dancing, but certain moves recur—like taking small backward hops with your feet close together. Further, most people's dance sequence seems to start with a short introductory stroll (*paseo*), then a sudden jerk (*ponche*), followed by a series of free moves (*piquetes*) imitated by the drummer, who is the real dance partner. For some reason, men here no longer seemed to be interested in dancing bomba, so the dancers are all female; several of them are children no more than eight years old. They take turns, each dancing a few minutes before the drummer, while the onlookers cheer, clap, and sing the choral refrains in a spirit of riotous fun.

Bomba, the most vital Afro-Rican music and dance idiom, is a product of the slave barracks and was described in chronicles dating as early as the 1820s. More than once it was used by slaves to distract their masters from impending revolts or escape breaks. I had previously been led to believe that bomba was a nearly extinct form, done only by doddering octogenarians or in lifeless stage renditions by folkloric groups, such as I had seen. In fact, as I learned in Loíza, it is still alive and even resurging. Locals say the Catholic priests in Loíza have consistently campaigned against bomba, denouncing it as pagan and vulgar. In fact, bomba is a secular dance with no particular religious overtones, although it is true that the lyrics are often uninhibitedly spicy (leading a 1960s study to conclude that bomba is "unsuitable for use in secondary school choral groups").[4] As for the dance, like most Latin dancing it is indeed erotic, but when well done it is too expressive, fresh, and downright beautiful to be vulgar (except perhaps to someone who has sworn to celibacy). Fortunately, in the past decade there has been a revival of bomba, drawing on the threads of tradition kept alive by grassroots enthusiasts in Loíza and elsewhere, and by the Cepeda family's school in Santurce, San Juan. Now one can take bomba classes in various schools in Puerto Rico and New York, and impromptu bomba pops up at various events, from parties to weddings. Further, almost everyone under thirty is familiar with its sound, as reggaetón idol Tego Calderón included a few traditional bombas on a CD, and even Ricky Martin, on his CD *Vuelve*, included a song called "Bomba," which, if not really a bomba, does contain an old bomba refrain.

PLENA AND BOMBA IN THE DANCE HALL

Since the 1920s, plena and, to a lesser extent, bomba have been performed and commercially recorded, in modified forms, by professional dance bands. One challenge for these genres has been that throughout the twentieth century, the realm of commercial dance music in Puerto Rico (and among "Newyorican" communities) tended to be dominated by Cuban-style music and, from the 1980s, by merengue. Moreover, even when Puerto Rican dance bands adapted plena and bomba, there was a marked tendency to use Cuban-style rhythms, arrangements, and instrumental mannerisms, so that the commercial plena and bomba risked losing their local flavor. The story of urban plena and bomba was in part a chronicle of the interaction of native Puerto Rican forms with imported Cuban genres, which Puerto Ricans have adopted as their own.

The first bandleader to popularize plena in a dance-band format was Manuel "Canario" Jiménez, a New York-based singer and longshoreman who, after being contracted by RCA, brought a modernized plena to large audiences in New York and Puerto Rico in the 1930s. American record companies had been recording island music for mainland consumption since 1909, when an industry trade journal announced a project to market "love songs in the original Porto Rican language, whatever that may be." (Who cares what it is? They're supposed to learn English anyway.) Canario, singing for both island and migrant audiences, retained much of the traditional plena's character by using the *pandero*, simple melodies, topical texts commenting on current events, mixed male and female choruses, and alternating verse-and-chorus structure (as opposed to the verses-and-*montuno* format of the *son*). At the same time, he filled out its traditionally sparse instrumentation with piano, bass, and trumpets. Canario sang both original compositions and traditional plenas, many of which showed the genre's characteristic proletarian irreverence, like "The Bishop Has Arrived":

Mama, the Bishop has come, the Bishop of Rome
If you could only see him, he's such a cute and pretty thing!

The Bishop doesn't drink rum, he prefers moonshine
If you could only see him, what a cute thing, when he's drunk![5]

Due to such flippant lyrics and the genre's generally informal character and plebian audience, plena enjoyed little social status, although the respected essayist Tomás Blanco hailed it as an admirably mulatto mixture in his 1935 article "Eulogy to the Plena."

In the late 1940s and 1950s, inspired by big-band swing jazz and the Cuban mambo, bandleader Cesar Concepción brought the plena *de salon* to a new level of bourgeois "respectability," with his big-band plena typi-cally performed at the fancy ballrooms for genteel audiences in tuxedos and evening gowns. In doing so, Concepción removed the plena far from its earthy proletarian roots in such a way that it came to be seen by many as *gallego*—whitewashed, bland, and overly refined.

In the 1950s, Rafael Cortijo, an Afro-Rican bandleader from Santurce, together with singer Ismael "Maelo" Rivera of Loíza and a similar band led by Mon Rivera, burst onto the Puerto Rican music scene with a raw, revitalized plena and bomba, successfully adapted to standard Cuban *conjunto* format. Much of Cortijo's repertoire consisted of Cuban-style *son* and *guaracha*, and his version of bomba—loosely based on the *sicá* rhythm—was far removed from its folk model. However, the band's renditions of both bomba and plena, for which it was particularly renowned, retained the genres' original earthy, barrio vitality and distinctly Puerto Rican character. Cortijo's lyrics, far from reiterating romantic clichés, provided evocative, often whimsical vignettes of Afro-Rican barrio life, whether about black magic ("Huy qué pote"), a racist murderer ("Negro bembón"), or a commuter choo-choo train in Santurce ("Maquinolandera"—or is it about sex?). Such songs constituted a new sort of urban folklore and placed black music squarely in the mainstream of island culture. Similarly, Rivera's "¿Alló, quién ñama?" dramatizing a contemporary textile workers' strike, linked the commercial plena with the genre's traditional usage in proletarian protests.

Unfortunately for the commercial plena, Rivera spent much of the '60s in jail on a drug conviction, and the "straight" members of the band re-formed as the salsa dynamo El Gran Combo in 1962 (still going, with renewed personnel, in 2005). Plena and bomba then receded from the dance arenas, which have since been dominated by salsa, merengue, and nowadays reggaetón. Plena is still performed by revivalist bands such as the Pleneros de Loíza, Plena Libre, and New York's Pleneros de la 21. Mean-while, throughout the trendy rise and fall of dance-band plena and bomba, the genres in their traditional forms have continued to thrive as vehicles of popular expression, completely independent of the commercial record industry.

Plena on stage: New York's Pleneros de la 21 (both this page by Peter Manuel)

Plena on the streets of New York

MUSIC AND THE PUERTO RICAN DIASPORA

Since the 1920s, Puerto Rican music has been as much a product of New York City as of the island itself, due to the fundamental role that the migration experience has come to play in Puerto Rican culture. The diaspora has been massive: About 40 percent of people of Puerto Rican descent live on the mainland. Moreover, many of those still residing on the island visit the mainland, and, of course, the mass media, visits by mainland relatives, and the effects of international capital make island society even more intertwined with that of the greater United States. As a result, Puerto Rican culture cannot be conceived of as something that exists only or even primarily in Puerto Rico; rather, it has become inseparable from "Newyorican" culture, which itself overlaps with black and other Latino subcultures in New York and, for that matter, with mainland North American culture as a whole.

Migration to the greater United States had been a steady trickle through the 1930s, and handfuls of Puerto Ricans had settled as far away as Hawaii to market their skill at growing sugarcane. In the 1940s, the trickle turned into a flood, as hundreds of thousands of Puerto Ricans took advantage of cheap airline tickets to try to escape poverty and find better fortunes abroad. Many moved to rural New Jersey and Connecticut to work in migrant labor camps. However, more than half settled in New York City and, especially, in East Harlem, which subsequently became known as Spanish Harlem or simply "the barrio." "Newyorican" (Nuyorican) subsequently became a convenient term, however problematic, for all migrants (many of whom, however, refer to themselves simply as Puerto Rican or "Spanish"). Altogether, some 2.8 million people of Puerto Rican descent now live on the mainland, as opposed to 3.9 million living on the island.

As migrants found themselves in the alien, English-speaking, stressful, and often violent milieu of New York's tenements, it was natural for them to try to make their surroundings more familiar by transplanting as much of island culture as possible to the barrio. Hence, taverns and clubs formed where migrants from island villages and barrios like La Perla could regroup and socialize. Enterprising Newyoricans built flimsy yet gaily decorated shacks (*casitas*) on vacant lots to serve as clubhouses. One migrant related, "I cannot live in Puerto Rico because there's no life for me there, so I'll bring it with me bit by bit; four land crabs from Vacía Talega, in the trip before, two fighting cocks, in my next, all of Cortijo's records."[6]

Music has been an important source of solace and recreation for the migrants, and Puerto Ricans have tried to maintain their traditional musics, whether they have settled in Harlem or in Hawaii (where their *jíbaro* songs are called "kachi-kachi" music, in reference to the scratchy güiro). Conditions favored the transplantation and flourishing of certain genres more than others; thus, trios and quartets playing Cuban-style *son* and bolero at parties and clubs proliferated through the 1940s, while *jíbaro* music and bomba did not thrive as much on the mainland.

As can be imagined, the migration experience was often difficult, if not traumatic, especially for illiterate *jíbaros* who moved straight from the countryside to Spanish Harlem. Migrants were gouged by landlords, victimized by thugs, ruthlessly exploited by sweatshop employers, and harassed or, at best, neglected by police. Even those eligible to vote in New York were disenfranchised by gerrymandering and English literacy tests until the mid-1950s. These and other features of tenement life exacerbated tendencies toward family disintegration, crime, and drugs. The travails of migration have been described in many books, but they are also extensively chronicled in the oral folklore of plenas, boleros, and *seises*, such as this 1927 song of Rafael Hernández:

> I came to New York hoping to get ahead,
> but if it was bad back home, here it's worse.
> Sometimes it's hot, and other times freezing cold,
> sometimes I look like a bundle sliding around on the snow.
> I don't like this, I'm going back to my hut.[7]

Coping with the language barrier and the unfamiliarity of the city was a perpetual frustration, especially for uneducated former *jíbaros,* whose travails were the subject of innumerable *seises:*

> One morning I went out to get medicine
> for my friend who was suffering with pneumonia,
> but since I didn't know how to get around in New York,
> I took the wrong subway, and it took me five days to get back.[8]

Another *seis* relates:

> I came to New York thinking that they spoke as much Spanish as English,
> but here they told me, "No you're quite mistaken,"
> when you want *bacalao*, you have to say 'co'fi' "[codfish]." ...
> I feel so ridiculous in the restaurant, when they ask, "Wha' you wan'?"
> and I have to point with my finger.[9]

Feelings of nostalgia and homesickness are particularly intense during Christmas season, which is an occasion for family reunions and celebration in

Puerto Rico, as elsewhere. An *aguinaldo* consoles migrants:

> You don't suffer in vain even if you're far away
> as long as the memory of your beloved homeland
> shines in your heart and remains there your entire life.
> If someday you may return, come with a kiss;
> your country, Borinquen, awaits you at Christmas.[10]

While the material problems of poverty, climate, and harsh work conditions have been formidable, the psychological stress of the diaspora experience was equally painful. Many Puerto Ricans, whether black, white, or mulatto, were exposed to humiliating ethnic discrimination on the mainland. The migration experience heightened the long-standing identity problem felt by some Puerto Ricans, already self-conscious about their status as perpetual colonial subjects. In a conformist society where schoolchildren were punished for speaking Spanish and the mass media excluded any people of color, it was natural for the first generations of migrants to feel ashamed of their ethnicity. Many Newyoricans did their best to assimilate and to raise their children without any sense of their Latino cultural heritage. For many such parents, it was a cruel irony to see their children being socially rejected despite their best attempts to Anglicize them. Indeed, it was a different sense of identity that inspired Newyorican *salsero* Marc Anthony to thank his parents, on the liner notes to his 1993 record, for making him speak Spanish at home. By that time, being Puerto Rican was no longer something to be ashamed of in New York.

We saw in the previous chapter how by the 1940s New York City had become a second center for the development of Cuban music. The city also came to be a center for Puerto Rican/Newyorican culture, but in a somewhat different sense. It was not that Puerto Rican music per se took New York by storm but, rather, that Puerto Rican musicians and audiences came to dominate the city's Latin music scene. One music historian, referring especially to Puerto Rican boleros of the 1920s–40s, describes the resulting paradox: "The bulk of what we today call popular Puerto Rican music was written and recorded in New York. Puerto Rico is the only Latin American country whose popular music was mainly created on foreign soil. The curious thing about this phenomenon is that it was precisely in those years that the popular Puerto Rican song became more Puerto Rican than it has ever been before or since."[11]

Such was the case particularly with the music of composer Rafael Hernández (d. 1965) and his Afro-Puerto Rican contemporary Pedro Flores, both of whom spent many years living, composing, performing, and recording in New York. Their songs—mostly boleros sung by one or two voices with guitar-based accompaniment—dominated Puerto Rican popular music in the 1930s and '40s and still warm the hearts of the older generations. Most of these pieces are sentimental love songs; some of the best-known ones obliquely address the migrant experience by combining nostalgia for the homeland with the memory of a loved one left behind. Flores's "Bajo un palmar" is typical:

> I had a blissful dream, which I wanted to make into a song . . .
> It was on a beach in my homeland so beloved . . .
> It was there that we were picnicking under a palm tree . . . .
> You were so precious . . . and I felt you breathing nervously in my arms.[12]

New York City became a center for Puerto Rican music largely because of its recording studios, its media infrastructure, and its concentrated market; indeed, New York has been the largest Puerto Rican city for several decades. But perhaps more important, it was in New York that musicians and audiences alike were exposed to broader cultural horizons. The Cuban *son, guaracha,* and bolero, which had already taken root in Puerto Rico, were the dominant styles in New York's Latin music scene, and it was natural for Puerto Rican musicians to form or join trios, quartets, or larger ensembles playing such music. Cuban music or diluted versions thereof were also gaining popularity among Anglo dance fans, especially after the hit success of Don Azpiazú's 1930 ditty "The Peanut Vendor" (El manicero)," a catchy *son* popularized under the misnomer "rhumba." To some extent, a "downtown–uptown" dichotomy emerged between the hotter, more authentic Latin music played for Puerto Ricans and Cubans in East Harlem and the slicker, smoother sounds played for Anglos in swanky lower Manhattan ballrooms. The most popular downtown-style bandleader was the Spanish-born, Cuban-raised Xavier Cugat, who commented, "To succeed in America I gave the Americans a Latin music that had nothing authentic about it."[13]

The Latin bands, whether small or large, "authentic" or "commercial," soon became filled with Puerto Rican musicians, many of whom had acquired formal music training in municipal bands back home. Puerto Rican musicians found themselves playing in all sorts of bands (including black, Mexican, and Anglo) for all sorts of situations, at times providing Anglo music for Latin audiences and at others, Latin music—whether real or stereotyped— for Anglo audiences.[14] Puerto Rican musicians thus became highly versatile and, in their own way, cosmopolitan, while adopting Cuban-derived styles as a basic musical lingua franca. By the late 1940s, Newyoricans like timbales player Tito Puente and his rival Tito Rodríguez (d. 1973) had become the top bandleaders and innovators, and the Latin dance music scene in New York

Rafael Hernandez

came to outstrip that on the island. (Even today, there are more salsa bands and clubs in New York than in Puerto Rico.)

As Newyorican culture has developed in its own directions, it has been natural for a gap to widen between it and island culture. Hence, some Newyoricans have come to regard islanders as provincial, while some islanders deprecate

Pedro Flores

their mainland cousins as deculturated half-breeds who cannot even speak Spanish properly, if at all. The history of emigrant Puerto Ricans has been, in part, the slow, painful process of establishing enough self-confidence (or righteous indignation) to take pride in their distinct ethnicity and culture and to assert its right to exist in a multicultural society. Such a conception of identity goes beyond merely establishing a beachhead enclave of transplanted traditional culture, an "island in the city"; rather, it involves building a new cultural identity that at once embraces island tradition and engages actively with mainstream society. In the words of scholar Juan Flores: "The Newyorican experience is showing how it is possible to struggle through the quandary of biculturalism and affirm the straddling position."[15] At that stage, it is the borders of the "island in the city" that become the fluid sites of the most dynamic and progressive forms of cultural creation.

In this transition from Puerto Rican to Newyorican (or "AmeRícan"), music has played a particularly crucial role. But it was really not until the late 1960s that Newyoricans on a mass level began to recognize and affirm the uniqueness and vitality of their culture. This new self-consciousness demanded a new form of musical expression—or, perhaps, a reinterpretation of an older form. That music, called salsa, is the subject of the next chapter. But first let's leapfrog past salsa to the even more modern sounds of rock and rap.

PUERTO RICO ROCKS AND RAPS

Since the late 1960s, many young Puerto Ricans, like their counterparts throughout Latin America, have become fond of British and American rock music, from the Beatles to Van Halen. These *rockeros* (or *roqueros*—that is, rock fans) tended to be whitish, middle or upper class, and more educated (especially in English) than Latin music fans. The latter were mostly working-class black and mulatto salsa enthusiasts, sometimes disparagingly called *cocolos* (loosely, "coconut heads"). In the 1970s and '80s, the tension between these two groups often became explicit, with the *rockeros* regarding *cocolos* as insular and unsophisticated, and the *cocolos* seeing themselves as proud Boricua (Puerto Rican) nationalists and the rockers as snobbish wanna-be Yankees. In the '90s this simple dichotomy ceased to be simple at all and eventually became analytically useless. One complicating factor was the emergence of Puerto Rican rock groups. *Rock en español* had become an international trend in Latin America and Spain, as local Beatles and Zeppelin cover bands eventually decided that rock didn't have to be in English and that it was OK for them to compose new songs in Spanish. In Puerto Rico, the latter 1990s saw the emergence of some talented groups, especially Puya and Fiel a la Vega.

Both groups regarded themselves as Puerto Rican to the core, singing about topics like the struggle to reclaim the island of Vieques, and if one were to tell them that they were just copying Yankee music, he might be hit on the head with a guitar. In effect, rock, like the earlier contradanza, bolero, *son*, and even merengue, had become incorporated into the fabric of Puerto Rican music culture in such a way that made the imported origins of this international musical style in many respects irrelevant.

A similar process happened with Puerto Rican rap, which became a lively fixture of the island music scene from around 1990, as cultivated by Vico C and later figures like Don Chezina and the early Tego Calderón. While we discuss rap and reggaetón further in chapter 4, here it may suffice to point out how Puerto-rap's emergence thoroughly obfuscated the *rockero*-vs.-*cocolo* divide: Rap is, on the one hand, clearly derived from the mainland, like rock, but on the other hand, in Puerto Rico it was very much a working-class black and mulatto thing—that is, on the *cocolo* side. By the time reggaetón exploded on the scene a few years later, the *rockero*-vs.-*cocolo* split no longer made sense. In effect, the Puerto Rican music scene has become more rich and diverse than ever, with artful and energetic cultivation of both strictly local genres like bomba, and other genres, such as dancehall, that were originally imported but now are *cien por cien* (100 percent) Boricua.

BIBLIOGRAPHY

Useful Spanish-language books include Pedro Malavet Vega, *Del bolero a la nueva canción* (Ponce, Puerto Rico, 1988), and *Historia de la canción popular puertor-riqueña, 1493–1898* (Ponce, Puerto Rico, 1992); María Luisa Muñoz, *La música en Puerto Rico* (Sharon, Conn.: Troutman, 1966); and Francisco López Cruz, *La música folklórica de Puerto Rico* (Sharon, Conn.: Troutman, 1967).

For literature in English, see Sue Steward *¡Música! The Rhythm of Latin America: Salsa, Rumba, Merengue, and More* (San Francisco: Chronicle Books, 1999), and articles by Jesus Quintero-Rivera, Juan Flores, and Jorge Duany in Vernon Boggs, *Salsiology* (New York: Greenwood Press, 1992).

RECORDS AND FILMS

JÍBARO MUSIC: *The Music of Puerto Rico, 1929–1946* (Harlequin HQ 2075); *Return on Wings of Pleasure: Pedro Padilla y su conjunto* (Rounder LP 5003). See also the records cited in the notes to this chapter, as well as any records by Ramito and Chuito (available on the Ansonia label).

COMPILATION: *Caliente = Hot: Puerto Rican and Cuban Musical Expression in New York* (New World 244).

FILMS: Jeremy Marre, prod., *Salsa: Latin Music of New York and Puerto Rico*, "Beats of the Heart series"(Harcourt Films, 1979), Ashley James, dir., *Bomba. Bailando el tambor* (Bomba, Dancing the Drum; 56 min.), ed. Maureen Gosling, prod. Roberta Singer (City Lore, New York Center for Urban Folk Culture, 2003). Best avoided are the glittery and overly produced films on bomba and other topics produced by Banco Popular.

4

Salsa and Beyond

THE *SON* SIRES A SON

The 1960s did not commence as an auspicious period for Latin music in the New York City area. The advent of small amplified ensembles and rock 'n' roll had contributed to the decline of big bands, and the mambo craze had fizzled out accordingly. The big Latin ballrooms, which had hosted the mambo bands of Machito and Tito Puente, were no longer profitable, and the closing of the Palladium in 1966 marked the definitive end of an era. There was little Cuban-style dance music in the media, except for a few programs deejayed by Anglo enthusiasts. A few major record companies (notably RCA) were producing some Latin music, but they seemed to regard it as ethnic throwaway music, to be packaged with cheap covers featuring a sexy woman and a conga and dumped in barrio grocery bins. Only two small record companies, Tico and Alegre, were marketing Latin dance music with any creativity and energy. Finally, the embargo against Cuba, designed to strangle the rebellious island and isolate it culturally, cut off influence from the most dynamic center of Latin dance music. But the decade ended up being an extremely fertile one for Latin music in the United States, and for American music in general. Indeed, the 1960s constituted a period of dynamic upheaval and reorientation for American culture.

Young Newyoricans in the '60s, like many first-generation migrants, lived a schizophrenic life. Typically, they spoke English at school and with their African American friends, who listened to soul and doo-wop, and spoke Spanish at home with their parents, who still cherished their records of boleros and *jíbaro* music. One product of this barrio melting pot was the boogaloo, which flourished briefly in the mid-'60s. The boogaloo, as popularized by Joe Cuba, Pete Rodriguez, and others, fused a hard-driving, medium-tempo *son*-type beat with gospel-style hand-clapping on the backbeat, and simple lyrics typically in English rather than Spanish (as in hits like "I Like It Like

That" and "Bang Bang"). But before the boogaloo attracted much national notice, it faded away. In retrospect, it represented at once a lively historical moment of ethnic interaction and a transient stage when young Newyoricans seemed to lack to confidence to sing in Spanish and cultivate a more distinctively Latino music style. In effect, the boogaloo (although it later took root in Colombia) was swept away by the Latino cultural revolution of the late '60s and '70s.

The sociopolitical ferment for which the 1960s are remembered was to some extent a phenomenon of white bourgeois youth. Frustrated by the stifling social conformism of the 1950s; empowered by allowances, cars, and the growing economy; and emboldened by their purchasing power and sheer demographic mass, middle-class baby boomers symbolically rejected much of their parents' culture and values, cultivating new styles of music, dress, art, politics, and recreation. The focal point for countercultural dissent was the Vietnam War, in which the government killed some 2 million Asians in trying to prop up a series of right-wing dictatorships.

Some of the causes and products of the 1960s counterculture had little resonance with Latinos and other minorities. While white middle-class youths seemed to be rejecting the American house-and-two-car dream as boring, minorities still wanted to achieve that dream and resented being denied it. And in many respects, the barrio remained a closed, Spanish-speaking world, where the Beach Boys, the Beatles, and legions of white pseudo-bluesmen were essentially irrelevant.

But the 1960s were also a period of upheaval for minorities, and there were significant areas of overlap between their turmoil and the middle-class-youth revolt. Minorities had made some economic progress, which at once empowered them and heightened their resentment of social discrimination. Opposition to the war united whites and minorities, and to the extent that the white youth counterculture constituted a genuine protest against social injustice, it marched hand in hand with the Civil Rights Movement. Most important, the '60s saw the intensification and increased militancy of the Black Power movement. Latinos were profoundly affected by this and started to conceive of themselves as more than just the "other" that was neither Anglo- nor Afro-American. Inspired by the Civil Rights leaders, the Young Lords, a group of sociopolitical activists, mobilized Newyoricans (and initially Chicago-based Latinos) to demand fair treatment and better social services for their city's large but previously neglected Latino population. The Young Lords achieved several of their material goals, but the most significant development was a new sense of pride in being Latino. For the first time, Latinos on a mass scale rejected the Anglocentric assimilationist goals that had led so

Tito Puente with singer Frankie Feliciano (Fran Vogel)

many Newyoricans to feel ashamed of their language and culture. The model of the Civil Rights Movement, the new interest in "roots," and, indirectly, the still smoldering Puerto Rican independence movement made the barrio a cauldron of militant assertiveness and artistic creativity.

The new social consciousness called for a new musical movement that could at once embrace Puerto Rican tradition and capture the spirit of the barrio in all its alienated energy and heightened self-awareness. The logical musical vehicle for this was not the perceivedly quaint and folksy *seis* or plena but modernized Cuban dance music—especially the *conjunto*-style *son*, which had been cultivated in Puerto Rico (by Cortijo's band, among others) and, alongside the mambo, by local bands of Tito Puente and Machito. In the process, the *son*'s Cuban origin, like that of the rumba now so avidly played by barrio street drummers, was de-emphasized, and the genre became re-signified as a symbol of Newyorican and, by extension, pan-Latino ethnic identity.

The rise of salsa was tied to Fania Records, which had been founded in 1964 by Johnny Pacheco, a bandleader of Dominican parentage and Cuban musical tastes. Fania started out as a fledgling independent label, with Pacheco distributing records to area stores from the trunk of his car. From 1967 on,

Fania, then headed by the Italian American lawyer Jerry Masucci, embarked on an aggressive and phenomenally successful program of recording and promotion. Fania's early roster included established performers such as boogaloo king Ray Barretto and Pacheco himself, who performed in a standard *típico* (loosely, "traditional") style of 1950s Cuban bands like the Sonora Matancera, using the *conjunto* format of two trumpets and rhythm section.[1] But the characteristic Fania sound came to be defined in the 1970s by the barrio-based groups that the label sought out and promoted.

Particularly influential was composer-arranger Willie Colon, a Bronx prodigy discovered and signed by Fania at the age of sixteen. Colon's early albums, with vocalists Hector Lavoe, Ismael Miranda, and Ruben Blades, epitomized the Fania style at its best and captured the fresh sound, restless energy, and aggressive dynamism of the barrio youth. As modern *salsero* Sergio George described it, "In my opinion, the true salsa sound of that era was the musical fusion of New York with Puerto Rico, with Cuba and with Africa; that whole fusion was for me the true roots of salsa in the late '60s, early '70s. It came out of a street sound, a barrio sound. People jamming in the park with the congas and somebody coming to sing . . . . That was the raw street salsa sound."[2]

Every commercial music genre needs a catchy label, and there was a natural desire for a handier one than "modernized Cuban dance music" or "the *son*/mambo/rumba complex." Hence, Fania promoted the term "salsa" (literally, hot sauce), which was already familiar as a bandstand interjection (and as the name of a Venezuelan radio show). To many, the term has always seemed to be an artificial, commercial rubric, designed partially to obscure the politically inconvenient Cuban origin of the music. The label seems especially meaningless when applied to *típico* musicians like Pacheco or to Tito Puente and Celia Cruz, whose musical styles evolved twenty-five years before the label was coined. (While Puente reconciled himself to the term, he also said, "The only salsa I know comes in a bottle. I play Cuban music.") Even mainstream salsa still follows the basic styles and formal structure of 1950s Cuban dance music. In defense of the term, however, one could point to various innovations that distinguished the new subgenre, such as the greater use of trombones, the use of timbales, and the occasional Puerto Rican elements (like singing "le-lo-lai"). Such innovations were especially prominent in the music of the salsa "vanguard" of the 1970s and '80s, whose outstanding figures were Eddie Palmieri and Ruben Blades. Palmieri is a unique bandleader, composer, and pianist whose best music combined dramatically original arrangements (often produced with arranger Barry Rogers), modern jazz-influenced solos, and an ineffable drive and power. Blades, whom we discuss later, is quite a

Eddie Palmieri (Fran Vogel)

different sort of character, whose brilliance was particularly reflected in his eclectic style and artful lyrics.

The most significant justification for the new term "salsa," however, was the way in which the music voiced the militant self-consciousness of the new generation of Latinos, becoming, as in the title of a Los Angeles radio program, *el alma del barrio*—"the soul of the barrio." This spirit was most explicit in song texts. Most songs dealt with love, in more or less traditional manners, but a significant minority openly reflected the new mood of the barrio, becoming soundtracks for early 1970s street protests. Some songs called for pan-Latin solidarity, as in Conjunto Libre's "Imágenes latinas":

> Indians, Hispanics, and blacks, we've been mixed into a blend,
> with the blood of all races, to create a new future;
> we've come to strengthen ourselves, to work and live
> within the entrails of the monster, as Martí put it.[3]
> From Quisqueya to La Plata, from the Pampas to Havana,
> we are blood, voice, and part of this American land;
> whether in the land of snow or underneath a palm tree,
> Latinos everywhere struggle for their liberty.
> We're Latin American, from the center, north, and south,
> with a present of struggle and a future of light.
> This is my Latin image, my new song,
> to tell you, my brother, to seek and find unity.

Other songs confronted American imperialism, whether directly or obliquely. Most characteristically, several songs portrayed the alienation, violence, and lurking malevolence of barrio life. Typical in this respect are early songs of Willie Colon, who styled himself "El Malo," or "bad." His 1973 "Calle luna calle sol" warns:

> Listen, mister, if you value your life,
> stay out of trouble or you'll lose it. . . .
> Listen lady, hang on to your purse,
> you don't know this barrio, here they attack anyone. . . .
> In the barrio of *guapos*, no one lives at peace;
> watch what you say or you won't be worth a kilo,
> walk straight ahead and don't look sideways.
> You may have a patron saint but you're not a *babalao* [Santería priest].[4]

In such songs, there is an ambiguous mixture of attitudinal stances. On one level, these songs are simply "telling it like it is," baring barrio reality in a nonjudgmental way. One could also interpret such lyrics as denunciations of the social system that produces such conditions. Colon's classic dictum "I'm bad—because I've got heart"[5] implies that the Hobbesian world of the barrio obliges a man to be tough in order to defend his sense of justice. But the lyrics also convey a sort of tension-ridden adrenaline high and suggest at least a hint of fascination with the ghetto's lawlessness and with the figure of the *guapo*, the macho hoodlum who has achieved power in the marginalized and oppressed world of the barrio. The song "Juanito Alimaña" (Johnny Varmint), written by Puerto Rican composer (and postman) Tite Curet Alonso and recorded by Colon and Lavoe, captures this spirit:

> The street is a concrete jungle full of wild animals;
> no one leaves home full of joy anymore.
> Here you can expect the worst, wherever you are.
> Juanito Alimaña swaggers to the cash register,
> nonchalantly draws his knife, and demands the money.
> He takes the bills, takes the pistol,
> then he disappears like the wind,
> and although everyone saw him, no one saw anything.
> Juanito Alimaña commits his daily crime,
> drinks his beer, has an orgy;
> people fear him because he's careful,
> you'd have to be mad to challenge him.
> If he gets arrested, he walks free the next day
> because a cousin of his is in the police.
> If Juanito Alimaña has brains, they're in the form of shrewd deceit.
> He's tight with whoever's in power,
> and although he steals from half the world
> and everyone talks about him, no one betrays him.

In their ambivalent portrayal of ghetto lawlessness, such songs foreshadowed hard-core rap, although they contain little of the latter's misogyny and celebration of violence for its own sake. Songs like "Juanito Alimaña" epitomize how distinct salsa's milieu was from that of the glamorous Palladium era or from the Cuban heyday, with its songs about quaint and colorful old Havana. From the Puerto Rican perspective, they also contrast the grim and violent barrio with the picturesque and forever-lost world of the *jíbaro*.[6] Salsa captured the new mood of Latinos in the 1970s, reflecting their consciousness of marginalization, their politicization, and their enhanced awareness of one another, all of which were reinforced by the mass media and the migrant experience. Salsa was rooted in the New York barrio, but because the modern urban alienation it described was common to so many other Latin American cities, salsa soon became an international phenomenon, a chronicle of the urban Hispanic Caribbean.

Salsa's international pan-Latin character was, of course, inherent even in the New York context. Both salsa's audiences and its musicians, though dominated by Newyoricans (and a few Cubans), included a wide variety of Latinos from other backgrounds. Among New York-based *salseros*, one could mention the Dominicans Johnny Pacheco and José Alberto and the Panamanian Ruben Blades (and, for that matter, the Jewish Americans Larry Harlow and Marty Sheller). Fania also continued to mine the island of Puerto Rico for talent, from Hector Lavoe to Tite Curet Alonso, who, like other stars on the label, received fame but no royalties from record sales. More significant, however, was the spread of salsa throughout the Spanish-speaking countries of the Caribbean Basin.

The case of Venezuela is representative.[7] Between 1935 and 1988, the country's population had gone from being 70 percent rural to 85 percent urban. By 1970, salsa, whether performed by local or foreign groups, had become the favored music of the urban lower classes, cherished especially for its barrio-oriented *malandro* (malevolent) edge. Initially, the predominantly white bourgeoisie tended to disparage salsa as *música de monos*—"monkey music"—just as their Yankee-oriented Puerto Rican *rockero* counterparts deprecated salsa fans using the racist term *cocolos*. But by the mid-'70s, salsa, especially as performed by local superstar Oscar D'León, had won over even the middle classes, and salsa record sales in Venezuela came to surpass those in New York.

Meanwhile, Colombia emerged as another vital center and mass market for salsa and came to replace economically troubled Venezuela as a transnational hub for salsa, generating its own superstars, Joe Arroyo and Grupo Niche. On a smaller scale, salsa went on to take root beyond the Latin world, especially in Sweden, Denmark, and even Japan, whose slick Orquesta de la Luz raised eyebrows throughout the salsa world in the early 1990s.

Unfortunately, there have been limits to salsa's ability to cross market boundaries. In the 1970s, when the style was at its peak, many had high hopes that it, like reggae, could cross over to the Anglo and world-beat markets. For promoters it would mean a taste of the commercial jackpot, while musicians could find a way out of the exhausting and exploitative club circuit. But salsa, despite Fania's commercially inspired efforts, never did catch on with the mainstream record audience. Carlos Santana's rock versions of Tito Puente songs—especially "Oye Como Va"–inspired a few Anglo rock fans to seek out the real thing, but on the whole, the language barrier and competition from disco and rock kept salsa marginalized in its ethnic enclave. Most Anglo buyers had little interest in what looked like corny big-band music played by short-haired slickers in matching polyester leisure suits.

Despite the failure of salsa's crossover dreams, the 1970s were the heyday of salsa and of Fania, which dominated the market. Mainstream acts like El Gran Combo, Ray Barretto, and Ismael Miranda churned out hits and kept the dancers on their feet, while innovators like Palmieri, Blades, and Jerry and Andy Gonzalez made the margins of the music scene shimmer with creativity. Composer, arranger, bandleader, and timbales player Tito Puente, who had been on the scene since the late '40s, was going strong, as was his contemporary, Cuban expatriate Celia Cruz. Particularly dynamic were the collaborations of composer-arranger Willie Colon with the soulful, *jíbaro*-voiced Hector Lavoe. And while salsa was no doubt a Latin thing, one of its most gifted bandleaders and pianists was Larry Harlow, *el judío maravilloso*— the marvelous (New York) Jew. By the early '80s, however, salsa found itself on the defensive against an onslaught of merengue and hip-hop and an internal creative decline. But before discussing that situation, let us look at the salsa life in general and at one of its most remarkable artists.

RUBEN BLADES: THE CUTTING EDGE

Most *salseros*, if asked to identify the single most distinguished figure in the field, would probably unhesitatingly name Ruben Blades. While pursuing law, acting, and politics, Blades, in his intermittent periods devoted to salsa, has produced much of the genre's most innovative, ambitious, and socially relevant music.

Blades grew up in Panama City, where he acquired a law degree while singing with local Cuban-style bands. In 1974, he moved to New York and, forsaking the courtroom for the recording studio, joined the roster of Fania

"Ruben Blades"
(Fran Vogel)

Records, which was then at its peak. Blades's charisma, razor-like voice, and boyish good looks might have guaranteed him some measure of success in themselves, but he had much more to offer. Unlike many singers, Blades is a skilled instrumentalist (guitar) and composer; many of the pieces he has authored or co-authored (sometimes in collaboration with Willie Colon) rank among salsa's most memorable and popular melodies and are full of innovative touches. His LP *Siembra* gained both critical acclaim and commercial success, selling more than 400,000 copies, which constitutes a hit by salsa standards.

Blades's music is particularly celebrated for his intelligent lyrics, which, departing from the normal *telenovela* (soap-opera) doggerel and "hey, let's dance" clichés, embrace a variety of social themes with incisive originality. Inspired by such writers as Gabriel García Márquez and Carlos Fuentes, Blades has written songs about everything from disarmament to the environment. His 1980 recording of Tite Curet Alonso's "Tiburón" (Shark), an allegorical indictment of American imperialism, along with his denunciation of U.S. economic warfare against Cuba, incurred death threats from right-wing Cubans in Miami, who banned his music from local radio stations. Perhaps Blades's most memorable songs are not the controversial political ones but those in which he strives to create, as he puts it, "a folklore of the city—not of one city, but of all the cities in Latin America."[8] His "Numero seis" was a lighthearted lament about waiting for the New York subway, while "Te están buscando" portrayed the plight of an illegal immigrant pursued by the law.

His most famous songs are epigrammatic character studies that personify, with a mixture of criticism and empathy, the vanities and travails of urban proletarian Latinos. The lyrics of "Juan Pachanga" portray a perfumed dandy whose suave exterior conceals an inner emptiness and loneliness; the song is also a driving dance tune, whose title became the name of a Queens salsa club. "Pablo Pueblo" describes the monotonous, pointless, and joyless life of a proletarian worker:

> A man returns in silence from his exhausting work,
> his gait is slow, his shadow trails behind.
> The same barrio awaits him, with the light at the corner,
> the trash in front, and the music emanating from the bar. . . .
> He enters the room and stares at his wife and children,
> wondering, "How long does this go on?"
> He takes his broken dreams,
> and patching them with hope, making a pillow out of hunger,
> he lies down, with an inner misery.

In "Pedro Navaja," whose text is a sort of existential snapshot of barrio life, a petty gangster and a hooker shoot each other in an incident whose background is unknown and essentially irrelevant:

> And Pedro Navaja fell mortally wounded to the sidewalk,
> watching this woman who, revolver in hand, tells him,
> "I was thinking that this just isn't my day, and I'm sunk,
> but look at you—you're really shit out of luck."
> And believe me, folks, that although there had been a noise,
> no one stopped, no one was interested,
> no one asked what happened, no one wept.
> Only one drunk, stumbling over the two corpses,
> pocketed their pistols, switchblades, and money, and walked on.
> And as he staggered merrily along, he sang, out of tune,
> the refrain that is the message of my song:
> *"Ay Dios,* life is full of surprises!"

The encounter portrayed in "Pedro Navaja," for all its wry and enigmatic depiction, was so evocative that it inspired a movie and a long-running play in Puerto Rico. In a musical milieu where hits come and go, the song, with its catchy melody, hard-driving *montuno,* and the innovative arrangement by Willie Colon, became a true classic, still beloved by young and old Latinos several decades after its appearance.

Blades has constantly tried to expand the horizons of Latin music. While he dislikes the word "crossover," he tried to break barriers between the compartmentalized Latin and mainstream markets. Seeking to reach English-speaking Latinos as well as Anglos, he recorded several songs in English, and his later LP covers include English and Spanish versions of his texts. Stylistically, some of his later music draws eclectically from reggae, merengue, and rock, and he has collaborated with artists as diverse as Joe Jackson, Linda Ronstadt, Lou Reed, and Elvis Costello. Blades, indeed, is the only salsa-based artist to have broken into the world-beat market while maintaining his preeminence in the salsa world. Nevertheless, Blades has never really attained superstar popularity, a fact that he accepts stoically: "I will never be a superstar. My role is to be different, to do what others won't do, and as a result, my fortunes will always fluctuate."[9]

Since the early 1980s, Blades has devoted much of his time to interests other than music. In 1984, he left salsa to earn a degree in international law from Harvard, and he also pursued a moderately successful Hollywood acting career. His most prominent role was in the 1985 film *Crossover Dreams,* in which he portrayed a *salsero* torn between the integrity of *típico* Latin music and his commercial ambition to cross over to the Anglo market and break out of the local club scene. From one perspective, Blades's preeminence as a *salsero* is paradoxical in that his commitment to music has never been more than sporadic and part time, involved as he has been in law, cinema, politics, and other matters. But seen from another angle, his ongoing involvement with nonmusical endeavors may have much to do with his greatness, since it is precisely his broader vision that has distinguished him from the ranks of mainstream *salseros* who, however talented, cannot seem to transcend the provincial club scene. As Trinidadian author C. L. R. James wrote, "What do they know of cricket, who only cricket know?"

In 1989, U.S. President George H. W. Bush ordered the invasion of Panama to depose his former CIA employee, the dictator Manuel Noriega, who had been involved in drug trading. After the invasion, which caused hundreds of Panamanian deaths and some 2 billion dollars' worth of damage, the nation's presidency fell into the immense lap of Guillermo Endara, a nincompoop under whose rule drug trafficking and corruption increased beyond the level of the Noriega era. Among those incensed by the invasion and its aftermath was Blades, who in 1993 returned to Panama to run for president, with the goal of rescuing his country from corruption and Yankee big-stick imperialism. His campaign failed, but Blades did not give up on public service. As of 2005, after cutting a hot CD with the Spanish Harlem Orchestra, he was off to Panama again to serve as minister of tourism. If such pursuits might seem far removed from singing, for Blades both endeavors have the same ultimate goal: "What I propose is to create what up to this point has been a mythical place: a Latin America that respects and loves itself, is incorruptible, romantic, nationalistic, and has a human perception of the needs of the world at large."[10]

STYLE AND STRUCTURE

In accordance with salsa's international popularity, the repertoires of some salsa bands have included a few jazzed-up Puerto Rican plenas and bombas and assorted elements borrowed from here and there in the Caribbean Basin and the United States. While some commentators have celebrated such eclecticism, mainstream salsa, in its basic style and structure, can be categorized basically as a modernized rearticulation of the Cuban *son*. The typical salsa song, then, coheres to the pattern of the modern *son* as described in chapter 2. Like the *son*, it commences with a "song"-like first section with solo verses, followed by an extended *montuno* with call-and-response vocals, instrumental breaks (mambo, moña), and—in live performance—improvised, jazz-influenced solos, all over a repeated harmonic-rhythmic ostinato.

A typical band consists of ten to fifteen people: the leader (who nowadays is usually the singer), two to five horn players, and those who play piano, bass, conga, bongo, and timbales (a kit including two drums and a cowbell), and perhaps one or two *coro* (choral refrain) singers. One of the vocalists might also play *clave*, güiro, or maracas, and the bongo player typically switches to second cowbell when the *montuno* begins. A variety of horn instrumentations are found, including the lean, crisp *conjunto* format of just two trumpets (used, for example, by Johnny Pacheco); a brassy four-trumpet section (Papo Lucca's Sonora Ponceña); or, more commonly, two trumpets plus two trombones, and perhaps a saxophone or two.

As in the Cuban *son*, the instrumental parts follow somewhat standardized accompaniment patterns, especially in the *montunos*. The schematized excerpt in Musical Example 13, loosely taken from Eddie Palmieri's "Ven ven,"[11] illustrates some of these basic features. The rhythmic ostinatos are two-bar patterns fitting into the *clave* structure, which, in this case, is "two–three" *clave*. Accordingly, the piano part hits the downbeat of the odd-numbered (for example, first) bars while gliding over the even-numbered (for example, second) bars. The "anticipated bass" skips—or rather, glides—over the downbeats, playing the chordal roots before the other instruments (here, the

Musical Example 13. Salsa excerpt

piano) reach the corresponding chord. The *coro* (choral response), which here is a simple "ven ven" (come, come), is answered throughout the *montuno* by the lead vocalist's semi-improvised "calls," or *sonejos*—in this case, "a bailar la rumba buena" ([come, come] to dance the lovely rumba).

Salsa songs are generally collaborative products of a songwriter and an arranger. The primary composer comes up with the basic tune and perhaps the lyrics and then has an arranger (who might or might not be a band member) compose and write out the ensemble (especially horn) accompaniment, including the instrumental interludes (mambos and moñas). This division of labor can be very effective, facilitating the input of, say, someone like Barry Rogers, who was not necessarily a gifted tunesmith but had great talent for arranging, composing, and playing accompaniment parts. Accordingly, it can be hard to ascertain how much of the distinctive "Eddie Palmieri sound" came from the input of Rogers (d. 1991), and sometimes a degree of tension may exist between composer and arranger in terms of division of renown and royalties.

THE SALSA LIFE

While salsa is an international music with mass followings, New York City, for all its problems, remains its capital and creative hub. Most of the big-name groups and record companies are based there, and despite the effects of merengue, hip-hop, and economic recession, New York still hosts the liveliest salsa-club and street-concert scene.

Latin percussion instruments: bongo, cowbell, Dominican tambora (atop a marimbula), güira, clave, maracas, güiro (Peter Manuel)

In terms of repertoire, prestige, and performance contexts, the New York salsa bands can be divided into two categories. The lower echelon consists of lesser-known bands that play cover versions of other groups' hit songs, performing at private parties and weddings and on the "*cuchifrito* circuit" of relatively cheap, unpretentious, and sometimes dangerous clubs (whose name derives from the fried snacks sold there). It is hard to estimate how many such bands exist, since they often consist of ad hoc ensembles hastily put together by a leader before a gig.[12] More visible, significant, and influential than these groups are the dozen or so big-name bands, which record, perform original songs, and have more fixed personnel. These bands occasionally play at private events, at which they may be obliged to play a few covers of hits, including merengues like "El compadre Pedro Juan." Mostly, however, they play at city or corporate-funded free concerts in parks and streets, at massive "salsa congress" conventions of dance enthusiasts, and, more regularly, at the eight or so fancy salsa clubs located in various places in the city. If all is going well, every band does two or three gigs a week, each consisting of two sets. Occasionally they will be busier and may even play a "double" or "triple," perhaps zipping off in a rented van to Philadelphia or elsewhere for a late-night gig after an afternoon park concert and a normal club date.

Ethnically, the New York musicians are a mixed bag of Newyoricans, Dominicans, Cubans, and a few Anglo horn players, like top-level trombonist and college professor Chris Washburne. As Washburne relates, the salsa life has its good and bad aspects. The pleasures are the camraderie among musicians, the glamor of being an entertainer and a minor star, and, of course, the exhilaration of playing such dynamic and exciting music. The bad aspects, however, are numerous and formidable, and for many musicians they eventually outweigh the rewards. First of all is the pay. From the 1970s to the '90s, this might average around $100 a night for sidemen; in recent years, the figure has almost doubled, but bands are playing far fewer gigs. One way or another, it typically translates into only about $13,000 a year—and it is very difficult to support oneself, not to mention a family, on that in New York City. Hence, most musicians have unglamorous day jobs, or in some cases they do studio work. Needless to say, working a forty-hour-a-week day job plus playing salsa until 4 A.M. two or three nights a week can be a grueling schedule. As Washburne relates, "If the music's hot, it's still a gas—but if the music's bad or the band isn't playing well, then it's *death*."

Musicians have to contend with other problems, as well. Fights occasionally break out at clubs and can terrify innocent musicians. Because work even with the big-name bands can be irregular, many musicians do freelance work with other bands at the same time. This practice can require a prodigious amount of telephonic juggling. Gigs can fall through for various reasons, including insincerity on the part of the club or the bandleader, and the sideman can be left double-booked or, even worse, idle on a Saturday night. Bands also have to put up with other sorts of chicanery, and every musician has tales of being ripped off, whether by bandleaders, club owners, or managers.

Washburne notes:

> Sometimes clubs book popular bands and advertise for them, just to attract crowds, and then they cancel those bands and have a cheaper band play. Sometimes we might play one set, and then the club owner tells us to leave, giving us just half-pay. That's understandable if it's a Sunday-night gig, and you can see that there aren't many dancers and the club is losing out, but sometimes it's for no good reason. On other occasions, especially with freelance gigs, you just don't get paid, and there's nothing you can do about it. I'm owed several hundred dollars that I'll probably never see. But most musicians are so hard up for work they'll go on working for the same people who occasionally rip them off. It's a mess, especially since nothing is written down.

Many such abuses could be rectified if salsa musicians were unionized, but the American Federation of Musicians has always ignored Latin bands, and post–Reagan America is hostile territory for unions in general. Further, salsa musicians, due to the nature of their work, are notoriously difficult to organize, as Ruben Blades found out when he tried to start a union in the 1980s.

Drugs have a certain presence in the salsa world, as they do in most popular-music scenes and cash-oriented sectors of the economy. In general, however, drugs are not nearly as pervasive in the salsa world as they were, for example, among jazz musicians in the 1930s and '40s. Most sidemen are more or less "straight," in accordance with their rigorous work regime and the need to be punctual, well attired, and well behaved onstage (and, to some extent, offstage as well). Unfortunately, some bandleaders have had serious problems with drug abuse. Tito Nieves and others have spoken openly about their former addictions, and a few singers, like Hector Lavoe and Frankie Ruiz, have paid the ultimate price. Drugs have also been part of the salsa scene in another way: Some club owners are believed to launder drug money through the cash-dominated club economy, and some groups and performances, whether in New York or Cali, Colombia, are sponsored by drug barons. Since the late '90s, the crackdown on the drug trade in the United States has reduced much of the drug-money involvement; unfortunately, it has also had the effect of significantly reducing the number of gigs that bands can play.

The business aspect of the salsa scene in the United States has tended to be dominated by a few impresarial moguls—typically one at any given time. In the 1970s, it was Fania's owner, Jerry Masucci, who energetically promoted the music while cheating artists of their royalties. Fania eventually dissolved and Masucci retired ("to play tennis") to Argentina (where he died in 1997). In the late '80s and '90s, the crown passed to another man, whom I shall call Ralph Mercado (since that is his name). Like Masucci in his time, Mercado expanded the salsa market with great entrepreneurial creativity and energy. He also managed most of the major bands and controlled most club bookings and big concerts. His record company, RMM, was the biggest salsa label of the era, and he allegedly wielded considerable influence (via "incentives" to DJs) over airplay on the two New York radio stations that play salsa regularly. Groups that, for whatever reason, did not work with Mercado would have a hard time getting gigs and recording contracts. Those that did work with him could do well, especially if able to conform to the paternalistic structure of his organization.

RMM could be likened to Motown, the 1960s soul label run by Berry Gordy in the manner of a family factory, complete with "house" composers and an authoritarian command structure. RMM's in-house musical wizard was Sergio George, a talented Newyorican who arranged and played piano on most recordings and who codified the smooth, brassy sound of modern pop salsa, influenced by R&B groups like Tower of Power. George's arrangements would be doled out, Motown-style, to the appropriate artists on the RMM roster, in consultation with Mercado. The result was the slick and commercially successful sound that still dominates New York's salsa radio slots. Like Fania, RMM was accused by musicians of failing to pay royalties, and a lawsuit led to the dissolution of the company in 2001 and Mercado's supposed banishment from the business. At present, a variety of record labels are now involved, with Sony Discos being particularly active.

Much of the crisp, flawless, mechanical slickness of modern salsa records (whose standards were set by RMM) derives from the way they are recorded. In the old days, a band, having played a set of songs for months in clubs, would book a few days in a recording studio and there perform the songs more or less "live" (that is, without overdubbing). At its best (in the recordings of Arsenio Rodríguez, for example), this practice allowed for loose, spontaneous interaction between musicians, quick recording sessions, and reasonably good audio fidelity. But in the modern pop-music scene, reasonably good is not good enough: Everything has to be seamlessly perfect, and twenty-four–track recording technology makes that kind of perfection possible. So with salsa, as with other forms of commercial music, it has become the norm to record most of the parts separately, by a handful of studio musicians rather than by the band that actually plays the songs in the clubs. (Also, songs are usually recorded before groups start performing them in clubs.) First, the piano and percussionists lay down their track, and then the horn players record their parts. In some cases, two horn players or even a single player will record the three or four parts. These, naturally, have to be recorded sequentially, but this is still generally cheaper than having four horn players record them "live," because that would require more musicians, and the greater likelihood of error would require more retakes.

The studio musicians—a select handful—are perfectionists, able to play a part flawlessly while sight-reading it for the first time. (When they hear the final song later on the radio, they may not even recognize it, since they record so much and often hear only their own parts.) After a day or two, the instrumental tracks for the entire record are completed, and the vocalist can spend another day or two recording his part. Spontaneous interaction is out of the question, which is one reason that some moldy figs prefer older records (for example, Cuban classics or early Fania), recorded more or less "live" in the studio.

But if many modern records tend to sound rather slick and commercial, it should be remembered that the dance-club scene is more important than records, both to audiences and to band members. The live version of a song is quite different from its recorded prototype. First of all, it is generally at least twice as long, with an extended *montuno* section often incorporating improvised solos. Further, the musicians—especially the rhythm section and, one hopes, the lead singer—need not slavishly follow the record but generally enliven the music with variations and flourishes, whether subtle or bold, which collectively electrify dancers and keep the other musicians grinning and energized.

New York's club scene, for all its problems, remains the throbbing heart of the salsa world. Admission is usually about twenty dollars for men and somewhat less for women. To sit at a table with a bottle of hard liquor, however, costs about two hundred dollars. On an average night, the audience of four hundred or so may include a few wealthy regulars and any number of working-class Latinos for whom this is a special occasion. (Anglos are also welcome, as are paying customers of any ethnicity.) While couples are in the majority, there are many unattached men and women who come to dance and socialize. In terms of club attire, Latinos dress up rather than down, and if you show up in jeans and sneakers, you will be turned away at the door, even if your hair is blow-dried.

Some people may sit and shout conversations, others may stand near the stage watching the band, but most come to dance. Indeed, it is worth reiterating that Latin dance music is designed to accompany dance. To attend a Latin dance club, whether in New York, Havana, San Juan, or Caracas, is to see two-hundred–plus people engaged in an extraordinarily rich and dynamic form of creative, artistic expression. This is not the shapeless shuffling and bobbing of mainstream American pop dance but, rather, a highly stylized and sophisticated couple dance. The basic foot (and hips!) pattern may be fairly standardized, but skillful dancers, with the man leading, combine it with such varied, dazzling, high-speed turns, twists, and spins that it becomes a high art form. Latin dance clubs also differ from rock clubs and other mainstream American dances in that one sees people of all ages on the dance floor, from gray-haired septuagenarians to nattily dressed twenty-year-olds—and the older dancers are often the best. There is little need for a youth countercultural dance-and-music movement when a dance style as rich as this has been around so long. Moreover, blacks, whites, mulattos, and even Asians are all dancing and mingling together, with an ease and naturalness that reflects the racial synthesis that produced Cuban dance music in the first place.

Since the 1990s, the New York and, to some extent, international salsa dance scenes have been enlivened by the rise of a new subculture of dance enthusiasts whose specialty is a preference for dancing "on two"—that is, taking the first step of the four-beat foot pattern on the second, rather than first or fourth beat of the measure (typically, for men, right-pause-left-right/left-pause-right-left). "On two" dancers also cultivate a more flashy style, with fancy footwork (called "shines") and complicated and dizzyingly fast turns. The dancers, whose core is Newyorican but who also include many others, especially of middle-class backgrounds, learn and cultivate these moves not only informally at the salsa clubs, but also at a network of commercial dance studios and deejayed "socials," at the big salsa congresses, and at various sorts of exhibition performances by dance companies. They prefer hard-driving, "old school" *salsa dura*, with prominent and easily audible percussion, and, as guided by websites, they gravitate toward the clubs that offer that sound.[13]

SALSA LITE?

Since its initial heyday in the late 1960s and early '70s, mainstream salsa has remained stylistically pretty much the same, adhering to the basic style and structure originally derived from the modern Cuban *son*. This continuity could be taken to indicate salsa's healthy stability and perseverance in the face of changing social conditions and the music industry's ongoing promotion of ephemeral fads. Alternately, the stasis of the salsa scene could be regarded as a failure to change with the times and an inability to expand, condemning its performers to the exploitative, unremunerative *cuchifrito* circuit. Salsa has not really changed much, and whether one thinks this is good or bad, the fact is that the genre has been on the defensive against merengue, rap, reggaetón, and other musics since the late 1970s. What happened to the brash, youthful music that took the Latin world by storm in the late 1970s?

Salsa LP cover from 1982 (Profono TPL 1403)

A complex combination of factors has kept salsa in a holding pattern for the past decades. Some of these factors have been external developments beyond the control of *salseros*. One problem has been the ongoing process of cultural and linguistic Americanization that has led so many Latino youths to shun salsa for English-language hip-hop and R&B. The Young Lords and their ilk may have persuaded millions of Latinos to be proud of their heritage, but inevitably many second- and third-generation immigrants have been losing their Spanish and assimilating into neighborhood Anglo- or, more commonly, Afro-American culture. For many of them, salsa is the old-time music of their parents' generation or of provincial islanders. In the '90s, a few *salseros* like Tito ("I'll Always Love You") Nieves tried to rein in such defectors by singing in English, but such experiments have not really caught on.

Another challenge for salsa was the merengue boom. Since the late 1970s, New York and Puerto Rico have been subject to a massive influx of Dominican immigrants (who now number some 800,000 in New York alone, constituting the largest immigrant group). The Dominicans have brought with them their national music, the merengue, which has since invaded the bastions of salsa's popularity and won over much of salsa's former or would-be audience. The Dominican bands are cheaper, their showmanship is snappier, the dance style is simpler, and a lot of Latinos—from New York to Venezuela just like merengue more than salsa, for whatever reason. It is fast, tight, intricate, and danceable, even if some hard-core *salseros* regard it as trivial and monotonous. Since around 2003, the amount of radio airplay devoted to salsa has been cut even further to make room for bachata and reggaetón. In retrospect, it was naïve of some zealous *salseros* of the '70s to imagine that salsa would be *the* music that would unite all of Latin America (or even Latin New York); rather, salsa is just one kind of Latin music—although an especially dynamic and diverse one—among several others, in a rich, diverse, and continually changing music scene. Just as Puerto Ricans have gone from constituting 80 percent of New York Latinos in 1960 to about 35 percent in 2005, so does salsa have to share the stage with other sorts of Latin music.

Some critics have tried to link salsa's difficulties to the directions the genre has taken since its heyday. By the late 1970s, salsa, whether in New York or Caracas, had largely abandoned its portrayals of proletarian barrio reality and its themes of Latino solidarity in favor of sentimental love lyrics. Of course, salsa is not the first art form to have to confront the dual and often incompatible functions of being educational or, alternately, being escapist entertainment. Some people may always prefer fantasy to social realism, and many Latinos who dress up to go dancing in plush salsa clubs do not want to hear songs about barrio murders—that's what they are trying to get away from. Accordingly, as salsa earned a stable niche in the record market, the music industry—starting with Fania in the mid-1970s—has tended to direct it away from its barrio orientation, to make it into a more bland, depoliticized pop—ketchup rather than salsa.

The trend toward sweet rather than hot salsa crystallized in the '80s with the emergence of *salsa romántica*, a slick, sentimental sound popularized by crooners like Eddie Santiago, contrasting with the more aggressive, proletarian, Afro-Caribbean *salsa dura* (hard-driving salsa). Accordingly, the new generation of *salsa romántica* bandleaders came to be not trained musicians and seasoned club performers like Willie Colon but cuddly singers distinguished by their pretty-boy (read: white) looks and supposed sex appeal (Sex Appeal also being the name of a contemporary group). Many of them, like Jerry Rivera, have been studio-bred creations of the commercial music industry who, in their occasional live performances, cling timidly to the recorded versions of their songs rather than improvising *soneos* in the *montuno*—an art that was the traditional mark of a *sonero*. Even contemporary stars like Marc Anthony seldom risk improvising lines. Puerto Rican–born singer Jorge Manuel "Giro" López articulates the new ideal: "Salsa used to have a nasty image, with its sexuality and rough performers, but my salsa is romantic, soothing, pretty . . . sort of like a rhythmic bolero, and that's today's salsa, which has changed a lot from the original style. Salsa used to be all about the timbales and bongó, but now it's about sweet and elegant words, and the girls like it much more than the earlier, macho salsa."[14] Singer Ray Sepulveda echoed this *romántica* approach, telling Chris Washburne, "You only need to sell to the young women, and they only buy love songs, so that's what we sing." The disappearance of improvised instrumental solos from records also took the avant-garde, jazz-related element out of recordings and situated salsa more firmly in the realm of pop. But whether one likes the *romántica* sound or not, it has attracted many younger listeners—especially women–to the market. It has also illustrated how salsa can depart, in general sound and orientation, quite markedly from the '50s Cuban *son*. Meanwhile, it is now rap—whether in English or in Spanish—that has replaced salsa as the real voice of the barrio.

The RMM years also saw the introduction of a new sort of eclecticism in salsa. In 1996, Sergio George produced a CD by the group Dark Latin Groove (DLG), whose hit song "No Morirá" fused salsa format with reggae dancehall chatting, the R&B-style vocal acrobatics of singer Huey Dunbar, and funky slapped bass lines (which Sal Cuevas had earlier played in songs like "Juanito Alimaña"). The group soon broke up, but such free mixings of elements from other genres continued to pop up in other songs and have long since ceased to raise eyebrows.

In the new millennium, problems notwithstanding, salsa remains essentially alive and well, within its limited sphere. Its market has grown in Latin America, and if some Newyoricans have failed to learn Spanish, New York remains full of newer immigrants—especially Dominicans—who help fill the salsa clubs. Indeed, there appear to be many salsa fans and even performers who have returned to Latin music after being lured away by the mainstream media's rock and rap hit parade. The 1990s saw former freestyle singer La India (Linda Caballero) and house-music vocalist Marc Anthony turn to Latin music as part of the new wave of salsa stars, attracting young followers with their updated images. The denim-clad, silver-voiced Anthony has enjoyed considerable crossover success, singing both pop ballads and salsa in both

English and Spanish. (An *intercambio* with Jennifer Lopez hasn't hurt his image, either.) For her part, India has enriched the scene with both her fine voice and her idiosyncratic brand of feminism. Her songs, like "Ese hombre" (That Man) and "Dicen que soy" (They Say That I'm . . .), became anthems for female salsa lovers, and her stage antics have provided much entertainment for fans and journalists. At a 1999 concert she leapt off the stage and attacked with a mike-stand a man who had tossed a wad of paper at her, and on another occasion she punched her musical mentor, Eddie Palmieri, sending his false teeth skittering across the floor.

As of 2005, the salsa scene features both *romántica* crooners and hardcore *salsa dura* artists, from youngster Ray Ruiz to the revivalist Spanish Harlem Orchestra. Some of the hottest music is played by the old guard. With Tito Puente and Celia Cruz passing away (in 2000 and 2003), Eddie Palmieri enjoys the status of a sort of reigning doyen of the New York scene, while in Puerto Rico, El Gran Combo—an institution since 1962—keeps pumping out hits. Elder musicians complain about the shortage of talented young instrumentalists, as high-school brass bands have been phased out and younger generations reared on rap fail to learn how to play instruments. Improvised instrumental solos—having largely disappeared from records earlier—are now even being cut out of live performances, as audiences want to hear short songs that simply duplicate the record. For their part, the "salsa congress" attendees and "on-two" zealots constitute a new set of patrons, although some salsa musicians feel that in playing for such audiences, their music is reduced to a mere accompaniment track with which the self-absorbed dancers don't have the sort of active engagement of the old days.

Salsa's perserverance is remarkable in the face of all the vicissitudes of the music business and the fickleness of audiences. Pablo Guzmán's words of 1979 remain at least partially valid: "New York still gets cold in winter. Latinos are still third-class citizens. Puerto Rico is still a colony. Which is why, in spite of the petty capitalists and those in media who block it from greater exposure, salsa will not die. It keeps us warm. And along with soul, country, rock, and jazz, it is one of the great kick-ass people's musics of the Americas."[15]

LATIN RAP AND REGGAETÓN

While salsa is simply too dynamic to die out, in increasingly opting for the *romántica* route, it may have lost the attention—and creative input—of many urban Latino youths who seek a meaningful expression of the proletarian barrio experience. Among English-speaking Newyoricans in the 1980s who were growing up with ghetto blacks and inundated with hip-hop culture, there developed a widespread tendency to adopt contemporary African American dress, mannerisms, and music. In the ethnic mosaic of New York City, the kindred rhythms of Jamaican New York dancehall reggae exerted a similar sway, especially as they had already been working their way into rap songs and island airwaves. Newyoricans like Charlie Chase had contributed to the early emergence of hip-hop and break-dancing, but by the mid-'80s the Latino input in rap was effectively marginalized as the genre became identified as a black (and secondarily, white) thang. But because adopting hip-hop could mean forsaking Spanish language and identity, an inevitable development was the emergence of Latin rap, mixing Spanish and English languages and musical identities in various proportions. The modern mass media have played crucial roles in Latin rap's evolution, as radio programs crisscross the English- and Spanish-speaking islands in the Caribbean night and satellite dishes bring MTV International to the entire region. Latin rap thus emerged as the expression of a common urban identity, especially as experienced in New York, where Latinos, Jamaicans, and African Americans have spliced their musics together like a set of patchwork designer jeans.

Gerardo's late-1980s "Rico Suave" was the first Spanish-language rap hit, and in its wake various forms of Latin rap emerged in Los Angeles, New York, and the Caribbean Basin. Like salsa, it has developed as an international genre, with offshoots and margins that lie outside the realm of Caribbean culture. For example, although we might wish to delimit a "Caribbean rap" category, it would be artificial to separate the music of the Chicano-oriented rapper Kid Frost from that of his Havana-born collaborator Mellow Man Ace—or both artists, for that matter, from their Newyorican colleagues Latin Empire. Accordingly, Latin rappers have come from all sorts of backgrounds. Gerardo's is Ecuadoran, El General hails from Panama via Brooklyn, and the Orishas are Cuban.

Most Latin rap has retained close stylistic affinities with African American hip-hop, although the use of Spanish thoroughly Hispanicizes its content. Latin rap has also tended to shun gangster rap's misogyny, anger, and nihilistic glorification of violence for its own sake. Latino culture is certainly patriarchal in its own way, but male Latin rappers do not seem to need to denigrate women as "bitches and 'ho's." What is more characteristic of Latin rap is humor, a delight in Spanish–English wordplay, and a self-conscious, eclectic, often postmodern borrowing and juxtaposition—all combined with an inclusive, rather than chauvinistic, affirmation of Latin identity. In Puerto Rico, Vico C celebrated cultural fusion in his slick and witty use of dancehall, merengue, rumba, rock, and boogaloo accompaniments and in his explicitly eclectic lyrics, as in his 1991 "Bomba para afincar":

> Puerto Rico has bomba to bounce, Venezuela has bomba to grab you,
> Colombia has bomba to enjoy. . . .
> I like to dress up, looking good in my rasta clothes,
> I want to include my chino, to unite all our blood,
> Mixing a little salsa with calypso, casting a spell.[16]

Since that era, Latin rap has neither declined nor taken the Spanish-speaking world by storm, but it has persisted in its somewhat limited milieu, perhaps being strongest in Puerto Rico, where rappers like Eddie Dee perpetuate the tradition of using rap as a vehicle for social commentary. Salsa musicians and other traditionalists may still see the Spanish-language rap audience as defectors from the Latin dance-music scene, and many elders worry that it establishes new avenues of influence for the nihilism and sexism found in gangster rap and dancehall. Spanish rappers themselves, however, tend to see their music as bringing rap-oriented Latino youth back into the realm of Spanish-language music. Latin Empire rappers have said that their audience consists largely of wanna-be-black youth who, by way of Latin rap, have rediscovered their ancestral language: "All the Puerto Ricans here, they want to buy English[-language] stuff. You know, but hopefully as more Latin rappers come out doing Latin-reggae, Latin-this, Latin-that, hopefully they'll start to have Latin sections in certain stores and everybody will be proud again of speaking their language."[17] Meanwhile, the English-language Newyorican rapper Fat Joe (of "Lean Back" fame) has managed to foreground Boricua (Puerto Rican) identity in his rap, after such elements were excluded for two decades. Tony Touch, renamed Tony Toca, also voiced this development:

> Yo down south, niggaz know about crackas and black people
> When I came up north, I started hangin' with Latinos
> the Borikens and Tainos and even the Arawaks
> It's the language that be dividin' the Spanish from the blacks.

Meanwhile, in using reggae rhythm and dancehall-style singing in his 1991 "Bomba para Afincar," Vico C was foreshadowing an even bigger wave of the future. Over the course of the '90s, "reggae en español" became increasingly popular in Panama, Puerto Rico, and elsewhere, with performers like the Puerto Ricans Lisa M and Roxanne Shanté, and the Panamanian El General, singing "inna dancehall style" over Jamaican "riddims" (recycled accompaniment tracks, discussed in chapter 7). In the first half of the next decade, reggaetón—as the genre was renamed—virtually exploded in the music scene as the new, pan-Latino party music of choice for the younger generation.

Reggaetón overlaps in many ways with rap, but on the whole it resembles dancehall in that the lyrics are sung rather than rapped and in that standard riddims are reused in song after song. In fact, most reggaetón uses only one riddim—what Jamaicans would call "Dem Bow," which sounds like a slowed-down soca beat. Another distinction is that while rappers like Eddie Dee may voice trenchant social criticism, reggaetón lyrics generally celebrate partying, dancing, and sex, with videos portraying the macho good life of gold chains, SUVs, and *gatas* (chicks) galore. As in dancehall, singers shout out snippets of patwa and call for lighters to flash, dancers sensually grind each other, and a "hype-man" might accompany the deejay/singer, filling in the anticipated rhymes to let the deejay catch his or her breath. When performing, some reggaetón singers, like rappers, seem to need to check their private parts manually every few seconds to make sure everything is OK down there. Despite such machismo, the scene has also accommodated at least one attitudinous rude girl to date: the Newyorican Ivy Queen (Martha Ivelisse Pesante, b. 1972).

One popular reggaetón artist of the new millennium has been the Afro–Puerto Rican Tego Calderón. Born in 1972, he is a decade or two older than most of his fans and lacks the poster-boy good looks of a Sean Paul, but his laid-back, perpetually behind-the-beat drawl and his often thoughtful, evocative lyrics have a distinctive expressivity that seems to charm millions. While he started out as a rapper (and taxi driver), many of his songs straddle the stylistic boundaries between rap and reggaetón (leading a few rappers to regard him as a defector to pop). His videos and his street slang foreground Afro-Rican life, but his songs are in other ways inclusive, as in his "Dominicana" eulogy to a Dominican woman. Many elders—that is, those older than twenty—disparage reggaetón as drowning out Latin music like salsa and fear that this new generation of performers is neglecting its roots and losing its musical chops. However, reggaetón, rather than being a simple copy of dancehall, has its own distinctive flavor, and Calderón's inclusion of traditional bombas on his CDs has given that venerable and hitherto marginal Afro-Rican genre an unprecedented degree of popular recognition. Meanwhile, reggaetón has made a certain kind of history in being the first Spanish-language music to penetrate mainstream U.S. top-40 airwaves, especially in the form of piggy-back remixes with rappers like Fat Joe. By 2005, millions of non-Latino teens were learning to shout along with stentorian hit choruses like Daddy Yankee's "Dáme más gasolina!" (Give Me More Gas).

NUEVA CANCIÓN

Meriting at least a brief elegy in the history of Hispanic Caribbean music is *nueva canción*—"new song"—which emerged in the late 1960s in Cuba, Chile, and elsewhere as a sort of self-conscious Latin American "protest music," emphasizing highbrow, progressive verses rather than dance rhythms and *telenovela* lyrics. Although to some extent inspired by the early Bob Dylan and other North American neo-folkies, *nueva canción* was motivated in part by an opposition to Yankee imperialism and to the inundation of North American commercial music. With most Latin American governments in the '70s and '80s consisting of right-wing regimes closely tied to North American political and economic interests, *nueva canción* emerged as a persistent, if marginal, voice of progressive opposition, advocating Latino and working-class solidarity and cultural renewal. Throughout Latin America, regional *nueva canción* styles have differed as artists have made self-conscious use of local folkloric musics, but all have been united by an underlying opposition to imperialism, sexism, and exploitation, and a commitment to the creation of a just, humane society. Perhaps above all, the *nueva canción* movement sought to avoid and counterbalance the cultural deformations caused by the capitalist music industry, with its sordid machinery of payola, advertisements, narco-dollars, liquor- and tobacco-industry sponsorship; its vested interest in maintaining the socioeconomic status quo; and its tendency to reduce all art to entertainment rather than enlightenment.

The *nueva canción* movement has had its distinctive local efflorescences in the Spanish Caribbean. We discussed Cuban *nueva trova* in chapter 2, noting how it was actively supported by the Revolutionary government. The marginal status of the *nueva canción* movement in the Dominican Republic has been more typical of its presence in Latin America. Dominican *nueva canción* emerged in the 1960s, during the years of Joaquín Balaguer's presidency, as the most explicit and outspoken music of dissent. As elsewhere, it has been an internally diverse movement, incorporating, for example, the quasi-folkloric group Convite, which reinterpreted Afro-Dominican traditional musics, and the sui generis folk-*rockero* Luis Díaz, who ended up moving to the United States to avoid persecution. A local variety of *nueva canción* also flourished in Puerto Rico, as represented by Roy Brown, Silverio Pérez, Andrés Jiménez, and the groups Taoné and Haciendo Punto (with some overlapping members).

If the workings of the corporate music industry are in some ways contradictory, the *nueva canción* movement had its own ideological and aesthetic dilemmas and contradictions. At the heart of these was the fact that, despite the sincere celebration of proletarian and folkloric values and concerns, most *nueva canción* artists and audiences have been from the educated bourgeoisie. From one perspective, their self-conscious usage of folk styles lacks the "authenticity" of its models, and only a few performers, like the Puerto Rican neo-*jíbaro* singer Andrés Jiménez, were able to straddle both genres comfortably. Another subject of controversy is that the search for a pan-Latin medium often led to the use of Yankee-style singer-songwriter soft rock as a musical lingua franca. When in the 1980s the Puerto Rican journalist and scholar Edgardo Díaz pointed out the irony of Pablo Milanés's singing "Canción para la unidad latinoamericana" (Song for Latin American Unity) in rock style,[18] he set off a furor that raged for weeks in local newspapers. By the new millennium, however, the sense of political mobilization of the Cold War years had ebbed, and such tempests-in-teapots no longer made news.

BIBLIOGRAPHY

The best book on classic salsa is Cesar Rondón, *El libro de la salsa* (Caracas, 1980), which, aside from being somewhat dated and in Spanish, is hard to find. See also the relevant chapter in Sue Steward, *¡Música! The Rhythm of Latin America: Salsa, Rumba, Merengue, and More* (San Francisco: Chronicle Books, 1999). A number of academic edited volumes on salsa have since appeared whose contents tend to be uneven in quality. A useful performer's and analyst's text is Rebeca Mauleón, *Salsa Guidebook for Piano and Ensemble* (Petaluma, Calif.: Sher Music, 1993).

RECORDS AND FILMS

See Jeremy Marre, prod., *Salsa: Latin Music of New York and Puerto Rico*, "Beats of the Heart" series (Harcourt Films, 1979). For audio recordings, see those by the artists mentioned and *Rough Guide to Salsa*, *Rough Guide to Salsa de Puerto Rico*, *Rough Guide to Salsa Colombia*, and *Rough Guide to Latin Jazz* (all on the World Music Network).

5

The Dominican Republic

The music and culture of the Dominican Republic pose what might seem a fundamental paradox: How could a country with a history of such oppression, poverty, and instability produce a national music of such manic exuberance as the merengue? Our attempt to answer this question requires situating Dominican music in the context of the nation's history and culture and exploring the relationship between the merengue and other local musics. In the process, we will see how the music of this troubled country has come to enjoy its own extraordinary vogue, interacting with the musics discussed in the previous chapters.

The early colonial history of Santo Domingo, as the Spanish half of the island of Hispaniola was called, superficially resembles that of Cuba and Puerto Rico. As in those islands, Christopher Columbus's arrival and Spanish rule led to the decimation of the Taino population (who called their homeland "Quisqueya"), the importation of enslaved Africans, and, after the exhaustion of the island's scanty mineral reserves in the 1500s, ensuing neglect and indifferent misrule by Spain. In other respects, however, Dominican history followed a different and, in many ways, more tortuous trajectory. Spanish sovereignty, tenuous from the start and then interrupted by French conquest in 1795, basically ended in 1822 when the newly independent Haitian government invaded Santo Domingo, occupying the region until 1844. With colonial rule over, Santo Domingo never developed an extensive plantation-based economy, and slavery never played a central role in the region's society. Nominal independence in 1844 failed to bring prosperity or stability, as the country remained undeveloped, insolvent, battered by hurricanes, and divided among regional strongmen (*caudillos*). Occupation by the U.S. Marines from 1916 to 1924 established a certain sort of stability while paving the way for the despotic dictatorship of Rafael Trujillo.

One of the legacies of the country's chaotic history and fragile sovereignty has been the failure to develop a strong and coherent sense of ethnic or national identity. Despite the fact that three-quarters of the population is mulatto, there has been, until very recently, little public acknowledgment of the country's Afro-Caribbean heritage. The middle and upper classes traditionally identified with Spain, and even the black and mulatto lower classes euphemistically refer to themselves as *indios* or *indios oscuros* (dark-skinned Indians) on their identification cards. While Dominican conceptions of race in general are remarkably fluid and tolerant, overt African heritage and blackness have tended to be associated with Haiti, which is still demonized. Accordingly, Dominican nationalism developed in opposition not to Spain but to Haiti and has traditionally been animated by fear and denial of Afro-Caribbean culture. The *negritud* movement, so influential elsewhere in the Caribbean, had little impact in the Dominican Republic, and until very recently there have been few local counterparts to the innumerable Cuban and Puerto Rican popular songs celebrating Afro-Latin identity.

Despite such attitudes and the historical remoteness of the slave-import period, the country's African heritage is evident, particularly in the veneration of West African- and Congolese-derived spirits (*misterios*) such as Yemayá and Kalunga. The worship of these spirits is not as formalized and standardized as, say, Cuban Santería. Rather, it tends to be mixed up with folk Catholicism, Haitian Vodou, the *espiritismo* founded by the French guru Allen Kardec (1804–69), and invocations of the Venezuelan healer Dr. José Gregorio Hernández (1864–1919). Still operant in various parts of the country are *cofradías*—brotherhoods, somewhat akin to Afro-Cuban *cabildos*—in which the *misterios* are worshiped and importuned with songs and dances accompanied by ensembles of long, slender drums called *palos* or *atabales*. Particularly distinctive and rich is the music of the Cofradía de los Congos de Espíritu Santo of Villa Mella. A non-liturgical form of *salve*—which otherwise denotes a Hispanic-derived liturgical song—is also sung in a highly Africanized style to the accompaniment of frame drums (*panderos*). Until the recent revival of these traditions (discussed at the end of this chapter), they were perpetuated largely in a few select communities.[1]

Another Afro-Dominican music tradition is *gagá*, a sort of local version of Haitian Rara. *Gagá* flourishes along the western border areas, which are heavily populated by Haitian migrants. In *gagá* celebrations, members of Vodou-related Rada cults form rowdy processions, playing interlocking rhythmic parts on bamboo tubes called *vaksin*, which they blow trumpet-style and strike with

Asa Dife performing *música de palos* (Peter Manuel)

sticks. In recent years, *gagá* processions have started to appear in the capital city and elsewhere.

THE *MERENGUE TÍPICO*

Despite the prevalence of such neo-African traditions, the Dominican Republic's most important musical genre, the merengue, is clearly a product of syncretic creolization, like other mainstream Caribbean musics. Although *merengue* (French, *meringue*; English, meringue) means whipped egg whites and sugar, as applied to music the word is believed to derive from the term *maringa* of Mozambique. The early history of the merengue is obscure, although as reconstructed by Dominican writers and by ethnomusicologist Paul Austerlitz,[2] it seems clear that one strain of the genre developed in the mid-1800s as a creole variant of the family of interrelated, syncopated couple dances variously called contredanse, contradanza, danza, and merengue in Cuba, Hispaniola, and Puerto Rico. A Haitian connection is quite likely, as suggested by an 1822 reference to merengue being performed for some Haitian patrons. (More dubious is the direct connection to the "merengue" of Colombian *vallenato* music; "merengue," like "mambo" and "tango," is just one of those words that pops up in all sorts of places, with or without stylistic continuities.)

This early salon merengue, like its counterparts elsewhere, may have been predominantly European in origin, but outside the ballrooms very different forms of merengue flourished, most with a marked Afro-Caribbean flavor in their lively rhythms and call-and-response final section. Merengue texts dealt with all manner of topics, serving as a rich oral tradition of social commentary. Like the Cuban contradanza and danzón, these folk merengue forms were denounced as vulgar and crude by the elite, although they thrived in regional variants throughout the country.

By the 1890s, the folk merengue—although originally played on guitar—came to be performed more commonly by an ensemble of diatonic button accordion, the metal güira ("wee-ra") scraper (which looks like a cylindrical cheese grater), double-headed tambora drum, and, occasionally, a bass instrument called "marimba." The marimba used for merengue is not the xylophone of Central America and Mexico but an African-derived instrument consisting of a wooden box with plucked metal keys. Like the Cuban *marimbula*, it is a bass instrument and is much larger than its African mbira-type ancestors. As in Cuba, until the mid-twentieth century the marimba was not even tuned, but simply served to fill out the ensemble sound with a bass timbre. The tambora is a barrel drum rested horizontally on the musician's lap; the left head, played with the palm of the left hand, is made from a male goatskin, while the other head, made from a female goatskin, is struck with a stick. (As the Dominican poet Manuel del Cabral rhapsodized, "Caribbean man, look at your dead goat singing.")[3] Folklorist Fradique Lizardo traces the origin of the tambora to Madagascar.

Traditional merengue has always differed from region to region, with distinctive styles like the *mangolina* of the southwest (in a brisk 6/8 meter) and the syncopated *pambiche* having their own distinctive flavor. However, it was the merengue of the densely populated Cibao Valley that came to be by far the most influential. By the 1930s, the *merengue típico cibaeño*—loosely, the typical or traditional merengue of the Cibao—had acquired a somewhat standardized, classic form, especially as popularized by bandleaders Toño Abreu and Nico Lora. This style uses the standard ensemble of accordion, güira, tambora, and marimba. The tambora mostly plays a short roll leading up to

Merengue típico group (José Quesada), with güira, sax, tambora, and accordion
(Vicente Fernandez/City Lore)

the downbeat, while the güira supplies a lively, scratchy, often mutating counterpoint. The most important instrument is the accordion, which, in the hands
of good players, provides a dazzling, shimmering, and constantly varying bar-
rage of crisp, staccato (*picadito*) accompaniment figures (better rendered on
button accordion than on keyboard accordion). Many *típico* ensembles also
came to incorporate a saxophone, playing fast arpeggios in harmony with the
accordion.

Many merengues traditionally started out with a short, march-like *paseo*,
in which couples would promenade around the floor, leading to a verse section, itself called "merengue," with a topical text; like the Cuban rumba and
son, the piece would then segue to an extended call-and-response section.
This more lively section was formerly called *jaleo* ("cheering," related to the
English "hello"), but is nowadays called "mambo" (there's that word again!).
The *merengue típico*, however, differs from the contemporary *son* in its instrumentation, its simpler harmonies (generally only alternating tonic-dominant
chords), and its relentlessly fast tempo. Its choreography is also simpler, consisting of a basic two-step pattern, with or without variations.

This *merengue típico cibaeño* came to thrive as folk entertainment in the
Cibao, performed especially at Sunday-afternoon fiestas (*pasadías*) and in

red-light bars in Santiago de los Caballeros, the provincial capital. The name of one of these taverns, the Perico Ripiao (Ripped Parrot), became adopted as a sobriquet for the Cibao merengue.

While horn-based, "*orquesta*" merengue subsequently went on to blare its way into international popularity, *merengue típico* has continued to thrive in the Cibao and especially in Santiago, which functions as a sort of Dominican Nashville. Today, *merengue típico* is generally played in a style popularized by Tatico Henríquez (d. 1976), called *merengue típico moderno*, with electric bass replacing the marimba. The accordion remains at the genre's heart, however, and the Cibao has continued to produce flashy and innovative players. In the late twentieth century, they included Francisco Ulloa, El Ciegito de Nagua, and even a few women, especially Lydia de la Rosa and the indomitable Fefita la Grande, who show that women as well as men can embody the aggressive feistiness, called *tigueraje* (tigerness), that Dominicans prize. *Merengue típico*, in contrast to horn-based *orquesta* merengue, has its own repertoire, including evergreens from Tatico's era and before. As we shall discuss later, *merengue típico*, far from declining, has been enjoying a dramatic renaissance in recent years.

THE MERENGUE AS NATIONAL SYMBOL

From the Spanish–American War of 1898 through the Panama invasion of 1989, the U.S. government has undertaken a series of military interventions and occupations in the Caribbean Basin designed to establish and maintain economic and political control over the region. From 1916 to 1924, it was the Dominican Republic's (first) turn, as U.S. Marines occupied the country to keep menacing European creditors at bay. The best that can be said about the occupation is that it generated an unprecedented degree of nationalist solidarity, in which Dominicans of all classes came to resent Yankee rule. (What's baseball got to do with it?) On the popular level, the occupation provoked prolonged guerrilla resistance and inspired several nationalistic merengues, including Nico Lora's "La protesta," which is still performed today:

> The Americans came in 1916,
> trampling Dominican soil with their boots. . . .
> The Yankee intruders, we'll drive them out with machetes.

Of greater lasting significance was the belated adoption of the merengue by the bourgeoisie of Cibao, which had hitherto shunned it (especially for its erotic lyrics) in favor of dainty waltzes, minuets, and foxtrots. Caught up in the nationalistic fervor, the provincial elite soon came to close their foxtrot and danzón parties with salon versions of the local merengue, as played by professional, sax-dominated big bands led by Juan Bautista Espiñola, Pavin Tolentino, and others. This trend laid the foundation for the genre's subsequent emergence as a national music.

Another foundation laid during the U.S. occupation was that of military dictatorship, as the Marines set up a National Guard and prepared the collaborator Rafael Trujillo to lead it. In 1930, Trujillo seized the presidency in a coup d'état and commenced a thirty-one-year dictatorship that colored every aspect of Dominican culture, including merengue. Trujillo brutally stamped out dissidence and promoted a culture of fear, sycophancy, and propaganda; even in front of the Nigua city insane asylum, a sign proclaimed, "We owe everything to Trujillo." Meanwhile, "El Benefactor" turned the country into his own private enterprise: By 1961, he and his cronies owned more than half of the nation's assets, and he had become one of the world's richest men—with the tacit support of Washington, D.C.

With the backing of the Catholic Church, Trujillo repressed Afro-Dominican religion and culture and revived anti-Haitian phobias. As his own grandmother was Haitian, he sometimes powdered his skin to lighten it. In 1937, he had some 20,000 Haitians on the border regions massacred and tried to get himself awarded the Nobel Peace Prize for settling the boundary.[4] While his land expropriations uprooted thousands of peasants, he prohibited large-scale urbanization and even tore up a railway to discourage travel. Under the guise of nationalism, he limited foreign investment (so that he and his family could monopolize the economy) and discouraged international musics like jazz and rock 'n' roll.

Of particular significance was Trujillo's influence on merengue. Trujillo was of humble origins, and he resented the elite sophisticates who had earlier barred him from their social clubs. In turn, Trujillo promoted the Cibao-style merengue, of which he was an enthusiast, as a populist symbol. Merengue groups accompanied him on his campaigns and tours, and hundreds of songs were commissioned to sing the praises of his policies and activities. At parties at his palaces, he liked to dance merengue, shouting "Viva Trujillo!" as he turned his partner, and occasionally imprisoning any musician who made a mistake. He required urban dance bands to incorporate merengues into their repertoires. The Santiago-based band of Luis Alberti was brought to the capital (now "Ciudad Trujillo") as a state ensemble and renamed Orquesta Presidente Trujillo; its 1937 hit "El compadre Pedro Juan" established the merengue's popularity in the urban salon. Such *orquestas* were heavily inspired by big-band swing jazz, using mambo-like sectional arrangements highlighting the trumpets and especially the saxophones, which have retained their importance to the present. At the same time, Alberti's occasional use of *típico* elements like the guira, tambora, and accordion bridged the gap between folk and salon merengues. Meanwhile, Trujillo's brother Petán, another merengue lover, inundated the public with merengue over the radio and television, which he dominated.

In effect—and by a 1936 decree—Trujillo turned a horn-based version of the Cibao merengue into the country's national music and dance genre. While the *merengue típico* and *orquesta merengue* remained tied to their separate social classes, the modernized Cibao-style merengue became what is still the single most significant unifying cultural entity in the nation.

THE MODERN MERENGUE

In 1961, the Central Intelligence Agency, fearful that Trujillo, like his neighbor Batista in Cuba, might be ousted by a popular insurrection, helped local conspirators assassinate El Benefactor. For months, the most popular merengue in the country was "La muerte del chivo" (The Death of the Goat), celebrating the event. Popular elections held the following year led to a landslide victory for the liberal Partido Revolucionario Democrático (PRD), headed by the intellectual Juan Bosch, who promulgated civil liberties, land reform, and labor-union rights and tried in general to dismantle the dictatorship.

Unfortunately, to Washington, D.C., these reforms smacked of communism, and after a right-wing military coup ousted Bosch in 1963, the administration of Lyndon Johnson endorsed the new dictatorship. By spring of 1965, however, the Dominican people had taken to the streets and were on the verge of ousting the junta. At this point, Johnson sent 22,000 Marines to invade the island, routing the popular forces and supervising rigged elections in which Trujillo's former right-hand man, Joaquín Balaguer (1906–2002), assumed the presidency. (This is called "making the world safe for democracy.") Thus began the next chapter in Dominican history—a semi-dictatorship that continued, with one inconclusive eight-year interruption, through the late 1990s.

In some ways, the Balaguer regime was a continuation of the previous dictatorship—Trujilloism without Trujillo. The power of the Trujillo elite and the military remained intact, labor unions were smashed, and in the early years, right-wing death squads terrorized the slums. Balaguer maintained his dictatorial power by regularly rigging elections, including those of 1994 (by which time he was blind and eighty-nine years old).

In other respects, the Balaguer years constituted a new era, with marked effects on music. One change was the dramatic urbanization of the country, fueled by the land acquisitions of multinational corporations like Gulf and

Western, which uprooted tens of thousands of farmers. Most of these displaced people flooded into the urban shantytowns, especially in Santo Domingo, whose population doubled in the 1970s. The character of the nation's culture has naturally changed, as a population that in 1960 was 70 percent rural is now predominantly urban.

Balaguer, in accordance with the wishes of his backers in Washington, D.C., dismantled Trujillo's barriers to foreign investment and opened the country to multinational corporations. Urbanization thus became coupled with internationalization, as foreign businesses, consumer products, and media networks came to pervade the country. The foreign presence was particularly visible— or, rather, audible—in the realm of music, as merengue, which had previously been able to monopolize the music scene, found itself in commercial competition with rock, pop ballads, and salsa. Whereas rock, pop, and salsa were backed by powerful multinationals, as of the early 1960s the Dominican record industry scarcely existed, because Petán Trujillo's dilettantish involvement in records and radio had scared off any would-be competitors while failing to produce more than a handful of records. Merengue and other local musics were thus at a distinct disadvantage in competing with foreign musics. On another level, the competition between local and foreign musics involved the development of new sorts of national identity, now conceived in relation to the broader world. As we shall see, a spiffed-up merengue, invigorated by the very foreign influences that threatened it, eventually came to triumph not only in its homeland but abroad, as well.

Rock music, in full flower-power by the mid-1960s, soon made inroads into the Dominican music scene and has occupied a small niche ever since, especially among bourgeois youth. But the language barrier, anti-Americanism (heightened by the 1965 invasion), and the love of Latin-style dancing have saved the Dominican Republic from disco domination. A different sort of foreign competitor has been the pop ballad, or *balada*, the international genre of sentimental love songs crooned by Julio Iglesias, José José, and others. The *balada* to some extent can be seen as a relative of the bolero and Latin American *canción* (a generic term for romantic songs that are not composed for dance), but it also constitutes a Spanish-language counterpart to the mainstream, commercial Euro-American ballads of Barbra Streisand, Englebert Humperdinck, and their like. In its pristine avoidance of social commentary, its orientation toward fantasy, and its dependence on multinational capital, the *balada* is at the opposite end of the musical spectrum from the anti-commercial protest songs that emerged in the late '60s from singer-songwriters like Luis Díaz and Sonia Silvestre. Whatever its effects may be, the *balada* continues to compete with merengue and, as we mentioned in chapter 4, with salsa on the airwaves, although it seldom functions as dance music.

The most immediate competitor to merengue has been salsa, which emerged in the late 1960s as Cuban-style music played primarily by Puerto Ricans as an expression of the New York City Latin experience. As we have seen, salsa soon became an international phenomenon, marketed and cultivated throughout cities of the Hispanic Caribbean Basin. However, salsa's role in Dominican national culture has been inherently ambiguous. On the one hand, it is a pan-Latin music and a dynamic symbol of Latino cultural resistance to North American "Coca-Colonization." On the other hand, while most Dominicans like salsa, they regard it as foreign in comparison to the indigenous merengue.

For those involved as performers or businesspeople in the Dominican music industry, the 1970s were a period of an intense musical war. Until the late 1970s, the merengue was definitely on the defensive, as the airwaves and record stores were dominated by North American pop, weepy *baladas*, and hard-driving salsa. By 1980, however, the tide was turning. For one thing, the Dominican recording industry was coming into its own; with Petán no longer intimidating entrepreneurs, several local record companies and sophisticated studios had emerged, able to produce slick, professional recordings that could stand their ground against the foreign imports. Dominican producers were also better poised to sway local radio disc jockeys with payola (which is legal in the Dominican Republic) than were foreign-based competitors. Further, salsa had lost much of its youthful vigor and freshness, and the trend toward bland, commercial *salsa romántica* was well under way.

The most important factor, however, was the emergence of a new, revitalized merengue that managed to combine the sophistication of the big-band salon merengue, the raunchy intensity of *perico ripiao*, and the best and most appropriate influences from its foreign competitors. The most innovative and significant figure in this development was bandleader Johnny Ventura (b. 1940). Starting in the 1960s, Ventura broke from the "sweet" sound of salon big bands like Alberti's, paring down the ensemble to a lean *conjunto* of two saxes and two or three trumpets. The key instruments were the saxes, which played crisp, staccato arpeggio patterns, interlocking percussively with the newly highlighted tambora to produce tight (*apreta'o*), machine-gun-like composite rhythms. Some of Ventura's songs perpetuated the merengue's tradition of social commentary, and his outspoken support for the PRD illustrated how the merengue easily shed its negative associations with Trujillo.

While maintaining some traditional aspects, Ventura enlivened the merengue with a variety of select foreign influences. He incorporated the sophisticated arranging style of salsa and adopted from disco the use of the bass drum, whose steady, crisp "thump-thump-thump" became a standard feature of merengue. Together with his partner and manager, William Liriano, Ventura, inspired by soul singer James Brown's revue, outfitted his band in flashy costumes and had them perform snappy dance steps on stage, and especially in his weekly television show, the "Combo Show." Some of these dances, like the '70s "el Pingüino" (the Penguin), became local crazes. Meanwhile, Liriano aggressively promoted the band on the island's concert circuit, realizing that this was one arena in which foreign musics could not compete. The band itself was packaged as a commodity, embodying a new image of merengue as glamorous and extravagant but, at the same time, indigenous. In effect, Ventura's band managed to refashion the merengue as a music that combined the best of the local and the international, and the traditional and the modern, while becoming an embodiment of Dominican *tigueraje*. Ventura's band soon became the model for commercial horn-based merengue groups (now called *orquestas*), and he continues to enjoy the status of a Tito Puente-like Dominican music doyen while also having had a parallel illustrious political career as a PRD leader. Also enlivening the scene from the late '70s was the innovative bandleader Wilfrido Vargas (b. 1949), who enriched the merengue with elements freely borrowed from zouk, rap, dancehall, salsa, and disco.

THE MERENGUE EXPLOSION

By the early 1980s, the merengue, revamped by Ventura, Vargas, and their followers, had definitively triumphed in its homeland, dominating the TV music programs and the playlists of the country's more than two hundred radio stations. More remarkably, the exuberant merengue went on to invade salsa's own homelands of Puerto Rico and New York City, putting salsa on the defensive and writing a new chapter in the history of Latin music.

To a large extent, the merengue has been personally carried abroad by the massive wave of Dominican migrants pouring out of the country, especially into New York City, since the 1970s. While Trujillo's policies had restricted emigration, the Balaguer regime encouraged it. Political opponents and dissidents were given the option of emigration or "disappearance," and the continued concentration of land ownership has driven thousands of dispossessed farmers into exile; other young Dominicans are simply *loco para irse*—"obsessed with leaving"—or motivated by the better economic opportunities in the United States. Because of the expense of emigration, many

Johnny Ventura
(Fran Vogel)

Wilfrido Vargas
(Fran Vogel)

emigrants have been members of the educated petty bourgeoisie, seeking better opportunities abroad.

In all, well over 15 percent of the Dominican population has migrated to the United States since 1961, including about 800,000 in New York and more than 300,000 in Puerto Rico. Many come illegally, especially by small boats plying the turbulent Mona Passage between the island and neighboring Puerto Rico; many boats have capsized in the white-capped, shark-infested waters, with hundreds of lives lost. Wilfrido Vargas has warned would-be emigrants in one song:

> Puerto Rico may be close, but go by air,
> if you get a visa you won't have problems with immigration;
> don't go in a *yola* [launch], don't kid yourself,
> because in the Mona Passage, the sharks will devour you.[5]

Once in the United States, some immigrants have ended up on welfare, and a few have enriched themselves as drug traffickers, but most have found jobs. New York City's Washington Heights—now nicknamed Quisqueya Heights—has become dominated and economically revitalized by "Dominican Yorks," who have also taken over many of the city's innumerable bodegas (or *colmados*, Latino mom-and-pop stores). On the whole, the Dominicans have distinguished themselves by their aggressive industriousness and their willingness to do hard work for little pay.

As merengue bands followed the Dominican migrants, dance clubs sprang up throughout upper Manhattan and the Dominican neighborhoods of Brooklyn and Queens (which is celebrated as the world's most ethnically diverse city). The sites range from plush venues in uptown Quisqueya Heights like Club 2000 to funky, hole-in-the-wall joints in Queens featuring *merengue típico*. But merengue's popularity soon spread beyond the Dominican community to pervade the Latin music scene. In the 1980s, many salsa musicians, promoters, and fans watched with dismay as their favorite clubs and radio stations switched to merengue formats, and barrios came to resound to the beat of the tambora.

Some of merengue's initial success was due to the willingness of the Dominican bands to play longer for less money. Moreover, the Dominican bands, true products of the MTV generation, wear garish outfits and perform flashy and often gimmicky choreography that most salsa musicians would scorn as silly. As one Dominican described the merengue bands in Puerto Rico, "They are musical guerrillas who go to Puerto Rico and place bombs where they play."[6] But the fact remains that a large portion of former or would-be salsa fans, whether in New York, Puerto Rico, or elsewhere, have simply come to prefer merengue. For one thing, the two-step merengue dance is considerably easier than the basic salsa footwork, and many younger Latinos and fumble-footed *rockeros* intimidated by virtuoso salsa dancers can easily boogie to the Dominican beat. Moreover, fads have their own logic, and just as salsa was getting stale, merengue appeared on the scene—spicy, hot, and eminently danceable. While some detractors have criticized the modern merengue's perceivedly glib superficiality, trivial lyrics, and commercial orientation,[7] the merengue's frenetic beat does not lend itself to a wide variety of textual sentiments. After all, merengue, like salsa, is dance music, and lyrical profundity may be less important in that sense than the intricate rhythms and exuberant arrangements.

By the early 1990s, merengue's relationship with salsa stabilized somewhat. The hard-core *salseros* of the '80s have realized that salsa is not going to be the definitive Latin American music, and, indeed, the Caribbean and New York music scenes have been greatly enriched and diversified by the merengue influx. A portion of the salsa audience may have been lost to merengue, but salsa is now holding its own, especially as an increasingly formulaic merengue accommodates itself to commercial success. Nowadays, New York's Latin radio stations typically alternate merengue and salsa with bachata and reggaetón, and some Dominican clubs in Manhattan feature both salsa and merengue bands. In fact, as second- and third-generation Newyoricans forget their Spanish and defect to rock and rap, the ranks of salsa fans are being replenished by Dominican immigrants. Within the New York merengue world, horn-based *orquesta merengue* tends to be preferred in upper Manhattan's Washington Heights community, many of whose constituents hail from urban Santo Domingo. But in Queens, where immigrants tend to be more recent and from the Cibao hinterland, it is *merengue típico* that rules, with several small clubs featuring live music.

Meanwhile, in Puerto Rico the "merengue invasion" has ceased to be a purely Dominican phenomenon, as Puerto Rican performers have joined the ranks of visiting Dominican bands. To some extent, singers like Olga Tañon and Elvis Crespo have popularized a distinctive style, perhaps a bit softer and slower than the current manic Dominican sound. In effect, the merengue is in the process of becoming—as did the Cuban *son*—an international genre that is part of the cultural patrimony of more than just the Dominican Republic.

Meanwhile, the international merengue boom has to some extent inverted the whole Dominican commercial music scene, so that its center of gravity, like that of Puerto Rican music, is now in some ways New York City (which Wilfrido Vargas refers to as "a province of the Dominican Republic"). As record executive Juan Hidalgo observes, "The capital of Dominican music? New York, of course." Because of piracy, a hit CD might sell only 10,000 copies on the island, but in New York it could sell 100,000.[8] Several major bands are based in New York, and some never bother to tour the Dominican Republic itself. In some respects, New York has become the tail that wags the dog, in accordance with the Dominican Republic's penetration by international capital and, for that matter, the fact that since 1961 Dominican political and economic policies have ultimately been determined in Washington, D.C.—that is, by the International Monetary Fund and the U.S. State Department.

There are other aspects, both positive and sordid, of the linkage of merengue to commercial capital. As to some extent with salsa, drug money is said to subsidize the merengue scene in various ways. More openly, many bands on the island are supported by ties (*patrocinio*) to businesses, especially beer, rum, and cigarette companies, which sponsor tours and concerts in exchange for exclusive contracts and advertising rights. But that's show biz!

MERENGUE STYLE AND DANCE

The essence of merengue is its intricate, composite rhythm, which combines frenetic speed with crisp, controlled instrumental parts. Typically, while the tambora roll highlights the downbeat of every other bar, the güira provides hissing variations on a steady "chick-chicka-chick-chicka" pattern, and the bass plays a steady half-note pulse. Meanwhile, the melodic instruments typically play fast arpeggio ostinatos, as in the excerpt from a *merengue típico* by Fefita la Grande ("Tengo un lio") shown in Musical Example 14.

Variations on these patterns are common. The bass player, for example, can provide a variety of effects, and in recent decades the traditional tambora roll has given way to a simpler pattern called playing "*a lo maco*" (like a frog), popularized in particular by Los Hermanos Rosario. At a fast tempo, such variations can make the beat anything but simple. When combined in different ways, different songs and sections of a single song may show considerable rhythmic variety within the basic framework.

The formal structure of the modern merengue often resembles that of the *son* in having an initial "song"-like section (itself called "merengue") with a text, followed by a longer mambo section, which, like the *montuno*, contains call-and-response patterns over a repeated chordal ostinato, punctuated by

Musical Example 14. Merengue excerpt

pre-composed horn interludes. In many cases, the harmonies to the entire song consist of alternating tonic–dominant (I–V) chords, so that the first and second parts are not as distinct as in *son* and salsa. Some merengues alternate mambo and verse sections (such as Vargas's hit "Abusadora"), and in some, the verse section is all but absent.

Saxophones are indispensable to dance-band merengue—unlike in salsa, where they are at best optional. Typically, the saxes play fast arpeggio patterns throughout the most of the song, effectively perpetuating the role of the accordion in traditional merengue. Their crisp, tight ostinatos are punctuated, often in a responsorial style, by trumpet riffs.

Many songs with more varied chord progressions were not originally merengues. In the 1980s, it became common for bands to take various popular songs, especially slow *baladas*, and perform them as merengues, adding snappy *jaleos* and, of course, doubling or tripling the tempo. Wilfrido Vargas did several such cover versions of French Caribbean zouk and konpa (*compas*) songs. This practice is known as *fusilamiento*, which literally means "firing." The implications of the term are ambiguous: For fans, it can imply that a song has been "fired up" and energized when done as a merengue; for critics, however, it implies that the original version has been butchered. Such borrowings of tunes are hardly unique to merengue; they are in fact commonplace in much Caribbean music in general, whether in the case of a Colombian *vallenato* song recycled as a bachata or a country-and-western tune reworked in reggae.

The basic merengue dance step is quite simple, consisting of rocking back and forth between the left and the right foot in time with the bass and bass-drum beats, in a pattern called *paso de la empalizada*, or "stick-fence step." Partners can embrace loosely or more intimately—*brillando hebillas* (polishing belt buckles), as they say. The two-step pattern is considerably easier than the basic salsa choreography. In both salsa and merengue, dancers can combine the basic step with a variety of turns, spins, and breaks. Many merengue dancers, however, restrict themselves to the basic step, so that it often seems that they are barely moving, or are doing so in some sort of viscous medium. Also, the embellishing turns can be done at slow tempo, unlike in salsa dancing, where the delight lies in their dizzyingly rapid and yet smooth execution. Thus, although merengue as music is celebrated as *subido* (fast and intense) its accompanying dance is often *bajado* (cool, subdued, and restrained).

BACHATA: SONGS OF BITTERNESS, SONGS OF LOVE

While the merengue was sizzling its way throughout the Dominican Republic and abroad, in the '60s and '70s a quite different kind of music was thriving in the countryside, largely ignored by the mass media. The early Cuban bolero—and some say, the term "*bachata*"—had been brought to the island by Cuban troubador Sindo Garay in the 1890s and had taken root as an informal, guitar-based romantic song. These songs were typically performed either by rural amateurs or by guitar-led ensembles that also played merengue and other genres. By the 1880s, accordion-based groups had become more popular, but the guitar ensembles, rather than disappearing, continued as a somewhat marginalized folk tradition. By the 1950s or so, these groups typically consisted of one or two guitars, maracas, and perhaps bongo and marimba, accompanying a solo male singer. Their repertoire consisted of Cuban *sones*, Mexican *rancheras*, local merengues, and, above all, sentimental boleros. The music was predominantly romantic, used by suitors to serenade their ladies, to accompany dancing at rural parties, and to soothe the sentiments of jilted lovers at neighborhood taverns. Many songs were full of ribald double entendres and made no pretensions to bourgeois respectability.

As the Balaguer regime opened the countryside to foreign investment, hundreds of thousands of farmers lost their land to American agribusiness firms like Gulf & Western and, in most cases, migrated to Santo Domingo. Many ended up living in shantytowns or "Villa Miseria" slums, with their mud alleys, open sewers, rat-infested garbage heaps, and flimsy shacks clinging precariously to the slopes of ravines. This was a world essentially ignored by the Balaguer regime, which preferred to devote its attention and the nation's resources to projects like the $250 million Columbus lighthouse monument overlooking the harbor. The shantytown residents may have enjoyed merengue but would have had few chances to hear live performances, which would occur primarily in expensive urban clubs that had restrictive dress codes and were oriented toward the local elite, like the residents of the affluent suburb stretching up the gentle hillside overlooking Santo Domingo's Avenida de los Mártires.

As the dispossessed peasants flooded into urban shantytowns, they brought with them their guitar-based *canciones de amargue* (songs of bitterness), as they were then called, and the music came to express the frustrations and longings of male slum dwellers. As disseminated on cheap, poorly produced 45s and cassettes, the music found new homes in tavern and brothel jukeboxes, in tape players in neighborhood *colmados*, and on street corners. As we have seen, peasant music in Puerto Rico and Cuba has enjoyed a certain idealized status in national ideology, but the Dominican lower-class guitar songs enjoyed no such paternalistic support. Dismissed by the bourgeoisie as *cachivache* (trivial, worthless), in the early '70s the music came to be called bachata, the word for a rowdy lower-class fiesta. However derogatory in origin, the term stuck, and by the early 1980s, bachata music, though largely shunned by television and radio and marketed mostly by humble street vendors, was coming to rival merengue in record sales and popularity. As bachata singers like Luis Segura, Leonardo Paniagua, and Julio Angel popularized the genre, its relationship to merengue took on aspects of a symbolic class war, pitting the homemade guitar against the noisy saxophone and the humble *colmado* against the elite club. If merengue is music for the feet and hips, bachata is music for the soul—the battered Dominican peasant soul, driven by poverty from the rural Cibao to urban slums and often on to Puerto Rico and upper Manhattan. Bachata's original milieu was the sector of society that Dominicans compare to *concón*, the burnt rice at the bottom of the pan—the poor who are exposed to the heat of poverty, toil, and oppression and who are unable to develop as well as the rest.

As Deborah Pacini Hernandez illustrates, however, bachata's originally proletarian character lay not in the presence of overtly political songs (of which there are hardly any) but in the ways that its sentimental lyrics expressed the concerns of its original core audience, the male shantytown dwellers. Most of the songs resemble sentimental boleros, and many seemed particularly suited to express the frustrations of devalued, discouraged barrio men in a milieu where men are often unemployed or dependent on working women and where transient liaisons between men and women were coming to outnumber stable marriages. Women, semi-liberated by enforced economic self-reliance and the breakdown of kinship relations, were coming to be regarded with ambivalence by men who felt socially and economically marginalized and superfluous. Many '80s bachata songs expressed these feelings of bitterness (*amargue*). Like innumerable boleros and Mexican *rancheras*, they often portrayed the man drowning his sorrows, cursing perfidious women, and offering bitter advice to other men, as in Confesor Gonzales's "No te amargues por ella":[9]

> I've lost my illusions about all women
> Because I saw what happened to a friend of mine
> He trusted his wife, he would have given her his life
> And he trusted her so much, she betrayed him with another....
> My friend, come sit at my table
> I'm going to offer a toast of liquor
> Don't get bitter for her
> A man is worth more than a woman.

Other songs lament the perceived corruption of urbanized women:

> I'm going to tell you about women who come to the capital
> After three days she gets so you can't put up with her
> And she starts to walk in the streets alone
> And she even deceives you with your own best friend.
> (Manuel Chalas, "Aquí la mujer se daña")

When not denouncing the perfidy of women, men boast of their sexual prowess:

> I'm like the dollar, valued all over the world
> And wherever I go, I get what I want.
> I wander here and there, seducing women
> And because of the way I am, I get what I want.
> (Manuel Chano, "Yo soy como el dólar")

In a more lighthearted vein are the *doble sentido* (double entendre) songs, with their thinly disguised sexual metaphors:

> I have a little car, that's a delight
> If I'm with women it goes faster....
> I keep my car in the carport,
> But I take it out for the woman next door.
> (Anthony Santos, "El carrito")

> I have a very strong tree, no one can knock it down....
> More than three hundred women came to the challenge
> They sawed for a while, but not one succeeded.
> (Juan Bautista, "El serrucho")

In the 1990s, both bachata and its social status changed dramatically. Under the influence of Anthony Santos and others, the tempo sped up to a moderate bounce that was considerably faster than the classic bolero, and the finger-picked acoustic guitar switched to a distinctive squeaky-sounding amplified-acoustic sound while still playing very standardized accompanimental arpeggios. With the use of better studios, the input of new musicians, and perhaps a natural process of maturation, the genre improved in general quality, as well. The angry, bitter, or proudly macho lyrics of the early years became less characteristic, giving way to gentle odes by Raulin Rodríguez and songs like Joe Vera's "Por tu amor," in which he promises to cook, clean house, make coffee, and take the kids to school to please his woman. Female bachata singers have even made their mark, such as Alexandra (of Monchy and Alexandra) and Melida Rodríguez. Even more dramatic than these changes has been the genre's meteoric rise to respectability and thoroughly mainstream appeal, as bachata quickly shed its lower-class stigma. Nowadays, although some merengue and salsa musicians may regard bachata as musically crude, just about everyone else likes it, regardless of social class. Bachata has become the nation's romantic music of choice, and macho origins notwithstanding, it is especially popular among women, many of whom prefer its sentimentality to merengue's manic glibness. It is also a popular dance genre, and one need not be sober to execute its simple one-two-three-hop choreography.

Whether in the Dominican Republic or on New York's Latin radio, bachata commands at least as much air time as merengue, and its appeal has extended well beyond the Dominican community, pervading Puerto Rico and Mexico. The new internationalism and inclusiveness of bachata is best shown by the New York-based group Aventura, whose hits come out in both English and Spanish versions. As for Aventura's music being strictly a Dominican thang, the group's CD *Obsesión* contains a song "Mi Puerto Rico," and its first CD shows its members standing next to a sign for the number 4 subway—which, as everyone in the world knows, leads not to the Dominican stronghold of Quisqueya Heights but to the Puerto Rican barrios of Loizaida (the Lower East Side) and the South Bronx (whence the group hails).

To some extent, bachata's definitive legitimization was due to the singer, songwriter, and bandleader who has emerged as the nation's most versatile and popular musician and who merits special attention in this chapter.

JUAN LUIS GUERRA

Juan Luis Guerra, like Ruben Blades, is a sui generis musician—in a class by himself. On the one hand, his music is too unique to be typical, but on the other hand, it illustrates the internationalization and growing sophistication of Dominican music. Guerra's musical education was somewhat unusual by Dominican standards: After training at the Dominican national conservatory, he went on to study at Boston's Berklee College of Music, where he was schooled in jazz and exposed to a wide variety of international musics. Returning to Santo Domingo, he formed a vocal quartet called 440, which performed original jazz-oriented songs in a style inspired by—or in some cases, directly adapted from—the U.S. group Manhattan Transfer. The quartet's music was oriented primarily toward urban intellectuals and university audiences, although his subsequent recordings have managed to retain this orientation while enjoying genuine mass appeal. Guerra's success derives both from his musical talent and his refined and sensitive lyrics, with which he has taken both bachata and merengue to new levels of profundity and expressiveness.

In the early 1990s, Guerra moved beyond the Latin Manhattan Transfer stage, foregrounding his own often strikingly original singing and incorporating diverse styles and influences. His output has included several merengues, which set new standards for harmonic and vocal sophistication. His "A pedir su mano" is a sort of merengue to end all merengues, with its brilliant and eclectic orchestration and searing chorus. In its Afro-pop-style inclusion of snippets of South African choral singing, its Congolese-derived tune, and the appearance in the video of scenes of *gagá* revelers, Guerra reasserted the Dominican links to Africa.[10] In his neoclassical version of the venerable standard "Mal de amor," he at once tipped his hat to the 1950s bands of Luis Alberti and Papa Molina and reinterpreted the song in an idiosyncratically modern fashion.

Some of Guerra's biggest hits, like "Burbujas de amor," have been love songs in a sort of bolero or bachata-*balada* style, through which he has out–Julioed his way to international renown as one of the leading Latin pop crooners. Such songs fit comfortably into the "Latin pop" category of MTV International (which excludes salsa and merengue). His implicit labeling of such songs as "bachata," as in his Grammy-winning 1991 CD *Bachata Rosa*, which sold more than 4 million copies, helped legitimize that hitherto marginal genre (although established bachata singers might regard him as something of an interloper). Other of his songs might be classified as a sort of neo-*nueva canción* in their singer-songwriter lyricism and their frank confrontation of social themes. His "Visa para un sueño," for instance, is a poignant portrayal of the desperate aspirations of visa applicants at Santo Domingo's U.S. embassy, while his bachata "Frío frío" draws from themes of the Spanish poet Federico García Lorca. His "Ojalá que llueva café" (Let It Rain Coffee) became an anthem to the nation's farmers. In other pieces, Guerra uses a *son*–salsa format, inviting comparison with the music of Ruben Blades. As Guerra said, "The newspaper gives me ideas. When I heard Ruben Blades doing this with salsa, that opened the door for me to think I could do the same with merengue."

And like Blades, he has taken his share of flak, as the video for his song "El Costo de la Vida" was banned in several countries because of its stark indictment of Latin American poverty.

Whether singing of love or of an inadequate Dominican hospital (as in "El Niagara en Bicicleta"), Guerra's lyrics are consistently original and incisive. For example, "Burbujas de amor" is, in its way, highly sexual, but the imagery is simply too surrealistic to be vulgar:

> I want to be a fish, to rub my nose in your fishbowl
> and make bubbles of love all over
> Oh, to pass the whole night awake, wet inside you!

Nowadays, however, since being born again he mostly sings and talks about God.

Guerra's success owes nothing to the machinations of the entertainment industry's promotion machine. He remains wedded to the small indie label, Karen, which he founded, and avoids interviews and generally shuns tours in favor of spending time with his family in the Dominican Republic. Literary allusions and self-conscious eclecticism aside, Guerra's mass appeal can be attributed especially to his tuneful melodies and inventive arrangements. One reviewer summarizes his talent: "If we were part of an award committee, we'd have to give the highest honors to Guerra for the diversity of his themes, the

Juan Luis Guerra (adapted by Peter Manuel)

incisive yet balanced social criticism, the philosophical depth, and for the taste and intelligence of the author, as much in the music as in the poetry."[11] The eclecticism and sophistication of Guerra's music illustrate how Dominican music has come of age, at once transcending and retaining its earthy folk roots and becoming an international art in its own right.

THE RETURN OF THE REPRESSED

In recent years, with the Dark Ages of dictatorship fading into the past and the Dominican Republic being increasingly enriched—economically and culturally—by emigrants and outside influences, the local music scene has undergone remarkable changes. One of these is that *merengue típico*, far from being seen as quaint and old-fashioned, has become more popular than ever in the Cibao, although it retains a rural or working-class orientation. In Santiago, aside from resounding from car stereos and in its customary venues of cockfights and thatch-roofed, rural-nostalgia-oriented clubs, *merengue típico* is regularly performed at dances held in the car washes and gas stations that are founded by entrepreneurial return migrants from New York. In the past few years, performers like Krisspy and Geovanni Polanco have popularized an even more modern frenetic "merengue al mambo" style that, while retaining the rustic accordion, reduces the initial verse section to a bare minimum, emphasizing instead the funky, responsorial mambo section.[12] In this current era of fusions and remixes, the New York-based group Fulanito (accompanied by *típico* accordionist Arsenio de la Rosa) mixes merengue with house and rap, and one even encounters Aguakate's "reggaetón ripiao" throwing dancehall into the mix. These trends are so hot—and the returning emigrants so well-heeled—that they are even being admitted into dances at Santiago's Centro Español, the elite bastion that had hitherto rigorously excluded the rustic *merengue típico*.

Another dramatic development involves the Afro-Dominican traditions of *salve* and *música de palo*. As suggested earlier in this chapter, these genres were traditionally confined to a few black neighborhoods; to the extent that they were known at all by others, they were typically scorned as a *cosa de negros* (black people's thing) that had nothing to do with "legitimate" Dominican culture. Then, starting in the years around 2000, a funny thing happened: Afro-Dominican music became not only recognized but downright fashionable. It's hard to pinpoint exactly why, but several factors may be involved, aside from a certain merengue fatigue. Although the born-again evangelist Juan Luis Guerra now has no use for Afro-Dominican religion, his foregrounding of *palo* music in the lyrics and video of his hit "A pedir su mano" clearly had some impact on popular attitudes. With reggaetón

Merengue at the car wash in Santiago (Sydney Hutchinson)

superstar Tego Calderón including traditional Afro-Rican bombas on his CDs, and the unprecedented visibility of Santería and its music in Cuba, the waves of Afro-Caribbean pride may have been washing up belatedly on Dominican shores. Finally, UNESCO's formal recognition of the Cofradía de Congo de Villa Mella in 2001 helped persuade many young Dominicans that their

country's Afro-Dominican heritage was a treasure rather than an embarrass-
ment. Whatever the reasons, in the early years of the new millennium, and
especially as starting in New York City, *música de palo* and stylistically similar versions of *salve* became hot dance music at parties, whether the music
was provided by one of the handful of extant CDs or by a live ensemble of
three drummers and singers. Such ensembles might consist of a few singers
with *panderos*, or an electrified "*salve electronica*" group, or it might be rendered *a palo limpio*—straight-ahead *palo*, as in the title of the popular cut
on merengue singer Kinito Mendez's CD. To this ardent drumming and
responsorial singing people now dance, more or less free-form style (rather
than merengue-style), often singing along with the newly familiar *salve* chants.
New folkloric and commercial groups have sprung up out of nowhere, and
elder rural groups, which used to perform for free at rituals, are now regulars
at club dates. As one such veteran told researcher Angelina Tallaj, "I never
thought we would get paid to do this!" Meanwhile, New Yorkers can take
classes in *palo* drumming and dancing at the Alianza Dominicana, and as
Tallaj relates, the National Conservatory in Santo Domingo, which used to
punish anyone who dared practice a merengue, has even instituted a course
in folkloric music. The times they are a-changing!

BIBLIOGRAPHY

See Deborah Pacini Hernandez, *Bachata: A Social History of a Dominican Popular
Music* (Philadelphia: Temple University Press, 1995), and Paul Austerlitz, *Merengue:
Dominican Music and Dominican Identity* (Philadelphia: Temple University Press,
1997).

RECORDS AND FILMS

Aside from records by the artists named, see *Afro-Dominican Music from San Cristobal,
Dominican Republic* (Smithsonian Folkways FW04285 1983); *Rough Guide to
Merengue and Bachata* (World Music Network); and *Merengue: Dominican Music and
Dominican Identity* (Rounder, 1997). For films, see Giovanni Savino, dir., *Bachata:
Music of the People* (60 min., 2003) and *Santo Domingo Blues* (dir. Alex Wolfe, 2005).

6

Haiti and the French Caribbean

MUSIC IN THE STREETS OF PORT-AU-PRINCE

On a hot, sunny January day in 1988 in Port-au-Prince, my friend Tony, a flute player, invites me to visit a rehearsal of a new popular music group he has just joined. We walk to the street, and Tony lets out a loud "psst" sound, flagging down a local bus. Called a "tap-tap," our bus is really a half-ton flatbed pickup truck with an elaborately painted wooden frame covering the cargo area. Piled atop our tap-tap are bags of charcoal used for cooking food, some fruit and vegetables, and a young man carrying two chickens. Tap-tap are decorated with paintings of Catholic saints, important people like Malcolm X, movie characters (Rambo was then a popular choice), and other people who display unique and admirable qualities. Slogans painted on the tap-tap, such as "Dieu qui décide" (God Decides) and "Psaume 34" (Psalm 34) serve to protect us from a fatal traffic accident, while other slogans, like "Miami Beach" and "Min Nou!" (Here We Are!), express the tap-tap owner's taste and personality.

We board the tap-tap on Avenue J. J. Dessalines, the main thoroughfare in Port-au-Prince. Since the vehicle is completely full, we opt to hang off the back of the truck, holding on to the roof rack for balance. We are in a superb position to observe the many types of musical activity found on the streets of Haiti's capital. Our tap-tap is mounted with large speakers that blare Haitian dance music called konpa (*compas*); a few of the passengers sing along with the recordings. As we pass the Mache Fè (Iron Market), young men peddle soft drinks by beating rhythms on *kola* bottles using their metal can openers. Other vendors use similar techniques to draw attention: The ice-cream vendor uses three bells suspended from a piece of wood to announce his arrival, while the shoeshine man rings a single bell. The meat-pie vendor sells his wares by

---

Chapter 6 was written by Michael Largey.

singing "hot meat-pie," and the peanut-brittle seller sings "praline"; both sellers hope to make passersby hungry with their not-so-subliminal messages.

On a street corner, two *twoubadou* (troubadors) perform for shoppers. The singer of the group sits on a large, empty tin can and taps out a rhythm on a small plastic bowl with a piece of wood. His partner beats out rhythms on an assortment of cans, tubs, buckets, and assorted scraps of metal. On the next corner, another *twoubadou*, also known as a *mizisyen ambilan* (walking musician), gives a performance as a "one-man band." He strums a homemade guitar pasted with photos from discarded magazines while playing a kazoo that has a car stereo speaker attached to its end. Strapped to his legs are two *tcha-tcha* (maracas), and his foot is beating out a rhythm on a *tanbou* (single-headed drum).

Our tap-tap turns up Avenue Delmas, heading toward Pétionville, a suburb of Port-au-Prince. I push the buzzer attached to the back of the truck signaling the driver to stop, and Tony and I jump off the back of the tap-tap. We pay our fare of 85 centimes apiece (about 18 cents) and begin the descent to Tony's rehearsal. We are the last to arrive, and some of the musicians have already begun to rehearse by the time we finish greeting everyone present.

Tony introduces me to Théodore "Lolo" Beaubrun, the leader of the group; Lolo's wife, Mimerose; his cousin Daniel "Dadi" Beaubrun; and the rest of the band. Lolo explains that the group's name is Boukman Eksperyans; it takes its name from the Vodou priest Boukman who in 1791 made a blood pact with a group of runaway slaves to overthrow the French colonial system. Lolo explains that the group's music derives its inspiration from the Vodou ceremony where worshipers dance to songs and ceremonial drumming meant to communicate with the *lwa* (spirits) of Africa.

Lolo steers me toward a stool in the cramped rehearsal space in the living room. From my vantage point, I can see the entire ensemble, including two female singers, Lolo on keyboard synthesizer, Dadi on the bass and drum machine, and several drummers playing a set of Vodou ceremonial drums from the Rada nation of spirits. Lolo asks the band to rehearse its new number, "Se Kreyòl nou ye," a song that uses a familiar *yanvalou* rhythm of "short-long-long-short-long-long-long" (a variant of the African-derived standard time line shown in chapter 1). The words of the song are striking, since they call for all speakers of Kreyòl (Creole, the national language of Haiti) to take pride in their native language and culture.

HAITIAN CULTURAL CROSSROADS

Haiti, like Cuba, is place where musical expression reflects the mixture of several different cultural influences. While most historians look at the history of colonial Haiti as a process of replacement of indigenous populations of Native Americans with Europeans and enslaved Africans, in reality the heritages of all three groups endure in present-day Haiti, albeit in different forms and to varying degrees.

Before Columbus's arrival in 1492, Haiti was populated by several Native American groups, including the Taino (the largest group), Carib, and Guanahatabeys (sometimes referred to as Ciboney) peoples. The Taino groups were led by *caciques* (chiefs) and spoke a language called Arawak; other Taino groups existed in nearby Cuba. Within the first twenty-five years of Spanish rule, about 90 percent of the Taino population of the island was wiped out by Spanish guns and diseases. Nevertheless, some Arawak words are still used in Haiti—for instance, "Quisqueya" (the Taino word for the island) and even the word "Haiti" itself, which means "mountainous land."

The Spanish ruled Quisqueya, which they renamed Hispaniola (Española), from 1492 until 1697, when, in the Treaty of Ryswick, Spain ceded the western portion of the island to France. The French called their new colony Saint-Domingue and turned it into one of the most profitable economies in the Western Hemisphere, leading Europeans to dub it "the pearl of the Antilles." French colonists, especially those who owned and operated the large sugarcane plantations, brought their European entertainments to Saint-Domingue, opening theaters for musical performances and sponsoring productions of popular French operas. There were more than 3,000 European dramatic and musical performances in Saint-Domingue between 1764 and 1791, most of which were imported from the theaters of France.

The colony's economic successes were, however, borne on the backs of Africans brought to Saint-Domingue as slaves. Working long hours at the arduous tasks of harvesting and processing sugarcane into molasses, rum, and sugar, Africans enjoyed few of the popular entertainments available to the French planters. Slaves were forbidden by law from attending French entertainments as audience members, but they were drafted as entertainers for wealthy planters. European accounts from the colonial period indicate that many slaves were adept on European instruments such as the violin, clarinet, and French horn.

While African slaves were familiar with several of the musical traditions of their French captors, most of their music-making was based in West African and Central African traditions of music. Slaves were brought to Saint-Domingue from as far north on the west coast of Africa as Senegal and as far south as Angola. Haitian historian Jean Fouchard claims that many Africans were brought to Saint-Domingue from the east coast of Africa, especially Madagascar and Mozambique (whence the word "maringa," or mereng, is also believed to derive). During their perilous voyages as human cargo across the Atlantic, Africans were not able to bring any physical artifacts from home. The drums they made in Haiti, called *tanbou*, were carved from Caribbean wood but used designs from drums made back in Africa. Other instruments, like the *ogan* (a struck piece of metal), were adapted by African musicians in Saint-Domingue. Africans also adapted instruments from Taino music, including the *tcha-tcha*, which functioned much like the West African *shekere* (gourd shaker covered with a beaded net) and the *lanbi* (blown conch shell), which was an adaptation of the Akan *abeng*, or blown cow's horn.

In addition to the planter and slave classes, there was a significant population of mostly light-skinned free people of color, called *afranchi*. As the offspring of white French men and African women, the *afranchi* had some legal advantages over the slave classes. *Afranchi* could attend some of the French colonial entertainments and could own land. They were forbidden, however, to hold administrative posts, work as lawyers or doctors, or wear clothing that resembled the styles favored by the wealthy white colonists. Despite the limitations placed on their participation in French planter society, many *afranchi* identified themselves culturally with France.

All of the social groups in Saint-Domingue (French planters, *afranchi* landholders, and African slaves) were interested in breaking free of French governmental control, although their reasons differed. The planters wanted to be free of the tribute they were forced to pay to the French government for the privilege of owning land. The *afranchi*, eager to be rid of the French planters, hoped to gain independence for Saint-Domingue and take over the plantations. The slaves were also eager to be rid of the French, but not so that *afranchi* landowners could merely take the place of the French planters. Some slaves sided with the French government, believing that the recent French Revolution, with its promise of "liberty, equality, and fraternity," would extend to them. Other slaves believed that their only hope of freedom lay in a complete break from France.

Slave resistance to the French took several forms. During the seventeenth and eighteenth centuries, many slaves ran away to inaccessible mountainous areas. These slaves were called *mawon* (from the French word *marron* and the Spanish word *cimarrón*, meaning "runaway slave"). The *mawon* formed communities and practiced small-scale agriculture and hunting. Many *mawon* went on covert trips back to their plantations in efforts to free friends and family members. On some occasions, *mawon* joined forces with Taino settlements that had escaped the extermination campaigns of the Spanish in the seventeenth century. Other slave-resistance efforts attacked the French plantation system directly. In the 1750s, a *mawon* leader named Makandal led an unsuccessful campaign to poison the drinking water of several plantation owners. Later, in 1791, another *mawon* called Boukman Dutty officiated at a ceremony at Bois Caïman, effectively declaring war on the French plantation owners.

The Haitian Revolution, which lasted from 1791 to 1804, brought the colonial period to an end but left political power in the hands of the *afranchi* elite. While French planters were either exiled or executed, the former *afranchi* class, now split into *milat* (mulatto, light-skinned) and *nwa* (noir, dark-skinned) factions, assumed control of much of the business of the new country. The vast majority of the former slaves were located in the rural areas and continued to work the land, but enjoyed few benefits from their newly won freedom.

Today, the vestiges of the plantation system endure in the form of social-class and color stratification. Elites, still divided into *milat* and *nwa* groups, vie for control of the country, while the predominantly dark-skinned rural population provides the tax base for the economy. While color prejudice is still felt in modern Haiti, class discrimination is the more pervasive and persistent impediment to social change.

CREOLIZATION IN HAITI: LANGUAGE

The different cultural heritages of Haiti have shaped not only the history of the country but also its language and religions. Unlike the Spanish-speaking Caribbean nations, Haiti has its own language, which is not intelligible to speakers of French. Haitian Creole (as it is known in English)—or "Kreyòl ayisyen," as Haitians call it—is a mixture of several different languages, including French, which makes up most of the language's vocabulary, various African languages, Spanish, some Portuguese, and, more recently, English. The term "creole" refers to a linguistic phenomenon that emerges when two groups speaking different languages come into contact and must find a way to communicate. The language formed as a result of this contact is called a pidgin. Normally, pidgin languages are used by people in contact situations: Pidgins tend to exist when different groups trade with each other but return home to speak a different language. When a pidgin language becomes a native language for a group, it is said to be a "creole" language.

Kreyòl was originally a contact language between the French slaveholders and their African captives. It eventually became the native language for the majority of the Haitian population; all Haitians, with the exception of some of those who have grown up outside Haiti, speak and understand Kreyòl.

Despite Kreyòl's widespread use in Haiti, elite Haitians, most of whom speak both French and Kreyòl, look down on Kreyòl as an "ungrammatical" use of French. As a result, Kreyòl was first recognized as the "national" language of Haiti only in the 1970s, and French is still the "official" language of government and business. Haitian education, which had been conducted almost exclusively in French, began to use Kreyòl as a language of instruction, but only for the first few elementary-school grades.

Elite prejudice toward Kreyòl and its rural speakers has political consequences, as well. Since non-elites have access neither to good education nor an environment to cultivate the French language, they are effectively cut out of the official domains of government and business. Elites have successfully blocked efforts to reorganize language instruction in Haiti, fearing that an educated, literate populace will organize itself and present a threat to the status quo.

Kreyòl's continued existence as the principal language of Haitians is due in part to its ability to change to meet the needs of Haitian speakers. Like most spoken languages, Kreyòl is in a constant state of transformation, incorporating new vocabulary and revitalizing older words and phrases to meet new demands. Kreyòl is famous for incorporating words that not only express new ideas but that also comment subtly on changes in modern society. For example, in the 1960s, Haitians called the used clothing shipped from the U.S. *kènèdi*, after John F. Kennedy, the U.S. president who established the Peace Corps. Now that JFK is no longer remembered in Haiti as a political figure, used clothes are called *pepe*. After the 1995 "intervasion" of Haiti by U.S. military forces to reinstall Haitian President Jean-Bertrand Aristide, Haitians heard U.S. soldiers calling their patrol colleagues "partner." As a result, Haitians coined the term "*patnè*" (partner) to refer to a close companion. Other examples of American commercial influence on Haitian language include laundry detergent, known as *fab* (after the popular American brand of soap), toothpaste, called *kòlgat* (Colgate), and cameras, called *kodak*.

CREOLIZATION IN HAITI: RELIGION

Vodou, the Haitian religion that blends several West African spiritual traditions with a veneer of Roman Catholicism, is similar in many respects to other African-derived religious traditions in the Caribbean.[1] Like the Shango religion of Trinidad, Jamaican Kumina, and Cuban Santería, Vodou uses music, dance, and spirit possession in its religious rituals. Vodou synthesizes the belief in African spirits, called *lwa* (*loa* in French), with the Catholic saints, resulting in multiple identities for popular religious figures. The Virgin Mary of

Roman Catholicism is frequently associated with the *lwa* of love and beauty, Ezili Freda, while St. Patrick, who is most often associated with driving the snakes from Ireland, is interpreted as a counterpart of Danbala, a *lwa* symbolized by a serpent. Initiates in the Vodou community, called *ousi*, dance to the music provided by drums, a small iron gong, and a rattle; their goal is to have the *lwa*, who are said to reside in Ginen (Guinea, or ancestral Africa), travel to Haiti and possess the bodies of their Haitian devotees. The *lwa* are said to "mount their horse" during a spirit possession; the worshiper becomes the vehicle of expression for the *lwa*. In a ceremony, people who achieve a spirit possession make gestures that enable others to recognize that a possession is taking place. Often, the worshiper appears to be in a physical struggle, making sudden and vigorous gestures that differ in character from the usual movements of the dance.

Once the *lwa* has mounted his or her "horse," the worshiper takes on the personality traits of the *lwa*. A worshiper possessed by Ogou, the *lwa* associated with ironsmithing, war, and the military, often calls for his machete and some rum, while an individual possessed by Ezili Freda might demand gifts of perfume, fine clothes, and jewelry. Other worshipers, recognizing the presence of a *lwa*, may stop and pay their respects to the visiting spirit; some may ask the *lwa* for advice or a favor.

Vodou ceremonies can be held anywhere, from an *oufò* (temple) in rural Haiti to the basement of an apartment building in Flatbush, Brooklyn. What is necessary for a successful ceremony is the creation of a sacred space where the *lwa* will feel welcome. The proper spiritual atmosphere is created in part by the ritual drawings of the *lwa* in cornmeal or flour, called *vèvè*. *Vèvè* act as signs to the *lwa* that a ceremony is taking place and that they are invited to attend. Each *lwa* has characteristic *vèvè* that symbolize different aspects of his or her personality. Ezili Freda, associated with love and beauty, has a *vèvè* with a heart design, while Ogou (a counterpart to Santería's Ogun), associated with iron and war, often has a machete as part of his *vèvè*.

Lwa also have their own music in the form of ritual songs. Ceremonies usually feature a series of songs intended to invite the *lwa* to participate in the ceremony. The first song is always sung to Legba (Eléggua in Santería), the *lwa* who guards the crossroads. His songs usually feature the phrase, "Papa Legba, ouvri bayè pou nou" (Father Legba, open the gate for us), a plea for Legba to give the worshiper access to the world of the spirits. Other songs follow in a prescribed order, each devoted to a particular *lwa*. Songs are in a combination of Kreyòl and *langaj*, a ceremonial language derived in part from ritual language used in some West and Central African religions. *Langaj* is a "deep" form of ritual language that defies direct, singular translations.

Souvenance, Haiti, 1988. A Rada drum ensemble: *segon* on the left; *manman*, or mother drum, played by master drummer in the center; and *boula* on the right (Michael Largey)

A woman possessed by "Gede" at a Vodou ceremony in Brooklyn (Chantal Regnault)

Frisner Augustin at the Petwo drum (Chantal Regnault)

Frisner at the Rada drum (Chantal Regnault)

Lwa are organized according to *nanchon*, or "nations," which take their names from geographic locations or ethnic groups in West and Central Africa. Lois Wilcken has called Vodou *nanchon* "confederations," recognizing the coalescence of different African spiritual practices into a single worship service. Ceremonies often salute the *lwa* of Rada, Petwo, Nago, Ibo, and Kongo with their songs and dances. Each *nanchon* probably had its own musical ensemble at one time, but today the major *nanchon* use either Rada or Petwo instruments.

The Rada *nanchon* uses an ensemble of three *tanbou* (drums) called *man-man* (mother), *segon* (second or middle), and *boula* (or *kata*). The ensemble is similar in function to the *tumba francesa* and *batá* ensembles of Cuba in the sense that in each it is the largest, lowest-pitched drum that leads the group. The *manman* is the largest drum and is played with a single stick and one hand. The master drummer plays the *manman*; he (most drummers are male) directs the ensemble and determines when the musicians will move to another rhythm or song. The *segon*, slightly smaller than the *manman*, plays rhythmic patterns and can vary the pattern slightly, but not as much as the lead drummer. The *boula* plays a steady rhythmic pattern and helps keep the other drummers coordinated. The drums used in the Rada ensemble are made from hardwoods and are covered with cow skin and tuned with pegs that are driven into the body of the instrument. The Petwo *nanchon* uses two drums made of softer wood than Rada drums; the goatskin heads are fastened to the body of the instrument with cords rather than pegs, and are always played with the hands.

Lwa have a reciprocal relationship with their devotees. Spirits provide good harvests, plentiful rain, and good mental and physical health in exchange for their followers' sacrifices. These sacrifices can either be a live sacrifice of an animal or *manje sèk* ("dry food"—that is, not consecrated with the blood of a live sacrifice). Often sacrifices accompany an important celebration such as an initiation or yearly feast. When such animals as chickens, pigs, bulls, and goats are sacrificed, their meat is consumed by the religious community. For large celebrations, such as the annual festival at Souvenance during Easter week, many animals are sacrificed, ritually offered to the *lwa*, and prepared for those present to eat.

Ask anyone from the United States what comes to mind when they hear the word "voodoo," and the responses will range from creepy to comical: Voodoo dolls, zombies, black magic, superstition, cannibalism, and devil worship are but a few of the popular ideas associated with Haitians and their religion. Movies like the James Bond adventure *Live and Let Die* and the more recent *Angel Heart* and *The Serpent and the Rainbow* satisfy a taste in the United

States for lurid depictions of black Haitians in so-called primitive orgiastic rites. These attitudes about Haitians are founded on racism and perpetuated by ignorance about Haiti, its people, and its culture.

While it is tempting to think that such images of Haitians are a relatively recent phenomenon, U.S. discomfort with its Haitian neighbors dates back to the early days of the Haitian Republic. In the decades after 1804, when Haiti became the first independent black republic, southern whites in the United States were concerned that the example of a successful slave insurrection would inspire a similar revolt on their plantations. Since the early nineteenth century, then, white U.S. fiction about Haiti has been concerned with the depiction of Haitians as savages, consumed by a thirst for white blood. Negative stereotyping of Haitians by white writers has persisted to the present in the form of movies and books that transform the religion of Haitians from a healing ceremony into a satanic ritual. Readers should be aware that despite the pervasiveness of pejorative images about Vodou, the fictionalized version of Haitian religious practices has little to do with Haiti, Vodou, or reality in general.

CARNIVAL AND RARA

During the week before Ash Wednesday, several Caribbean nations celebrate what is collectively known as Carnival. Trinidad is perhaps the most famous for its celebrations, complete with huge masquerade bands, fantastic costumery, and festive dancing and music making. The celebration can last up to a week before Ash Wednesday, but the preparation for the event often takes months. Many participants in the festivities, especially those involved in the construction of costumes, begin their work the previous year.

In Haiti, the celebration of Carnival (Kanaval in Kreyòl) is also accompanied with parades featuring floats called *cha madigra*, popular music provided by Haitian dance bands mounted on the backs of flatbed trucks, and masses of dancing revelers moving through the streets. The *cha madigra* are usually sponsored by local businesses, which hire young women to sit atop the floats and wave to the crowd. Haitian companies such as Freska (a popular toothpaste firm), and Royal (a margarine producer) use the opportunity to plug their products and to associate themselves with their Haitian audiences. Since Haiti is predominantly an import market, local producers have to compete with less-expensive American and French brands of merchandise. Carnival and its association with Haitian traditions give local manufacturers a forum for promoting their goods as "authentically Haitian."

Foreign products also sponsor floats and masqueraders; the aspirin manufacturer Bufferin hired a group of masqueraders to ride papier-mâché horses emblazoned with the Bufferin logo back in the late 1970s. Non-Haitian products can also be the target of ridicule by Carnival participants. In the film *Divine Horsemen*, filmmaker Maya Deren included a group of masqueraders carrying signs for "Ex-Lax," a product that is the butt of many jokes in the United States, as well.

The association of Carnival and commercialization dates back to the 1920s, when the Haitian government became active in the promotion of the celebration. During the American occupation of Haiti (1915–34), the government of Louis Borno was sensitive to the criticism that it had sold out to American interests. Because Carnival is also a time for voicing social criticism, the Haitian government is frequently the target of Carnival songs and jokes. By making Carnival more of a commercial venture and downplaying the critical nature of Carnival song lyrics, the government, with the tacit support of the elite members of Haitian society, hoped to keep Carnival under official control. By involving Haitian manufacturers in the celebration, attention could be focused away from criticism of the political regime.

Carnival is also a time for competition among rival groups of masqueraders, dancers, and musical organizations. With the advent of electronic sound amplification, popular music bands today ride through the streets of Port-au-Prince playing for enthusiastic crowds. Bands congregate near the customs office and engage in a mock battle; each aims to capture the attention of the crowd and, in so doing, push the competition out of the limelight.

Public behavior during Carnival is very different from everyday life. In Port-au-Prince, masses of people crowd the main streets, pressing up against one another in an effort to see the masquerades and musicians pass by on the *cha madigra*. During one Carnival celebration, I had the opportunity to witness Carnival crowd dynamics firsthand when I was having a drink at a bar in Port-au-Prince called the Rond Point. Located at a crossroads near the French Institute of Haiti and the American embassy, the bar was one of the meeting places for competing bands. The management of the Rond Point had already removed the plate glass windows from their frames so that exuberant dancers would not fall through the sheets of glass. As the crowd swelled, my friends and I decided to go outside and experience the Carnival atmosphere up close. As we reached the street, the press of people made it impossible to move; people were so tightly packed together that individuals moved involuntarily with the motion of the crowd. At one point, I was lifted off the ground and carried several feet.

In most Caribbean countries with a Carnival tradition, Mardi Gras, the "Fat Tuesday" before Ash Wednesday, is the final day of festivities. On Wednesday morning before the Lenten season begins, the Carnival paraphernalia are burned, the musical instruments are "put to sleep" until the following Carnival season, and people return to their routines. In Haiti, Carnival is immediately followed by a festival that lasts until Easter Sunday and is known as Rara.[2]

Rara refers to the street celebrations held in Haiti from the beginning of the Lenten season until Easter Sunday. While the most intense Rara activity is usually during the week before Easter, each Sunday during Lent revelers roam the streets of Haitian cities, towns, and hinterlands in search of an audience. Léogâne, a town 30 kilometers west of Port-au-Prince, is especially well known as a center for Rara music. Music is provided by the *bann rara* (Rara band) on homemade instruments such as the *kòne* (a pressed zinc trumpet that can measure more than three feet), the *vaksin* (a large, single-note bamboo trumpet played in groups of three or more), the *tanbou* (single-headed animal-skin–covered drum), the *graj* (a metal scraper similar to those used in Dominican merengue bands), the *kès* (caisse, snare drum), *tcha-tcha* (maracas), as well as any struck object carried by dancing participants. Rara bands in Léogâne also play brass instruments such as trumpets, trombones, baritone horns, and sousaphones (called *elikon* or *kontrabas*), which has caused some people to call Léogâne Rara too much like Carnival. Léogâne residents are quick to point out, however, that despite the overwhelming volume of the Rara bands' brass sections, it is always possible to hear the core instruments of rara: the *tanbou*, the *vaksin*, and the *graj*. Usually, members of the Rara band who are not playing the instruments listed earlier provide rhythmic ostinatos on soft-drink or beer bottles (the local brand, Prestige, is popular, but its stubby neck makes it difficult to handle; many participants go for the longer-necked Dutch import Heineken or a Coke bottle.)

Like their counterparts in Carnival celebrations, Rara members also engage in boisterous behavior during their sojourns into the streets. Song texts often refer to political topics or events in recent history; many texts are downright obscene. Often, the ribald nature of the texts masks a deeper meaning, sometimes in the form of political satire directed at the regime in power. I have heard that one Rara song about a woman who decided to straighten her pubic hair with a hot comb was directed at Michèle Bennett, the wife of the former Haitian dictator Jean-Claude Duvalier.

As Elizabeth McAlister notes, Rara has tended to be dismissed as a form of "rural Carnival" in which pent-up farmers "blow off steam" in a drunken orgy. This view has been perpetuated by elite Haitians who see the celebration of Rara as a dangerous, lower-class phenomenon. But Rara should also be seen as a religious celebration in which the normally stationary practice of Vodou is taken to the street. Rara bands often fulfill religious obligations during their

Two *vaksin* players using PVC tubes along with a Petwo drummer and others (Michael Largey)

nocturnal processions. The Rara band Ti Malis K-Che (The Rara of the Clever Children in Hiding, usually called "Ti Malis") from Léogâne always performs a Vodou ceremony under a large mapou tree before it begins its processions on Good Friday. Band members and the Rara-band instruments are given a ritual bath steeped in leaves collected by a *doktè fèy*, or leaf doctor. The bath serves to protect the musicians and their instruments from the dangers of the street processions.

Since many bands take to the streets in Léogâne during Rara, competition can be fierce and, at times, physically dangerous. Exuberant musicians and

Two *vaksin* players using PVC tubes along with a Petwo drummer and others (Michael Largey)

fans clash when their favorite bands meet on the street. For bands that have long-standing feuds, these encounters have sometimes been memorialized in song. For example, in 1954, the members of Rara Laflè di Woz (Rose Flower Rara) attacked the village of Kansay, home of Ti Malis. According to the story from Ti Malis's point of view, several band members were killed, and their property was stolen or burned. Ti Malis members wrote a song called "Senkantkat" (Fifty-Four) that commemorates the attack and excoriates the members of Laflè as "pig thieves." "Senkantkat" continues to be a popular song in Ti Malis's repertoire, even though the attack took place more than fifty years ago.

Rara bands pride themselves on their ability to fill the streets with dancing and singing participants. If band members spread out too much in their procession, the "full" feeling of the march dissipates, and the band runs the risk of *kraze*, or breaking down on its route. However, a band that keeps its members too close together may be described as *rèd*, or hard, unable to move from its position on the road. Automobile traffic is frequently slowed or blocked during Rara season; angry motorists beep their horns and run the risk of enraging the Rara crowd. Drivers who dance in their seats are waved through the crowd since their movements tell the Rara band that its musical message has gotten through. In many parts of Haiti, impatient motorists pay a small toll to hurry their safe passage through the Rara throng.

At first encounter, a large group of people dancing and singing their way through the streets may seem like an undifferentiated mob. While the informal membership of the procession can and should swell dramatically during the Rara celebration, the principal members of the *bann rara* constitute an organized, hierarchically structured group. The patron of the Rara is the *prezidan*. He or she usually purchases the more expensive instruments, costumes, flags, and celebratory paraphernalia for the members. The *kolònel* (or colonel) leads the band in its street marches and can be recognized by the whip and whistle that he or she uses to move the dancers along their route. Male dancers and baton twirlers, known as *majò jon*, dress in multicolored scarves somewhat reminiscent of the Jamaican "pitchy-patchy" character of *jonkonnu*. They work with the female dancers, known as *renn* (queens) to bring as many spectators into the procession as possible. *Renn* frequently work in pairs, engaging male audience members with friendly, mocking, and vaguely suggestive dancing.

Renn are also responsible for collecting tolls from participants. One Sunday afternoon during Lent in Haiti, I was enjoying a pizza with a friend at a street-level cafe. We didn't pay much attention to the growing volume of a nearby *bann rara*, so before we knew what happened, we were surrounded by a group of thirty or more. The two principal *renn* danced at the front of the group, asking us to join in the procession. We answered that we would love to participate, but, unfortunately, our pizza had just arrived and we were going to have to eat it before it became cold. One of the *renn*, sitting in my lap, acknowledged that cold pizza would be a terrible waste, so she and her compatriots took our slices and continued down the street. We couldn't help but laugh at our situation: We had paid the price for refusing to participate in the rara celebration.

MISIK TWOUBADOU

First-time travelers to Haiti might have their initial encounter with Haitian music on the tarmac of the Port-au-Prince airport. Often, the airport authorities hire musicians to perform Haitian folksongs, other popular songs from elsewhere in the Caribbean, or an occasional arrangement of some current American song hit for the entertainment of the arriving passengers. These musicians, called *twoubadou*, can also be found in larger restaurants, playing requests for patrons for small donations, or performing outdoors for celebrations. Troubadours perform in small ensembles, usually featuring a guitar or two, a pair of maracas or a *graj*, a *tanbou*, and a large lamellaphone with three to five keys called *manibula*, *maniba*, or *malimba*, depending on the geographic region.

As Gage Averill points out, despite the relatively recent development of *misik twoubadou* in Haiti, most Haitians assume that the genre is an indigenous Haitian music, presumably because of its association with rural (and poor) musicians. Derived from the *guajiro* traditions of Cuba and related to the *jíbaro* musical tradition of Puerto Rico, *twoubadou* music was brought by itinerant Haitian sugarcane cutters who traveled back and forth to Cuba to harvest the seasonal crop. The instruments in the ensemble are portable, since most *twoubadou* had to carry all of their possessions back and forth between Haiti and the sugarcane fields abroad.

Migrant labor has played an important role in Caribbean history since the era of colonial domination. Cash crops such as sugarcane and coffee require labor-intensive processes to get goods from the fields to the market. Haitians have been part of a network of migrant labor since the late eighteenth century, when Haitian workers routinely traveled to Cuba to participate in the sugarcane harvest. Haitian migrants have also shaped the musical styles in the areas they work. *Tumba francesa* is the Cuban term for Haitian-derived recreational drumming and dancing; the style is still practiced among expatriate Haitian cane cutters. In the Dominican Republic, Haitian sugarcane cutters, who live in cane-harvesting camps, celebrate Rara, albeit in a slightly altered form. Called *Gagá*, the Dominican version of Rara features the same emphasis on colorful costumes, revelry in the streets, and political satire in the form of street theater. *Gagá*, like Rara, has ties to the Vodou religious system, except the *lwa* associated with the *Gagá* festival have identifiably Dominican attributes.

Misik twoubadou has always had a following in Haiti, especially in small nightclubs where combos of two guitars, maracas, *tanbou*, and a pair of vocalists serenade dancers with Haitian, Cuban, and Brazilian music. Perhaps the most famous contemporary exponent of the *twoubadou* style among popular entertainers in the latter twentieth century was Jean-Gesner Henry, better known as Coupé Cloué (1925–98). Nicknamed for the soccer moves *coupé* (cut) and *cloué* (nail), Coupé Cloué was renowned for his sexually suggestive lyrics. Recently, commercial artists have embraced the *twoubadou* sound, releasing several albums in recent years that foreground the guitar and the rhythms of Cuban music. One of the more successful releases is *Haitiando*, a three-CD series of Cuban music translated into Kreyòl and sung to the music of the two-guitar ensemble. The *Haitiando* series makes the often forgotten connection between Haitian and Cuban music explicit with their translations of popular Cuban songs into Kreyòl.

HAITIAN DANCE MUSIC

Dancing is an important part of Haitian life.[3] As we have seen in the case of Vodou, the religious experience of spirit possession is usually accompanied by dancing, singing, and drumming. Carnival and Rara celebrations feature exuberant dancing and movement in the streets. Dancing is also a social activity, used for celebrations such as church socials and informal parties, as well as evenings out with friends. In small restaurants, social dance music is provided by the relatively small *twoubadou* groups, while larger clubs with big dance floors often feature dance bands reminiscent of the American big bands in size.

Social dance music has been one of the most heavily creolized music forms in Haiti. European dance forms such as the contradanse (*kontradans*), quadrille, waltz, and polka were introduced to white planter audiences during the colonial period. Musicians, either slaves or freed people of color, learned the European dance forms and adapted them for their own use.[4] One of the most popular African-influenced dance styles was the Haitian mereng (*méringue* in French), related to the Dominican merengue. Along with the *carabinier*, the mereng was a favorite dance style of the Haitian elite and was a regular feature at elite dances. The Haitian expression "Mereng ouvri bal,

mereng fème bal" (The mereng opens the ball, the mereng closes the ball)
alludes to the popularity and ubiquity of the mereng as an elite entertainment.
In nineteenth-century Haiti, the ability to dance the mereng, as well as a host
of other dances, was considered a sign of good breeding.

Like other creolized dance styles, the mereng was claimed by both elite and
proletarian Haitian audiences as a representative expression of Haitian cultural
values. Elite Haitian composers, many of whom were trained in Europe and
wrote in a European-influenced style, used the mereng as a vehicle for their
creative talents. Composers such as Occide Jeanty; his father, Occilius; Ludovic Lamothe; Justin Elic; Franck Lassègue; and Fernand Frangeul wrote
mereng for solo piano and sometimes for small groups of wind instruments.
Often, these elite mereng were named for people, such as Occide Jeanty's
"Maria," or events in the composer's life—for example, François Manigat's
"Eight Days while Staying in Cap (Haïtien)."

The mereng is based on a five-note rhythm, or quintuplet, known in French
as a *quintolet* and in Spanish as a *cinquillo* (see chapter 2). The quintolet
is unevenly subdivided, giving an approximate feeling of "long-short-long-
short-long." While the concert mereng tended to use the syncopated version,
Haitian piano soloists, like Ludovic Lamothe, tended to play the *quintolet*
more like five even pulses, giving the mereng a smoother, subtler feel.

Occide Jeanty's "Maria" was written for the Musique du Palais, the official presidential band for the Haitian Republic. Jeanty was chief director and
composer for the group and wrote most of the band's performance repertoire.
The *quintolet* in "Maria" is the syncopated version, appearing first in the saxophones and horns, then answered by the flutes, clarinets, and trumpets. Most
mereng for concert band followed this pattern, keeping the *quintolet* figure
moving from low to high register, thus allowing the melody to alternate the
mereng rhythm with sustained, heavily vibrated notes. The percussion parts
also alternate the musical pulse and the *quintolet* rhythm, giving the mereng
an additional lilt.

Mereng were also used by proletarian audiences during Carnival time, especially in the nineteenth century. Unlike the elite mereng, intended for use
on the dance floor, the Carnival mereng were directed at the elite members
of Haitian society, either criticizing unpopular people in power or ridiculing their idiosyncracies. The formulaic insults of the Haitian Carnival mereng
bore some similarity to the early calypso *picong*, or "stinging," style.

While the mereng remained a popular dance form for Haitians well into the
twentieth century, other musical forces made their influence felt in Haitian
dance music. American big bands gained popularity in Haiti in the early twentieth century due to the presence of U.S. Marines from 1915 to 1934, the

presence of radio, and the back-and-forth travel of elite Haitians to France. Haitian bands incorporated American jazz into their repertoires, performing popular tunes for American as well as Haitian audiences. One Haitian president, Nord Alexis, was so fond of the "new American" style that he hired Ford Dabney, the popular American jazz-band leader, in 1904 for a three-year stint as an official musical adviser to the Haitian presidential band.

After the American invasion of Haiti in 1915, some Haitians viewed the popularity of music from the United States as a threat to the vitality of Haitian music, specifically the mereng. While Haitians in the countryside formed resistance militias to repel the American Marines, elite Haitians, located mostly in urban areas, chose to show their displeasure with the American occupation with forms of "cultural resistance," including music, dance, literature, and visual arts. Rejecting the culture of the invading Americans as vulgar and uncouth, some Haitian intellectuals recommended turning to the rural roots of Haitian culture—specifically, the Vodou religious ritual. The Haitian physician, ethnographer, and politician Jean Price-Mars wrote *Ainsi parla l'oncle* (So Spoke the Uncle) in 1928, exhorting Haitians to explore the folktales, music, and religion of the working rural masses. Price-Mars believed that research into the folklore of the Haitian countryside could inspire a national artistic movement that would challenge European domination of aesthetic judgment.

There were several musical responses to Price-Mars's call for a national Haitian music. Classical composers like Justin Elie, Ludovic Lamothe, and Werner Jaegerhuber wrote orchestral and chamber music using either Vodou melodies or tunes inspired by Haitian religious ritual. Others, like the leaders of popular dance bands, introduced the drum, scraper, and melodies from the Vodou ceremony into a big-band format. Perhaps the most famous of these "Vodou-jazz" groups was Jazz des Jeunes (Youth Jazz), which used Vodou rhythms such as the *kongo*, *ibo*, and *yanvalou* in musical arrangements that were based on dance-band formats. Teamed up with singer Lumane Casimir, Jazz des Jeunes cultivated a sound and look that appealed to the Haitian public; band members dressed in "folkloric" garb of colorful cloth, while dancers moved to the Vodou-influenced rhythms. Jazz des Jeunes was also active in the promotion of a "noirist," or pro-black, political platform in support of Dumarsais Estimé, the first dark-skinned Haitian president who was not a puppet of the light-skinned Haitian elite. In addition, folkloric dance became popular in the 1940s as elite Haitians reconsidered their relationship to cultural practices influenced by Vodou. In 1941, the Haitian government sent a troupe of folkloric performers led by Lina Fussman-Mathon to the National Folk Festival in Washington, D.C. Despite the fact that Vodou ceremonies were forbidden in Haiti at the time, the Haitian government enthusiastically supported this staged version of Haitian ceremonial music and dance.

Latin music, especially from Cuba, was also a shaping influence on the development of Haitian dance music. *Twoubadou* music, mentioned earlier, was an important Latin-influenced genre that found a ready audience among Haitian dance bands in the early twentieth century. With the arrival of the phonograph and radio in Haiti during the 1920s, more Haitian audiences were listening to the sounds of Cuban *son* bands such as the Sexteto Habanero, Septeto Nacional, and Trio Matamoros. Haitian bands adapted the sounds of the Cuban trios, using the two-guitar, maracas, and single-headed–drum ensemble. In the 1940s and '50s, larger Latin bands grew in popularity throughout the Caribbean. Arsenio Rodríguez, the blind Cuban *tres* player, toured several Caribbean islands during the 1950s with his band, featuring an expanded brass section.

Haiti's closest neighbor, the Dominican Republic, exerted its musical influence over Haitian music through its exportation of the Dominican merengue dance. While the Dominican Republic had several different styles loosely referred to as merengue, the most popular in the 1950s was that of the Cibao region, promoted by the Trujillo regime as a symbol of Dominican national culture (see chapter 5). Dominican radio stations, playing the Trujillo-praising merengues in a big-band format, reached the radios of Haitian middle- and upper-class audiences. Orchestras under the directorship of Luis Alberti and Antonio Morel were staples on the Dominican radio stations received in Haiti.

The influence of the Dominican merengue on Haitian popular music did not, however, mean that Haitians were eager to embrace the politics of the *merengue cibaeño*. Dominicans and Haitians have had a rocky relationship since the invasion of the Dominican Republic by Haitian military forces in 1822. While the political tension between the two countries has been expressed by overt military action, such as Trujillo's massacre of tens of thousands of Haitian cane cutters in 1937, Haitians and Dominicans also fight for their national dignity using the provenance of the merengue as a weapon. Intellectuals from both countries have written extensively on how the merengue originated in their homeland. Haitian historian Jean Fouchard's book *The Méringue, the National Dance of Haiti* was written in part to counter Dominican claims that the current popularity of the merengue was due to the Dominican interpretation of the rhythm; Fouchard thought the Haitian mereng's influence on the more recent Dominican version was the reason for the dance's success. To Fouchard's ears, only the reinstatement of the original Haitian mereng could save Haitian orchestras from adopting the "foreign-sounding" Dominican merengue.

Despite intellectuals' bickering over the origins of the merengue, Haitian musicians were eagerly adopting the Dominican style to their bands. Nemours Jean-Baptiste and his group, the Ensemble aux Calebasses, altered the merengue beat slightly and in 1955 named their invention *konpa dirèk* (*compas direct* in French), or "direct rhythm." Weber Sicot, a former saxophonist in Nemours's band, formed his own group, Cadans Rampa de Weber Sicot, and introduced a variation on the *konpa dirèk* beat that he called *kadans ranpa*, or "rampart rhythm," a reference to the "ramparts" from which Sicot would challenge his new rival for Haitian musical supremacy. The musical rivalry of the two orchestras worked as a promotional device. Fans of both bands formed clubs that adopted official colors and flags for their musical "teams."

In the early 1960s, the British invasion that swept the United States came to Haiti in the form of rock music. Children in upper-class Haitian families with access to radio and phonographs formed small, electric-guitar–based combos that they called *yeye*, a not-too-subtle reference to the "yeah, yeah, yeah" lyrics of the Beatles that took audiences in the United States by storm in the early 1960s. (The term "*yeye*" was also used in France in the mid-'60s when the singer France Gall performed teenage bubble-gum pop.) When these *yeye* bands added *konpa dirèk* repertoire to their playlists, the resultant sound was called *mini-djaz*—"mini" referring to the latest American craze of miniskirts, and "djaz" being the Kreyòl spelling of "jazz." *Konpa dirèk* bands, or simply konpa bands, began to scale down their numbers to compete with the smaller, more flexible *mini-djaz*. Groups like Tabou Combo, subsequently one of the most popular *mini-djaz*, started as a small, neighborhood group in Pétionville, the elite suburb of Port-au-Prince. Other groups that came from Pétionville include D. P. Express (the "D. P." is from the band's former name, Les Difficiles de Pétionville), and Les Frères Dejean.

Lyrics for *konpa dirèk* tended to focus attention on either the rivalry between bands or relationship trouble. Often, the words had double entendres, either in a suggestive, sexual manner or in a more veiled social critique. Tabou Combo's "Mario, Mario" derides class prejudice against musicians, calling for the sympathies of the audience to favor Mario, a musician *san fanmi* (without family or without connections), in his pursuit of Miss Entel (or Miss So-and-so). Another Tabou Combo hit, "Konpa ce pam," praises konpa as an important vehicle of communication among black people in the African diaspora.

> Kolonizasyon fe tout moun depandan
> Sa pale franse, angle, panyòl.
> Men yon gwo fason pou nou kominike
> Lè misik frape, tout moun vibre.

Colonization makes all people dependent
It makes them speak French, English, and Spanish.
We have a way for all to communicate
When the music sounds, everyone starts moving.[5]

POLITICS AND THE HAITIAN DIASPORA

In 1957, Dr. François Duvalier was elected to the Haitian presidency by a narrow margin. Although Duvalier was not a seasoned politician, he was a trained physician and was well known among Haitian voters as one of the people responsible for the eradication of the tropical disease yaws in Haiti, thus earning him the sobriquet "Papa Doc." Duvalier campaigned on a "noirist" platform, calling for an end to the political control of the country by the Haitian mulatto elite. After the election, however, it became clear that Duvalier had no intention of reforming Haitian government. After a series of bloody purges designed to eradicate his political opposition, Duvalier declared himself president for life in 1964.

Duvalier's rule was characterized by violent repression of dissent, torture of political rivals, and the establishment of a secret police force called the Volunteers of National Security (VSN), more commonly known as the Tonton Makout. Duvalier feared the power of the regular Haitian army and started the Tonton Makout to protect himself from a coup d'état. The Makout secret police were an unpaid militia with presidential authorization to extort money from local citizens. Often the local magistrate, called chef de section, was also a Makout who routinely demanded bribes in exchange for protection.

The VSN was given the nickname "Tonton Makout" to evoke a sinister image intended to intimidate the Haitian populace. Tonton Makout, or "Uncle Strawbag," was the bogeyman of Haitian folklore who stalked small children and swept them up in his bag. Blue denim uniforms and dark sunglasses were the trademark of the Tonton Makout, images borrowed from Vodou religious imagery: Blue denim is the cloth of Kouzen Azaka, a Vodou spirit associated with agriculture, while dark sunglasses belonged to the Gede spirits who guard the cemetery and preside over the dead. Duvalier associated himself with the Vodou image of Baron Samedi, the chief guardian of the cemetery and most sinister of the Gede spirits.

Most Haitians who lived through this period have stories to tell about being terrorized by Tonton Makout. Many have relatives who were "disappeared" by the VSN; others relate stories about local Makouts who wielded their power over their neighbors. I once had a run-in with a Makout in the National Cemetery in Port-au-Prince. A Haitian friend had taken me to see

François Duvalier's mausoleum; a Makout with an ancient bolt-action rifle was guarding the tomb. When we approached the grave, the Makout pointed his rifle at us and told us to fetch him a bottle of rum and a pack of Comme Il Faut cigarettes. My friend said "*wi, msye* (yes, sir)," and we scurried off to make our purchases. On our way to the corner store, I asked my friend what would happen if we didn't comply with the Makout's order. He told me that we could risk evading his request, but that if the Makout found out who we were, the reprisals for refusing to buy him booze and smokes could be very serious. It was a risk that neither of us wanted to take, since the reputation of many Makouts was to punish any form of disobedience with violence. Tonton Makout were understood to be personal emissaries of Duvalier. Refusing a Makout's order was tantamout to defying the Haitian dictator himself.

A popular joke from the early 1980s captures the feelings of dread most Haitians had of Duvalier. A woman had a sick child, so she took him to the *ougan* (Vodou priest) and asked the priest to cure the child. The *ougan* told the woman, "Place a picture of Satan on the child's forehead at midnight tonight, and when the child wakes up, your son will be cured." The woman went home and looked for a picture of Satan, to no avail. Since all Haitian homes at the time had a photograph of Duvalier on the wall, the woman placed his picture on her son's head at midnight. When she awoke the next morning, she found, much to her horror, that her son was dead. Distraught, the woman went back to the *ougan* and told him what happened. The *ougan* asked, "Did you put a picture of Satan on the boy's forehead, just as I told you?" She responded, "Well, not exactly. I put a picture of Papa Doc on him instead." "Oh my God," the *ougan* gasped. "The medicine you used was too strong!"

Duvalier ruled Haiti as a dictator from 1964 until his death in 1971. Before his death, he altered the Haitian Constitution, allowing him to pass on the presidency for life to his nineteen-year-old son, Jean-Claude Duvalier. Known as "Baby Doc," Jean-Claude's rule of Haiti was characterized by a continuation of the exploitative practices of his father. In 1980, Jean-Claude married Michèle Bennett, a wealthy socialite and daughter of a corrupt light-skinned businessman. The marriage alienated Jean-Claude from his power base and set the stage for a more repressive period in Haitian politics.

Upper- and middle-class Haitians began leaving Haiti in large numbers in the early 1960s, settling in the United States, Canada, France, and Zaire. Most of the Haitian emigrants settled in urban areas such as New York City (especially Brooklyn, Queens, and Manhattan), Boston, Montreal, and, more recently, Miami. Expatriate Haitian communities continued to grow throughout the Duvalier reign, creating a large and culturally active Haitian network outside the country. Haitians living in the United States have become an important source of revenue for families still living in Haiti, sending millions of dollars home to family members annually. Their remittances constitute the single largest contribution to the gross national product of Haiti. Haitians abroad became known as the "tenth department," an addition to the nine departments, or states, in Haiti proper.

Songs of protest against the Duvalier regime first developed in the Haitian diaspora, especially in New York. The anti-Duvalier, pro-democracy cultural movement that arose in the United States and Canada among expatriate Haitians was known as *kilti libète* (freedom culture). Farah Juste was perhaps the best known patriotic singer from the period just after Duvalier's death. Her early work with Soley Leve (Rising Sun) firmly established her as an outspoken critic of the Duvalier regime. When she started her solo career in the early 1970s, her credibility and popularity kept her a regular feature of musical presentations sponsored by Haitian organizations in the diaspora.

Within Haiti, other politically motivated singers were starting to speak out against the excesses of the Duvaliers. Manno Charlemagne and Marco Jeanty were perhaps the earliest protest singers to actually record in Haiti in 1978–79. After Baby Doc's marriage to Michèle Bennett, several *mini-djaz* groups joined the growing numbers of critical musicians willing to voice their dissatisfaction with the Duvaliers. Songs such as "Libète" by Magnum Band lamented the deaths of Haitian *bòt pipèl* (boat people) who took to the seas in small boats in hopes of reaching the United States.

At the height of the boat-people crisis, many Haitians expressed their frustration with the Duvalier government by telling the following joke. One day, Jean-Claude Duvalier wondered why so many people were leaving Haiti by boat. He decided to find out for himself, so he dressed as a peasant, putting on a straw hat, sandals, and old clothing, and walked to the wharf. He noticed that the wharf was full of people (in Kreyòl, the wharf is described as *"nwa ak moun,"* or "black with people," since Haitians are black). He talked to the captain of a boat and negotiated a price for safe passage to Florida. "You have to pay three thousand dollars tomorrow morning when we set sail," barked the captain, "and three thousand when you arrive in Florida." Jean-Claude agreed and returned to the National Palace. The next morning, he walked to the wharf and found, much to his surprise, that the wharf was empty (in Kreyòl, *"lari a blanch,"* or "the road was white"—that is, without black people). Jean-Claude asked the captain where all the passengers were. The captain replied, "Well, your Excellency, when they heard that you were leaving, they decided that they didn't need to go." When telling this joke, most Haitians stand knock-kneed and imitate Duvalier's nasal voice saying, "How did you know it was me?"

As the political pressure against the Duvaliers mounted, the dictatorship showed signs of weakening in the early 1980s. Jean-Claude, Michèle, and a retinue of Haitian military leaders left Haiti on 7 February 1986 aboard a plane furnished by the U.S. government. The ouster of the Duvaliers was followed by a period known as *deshoukaj* (or *deshoukay*), the "uprooting" of the dictatorship. The Kreyòl verb "*deshouke*" refers to pulling out a plant by the roots to ensure it will not grow back later. The homes of exiled supporters of Duvalier were stripped of their contents; even door frames, plumbing, and roof joists were taken to wipe away the traces of the former regime. Members of the Tonton Makout were captured and subjected to vigilante justice by irate local crowds.

Songs provided another, albeit less violent, outlet for the collective frustrations of the Haitian people. Immediately after the fall of the Duvalier regime, the Frères Parent released their album *Operation Deshoukaj*, which featured the full side of a twelve-inch LP for the title track. Their denunciation of the Tonton Makout included a "score of Makout–zero, the Haitian people–double score!" as well as a forecast that the departed dictator Duvalier would not be welcomed in hell by the devil. Other artists used familiar Haitian images to urge their expatriate listeners to return to Haiti and help restructure the society. Carole Démesmin, a Vodou *manbo* (female priest) and popular singer, released a song called "Tounen Lakay" (Come Home or Return to the House) on her *Lawouzé* album, urging Haitians to return home for the rebuilding of the country. She sings, "*N ap bat tanbou jiska soley leve*" (We'll hit the drum until the sun rises), referring to the anti-Duvalier movement, Soley Leve, of the early 1970s. The group Sakad's "Rebati Kay-La" (Rebuild the House) also likens the Haitian state to a house badly in need of repair.

CONTEMPORARY HAITIAN POPULAR MUSIC

The *mini-djaz* and *konpa dirèk* styles of the 1960s and '70s were supplemented in the '80s with the emergence of the music of the *nouvel jenerasyon* (new generation). Actually, the *nouvel jenerasyon* style was part of a long association between Haitian musicians and the more avant-garde sounds from American jazz. Gérald Merceron, a lawyer and self-taught musician, organized his own record company and produced several albums with the help of the musical director of Radio Métropole, Herby Widmaier. Calling their musical creations "*la nouvelle musique haitienne*" (the new Haitian music), Merceron and his friends Lionel Benjamin, Carole Démesmin, and Widmaier mixed several genres on their *Bokassa Grotraka* album, including an arrangement of the Haitian folksong "L'Artibonite" for full orchestra. Merceron's experimentation with Brazilian, Central African, and American jazz and avant-garde styles set the stage for others to incorporate new sounds into the *mini-djaz* dance-band format.

The *nouvel jenerasyon* sound is difficult to summarize since it is more of an attitude toward music than a strict genre. Ralph Boncy, a Haitian poet and amateur musicologist, characterized the *nouvel jenerasyon* as a cultural movement and identified such attributes as the importance of Kreyòl names for Haitian musical groups, a return to the music of the countryside for inspiration, increased emphasis on the text as a literary product, and standardized song lengths. A good example of the *nouvel jenerasyon* sound is "Tout moun ale nan kanaval" (Everyone has gone to Carnival), a love duet in which Emeline Michel and her singing partner, Sidon, lament the loss of their relationship. The relaxed tempo and sparse instrumentation of this song is in marked contrast to the sometimes frenetic guitar and constant percussion drive of the *mini-djaz* sound.

> Everyone has gone to Carnival.
> I stay by myself, it's not too bad.
> I don't want to go dance.
> You know what I'm thinking about.

Emeline Michel has emerged as one of the most popular *nouvel jenerasyon* singers. She achieved notoriety outside Haiti for her up-tempo song "AKIKO" (pronounced "Ah-Ka-Ee-Ka-Oh"), which was a radio hit on world music programs. Michel combines konpa-oriented dance numbers with songs that have a wider appeal outside Haiti. Her "Kotow Moun" (Where Are You People?) asserts that, despite external differences between people from different cultures, "*istwa nou mele*" (our histories are tied up with each other). The song features a "shout-out" to various places in and out of Haiti where Haitians live (Gonaïves and Martinique), as well as places that are associated with the African diaspora (Soweto, Brazil, and Senegal) and places that have no particular association with Haiti (Rotterdam, Australia, and Singapore). She also sings contemplative songs like "Pè Letènèl" (Eternal Father) that refer to the dangers of life in Haiti in recent years. The song was inspired by her experience of being carjacked in Haiti along with the zouk singers Jocelyne Béroard and Tanya Saint-Val.

Beethova Obas is another popular *nouvel jenerasyon* singer whose spare style and emphasis on lyrics connects him with the recently revived *twoubadou* style. Obas was the first winner of the "M Renmen Ayiti" (I Love Haiti) song contest in 1988, sponsored by American Airlines. His song "Planet La" (The Planet) reminds listeners that the welfare of humanity is dependent on the continued prosperity of planet Earth.

Ever since the emergence of *mini-djaz* in the 1960s, middle-class Haitian musicians have been drawn to the popular-music business in Haiti, despite pressure from their families to follow a path toward a more "respectable" profession. One such band is Zèklè (Lightning), a group that formed in the 1980s and featured synthesized keyboards and sophisticated lyrics. More recent bands that appeal to a middle-class Haitian audience include Carimi, whose hit "Ayiti" (Bang Bang) laments the political changes in Haiti, especially the increased influence of the United States in Haitian affairs. Without mentioning specific politicians, the lyric claims that the U.S. Drug Enforcement Agency and Federal Bureau of Investigation "are taking over the country and controlling me."

Other contemporary singers are best known for their participation in dance music, especially songs associated with Carnival. In the mid-1990s, "Sweet Micky" (Michel Marthelly) captured audiences' attention with his use of English in "I Don't Care," a song that called for Haitians who were dissatisfied with the situation in Haiti to "debake" (leave). The refrain for the song, "I don't care / I don't give a damn / I don't give a shit," captured the sentiment among many Haitians that the problems of the country were simply beyond their control. T-Vice has been a staple of Haitian dance music since the 1980s, when the group was known as Miami Top Vice (after the popular television show *Miami Vice*); later, it shortened its name to Top Vice and eventually to T-Vice. In 2002, T-Vice had a popular Carnival hit called "Elikoptè" (Helicopter) in which the group's members described themselves as returning to Haiti in a helicopter in time for Carnival so that they could play their music to "three million people with their hands in the air."

MISIK RASIN, RAP, AND RAGGA

Ever since Jean Price-Mars's invitation to Haitian artists to make use of their Vodou heritage, musicians have tried to bring the sounds of ceremonial music into their own works. In the 1940s and '50s, groups like Jazz des Jeunes and Orchestre Saïeh sang songs that borrowed the rhythms and lyrical style of both Vodou and Rara. At a time when actual Vodou ceremonies were banned in Haiti and Haitian elites disapproved of all things associated with Vodou, Vodou jazz thrived among middle-class black audiences in Haiti.

Inspired by the successes of Jazz des Jeunes, Haitian musicians in the waning days of the Duvalier regime incorporated the sounds of Vodou and Rara into their music. Although the term "Vodou-jazz" was coined to describe the music of early bands like Jazz des Jeunes, later bands used the formula of folkloric themes, Vodou-influenced rhythms, and dancers to revitalize the Vodou-jazz idiom. In the middle of the 1980s, the band Foula, under the direction of lead drummer "Aboudja" Derenoncourt, fused American-influenced jazz and a battery of Vodou drummers to create a new sound in *misik rasin,* or "roots music." After the fall of the Duvalier regime in 1986, several other groups joined the *misik rasin* scene, including Sanba Yo, Sakad, Boukman Eksperyans, RAM, and Boukan Ginen.

As we saw in the introduction to this chapter, the group Boukman Eksperyans is named for the slave leader who incited the slave insurrection in the late 1700s. The group and especially its leader, Théodore "Lolo" Beaubrun, were outspoken critics of the military regime that deposed Haitian President Jean-Bertrand Aristide in 1991. During Aristide's exile, Boukman was the target of government reprisals for fusing Vodou rhythms with politically critical lyrics. The song "Jou nou revolte" (The Day We Revolt), from the 1992 album *Kalfou danjere* (Dangerous Crossroads), both recalls the day Haitians revolted against oppression in the revolution against the French and foretells the revolution that is to come when the military is overthrown and Haiti's elected government is restored. Boukman's earlier album, *Vodou Adjae,* contained fewer references to direct political action but emphasized the importance of maintaining the Vodou heritage of Haiti. Songs like "Se kreyòl nou ye" (We're Creole) ridiculed the Haitian elite's disdain for the country's national language, saying that "some Haitians would rather speak French, English, or Spanish rather than Kreyòl."

As Gage Averill has noted, Boukman Eksperyans's 1990 Carnival song "Kè m pa sote" (My Heart Doesn't Leap, or I Am Not Afraid) played a role in the downfall of the military junta that held power in Haiti from 1988 to 1990. Using the Haitian concept of *pwen* (point) to make an indirect criticism of the regime in charge, Boukman's lyrics lamented the desperate situation in the country and, invoking the warrior spirit Ogou Badagri, called for the spirits to help make a change. Shortly after antigovernment protestors used "Kè m pa sote" as a theme song, the government resigned.

The group Boukan Ginen was formed by Eddy François when he left Boukman Eksperyans in 1990. Their name, which translates as "African Fire Pit," reminds listeners that the *misik rasin* sound traces its roots back through the African ancestry of all Haitians. In its song "Afrika," Boukan Ginen calls on Haitians to return symbolically to Africa and to recognize the importance of African culture to black people in the Americas.

Some *misik rasin* groups go beyond invoking the importance of African ancestry and use actual Vodou ceremonial music in their performances. Rara Machine's 1994 *Voudou Nou* (Our Vodou) CD features a song called "Badè." As Elizabeth McAlister has pointed out, Rara Machine adapted this chant from a prayer chant at La Souvenance, a well-known center for Rada religious activity near Gonaïves, Haiti. The chant is sung in Kreyòl and *langaj*, the language of the spirits. "Badè" begins with a *lanbi*, or blown conch shell, and shakers that emulate the sound of the *ason*, or sacred rattle.

Most *misik rasin* groups rely on Kreyòl lyrics and Vodou rhythms for their characteristic sound. One group that incorporates English lyrics into its Vodou-influenced style is RAM, the brainchild of Richard A. Morse (a.k.a. "R.A.M."). Morse is the son of Emerante de Pradines Morse, a famous Haitian singer and herself the daughter of the legendary "Kandjo" de Pradines. Morse is also the owner of the Hotel Olaffson, a place made famous by Graham Greene's 1965 novel *The Comedians* about the François Duvalier regime. Before the decline in tourism to Haiti in the 1980s, the Olaffson was a popular destination for wealthy foreigners: Mick Jagger of the Rolling Stones was a frequent guest in the 1970s. Morse revived the practice of putting on performances of folkloric dance and assembled a music and dance troupe. Morse's wife, Lunise, is a skilled Haitian folkloric dancer and the leader of the hotel's biweekly Haitian dance performance. RAM achieved international popularity with its 1993 hit, "Ibo Lele: Dreams Come True," which was featured in the soundtrack to Jonathan Demme's Oscar-winning film *Philadelphia*, starring Tom Hanks and Denzel Washington.

The success of groups like Boukman Eksperyans, Boukan Ginen, and RAM outside the local Haitian recording market have inspired groups outside Haiti to explore the sounds of Vodou rhythms. Once such group, Simbi, is based in Sweden and sings a mixture of traditional songs, other *misik rasin* music (Simbi covered Boukman Eksperyans's "Pwazon Rat," for example), and its own original compositions written in Kreyòl. On its *Vodou Beat* CD, the group sings a traditional *chan* (song) to Simbi, a Vodou *lwa* associated with water. The music for its song "Simbi" includes funk bass and an energetic baritone saxophone line that turns this ceremonial lyric into a swinging dance number.

While konpa, *nouvel jenerasyon*, and *misik rasin* appeal to many Haitians young and old, several genres—namely, Afro-American–derived rap and Jamaican-style raggamuffin (or "ragga")—have been adopted by younger Haitian singers. One of the earliest Haitian *rapè*, or rap artists, was George "Master Dji" Lys Hérard. Master Dji released his hit "Sispann" (Stop or Suspend) as a call to end the political violence after the aborted election of 1987, in which Haitian voters were massacred at the polls on Rue Valliant in Port-au-Prince. Hérard's collaboration with other Haitian *rapè* on *Rap and Ragga: (Match La Rèd* [The game is worse]) intersperses more of the lover's-style rap, as in "Manmzèl" (Mademoiselle), with politically charged music, such as "Conscience noire" (Black conscience) by Supa Denot and T-Bird.

As Haitian rap has become popular, especially with young Haitian audiences in Haiti and abroad, Haitian *rapè* have reached out to constituencies in the diaspora with music and lyrics that reflect their new, transnational identities. Papa Jube (pronounced "Jubee") is a New York-based *rapè* whose work self-consciously fuses different Caribbean styles. His "Konpa Ragga" combines the konpa dance beat with a chanting style that is similar to Jamaican ragga. Other rap artists, like Original Rap Staff, align themselves more closely with African American hip-hop styles. Original Rap Staff's "Whose Style Is This?" rhetorically challenges African American rap artists by asserting that its Haitian version of hip-hop is an improvement over the original. By mixing Kreyòl with rap-inflected English, Original Rap Staff lays claim to the growing West Indian audience. In a humorous twist, the lead singer in "Whose Style Is This?" proclaims "*mwen soti Ayiti*" (I am from Haiti) in a New York accent, thus substantiating his claim that he speaks for Haitian rap audiences everywhere.

One Haitian artist who has successfully crossed over into the U.S. recording market is Wyclef Jean. Wyclef came to prominence as part of the group the Fugees, with Lauryn Hill and fellow Haitian artist Prakazrel "Praz" Michel. In his 1997 solo album *Wyclef Jean Presents the Carnival, Featuring Refugee Allstars*, Wyclef intersperses lyrics in English and Kreyòl and doesn't provide translations of the Kreyòl lyrics for his U.S. audience.

In "Jaspora" (Diaspora), Wyclef laments the situation of Haitians living abroad, observing that "*jaspora pa respecte jaspora*" (expatriate Haitians don't respect one another). In "Yelé," Wyclef begins with a Kreyòl dialogue in which the singer tells his friend that he was robbed of his new Fila sneakers while walking through Flatbush, Brooklyn. The friend asks, "Did you shoot him?" and the singer says no, he was reminded of a psalm that his father taught him in which people need to "*chache Bondyè*" (search for God).

Haitian rap reflects the complexity of the Haitian experience in the twenty-first century. Haitians in the diaspora, especially in the United States, exert a strong influence on the musical tastes of young Haitians. As the earlier examples illustrate, Haitians continue to grapple with issues of identity, loss, and hope as they assert themselves in a cosmopolitan music market.

MUSIC IN THE LESSER ANTILLES: MARTINIQUE, GUADELOUPE, DOMINICA, AND ST. LUCIA

The musical soundscape in the French, or former French, Lesser Antilles is similar to Haiti's, since both areas rely heavily on radio for the dissemination of local music.[6] Martinique, Guadeloupe, Dominica, and St. Lucia all

Gwoka musicians sitting in at a Saturday afternoon jam session on *la rue piétonne*, Poite-à-Pitre, Guadeloupe, 2003 (Ken Bilby)

have Carnival traditions in which masked revelers take to the streets during the week before Mardi Gras. While foreign music like calypso and soca enjoys a brief popularity during the Carnival season, the islands of the Lesser Antilles have their own musical traditions that are enjoyed during the rest of the year. According to the ethnomusicologist Dominique Cyrille, there are three distinct French Caribbean dance repertoires: a rural dance tradition that draws on African cultural antecedents; a creolized repertoire that includes biguine, *maziouk* (or mazurka), and waltz, which was danced in quadrille sets or separately; and a contemporary repertoire that includes zouk.[7] The rural traditions of *gwo ka* (big drum) in Guadeloupe and *ka* (drum) in Martinique are two practices that fell out of use in the mid-twentieth century only to be revitalized in the 1980s.[8] The Martinican musician Dédé Saint Prix and his group Avan Van helped resuscitate *misik chouval bwa* ("wooden horse" music or "merry-go-round" music), which features a bamboo flute, a *ka* drum, a djembe drum, a bass, and *tibwa* (from the French petit bois or "little sticks" played on a piece of bamboo).[9]

Creolized dance forms emerged from the contact between slaves and slaveholders. These include the Martinican *bèlè*, which features dancing and group

Jing-ping band, Woodford Hill, Dominica, 2000 (Ken Bilby)

singing, often led in a call-and-response format with a song leader. According to the ethnomusicologist Julian Gerstin, the *tanbou bèlè* is played transversely (lying on its side) with the drummer using the heel of the foot to control the pitch. In addition, *bèlè* drummers play one-handed rolls using their thumb and ring fingers.[10] The *bèlè* dances (including *bidjin bèlè* or "béguine" *bèlè*, *bèlè pitché*, *gran bèlè*, and *bèlè marin*) all use the choreography known as quadrilles (*kwadril* in Kwéyòl). The quadrille, a set dance similar to the Haitian *kontradans*, is related to dances popular during the early colonial period. In Martinique as elsewhere, Afro-Caribbeans inserted their own aesthetic sensibilities into the dance, despite the quadrille's constrained dance movements, relatively static rhythmic patterns, and connection to European-derived dance traditions. Quadrilles and other European-derived dances might be played by a variety of ensembles, generally pairing a melodic instrument like the accordion with various percussion instruments. The *jing-ping* ensemble of Dominica depicted above features an accordion, a *syak* scraper (like a güira), a *tambou* frame drum, and a tube, called *boumboum*, which is blown like a trumpet, filling out the ensemble with bass timbres. The quadrille's popularity waned in the countryside during the mid-twentieth century, but cultural activists have promoted the dance as an important part of island heritage.

Unlike Haiti, which has been independent since 1804, two of the islands of the Lesser Antilles, Martinique and Guadeloupe, are *départements*, or states, of

France. These islands, along with St. Lucia and Dominica, have predominantly black populations, descended from African slaves. St. Lucia and Dominica are independent nations and have a greater legacy of English colonialism; English is the language of state for both countries, but people on both islands speak French-based creole languages with a high degree of mutual intelligibility.[11]

The musical styles of the four Antillean islands under consideration here are also mutually intelligible, due to the long process of musical cross-fertilization in the area. Zouk, a dance music that emerged in the 1980s, is popular throughout the region. It can be seen as a synthesis of several popular Caribbean musical styles, including biguine, *cadence-lypso*, Haitian konpa, and several popular music styles from the United States.

A significant antecedent for zouk is biguine, a musical style from Guadeloupe and Martinique and a favorite among dance orchestras from the 1930s to the '50s. The basic biguine rhythm, played on the *tibwa* or drum set, is a variant of the *cinquillo* rhythm found in Haitian mereng and in the cymbal part of *konpa dirèk*. During the 1930s, biguine orchestras played for dances held in a variety of locations including dance halls, church parties, birthday parties, and private affairs. During the 1940s and '50s, as radio connected the islands of the Caribbean and touring musicians from other islands visited the Lesser Antilles, Guadeloupean dance bands absorbed aspects of Cuban dance music, Haitian *konpa dirèk* and *kadans ranpa*, and jazz from the United States.

Zouk also traces its ancestry to *cadence-lypso*, or *cadence*, the local dance music from Dominica. *Cadence* is popularly believed to be a fusion of the Haitian *kadans ranpa* and calypso from neighboring Trinidad and Tobago. Exile One, a Dominica-based group led by Gordon Henderson, experimented with calypso fusion in the early 1970s and created a calypso-influenced dance music that used Kwéyòl lyrics. Like the politically inclined calypso, *cadence* lyrics often included social commentary on local events or reflections on issues of identity. The Midnight Groovers are another popular Dominica-based band that uses Rasta-inflected lyrics to target social issues that face Caribbean peoples.

Claiming its fundamental rhythmic organization from the *cinquillo*-based genres of *konpa dirèk*, *kadans ranpa*, and biguine, zouk has moved away from the big band ensembles once popular in Guadeloupe and Martinique in favor of a sparer, more electronically influenced sound. Most successful zouk bands feature synthesizers, digital samplers, and drum machines programmed to imitate such popular local percussion instruments as the *tibwa*.

The first major zouk group to emerge was the Guadeloupan-based ensemble Kassav'. Deriving its name from cassava, the starchy root that is a part of the Caribbean diet, Kassav' released its first album in 1979 and has continued to be a powerful force in the popular-music scene in the Lesser Antilles. While most commercial popular music in Guadeloupe and Martinique had previously been in French, Kassav's lyrics are in Kwéyòl, emphasizing the group's connection with its local audience. The band also regularly features dancing as part of their live act to promote audience involvement.

In 1984, Kassav' released its first international hit, "Zouk-la sé sèl medikaman nou ni" (Zouk Is the Only Medicine We Have). As Jocelyne Guilbault has observed, the song is "the perfect example of a song based on the greatest economy of means to produce a maximal effect."[12] Using only bass, drums, electronic keyboard, and spare vocals, the song asserts that zouk is necessary for people's survival in a harsh world.

In its 1985 hit "An-ba-chen'n la" (Under the Chain), Kassav' sings of the importance of bringing its musical message to others and increasing outsiders' awareness of the Antilles and its people:

> We must often leave our country
> In order to bring our music to others.
> It's time for everyone to know that the Antilles exists
> And that it is love that commands us.

The Kassav' member Patrick Saint Éloi wrote "An-ba-chen'n la" after visiting a museum in Senegal in which artifacts from the slave trade were on display.

Other popular zouk artists include Eric Virgal, known for his renditions of "zouk love," or the more romantic, slow-tempo ballad; the late Edith Lefel; and Joelle Ursull, the first Antillean representative for France in the 1990 Eurovision contest. The group Malavoi performs zouk as well as the older genres of biguine and quadrille and the foreign styles of merengue and *son*. While Malavoi shares its producer, George Debs, with Kassav', the group maintains an eclectic repertoire with an unusual array of acoustic instruments, including violins. Malavoi's lyrics often portray Martinique as a focus of nostalgic longing and painful memories. In its 1983 song "Malavoi," the band sings of the *malavoi* variety of sugarcane, which, due to its high sugar content, was the preferred product for the slave plantations. The sweetness of the highly prized cane contrasted with the bitterness felt by those workers who harvested it as slaves.

In the late 1980s and '90s, while zouk took on a new life in Cape Verde and its diaspora communities, it seemed to stagnate in the French Caribbean itself, leading some artists to turn toward other alternatives for their musical inspiration. Two contemporary singers who have turned toward Rastafarian-oriented "roots" music are Kali and Pôglo. Martinique-born Kali (Jean-Marc Monnerville) came from a family of musicians and trained for a musical career in France. His early career featured fusions of zouk with Jamaican reggae; eventually he found inspiration in some of the earlier genres of *maziouk* and biguine. The 1988 recording *Racines* (Roots) features Kali on banjo, an instrument that evokes the old-fashioned musical trends he drew on for his new style. Kali was chosen to represent Martinique in the 1992 Eurovision song competition, and while he did not win, he dispelled audiences' impression that the French Caribbean produced only zouk.

The singer, painter, and poet Pôglo (Eric Lugiery) infuses his songs with Rastafarian imagery to emphasize the connection between the struggles of black people around the world. His song "Lèspwa" (Hope) evokes the Rasta colors of green, gold, and red and calls on listeners to turn to Jah, or God, to achieve "the victory of kindness over violence."

Other responses to zouk's stagnation included the creation of a new dance-oriented style called *bouyon*. Taking its name from a soup or stew in which flavors intermingle as they simmer on a slow fire, *bouyon* combines aspects of 1970s *cadence-lypso*, zouk, soca, and Dominican *jing-ping*, that features accordion, a scraper, a large frame drum, and a bamboo trumpet similar to the *vaksin* of Haitian rara. In 1988, the band Windward Caribbean Kulture (WCK) began experimenting with *cadence-lypso* and *jing-ping*, using electronic instruments to imitate the sounds of the acoustic *jing-ping* ensemble (in much the same way that *misik rasin* groups in Haiti programmed drum machines to produce Vodou-inspired rhythms). With its second album, *Culture Shock*, WCK coined the term *"bouyon"* for its new style.

From *bouyon* to zouk, French Caribbean artists have produced music that selectively retains aspects of Antillian identity while incorporating new sounds and technology. Maintaining a balance between its need for international and local appeal, French Caribbean musical genres continue to stimulate their audiences with cultural ideas set to a dance beat.

BIBLIOGRAPHY

Literature on Vodou and its music includes Lois Wilcken (with Frisner Augustin), *Drums of Vodou* (Tempe, Ariz.: White Cliffs Media Company, 1992); Jean Price-Mars, *So Spoke the Uncle* (*Ainsi parla l'oncle* [1928]), trans. Magdaline Shannon (Washington, D.C.: Three Continents Press, 1983); and Karen McCarthy Brown, *Mama Lola: A Vodou Priestess in Brooklyn* (Berkeley: University of California Press, 2001). For Haitian popular music, see Gage Averill, *A Day for the Hunter, a Day for the Prey: Music and Power in Haiti* (Chicago: University of Chicago Press, 1997). For Haitian Rara, see Elizabeth McAlister, *Rara! Vodou, Power, and Performance in Haiti and Its Diaspora* (Berkeley: University of California Press, 2002). For French Caribbean popular music, see Jocelyne Guilbault, Gage Averill, Édouard Benoit, and

Gregory Rabess, *Zouk: World Music in the West Indies* (Chicago: University of Chicago Press, 1993); Brenda F. Berrian, *Awakening Spaces: French Caribbean Popular Songs, Music, and Culture* (Chicago: University of Chicago Press, 2000). Other interesting publications include Jean Fouchard, *La méringue: Danse nationale d'Haïti* (Port-au-Prince: Éditions Henri Deschamps, 1988); Ernest Mirville, *Considérations Ethno-Psychanalytiques sur le Carnaval Haitien* (Port-au-Prince: Collection Coucouille, 1978).

RECORDS

Angels in the Mirror: Vodou Music of Haiti (Ellipsis Arts CD 4120); Boukan Ginen, *Rev an Nou* (Xenophile 4029); Boukman Eksperyans, *Vodou Adjae* (Mango 162-539 889-2), *Kalfou Danjere* (Dangerous Crossroads) (Mango 162-539 972-2), *Libète (Pran Pou Pran'l)/ Freedom (Let's Take It)* (Mango 162-539 946-2), *Revolution* (Tuff Gong 54270-2); Verna Gillis and Gage Averill, eds., *Caribbean Revels* (Smithsonian Folkways C-SF 40402); Carole Démesmin, *Lawouzé* (Shap 1003); Frères Parent, *Operation Deshoukaj* (Mishga 002); Papa Jube, *Liberasyon* (Melodie Makers CD 1023); Rara Machine, *Voudou Nou* (Shanachie 64054); RAM, *Aïbobo* (CinéDisc CD 12191); Elizabeth McAlister, ed. *Rhythms of Rapture: Sacred Musics of Haitian Vodou* (Smithsonian Folkways SF CD 40464); Sweet Micky, *Best of Sweet Micky* (Déclic Communication 50657-2); *Haiti Kanaval Konpa 2002* (Metrosonik 002); Tabou Combo, *The Music Machine* (Mini Records MRSD1070), *Aux Antilles* (Zafem Records TC 8056CD); *Konbit: Burning Rhythms of Haiti* (A&M CD 5281); *Haiti: Rap and Ragga (match la rèd)* (Déclic Communication 319-2); Wyclef Jean, *Wyclef Jean Presents the Carnival Featuring Refugee Allstars* (Ruffhouse/Columbia CK 67974); *Alan Lomax Collection: Caribbean Voyage: The French Antilles: We Will Play Love Tonight!* (Rounder 1733); *Caribbean Voyage: Martinique—Cane Fields and City Streets* (Rounder 1730); *Music of Haiti: Volume 1, Folk Music of Haiti* (Smithsonian Folkways Records FW04407 1951); *Music of Haiti: Volume 3, Songs and Dances of Haiti* (Folkways FW04432 1952); *Rough Guide to the Music of Haiti* (World Music Network).

7

Jamaica

There is probably no country in the world that, relative to its size, has had such a disproportionate impact on world culture as Jamaica. In the space of a few short decades, this postcolonial island nation of some 2.5 million people, with all its economic woes, has accomplished a feat that few other countries (and then only major economic powers such as the United States and Great Britain) have been able to swing: Jamaica has conquered the world with its music.

Jamaican popular music has gained the stature of a global musical currency, alongside jazz, rock, and rap. Nor has its international impact been limited to shallow commercial exploitation. In complex and varying ways, reggae has been adopted by a wide range of local communities around the world—Hopi and Havasupai Indians in Arizona, Palenquero Maroons in Colombia, urban youths in Nigeria and South Africa, working-class skinheads in Britain, Maoris in New Zealand, and aboriginal Australians, to name a few—as an expression of something deeper than mere entertainment. Some are moved by its spiritual values, others by its emphasis on pan-African identity or its expressions of class consciousness, and yet others by its message of universal liberation. For its part, dancehall has become just as globally popular, especially as it becomes adopted as a vehicle for local self-expression, in local languages, in places as diverse as Korea and the Congo. But underneath the carefully crafted pop sheen of much of the island's exported music—not to mention the less polished music produced for purely local consumption—lie deep and distinctive cultural wellsprings.

KUMINA CULTURE, 1976

Sitting at the dinner table across from me was an eminent patron of the arts, a grande dame known for her creative work in the local theater

Chapter 7 was co-authored by Kenneth Bilby (roughly to pp. 191–93) and Peter Manuel.

movement, which had been gaining ground since Jamaica's independence in 1962.

"I am a baan-ya," she told me in stilted patois, explaining that this was the Jamaican way of saying that she was a "born-here" person, a true native of the island. I (Ken Bilby) could tell that she wanted to dispel any doubts that might have been raised by her European features and rather British-sounding accent: After all, she was about to assert her authority on matters Jamaican, including Kumina, a Jamaican religion deriving mostly from traditions brought to Jamaica by African contract workers from the Congo in the mid-1800s. I had started a polite conversation about the Kumina drumming one might hear on any given night in certain neighborhoods of Kingston but quickly found myself being corrected. Kumina, she informed me, was the last vestige of true African culture in Jamaica and was certainly not a feature of urban life. In fact, she said, it had nearly disappeared even in the remote country districts. Besides, Kumina was a ritual involving animal sacrifice, and such things were not permitted in town.

One reason this conversation has stuck in my memory is that it provided me with a striking lesson in the width of the gulf that separates "uptown" (the social and literal space inhabited by the economically privileged minority) and "downtown" (the realm of the huge majority of disenfranchised ghetto dwellers) in Kingston and, by extension, in other parts of Jamaica. It is a social division that is fundamental to life in urban Jamaica, and nowhere is it more clearly reflected than in the history of Jamaican popular music.

The uptown cultural expert sitting across from me did not know that I had spent most of the night before at a Kumina ceremony in Hunts Bay, one of many impoverished, ramshackle neighborhoods in West Kingston— a downtown area that children of "respectable" Kingstonians are taught to avoid. There had been nothing unusual about the occasion. A member of the community who had died was being commemorated and was being asked for spiritual aid. What was out of the ordinary was that I, a foreigner, was present. The reason I was there was that the organizers of the Kumina ceremony had needed to find a way to transport a goat from the village of Freetown in distant Clarendon parish to Hunts Bay on sudden notice. Some Kumina drummers from Spanish Town, with whom I had been studying, knew that I had a rented car and had tracked me down to ask for help.

I remember the drive well. We arrived in Freetown to find that another Kumina dance was already in progress there. As we approached, flecks of light came rippling through the slats of the bamboo dancing booth, and shadows played across the ground. Someone came and guided us into the booth, where we were served Red Stripe beer while one of my companions was invited to sit in on the drums. The music reminded me of a popular Ghanaian style called *kpanlogo*, but with a deeper, more resonant bass pattern, a rhythm like the beating of an excited heart, which I had been told was the spiritual root of Kumina, the "heart-string" connecting the living and the dead. The drummers were doing their work well: A man with a piece of red cloth tied around his head spun around with a few jerking steps and fell into a graceful dance between the drums. After a few moments, he approached me and took my hand, staring me in the eye and saying something totally unintelligible to me. "African language," some bystanders told me. "He's thanking you." Later, as we lowered the goat into the trunk, its hooves bound with rope, one of the drummers explained that the spirit of an "old African" had used the dancer's body to speak to me and offer thanks for the use of the car.

All the way to Spanish Town, the bleating of the goat in back made me uncomfortable. Someone suggested that we stop on the edge of the town for a drink before continuing on to Kingston, so we pulled up to a zinc fence with a small crowd of young men in front. Inside, the small makeshift bar was dwarfed by a massive bank of speaker boxes. The vibrations blasting out of them seemed to penetrate every fiber of my body. It was the loudest music I had ever heard—louder even than the overdriven Marshall amplifiers of a hard-rock concert, but with one main difference: the loudness was concentrated in the all-enveloping rumble of the bass rather than in the searing treble of live guitar-driven rock. The naked speaker cones jumped right out of the boxes at us, along with the words: "Jah live, children, yeah." Bob Marley's defiant answer to those who were ridiculing the Rastafarians by pointing to the death of their divinity, Ethiopia's Emperor Haile Selassie, had just been released, and the streets were buzzing with Rasta reaction. After all, how could God die?

Back in the car, the Kumina drummers rolled a couple of cone-shaped marijuana cigarettes, or "spliffs." While lighting up, one of them, Bongo Jack, told me, "Some people call the herb 'ganja,' but in the African Congo language we call it *diamba*. The Rastas have learned the truth that the old Africans always teach us, you know; it's the wisdom weed." The younger drummer sitting in back nodded his head in agreement. Emblazoned on his T-shirt was the silk-screened image of a wild-haired Bob Dylan in dark sunglasses.

My passengers warned me to stay alert and keep an eye out for Babylon; a police blockade might appear at any moment. Once again, Marley's trenchant lyrics captured the moment. His famous refrain "three o'clock roadblock" kept circling in my head. As we zoomed through Central Village, Jack pointed out the Spanish Town Cask and Drum Company on the left, where Rasta *kete* drums were made to order. We had just heard the sound of one of these

Kumina drummers, Spanish Town, Jamaica, 1975 (Ken Bilby)

drums, called the repeater, in Marley's "Jah Live." Jack explained that the Rasta repeater was "coming off the same root" as his own Kumina drum but was designed a little differently. In fact, he knew some other "Bongo men"— Kumina players—living in the Spanish Town area who liked the unique sound of the repeater drum and used it sometimes when playing for Kumina dances.

As we approached the outskirts of the capital, the smell of burning sugar-cane came wafting into the car. The night sky ahead glowed an ominous red. It was January, and national elections were around the corner. The political violence was escalating, and everyone and everything seemed to be on edge, especially in war-torn West Kingston. My guides made sure that I made no wrong turns, for our destination was only a few blocks away from a section of the city that had been reduced to cinders a couple of days before, the latest casualty to the wave of political terror sweeping over West Kingston. Here we were only a few miles from uptown Kingston, yet we were worlds apart.

We turned a corner and pulled into a yard. There we were met by a couple of "gatekeepers," who guided us into a partially hidden recess where the car would be safe. Once the goat was out of the trunk and in the right hands, we were led through an opening in a zinc fence into the yard where the Kumina was being held. At least two hundred people were present, all of them strangers to me. Several did not remain strangers for long, though. Every few minutes, a new person would come up and introduce himself or herself, telling me to feel welcome and not to be afraid, for although these were "dread" times in West Kingston, I had nothing to worry about: I was fully "protected" here at the Kumina. It was, I realized, a major ceremony. Friends and relatives from all over the eastern part of the island had come together to do their part. One man introduced himself to me as a Maroon from a community in the Blue Mountains, where descendants of escaped slaves had maintained their own culture and identity. Maroons and Kumina people, he said, were from "different nations." He told me to enjoy the Kumina, and suggested that I visit his village in the hills if I wanted to hear Maroon music, which, he said, was even "deeper" than Kumina.[1]

The feeling of harmony within the Kumina yard was underscored by the music. Early in the evening, a large group, mostly women, congregated on the side to sing "Sankeys" (a term applied by Jamaicans to a large variety of hymns, some of which were learned from the popular nineteenth-century hymnal published by the evangelist Ira David Sankey). The performance was loosely organized, with people coming and going as they pleased. Yet it held together nicely. Everybody seemed to know the words by heart, and many showed an uncanny ability to improvise individual melodic parts that somehow managed always to become woven together into a rich harmonic fabric. The sound was clearly derived from Protestant hymnody, but the performance style was wholly unlike the hymn singing found in most European or North American churches. People sang at the tops of their voices, swayed their bodies to the mellifluous rhythm, gesticulated, and leaned on one another's shoulders. Several of the singers stopped from time to time to take a swig of *kulu-kulu*, the raw, overproof white rum that was being passed around.

Before long, the impromptu choir was singing psalms. A woman had worked her way out front, Holy Bible in hand, and the gathering was now "tracking" along with her. As the song leader read out the text, one line at a time, the others repeated after her in a complex, polyphonic chorus. The improvised melodic parts snaked over and under one another, creating surprising harmonies and dissonances. The ethnomusicologist in me told me that this particular kind of call-and-response singing, though clearly traceable to the tradition of "lining out" psalms that first became established in seventeenth-century rural Britain, was also fully compatible with the antiphonal style of music making brought by enslaved Africans to Jamaica. This was not just an idle thought, for I was well aware that Rastafarians sometimes performed hymns and psalms in the exact same way at their own ceremonies, which they called *nyabinghi*, viewing them as an expression of their African identity. I was also aware that the Afro-Protestant musical heritage of which this tradition was a part had made a major contribution to Jamaican popular music through Rastafarian reggae and other channels.

There was no doubt whatsoever about the African origins of the drumming that was now picking up momentum in the center of the yard. The three drummers were seated on their instruments, which were turned on their sides. Two of them played rock steadily, keeping to a single, unvarying heartbeat pattern. On top of this, the lead drummer created excitement with skillful improvisations. All of the drummers used their heels against the skins to vary the pitch.

Next to them was a "center pole," through which certain spirits, summoned by the drums, could travel on their way to the bodies of the dancers they chose to possess. Around this center, a ring of dancers slowly rotated with a gentle counterclockwise motion. Throughout the night, this circle continued to revolve in time, contracting or expanding as dancers left and were replaced by others. The combination of sound and motion was subtle and beautiful. Even when the drumming became especially hot, lifting the excitement to a new peak, the dancing remained cool, graceful, and disciplined, with only an occasional disruption whenever one of the dancers' bodies, suddenly seized by a visiting spirit, was thrown temporarily into convulsions.

As daybreak neared, the goat made its final appearance, borne on the shoulders of one of the drummers who had accompanied me on the journey from Clarendon. Moving into the ring, the man danced the goat several revolutions around the center pole, waving a machete in his hand. The air was filled with one of the "African country" songs of Kumina:

tangalanga mama gyal yu kalunga
tangalanga besi-oo kalunga
tangalanga besi mama kalunga
tangalanga besi-oo kalunga

With no warning, the man stepped inside the ring and placed the goat on the ground. For a minute or two, the animal lay still on its side, while the man rejoined the moving circle. And then, as the ring came around one more time, it happened in a split second: The goat suddenly stretched out its neck. Without missing a beat, the dancer spun around and brought the blade down, severing the head with a single blow.

To the east, the angry hue of the Kingston night was giving way to a blood-red dawn. Within a few hours, the sleepless maids and construction workers would be back on the job, while their unemployed friends and relatives, as usual, would be wandering the streets and gutters in search of a meal, and uptown Kingston would be none the wiser.

ROOTS MUSIC IN THE MID-TWENTIETH CENTURY

The Rastafarian brethren have a saying: "The half has never been told." This adage seems particularly true of Jamaica's musical history. Indeed, there is reason to believe that the story of Jamaican popular music will never be told in its entirety, not only because of the difficulty of teasing out the diverse strands that contributed to the music's early development, but also because of the unusual fluidity and complexity of the social milieu in which it emerged. During the decades leading up to the 1960s, when the seeds of Jamaica's indigenous popular music were being planted, West Kingston was a new and rapidly expanding urban fringe made up of migrants from various parts of the island. Recently arrived from "country," these sons and daughters of peasants—among them, the poorest of the poor and the least schooled of Jamaica's unlettered masses—were seen as scarcely worthy of the attention of those in a position to record in print the latest trends in Jamaica's social and cultural life. Yet it was they who laid the foundations of what was to become a thriving urban musical culture.

Located at the interface of the rural and the urban, the traditional and the modern, many of those who made important contributions to Jamaica's emerging popular music did so anonymously, in the course of their daily lives. The paths of musical influence were often convoluted and indirect, products of the innumerable musical encounters, both planned and spontaneous, that formed part of everyday social life in Jamaica's new urban spaces. Whether at church, in dance halls, at *buru* gatherings, in Kumina yards, or in any number of other musical contexts, these ordinary Jamaicans, possessing little or no formal musical training, regularly made music that fulfilled a variety of social functions. For them, the act of making music was enmeshed in community life. As humble practitioners of rural folk musical traditions transplanted to the city, most of these individuals went unheralded, and most of them are probably destined to remain unknown. Nonetheless, their voices echo down to us in the present.

The older musical languages that were available in West Kingston during the formative period of Jamaica's urban musical culture were many. Neo-African drumming traditions, some of them going back to the ceremonial and social dances held on slave plantations during the eighteenth and nineteenth centuries, had survived in several parts of the island. Among these were the *etu, tambu,* and *gumbe* traditions, concentrated in the western part of the island, and the *buru* tradition, found primarily in the central parishes of Clarendon and St. Catherine. Like Kumina drumming, some of these neo-African styles were tied to African-derived forms of religious worship. Most of them employed an ensemble of two or three drums, one of which led with improvisations while the others provided supporting rhythms, and an assortment of percussion instruments such as rattles and scrapers. European influence was almost absent from these styles. Less familiar were traditions like the music played on the benta, a monochord made of a long bamboo log, played, as shown on page 185, with a gourd and a pair of sticks, used to accompany songs at wakes.

Much more widespread than these surviving neo-African forms were the musical expressions of Jamaica's hundreds of rural Afro-Protestant churches and sects, most of them variants of the general form of worship known in Jamaica as *pocomania* (sometimes spelled pukKumina), or "Revival." These indigenous religions were forged out of the nineteenth-century encounter between the religious concepts brought to Jamaica by enslaved Africans and the teachings of European missionaries. Like their religious practices, which included possession by both ancestral and biblical spirits, the music of these groups blended African and European influences. Many Revivalists used a combination of two or three drums—one or more "side drums" played with sticks (often equipped with a homemade snare) and a bass drum played with a padded beater—to accompany their singing. Sometimes other percussion instruments and hand clapping were employed, as well. While the melodic style of many Revivalist hymns, such as the ubiquitous "Sankeys," was European-derived, some songs were of more mixed derivation, and certain other features of the music, such as the drumming and the form of rhythmic breathing known as "groaning" or "sounding," betrayed a clear African influence. These *Poco* or Revival churches were scattered across the island. Over time, they spread to the larger towns and cities, and today they remain a force to be reckoned with not only in the Jamaican countryside but also in poor urban neighborhoods.

Not all of the older musical traditions available to Jamaicans during this period were religious. Before the 1950s, the closest thing to an indigenous popular music in Jamaica was the mento. Though its exact origins are obscure, it is clear that the mento was born of a creolizing process that blended elements of a variety of European social-dance musics with African-derived stylistic features. Varieties of European-derived ballroom dances such as the quadrille, the lancer, and the mazurka were popular in Jamaica both during and after the era of slavery, and the instrumentation, harmonic structures, and melodic contours that typified them contributed much to the music played by village bands across the island until recent times. To the fiddles, flutes, and guitars of these rural bands were added banjos, rhumba boxes (bass instruments with plucked metal keys), drums, rattles, scrapers, and other instruments wholly or partly of African origin. This creole social-dance music, originally

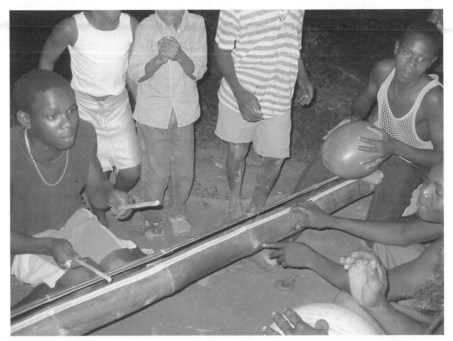

A benta being played in Islington, St. Mary, Jamaica, 2002 (Ken Bilby)

European-sounding, eventually acquired a new rhythmic feel because of the African-derived aesthetic preferences of the musicians who played it.

It is not clear exactly how and when mento emerged from this background, but its linkage with these older, creolized European dance styles can still be heard in the common practice of replacing the fifth (or sometimes sixth) fig- ure at quadrille dances with a "mento" (sometimes called a "round dance"). By the 1940s, the term "mento" had already come to embrace a fair amount of variation. Mento could be performed by ensembles consisting of little more than a harmonica and a few percussion instruments, by rural string bands fea- turing banjo and guitar, or even by large orchestras that included piano, trap drums, and a brass section. The musical style called mento had also long been associated with a genre of topical songs reminiscent of other Caribbean styles, such as calypso. Indeed, by the 1940s, mento was already being influenced by Trinidadian calypso (and was itself exerting an influence on the music of the other islands). Cuban influence is also suggested by the frequent use in mento of the "rhumba box"—like the Cuban marimbula—as well as the fact that in some rural parts of the island, the words "mento" and "rhumba" (a common misnomer for *son*) are used interchangeably to refer to the same musical style.

(In its original rural form, played in the eastern part of Cuba, the *son* sounds rather similar to mento as played by Jamaican string bands, making use of similar instrumentation.)

Add to these musical forms several kinds of work songs used to accompany a wide variety of chores in rural Jamaica, and the list of potential musical resources expands. Nor does the list end there. We must not forget the fife-and-drum music, of mixed African and European parentage, associated with the masked dance known as *jonkonnu* (or "John canoe") in most parts of the island. The list goes on; a host of other, less-well-known musical traditions could be cited. Some of these, such as the "digging songs" used in cultivating and planting crops or the "ring-game" songs used for rural entertainment, have long been leaving their mark on mento. In fact, certain songs commonly performed as mentos today actually originated as digging songs or ring-game tunes.

This ongoing tendency to absorb songs, melodies, and other stylistic elements from a variety of sources helped to make mento a sort of generic Jamaican folk music—a kind of synthesis of Jamaica's varied traditional musics. Over time, it became the closest thing to a Jamaican "national" music, known and appreciated across the island. Unlike many of the other forms mentioned here, mento had no special association with any particular community, region, religion, or social group within Jamaica (though it continued to be identified with its rural Jamaican roots). As a musical form capable of speaking to those who were flowing into the capital city from all over the island, mento was well positioned to serve as the basis of Jamaica's first wave of indigenous popular musical expression.

Following World War II, the nightclubs of downtown Kingston were driven by the music of dance orchestras, or "road bands," modeled in part on the African American big bands of the United States. Jamaican bandleaders presided over a steady diet of North American jazz and swing standards, supplemented by an occasional Cuban number. Other Caribbean styles, such as merengue and calypso, were also popular on the dance floors. Jamaica's own mento, however, was viewed with a certain ambivalence by these pioneering urban dance bands. Some looked down on it as "coming from country" and dismissed it as unsophisticated; others performed it with relish. Regardless of how they viewed the style, almost all bands featured at least an occasional mento to satisfy audience demand.

In contrast to these new dance bands, the older guitar-and-banjo mento bands that could also be found in the environs of Kingston at the time seemed to be on the wane. Some of them, however, found new life performing in tourist venues, where they often presented themselves as "calypsonians" in an attempt to benefit from the popularity then enjoyed by the somewhat similar Trinidadian calypso. Despite this misleading use of language, most Jamaican "calypsonians" were really mento singers who continued to perform in the indigenous Jamaican style.

MUSIC INNA DOWNTOWN STYLE: RECORDING THE UNRECORDED

When a businessman named Stanley Motta opened the first commercial recording venture in Kingston in the late 1940s, mento was the kind of music that caught his attention. Thus it was that the first local popular music that began to circulate on record was a form of mento that, though somewhat urbanized and occasionally featuring new instruments such as piano and traps, remained for the most part very close to its rural roots. Like the rural mento tradition from which their music was derived, these artists' recordings sometimes contained social commentary, but more often they consisted of reworkings of older digging songs or ring-play tunes. A portion of their output also reflected the increased emphasis on bawdy or suggestive lyrics acquired by mento in the context of urban clubs, where the pelvic-centered dance movements associated with the style had become more pronounced and had taken on a more erotic cast.

These early efforts at recording mento were overshadowed in the late 1950s by a new phenomenon, the "sound system," which would play a crucial role in Jamaican popular music over the next few decades. Indeed, it continues to play a vital role even today. In neighborhoods with limited financial resources, live dance bands were seldom affordable. The advent of increasingly powerful audio systems provided a solution: The owner of a set consisting of little more than a turntable, a few heavy-duty speaker cabinets, and a souped-up amplifier or two could now produce sufficient volume to draw large crowds to yard parties and "blues dances" and keep them dancing through the night. By the late 1950s, such sound systems were proliferating in downtown Kingston. Two of the early operators most often mentioned in accounts of this period are Clement "Coxson" Dodd (1932–2004, whose system was known as Sir Coxsone's Downbeat) and Duke Reid (known as The Trojan). Although these two stand out for the tremendous influence they had and for their longevity, literally dozens of less-well-known sound systems—sporting evocative names such as Admiral Cosmic, Count John the Lion, and Count Piah the Bluesblaster—operated in the metropolitan area in the early days. These systems played what their urban patrons wanted to hear: the hot African American rhythm 'n' blues then reigning in the United States, with special preference shown for the New Orleans sound. But most of them made room for a certain amount of variety, spinning an occasional Cuban dance number, perhaps, or a calypso, and almost all of them played at least some mento records. The many competing sound systems at this time also included a number of mobile sets that toured rural areas and catered to more traditional tastes, and they tended to play a larger proportion of mento tunes.

A major impetus for the development of a local recording industry came when North American R&B began to take a new direction toward the end of the decade, so that it became increasingly difficult for sound-system operators to import U.S. recordings in the styles favored by Jamaicans. In this fiercely competitive world of small entrepreneurs, the ability to obtain exclusive copies of "hot" records and to keep them out of the hands of other operators could make or break a sound system. To offset the dwindling supply of records from the United States in the preferred style, some sound-system operators invested in basic recording equipment and began pressing records of local artists performing R&B. Two of the most important recording studios in the history of Jamaican popular music, Coxson Dodd's Studio One and Duke Reid's Treasure Isle, got their start in this way, as did a number of others.

Before long, these local recordings were displaying subtle evidence of stylistic change. Jamaican R&B was beginning to differ, though only slightly, from its North American counterpart. All of these circumstances—increasing rural—urban migration, the growing popularity of sound systems, the birth of a local recording industry, and the growth of a Jamaican style of R&B, increasingly taking on a sound of its own—coincided with a unique and critical period in Jamaican history. The Federation of the West Indies, to which Jamaica had belonged since 1958, was disintegrating, and Jamaica was on the verge of political independence, which was finally achieved in 1962. The prevailing mood of nationalistic pride encouraged an increasing openness toward indigenous cultural expressions—at least in the arts—and stimulated a certain amount of conscious musical experimentation with rural folk forms. It was in this general climate that Jamaica's first truly new and distinctive form of urban popular music, known as ska, emerged.

Most observers agree that the style that came to be known as ska developed gradually, as Jamaican studio musicians began to alter the basic rhythmic structure of the U.S. R&B music that they were accustomed to playing. This process of modification continued imperceptibly for some time, until eventually it could be said that a new, distinctively Jamaican style had come into being. But here the consensus ends. Precisely because this emergent popular music was a product primarily of downtown musicians, producers, and audiences, beyond the pale of "respectable" uptown society, the circumstances

Selector (Coxson Dodd) with deejay (UrbanImage.tv/Bernard Sohiez)

Guarding the sound system
(UrbanImage.tv/Adrian
Boot)

of its genesis were not carefully documented by the local media. In fact, they were hardly documented at all, and today we are left with little more than the recordings themselves and the testimonies of those who participated in their making. As a result, there is a good deal of controversy and sometimes even acrimonious debate over the question of origins.

Some have taken the position that reggae, apart from the R&B contribution, is derived essentially from mento; others say that it owes most to Revival and other Afro-Jamaican cult rhythms; and yet others say that it can be traced to *jonkonnu* music, or even to military drumming. The problem with such competing claims, aside from the fact that it is virtually impossible to prove or disprove them, is that they presume a simple, linear path of development from a single, original Jamaican source, with each new "stage" of the music (such as rock steady, reggae, or dancehall) representing a stylistically uniform extension or outgrowth of the one that preceded it. Throughout all the stages, the influence of the main, original source is supposed to have remained predominant. But Jamaican popular music has evolved in a considerably more disorderly manner than this and has always been stylistically more heterogeneous and complex than such a view would suggest. In fact, if one allows for the possibility of constant, multiple influences from many traditional Jamaican sources, varying in importance over time, then all of the arguments for different origins can be said to have some validity. Indeed, I would argue—as a number of others have—that the urban popular music of Jamaica, like mento before it, represents nothing less than a synthesis of many diverse stylistic influences, both Jamaican and foreign, the balance of which has continued to shift over time.

From this perspective, it is pointless to debate, for instance, whether the characteristic driving rhythm played by horns and other instruments in ska (and apparently carried over to the guitar and piano in much reggae) is derived from the hand clapping of Revival churches, the beat of the timekeeping Rastafarian *funde* drum (in one particular early style of *nyabinghi* drumming),

Musical Example 15. The ska rhythm

or the strumming of the banjo in mento, all of which display a similar emphasis on the offbeat. Both ska and reggae would remain open to stylistic influences from traditional sources, some of which might result more from a kind of organic "osmosis" than from conscious intent.

There is no doubt that local studio musicians have brought to Jamaican recording sessions a wealth of varied musical experience. For example, most members of the Skatalites, a seminal ska band, received formal training at the Alpha Boys School, an orphanage and home for the underprivileged in depressed West Kingston, where they and many other prominent local artists learned the rudiments of European classical music, jazz, and marching music and discovered the joys of brass-ensemble playing. They were also well versed in U.S. R&B, as they had to be to survive as session musicians during the period leading up to the birth of ska. Meanwhile, trumpeter Johnny "Dizzy" Moore claims that, rather than any of the traditional Jamaican styles, it was the European "martial" drumming he encountered during his time at Alpha and later in the army that had the strongest influence on his playing and that it was this that led to the development of the ska "beat." In contrast, tenor saxophonist and fellow Alpha alumnus Tommy McCook cites as a rhythmic inspiration the regular visits he made to the camp of Rastafarian master drummer Count Ossie (Oswald Williams), beginning in the late 1940s, where he would often sing along with the Rasta chants and sometimes jam on saxophone with the drummers. Clearly, if one were to poll a larger number of early Jamaican studio musicians or to probe in greater depth, a yet broader range of experience would come to light, and a number of other opinions regarding sources would doubtless emerge. Thus, much of "the half that has never been told" remains untold to this day.

ROOTS AND CULTURE: DOWNTOWN TRIUMPHANT

The 1970s were a momentous decade for Jamaica. They were a period of great sociopolitical upheaval and the era that saw the full flowering of reggae—or, more specifically, the style that retrospectively came to be known variously as roots reggae, classic reggae, or foundation reggae (as opposed to dancehall). The '70s can also been seen as the period in which various trends in Jamaican music came to fruition. One of these was a process of maturation in which Jamaican popular music, after getting off to a rather late start, quickly acquired a level of extraordinary sophistication and expressive power. If much '60s ska consisted of little more than tentative cover versions of American R&B tunes (with that certain Jamaican rhythmic twist), by the early '70s top reggae artists like Bob Marley and producers like Lee Perry were in complete control of their idiom, fully endowed both with inspired ideas and the technical ability to realize them.

A concurrent trend was the intensifying international dissemination of Jamaican music, which, unlike Cuban music, had enjoyed no particular foreign presence until the "My Boy Lollipop" ska hit of 1964. In 1968, a bigger impact was made by the independent, black-and-white feature film *The Harder They Come*, which merged the figure of a famous rude boy with that of an aspiring reggae singer, played by the real-life singer and composer Jimmy Cliff. The film became a cult classic in the United States and the United Kingdom, and Cliff's LP by the same name soon became a standard fixture in Anglo-American record collections, alongside Led Zeppelin and the Beatles.

The biggest international stardom, however, was enjoyed by Bob Marley (1945–81), especially after he signed with Island Records' owner, Chris Blackwell, in 1972. Under Blackwell's guidance, Marley beefed up the Rasta look, foregrounded the electric guitar, added the gospel-sounding female backup trio, the I-Threes, and started producing nicely packaged LPs rather than singles. To American and British youth who had come to feel that rock had lost its countercultural edge, reggae and especially Marley's music seemed like a fresh sound—tuneful, rhythmically compelling, idealistic, and somehow untainted by commercialism. Marley and the Wailers (as of '74 without former sidemen Peter Tosh and Bunny Wailer) went on to attain phenomenal global appeal, successfully touring the United States, Europe, and Africa and inspiring fans and imitators everywhere from Senegal to Sri Lanka.

Perhaps paradoxically, the international vogue of reggae paralleled a process of indigenization in which Jamaican popular music became in many ways more distinctly Jamaican. Along with the post-independence search for a national identity came the growing feeling that Jamaicans should return to their roots for inspiration. Although recordings in the transitional rock-steady style (ca. 1966–68) continued to draw heavily on North American soul music, the underlying rhythm, with its characteristic medium-tempo chugging, had become more distinctively Jamaican, perhaps influenced by the mento that rural migrants brought from the countryside. By 1968, when reggae proper became established on the scene, indigenous influences were becoming even stronger, partly as class-consciousness was converging with increasing cultural assertiveness. The popular expression "roots" came to refer as much to the downtown ghetto experience of suffering and struggle as to the African sources of Jamaican culture. Accordingly, by the '70s, cover versions of American songs had given way to original compositions, and reggae had acquired such a distinctive sound that it couldn't be regarded as simply a spinoff of American music.

o G o   o G o   o G o   o G o

Musical Example 16. The classic reggae rhythm (o = organ, G = guitar)

The "Jamaicanness" of reggae style may derive from a number of sources. Some have argued that reggae's slower tempo and distinctive syncopation comes from mento, with its similar banjo or guitar strumming patterns, especially as introduced by migrants from the countryside in the late '60s. Indeed, the seminal 1967 reggae song "Nanny Goat"—whose "riddim" (accompaniment track) was endlessly recycled—was unmistakably mento-based, as were other songs. Also noteworthy was the Afro-Protestant musical contribution. Even the Wailers, before fully embracing the Rastafarian faith, recorded a number of Revival-influenced spiritual songs during the ska period. With the ascendance of Rasta-oriented reggae, those elements of traditional Rastafarian *nyabinghi* music that derived from Revivalist sources were transferred to urban popular music, lending much of '70s reggae a hymn-like quality that would be familiar to the ears of churchgoers all over rural Jamaica. The melodies and chord progressions of many Rasta reggae songs, as well as the biblical language and prophetic messages that typify the genre, owe much to Revivalism. Yet another influence was local versions of Afro-American gospel singing, whose inspiration is particularly audible in case of the Maytals.

Much Jamaican music had become local in lyric content as well as in style. Local producers, who emerged from the sound systems, aimed for the largest record-buying market, and in Jamaica this meant the struggling masses of ordinary citizens. Thus, it was not long after the appearance of ska that popular music in Jamaica began to reflect the social tensions caused by the glaring divisions between elitist, bourgeois, uptown society and disenfranchised but increasingly self-conscious and assertive downtown. Many ska songs of the '60s sang of the shantytowns, of the travails of the "sufferers," and, ambivalently, of the rude boys who, in a milieu of poverty and instability, sought respect in street-corner machismo and petty or not-so-petty crime. In 1976, Max Romeo epitomized this class tension in a reggae song that told of how "uptown babies don't cry, they don't know what suffering is like." And when Bob Marley, on the brink of international fame, sang, "Dem belly full, but we hungry," those living uptown felt compelled to listen. These musical developments both reflected and helped shape major changes taking place in Jamaican society.

RASTA AND REVOLUTION

Linked to these trends was the rapid growth of the Rastafarian movement, especially among poor urban youth. By the 1970s, the Rasta emphasis on African roots, black redemption, and social awareness had become the dominant force in Jamaican popular culture. The roots of Rastafari lie in the teachings of Marcus Garvey, an early advocate of black pride and mobilization. Born in Jamaica in 1887, Garvey attracted some notoriety as a labor activist there and among Panama Canal workers and left Jamaica for the United States in 1916, hoping to seek a more receptive audience for his evolving creed of Afrocentricity and black self-reliance. In the United States he founded the United Negro Improvement Association (UNIA), which urged black people to take pride in their African ancestry and bypass white domination by developing their own networks of support and sustenance and, ultimately, by "returning" to Africa. He founded a steamship line, the Black Star Line—at its peak consisting of four ships—which sought to establish trade links between black communities in the Americas and, eventually, Africa. The UNIA attracted tens of thousands of followers, along with the interest of the FBI, which regarded Garvey as a troublemaker. The young J. Edgar Hoover, who would later persecute Martin Luther King Jr. so effectively, set out to neutralize Garvey, who was imprisoned in 1925–27 for financial irregularities and then deported. Back in Jamaica, he continued preaching and developed a small but devoted following; he later moved to England and died in poverty in 1940.

In 1927, Garvey reportedly gave a speech urging followers to "look to Africa, where a black king will be crowned." And lo, in 1930 it came to pass, as one Ras Tafari Makonnen, with great pomp and circumstance, declared himself emperor of Ethiopia, taking the name Haile Selassie. Ethiopia, although it had no cultural connections to the slave trade or to black America, had already enjoyed a certain visibility among African Americans. It was the only independent country in a black Africa otherwise carved up by European colonial powers; it was also predominantly Christian, and the term "Ethiopia" had long been used as a synecdoche for "Africa" in general (including in the St. James Bible). Thousands of Jamaicans began worshiping Selassie as God, the returned Messiah, and Garvey as his prophet. The fact that both Garvey and Selassie (a devout Christian) disowned this belief made little difference to the growing number of Jamaicans who, alienated both from orthodox Christianity and African-based religions like Kumina, sought an alternative faith that celebrated rather than disparaged their African ancestry.

Rastafari evolved in many respects as a reinterpretation of Old Testament beliefs, taking inspiration from the tale of the "chosen people" taken in bondage from their home, Zion, to Babylon, where they lay and wept. "Babylon" thus encompassed Jamaica, the New World, and the entire "shitstem" of white neocolonial domination (even if enforced by black cops, or "Babylon bwoys"). More implicitly, it was a state of mind to be transcended. Rasta preached going "back to Africa," which could be interpreted in a figurative sense, of reorienting one's sense of identity, or literally, as in the case of the hundreds of gullible Jamaicans who purchased steamship tickets to Africa in the '50s, only to find they had been duped by scam artists. The Old Testament was also the source for dietary restrictions on alcohol, salt, pork (or all meat), and shellfish. For its part, the flaunting of long dreadlocks derived both from the tale of Samson and Delilah as well as a desire to invert traditional racist notions of "good hair" (straight) and "bad hair" (dark and kinky). In Rasta imagery, the biblical lion (of Judah) became the quintessential animal role model, perhaps in contrast to the humble Anansi the spider, the African-derived trickster figure. Although ganja (marijuana) was celebrated as a vehicle of spirituality, Rastas cultivated an ethic of clean and healthy living, represented in its own way by Marley and friends, who could often be seen jogging around Kingston and playing soccer.

Rastafarian musicians during a Sunday service at the African Reform Church of God, Braes River, St. Elizabeth, Jamaica, 2000 (Ken Bilby)

Despite its idiosyncratic Afrocentricity, Rasta had little to do with the real Africa, which functioned more as an imaginary utopia. Rastas had little use for the surviving aspects of West African culture in Jamaica (like Kumina) and instead looked over the heads of their West African cousins to focus on remote and culturally unrelated Ethiopia. Perhaps most important, however, was the way that Rasta, for all its contradictions, enabled or even obliged Jamaicans to confront and challenge the Anglocentric, colonial mentality that had dominated local ideologies for so long. Hence, while Rastas never constituted more than a small minority of Jamaicans, many others felt inspired by aspects of their image.

A Rasta ethic and lifestyle came to coalesce in the Pinnacle commune led by Leonard Howell, and the breakup of that community in 1954 served to spread the faith as brethren relocated in cities, paving the way for the dramatic growth of the movement in the '70s. Reggae became closely linked to Rasta, most visibly in the image of Marley, and the two movements thrived together, preaching spiritual renovation, lamenting the domination of Babylon, and predicting its fall ("Babylon, your throne gone down"). As the British-based group Steel Pulse sang:

> I curse the day they made us slaves
> How can we sing in a strange land? . . .
> One God, one aim, one destiny
> Rally round the [UNIA] flag, the red, gold, black, and blue
> the right direction: Africa, Africa.

The merging of Rastafari consciousness with reggae led to one of the most fertile periods of Jamaican popular music. This new surge of musical creativity helped to spur a Rasta "cultural revolution" that affected the entire society. Even many sons and daughters of the upper and middle classes began to take on the trappings of the Rasta faith. The international success of Bob Marley and the growing interest in the Rastafari movement in other countries helped enlarge the market for reggae in other parts of the world, which in turn gave a boost to the local music industry.

Hard-core Rastas shunned sociopolitical activism, regarding politics as a corrupt "shitstem" that would be swept away in the impending apocalypse. Progressive politicians like Michael Manley and internationally oriented artists such as Marley implicitly presented a more moderate form of this creed, in which anticipating the fall of Babylon could be interpreted as a fundamental optimism cohering with the general spirit of the '70s. Like their counterparts in other recently independent countries, many Jamaicans felt that they were poised to throw off the yoke of neocolonial (especially American)

Bob Marley (adapted by Peter Manuel)

domination, allying themselves as need be with the Soviet bloc and other Third World countries. In 1972, Manley (1924–97) and the People's National Party (PNP), riding a crest of mass mobilization and enthusiasm, came to power with a moderate socialist platform of demanding better payments from the multinationals mining Jamaica's bauxite, distributing that wealth to the poor, and seeking assistance from any quarter, including accepting Cuban doctors. Manley courted the Rastas and reggae fans in general, and many reggae songs praised the PNP and its idealistic commitment to the "sufferers." Echoing in worldly terms the impending fall of Babylon, many PNP supporters thought that Jamaica and the Third World could at last overcome imperialist domination. Innumerable reggae songs focused on a set of interrelated themes of shantytown life, social justice, Rastafari, socialism, and a general sense of optimism, as in Marley's "Small Axe," portraying him felling with his hatchet the huge tree (of imperialism? Babylon? exploitative record companies?).

The '70s were the heyday of roots reggae, with Marley, Jimmy Cliff, Peter Tosh, Toots and the Maytals, and other groups enjoying healthy local and foreign record sales and international stardom. Yet by mid-decade their music, although respected on the island, was already regarded by most young Jamaicans as a distinctly "international" and already somewhat old-fashioned style. Unlike in the Spanish Caribbean, few live bands performed in Jamaica, where roots reggae had evolved largely as a studio art form, whose leading exponents were generally on tour "a' foreign." Instead, when young Jamaicans went out to dance on a Saturday night, they danced to the beat pumped out by that distinctly Jamaican entity: the sound system.

As we've seen, the basic elements of the sound systems had dominated Jamaican musical life from the '50s: a towering bank of speaker cabinets, each big enough to house a family; a "selector" with one or, later, two turntables, choosing from a collection of 78s that included not only familiar hits but also exclusive, custom-ordered specials; a throng of devoted followers, who were not above attacking members of a rival "sound"; an accompanying informal economy of hawkers, hookers, and hangers-on; and, increasingly in the '70s, the charismatic focal figure of the deejay, who "chatted," in a half-sung, half-rapped manner, over the instrumental B-side of a record. While the international market and local radio promoted Marley and roots reggae, it was the young deejays like U-Roy and Big Youth and innumerable aspiring stars who entertained dancers in ground-level Jamaica itself, chatting about the pleasures and vicissitudes of street life and "bigging-up" (praising) the sounds, their audiences, and themselves. The parallels with rap, which emerged in the Bronx around 1980, are striking, and some have argued that Jamaican immigrant and sound-system operator Kool Herc played a seminal role in adapting his talents to the New York scene. Like early rap, the deejays' art was primarily live rather than recorded.

Besides hits and their B-sides, the records played by the sound systems often featured a new genre called "dub," consisting of innovative remixes of contemporary hits. The starting point for a dub record was the instrumental flip side of a record, which sound systems would play for deejays to chat over, or for dancers to sing over. From the early '70s, recording engineers like King Tubby and Augustus Pablo (d. 1999) took the art of remastering a step further, manipulating filters, faders, echo effects, and the like to alternately cut out and then reintroduce various tracks (drums, back-up vocals, guitars etc.), adding reverb and other effects and perhaps even bringing back snippets of the original lead vocal. Though produced in the studio, dub was meant to be heard "live" in the sound-system dance, where dancers and listeners would revel in the surrealistic deconstruction of familiar songs, now presented as perpetually mutating rhythm tracks conceived and ideally consumed under the spiritually medicinal effect of ganja. Sound-system operators would often appear at the studio of King Tubby or another mixologist on the morning before a show, requesting a fresh dub for the evening's entertainment. Together with the deejays, the constant flow of fresh dub versions provided a sort of spontaneity to sound-system shows that more than made up for the absence of live bands.

Meanwhile, the dub records enjoyed their own market appeal, sometimes even outselling the records they were based on.

Dub, as a remix genre, should not be confused with dub plates (discussed later), rub-a-dub-dancing, or dub poetry. The socially conscious lyrics of dub poetry exist in both written and aural form—in the latter case, performed with reggae beats. Among its major practitioners are Oku Onuora, Mutabaruka, the late Michael Smith, Jean Binta Breeze, and the London-based Jamaican poet and music historian Linton Kwesi Johnson.

THE END OF AN ERA AND THE DAWN OF A NEW ONE: FROM REGGAE TO RAGGA

As the 1970s progressed, events conspired to crush the PNP's heady aspirations of chopping down the tree of imperialist domination with its small axe. The formation of the Organization of Petroleum Exporting Countries (OPEC) and the quintupling of oil prices in 1973, while constituting a bonanza for nearby, oil-endowed Trinidad, hit the Jamaican economy like a steamroller, and the prospect of getting more money from bauxite sales turned out to be illusory. Washington, D.C., which resented Manley's playing footsie with Cuba, discouraged American tourism and started funneling weapons via the CIA to Manley's rival, Edward Seaga ("CIAga," according to graffiti), leader of the more status-quo Jamaican Labour Party (JLP). Rivalry between the two parties degenerated into bloody gang warfare, culminating in the deaths of more than seven hundred people in the 1980 elections.

In that election, frustration with PNP corruption and failures led to victory for the U.S.-friendly Seaga—just as the elections of Ronald Reagan and Margaret Thatcher marked decisive right turns in United States and the United Kingdom. The mood of the Jamaican public seemed to change overnight. No longer at the forefront was the vision—whether socialist or Rasta—of overthrowing imperialism, casting down Babylon, or returning to Africa. For its part, roots reggae, linked to this declining spirit of messianic optimism, suffered further setbacks. The death, from cancer, of Marley in 1981 was followed by the gang-style murder of Peter Tosh in 1987 and a most indecorous scramble for Marley's inheritance. The gifted, if highly eccentric, producer Lee Perry burned down his studio in 1979 and dropped out of the scene. Youth interest shifted decisively from roots reggae to the artful chantings of the deejays, which in the mid-'80s came to be called "dancehall." In a situation where denouncing the government could be mortally dangerous, the deejays retreated to the politically safe topics of sex and boasting.

In considering the dramatic contrasts in style and aesthetics between roots reggae and dancehall, it is tempting to regard Jamaican music as having completely reinvented itself in the early '80s. Such a view, however, would be somewhat inaccurate. For one thing, roots reggae did not fizzle out entirely. Indeed, it took on a new life overseas, in the form of British-based bands like Aswad and Steel Pulse, and in the music of African bandleaders like Alpha Blondy of Ivory Coast and Lucky Dube of South Africa. Further, Jamaicans like Beres Hammond, Barrington Levy, Gregory Issacs, and Frankie Paul, and even the Haitian Wyclef Jean, perpetuated the style, and the '70s songs of Marley and others continued to enjoy popularity as "classics."

Moreover, 1980s dancehall did not evolve overnight, as if from a vacuum, but can be seen as the logical evolution of the deejay/sound-system music that had dominated the island's dance-music scene throughout the '70s. Perhaps the main change in the late '70s was that what was once, like early rap, a primarily live art form now came to be widely marketed on records. While U-Roy is regarded as the first to record his chats (in the mid-'70s), in the early '80s he was out-chatted by a new crop of deejays. The most prominent of these was Yellowman, an albino orphan who deserves credit for successfully promoting himself as a sex idol ("the girls dem a mad over me"). By the end of the decade, with the emergence of deejays like Ninjaman, Super Cat, Shabba Ranks, and the often lyrically artful Buju Banton, Spragga Benz, and others, the modern idiom of dancehall was in full flower.

The stylistic differences between roots reggae and dancehall (outside Jamaica variously referred to as ragga, dub, bubbling, or rub-a-dub) are so pronounced that it seems odd that they both are referred to as "reggae." The trademark "skank" rhythm of classic reggae persisted in many '80s dancehall songs, but by the end of the decade that beat was just one possible rhythm among many and is seldom heard in modern dancehall. The Ur-format of guitar, bass, and drums (and possibly organ) also became at best optional, if not obsolete, especially after the vogue of the 1985 hit "Under me Sleng Teng," with its purely synthesized accompaniment (according to some usages, the trademark of "ragga"). Even the language of the two genres differed: Much classic reggae used standard English, often with a biblical flavor, while dancehall reveled in the expressive power of Jamaican patois/patwa, often delivered at high speed, and if Yankees or local uptown elites had trouble following it, then too bad for them. Moreover, much roots reggae generally used conventional "song" format, with original compositions with flowing melodies, changing chord progressions, and verses and refrains. Dancehall, by contrast, typically features the deejay intoning verses in what is often a short, repetitive tune ("chune") superimposed over a "riddim" (rhythmic accompaniment), which generally consists of a repeated, and often digitally generated or reproduced, ostinato. Unlike rap, the verses are usually sung in a simple, repeated melody rather than spoken, but deejays are in some respects classed differently from roots-reggae–style "singers," and if a deejay like Shabba Ranks intones quite out of tune with the tonality of the riddim, no one seems to mind.

The riddims themselves acquire a special importance and have a unique role in the music system. Rather than being originally composed for each song, many riddims are recycled—like many other things in a low-income place like Jamaica. The reuse of riddims, indeed, had begun in the 1960s, as producers found they could remix old materials from their vaults to provide backing for new releases, thus reducing their dependence on session musicians and arrangers. Nowadays, a dozen or so riddims may be in vogue at any given time. Many of them used to derive from the B-sides of Coxson Dodd's Studio One roots reggae classic songs, like "Nanny Goat," but by the latter 1980s, most were original creations of producers. The riddim could be named after the original song that popularized it (hence the "Sleng Teng" riddim), or it could be given a name by its producer (as in the "Diwali" riddim of the Miami-based producer Lenky Marsden). Typically, the producer, having created a new riddim (or an imitative "re-lick" of an existing one), would hire deejays to "voice" over it and would handle the marketing of the resulting recording himself. A deejay could voice (both live and on record) the same verses over different riddims, and, conversely, he could record and sing different voicings over the same riddim. In a dance club, the selector might play a medley of songs using the same riddim—a technique called "juggling." (The use of a digitally generated ostinato invites comparison with hip-hop, but in rap there is no custom of recycling beats or riddims in innumerable different songs.)

While some critics complain that the reliance on pre-existing riddims is uncreative, it should be noted that many deejays are very prolific, often recording thirty to forty songs a year. Accordingly, each week as many as two hundred seven-inch singles are released on the Jamaican market. The deejay (or "artist") must compose or somehow acquire both lyrics and a tune. Many of the tunes are original, but many others, like riddims, are recycled from earlier recordings, and there is also a certain free-for-all borrowing of snippets from other sources, be it Michael Jackson or Curtis Mayfield. The reliance on pre-existing riddims is also democratic in the sense that both the established star and the newbie are competing, as it were, on the same turf; no one can hide behind the producer's talent.

Producers of hot riddims, like Marsden and the veteran duo of Sly Dunbar and Robbie Shakespeare, are driving forces of the music. Some producers, like Dave Kelly, are also composers who dole out their songs to appropriate artists. In Jamaica, most recordings, as produced in small but well-equipped home studios, consist of seven-inch vinyl singles, but especially due to local piracy artists certainly aspire to get material on CDs put out by foreign labels like VP Records (New York), Jet Star, and Greensleeves (Britain). A riddim can typically "buss big," on records and in shows, for several months or a year, before becoming a "dead stock."

While aficionados appreciate the talent and importance of behind-the-scenes producers, and the sound systems are the key institutions in dances and clashes, there is no doubt that in the realm of recorded music as well as at special concerts, the focus is on the deejay or artist. The best of them command catchy tunes, clever, pithy verses, strong voices, and an electrifying performance style. Their voices have variously included the booming baritone of Shabba Ranks, the dour monotone of Cutty Ranks, the smooth and silky tone of Sean Paul, the gruff, almost spooky voice of Elephant Man, and the gravelly, orchestrally rich rasp of Buju Banton, Sizzla, and Capleton.

TELLIN' IT LIKE IT IS, FROM "CONSCIOUSNESS" TO "SLACKNESS"

If dancehall differs dramatically from roots reggae in style, it also encompasses a broad range of values, some of which contrast markedly with those of classic reggae. Revivalist Rasta ideals of casting down Babylon and returning to Africa certainly persist in the "conscious" dancehall of Capleton, Sizzla, Luciano, and others. At the same time, other aspects of dancehall culture seem antithetical to those of the preceding generation. If Marley celebrated spiritual values over materialism, modern deejays sport gold chains and drive luxury cars. And in contrast to Rasta's pieties and invocations of Africa, much dancehall foregrounds the nitty-gritty perversities of street-level reality: the violence, the struggle for respect, and the pleasures of dancing and, last but not least, of sex. As young, downtown deejays reclaimed Jamaica's indigenous popular music from the pretensions of international marketers aiming to please cosmopolitan audiences, it became harder for foreign consumers of that music to romanticize the experience from which it springs or to see in it an entirely "progressive" response to social injustice.

The diverse values of dancehall culture, like those of classic reggae, are evident in the public personae of the stars, the album covers, the dress and behavior of fans, and perhaps most overtly, the song lyrics. To be sure, listeners may often ignore the lyrics, especially on the dance floor, and like rap, the main emphasis even of the verses may be less their message per se than their driving delivery and the artful, rhythmically compelling play of rhymes, alliterations, and other devices. But there is no doubt that lyrics are an important dimension of dancehall, just as they are in rap, constituting both a uniquely expressive art form and an articulation of a worldview.

With dancehall releases and unrecorded live songs numbering in the thousands each year, song lyrics address an infinite variety of themes. Many might be classified simply as "topical" in their documentation of the vicissitudes of Jamaican daily life, from Beenie Man's anti-gun "No Mama No Cry" to Lovindeer's 1988 "Hell of a Blow-Job" regarding, of course, Hurricane Gilbert. A random look at one song—Buju Banton's "Deportee: Things Change"—may give some idea of the realism typical of dancehall lyrics. This song portrays the fate of young man who makes it "a' foreign," living the good life with "Benz and Lexus" and girls massaging his shoulder and pouring his coffee. But he has ignored his family and friends at home, only to be deported as a criminal, and arrives broke and friendless:

> Yuh neva used to spen' no money come a yard
> Yuh wretch you, yuh spen' di whole a it abroad
> Squander yuh money now yuh livin' like dog
> Boy get deport come dung [down] inna one pants . . .
> Mama dung inna di hole, an' 'im don't buy her a lamp
> Not a line, not a letter, nor a fifty cent stamp.

Unlike some roots reggae songs that ethereally praise a mythical Africa or bewail Babylon, "Deportee" portrays, with specific, concrete imagery, the ups and downs and moral failures of a real-life individual who seeks success in Brooklyn or Notting Hill rather than Ethiopia. Many other dancehall songs can be seen as perpetuating, albeit with more detail, the orientation of ska and roots reggae toward the shantytown "sufferers," as in Bounty Killa's verses:

> Born as a sufferah, grew up as a sufferah
> Struggle as a sufferah, make it as a sufferah
> Fight as a sufferah, survive as a sufferah
> Yutes inna di ghetto, well di most a dem a sufferah.

In songs like "Untold Stories," Buju Banton seemed to be taking up the mantle of Bob Marley in his poignant depiction of the travails of the underclass:

> What is to stop the youths from getting out of control?
> Filled up with education yet don't own a payroll
> The clothes on my back has countless eyeholes.

In such conditions, the quest for street-corner status generates another favorite song topic: gun talk. Many '60s songs, like Marley's "Simmer down" and Desmond Dekker's "007," had sung of the rude boys in a noncommittal manner. Overshadowed in the '70s by the spirituality of Rasta roots reggae, in the '80s rude boy culture came back in the music with a vengeance and was often unequivocally celebrated, as in Vybz Kartel's "Guns like Mine":

> Dem nuh got no guns like mine, no KG-Nine
> A coppershot a buss dem big head and bruck spine
> Me gun will tear yuh like a table cloth . . .
> People find yuh body piece piece and think a chicken parts.

The glorification of guns and violence may be primarily rhetorical, especially insofar as it expresses the theatrical rivalry between deejays. As Shabba sings, "When me talk about gun it is a lyrical gun, a lyrical gun dat people have fun." Similarly, producer Scatta Burrell says, "It's better than taking up a gun a pointing it in a man's face."[2] But it is also more than just metaphor. Fistfights have erupted on stage between artists, such as celebrated ones between Bounty Killa and Beenie Man and between Ninjaman and Vybz Kartel. A number of artists, including Peter Tosh, Tenor Saw, Mickey Simpson, King Tubby, Henry "Junjo" Lawes, Bogle, and Pan Head, have been murdered, and Marley himself was shot in 1976. Accordingly, counterbalancing the gun-talk songs is the equal number of songs—by some of the same deejays—that call for unity, peace, and an end to street violence. Hence, Buju Banton, grieving the loss of Panhead and Simpson, sang in "Murderer":

> Murderer! You insides must be hollow
> How does it feel to take the life of another?

The macho gun talk overlaps with another favorite theme, consisting of the boasting of the deejay. In rude-boy tradition, many deejays assume mafia-style sobriquets, like Bounty Killa, Ninjaman, or Shabba Ranks (the name of a famous gunman). Deejays can boast about their abilities as fighters, their skill "'pon the mike" (as proved by the song itself), or their popularity with the ladies. Hence, Shabba is "Wicked inna bed," and Super Cat says, "Me big an me large, nuff gals gimme massage."

The contrast of such lyrics with those of Rasta-oriented roots reggae is striking. Some people regard them as shallow and narcissistic compared with the idealism of the Rasta singers, but such songs also reflect what could be seen as a healthy sense of self-empowerment. Rather than singing of the ancestral victimhood of slavery, or the righteous defiance of the Rasta, the quintessential dancehall deejay might more typically celebrate his worldly success and attainment, as embodied in his Benz, his vocal skills, and his "truckload a' girls."

Indeed, whatever dancehall's merits or shortcomings, dancehall is the music of the new generations of downtown sufferers and rudies, and it speaks resolutely to their own experience and does so in the contemporary language of the still growing Kingston underclass. Many youths of this class defiantly adopted the derogatory term "ragamuffin." In the words of the ragga singer Half Pint, "Raggamuffin [is] a youth who grow up outside where him can stand the weather and no havin' no flu, him can stand hunger, him can stand a pain, him can endure."[3]

The affirmative and upbeat tenor of dancehall is also evident in its orientation toward dancing (as the name suggests). Innumerable songs, especially by artists like Elephant Man, concern dancing itself. The music is intended to be heard not on an iPod in the subway but in a yard or club, where women joyously display their bodies and custom-made attire and dominate the dance floor, often dancing together rather than with men. New dance moves emerge every few months. The basic movements of Latin styles like salsa/*son* and merengue have been around for seventy years, but each year sees several new dancehall styles. Women are particularly active as performers, promoters, and sometimes even creators of the new styles, which they learn from friends, videos, or demonstrations at stage shows. Some of the most popular dances are inventions of professional choreographers, such as John Hype, who promotes some of his creations in the context of shows and videos with Beenie Man. All the dances have names, such as Bogle, Pedal an' Wheel, Sesame Street, and Jerry Springer. Some, like Thunder Clap, are associated with particular riddims. Many are mimetic, such as Signal da Plane (light up your cell phone, wave it around), Internet (move your fingers as if typing), Butterfly (flap your knees like wings), Mock di Dread (whip your hair around like a Rasta), and Log On (pretend you're stomping on a gay man—more about that later). But don't go trying these dances, as they're already out of date, and as Sean Paul warns:

> So from ah gyal nuh up to date we deport dem
> Cyar [can't] keep up to de change we report dem.

It remains to mention the broad category of dancehall songs that concern "slackness" (lewdness, ribaldry), as opposed to "consciousness" or "culture." Slackness, far from being new, was a prominent feature of traditional mento, and it certainly persisted in classic roots reggae–from Marley songs like "Bend Down Low" and "Lick Samba" to Clancy Eccles's "Open up!" (You pussy sweet, gyal!). However, in the roots reggae period, slackness was to some extent overshadowed by more spiritual songs. But in the early '80s, when Yellowman asked his audience what they wanted, consciousness or slackness, the crowd's shouted answer was unanimous and for many yardies represented a gleeful and explicit rejection of the pristeen snobbery of the "uptown" bourgeoisie. Hence, the paeans to pumpum, the sexual braggadoccio, and the anatomical details of "Titty Jump." As one Jamaican student pithily wrote in a term paper, "Dancehall artists sing about everything from politics to punanny. Mostly punanny." Sizzla's songs, for example, range from the pious "Explain to the Almighty" to the X-rated "Pump Up Her Pum Pum." The very name "dancehall" ultimately derives from its slackness, which kept much of it banned from the radio ("Not Fit for Airplay," or NFAP) and hence relegated only to the dance venues. But ultimately more important than the degree of slackness in dancehall may be the *kind* of slackness and the ways that men and women are portrayed—a topic that needs further comment here.

FEMALE DEGRADATION OR LIBERATION?

A foreign critic looking for instances of what at least *looks* like sexist objectification in dancehall culture could write volumes. Videos typically portray the male stud surrounded by scantily clad models; CD compilation covers look like porno ads; and lyrics routinely objectify women as punnanies rather than personalities. The portrayal of sex often seems violent and aggressive. "Me ram it and a jam it till the gal start to vomit," sings one deejay, while Buju chants, "Gal me serious, haf to get ya tonight, haf ta get your body even by gunpoint." Other songs have titles like "Bedroom Bully" and "Kill the Bitch," and deejays like Beenie Man (in "Yaw Yaw") boast about how many women they impregnate. The image of having a "trailorload a' girls," while indeed a reality for a few stars, could be seen as catering to the most adolescent male fantasies. Several songs by male deejays, perpetuating a rich African American art of witty insults (as in the "dozens"), mock women for their perceived imperfections, as when Elephant Man sings:

> Tanya Stephen, Lady G, Lady Saw wi love dem,
> Saw knee knock, G have a belly problem,
> Tanya Stephens foot big like Captain Bakery bread dem.

However, the ambivalence in such verses can also reflect how dancehall culture is contradictory and in many ways celebratory in its portrayals of women. Rastafari, as articulated by reggae singers, kept women in the background and had a certain streak of misogyny, with Peter Tosh calling women "instruments of the devil," and Marley saying, "Woman is a coward, man strong." But dancehall, for all its frequent vulgarity, foregrounds women, and especially their sexuality, in a way seldom encountered in classic reggae. Hence,

Beenie Man's "Slam" praises the sexual prowess of ghetto gals, and songs like his "Girls dem Sugar" and Buju's "Gal ya Body Good" eulogize women with a hefty "Coca-Cola bottle shape." Songs like "Tight Pum Pum" may objectify women, but they also praise them—or, at least, parts of them— and women are well aware that their sexuality and desirability can enable them to exert a sort of power over men. Women at dances who strut their stuff in batty-riders (tight shorts) and "bare-as-you-dare" outfits revel in the desire they can stimulate, as articulated in songs like Red Rat's "Tight up Skirt":

> Hey you girl inna tight up skirt, ya mek me head swell til me blood vessel burst
> Hey you girl inna de tight up shorts, ya speed up ten more beats to me heart
> hey you girl inna de tight-up blouse, everytime you pass me you get me aroused.

As Carolyn Cooper points out in her book *Sound Clash,* the lyrics of several songs by Shabba Ranks, for all their slackness, encourage men to respect their women and urge women to demand good treatment from their men. The specific favors in question can be more pragmatic than sentimental, as when he enjoins women, in inflationary times, "Aren't you gonna raise the price of your pussy too?" Similarly, in "Flesh Axe" he tells men,

> But every woman need mega cash fi buy pretty shoes an pretty frock
> Woman love model an dem love fi look hot
> She can't go pon di road and look like job lot
> Every woman a go call her riff-raff look like a old car mash up an crash.[4]

There are only a few female artists around to challenge the male frater-nity of deejays, and their songs present different sorts of female perspectives. The message of Ce'cile's "Respect Yuh Wife" is as straightforward as its ti-tle suggests, and equally assertive is Tanya Stephens, who, mocking her ex's "toothpick," tells him, "Well you used to work me once but you can't touch me no more." Often the images are more controversial, as in the case of Lady Saw, who embodies some of the contradictions of dancehall as a whole. Saw is a powerful and talented singer who can "ride the riddim" as well as the best male deejays. She sings in different styles about a variety of topics but is best known for songs like "Stab out the Meat," in which she describes her lovemaking at a level of detail that makes Yellowman sound like an altar boy. In her stage shows she is liable to grab the nearest man, throw him to the floor, and simulate sex with him. From one perspective, such antics constitute a soft-core porn show, aimed at the male gaze of hooting and hollering men. From another view, though, she presents the image of an empowered woman, in full control of her sensuality, demanding that her man be strong and "solid as rock." Far from being a passive boy toy, she sings,

> When me waan me man me just demand me ride
> take out me whip and like a jockey me a glide.

Whether her persona is liberating or degrading to women may depend on one's point of view.

The general status of women in Jamaican society suggests another perspective on dancehall. Many Jamaican women are economically dependent on men, but they are proverbially strong rather than submissive and are celebrated for the rhetorical skill and vigor with which they can "trace" or verbally humiliate men with a torrent of abuse. Moreover, there is a strong tradition of women's independence (bred in part by generations of absent fathers). Many women have been owners of small farms since the 1800s, and many operate market stalls. More significant, for several decades women have constituted about two-thirds of college students and graduates and are increasingly coming to rival male dominance of urban white-collar professions. From one perspective, the up-front sexual politics of dancehall represents a sort of grassroots negotiation of positions in a changing society.

LOVE MUSIC—OR HATE MUSIC?

In fall of 1992, Buju Banton's song "Boom Bye Bye" was enjoying steady airplay in New York, and its verses, unlike those of many dancehall songs, were sung slowly and clearly. When a "translation" was circulated, explaining that "batty boy" meant "gay," many listeners could easily follow the vicious message:

> Two men necking and a lay down inna bed . . .
> send for the 'matic and the Uzi instead
> shoot the batty boy come let we shoot dem . . .
> Boom bye bye in a batty boy head.

Complaints were made, the media took notice, and a minor uproar ensued. The *New York Post*'s headline screamed "Hate Music," and protests were staged against the stations that played it. When Shabba Ranks defended Buju and offered the humble opinion that gays should be crucified, his scheduled appearance on the *Tonight Show* was canceled, and he was dropped from a high-profile tour with Bobby Brown. With the cancellation of a prominent New York concert, Buju's own international career had also definitely hit a speed bump. And when he stated that he didn't actually advocate anti-gay violence, he was derided by Jamaican deejays and journalists for kowtowing to the "special interest" group of panty-clad Yankee "chi-chi men," and he subsequently revoked his apology.

In retrospect, what seems remarkable is not Buju's song but the fact that it was singled out among so many hundreds of other gay-bashing dancehall songs such as are still played on U.S. radio and that often have titles like Capleton's "Burn Out the Chi Chi." Despite—or perhaps because of—the increasing public space being achieved by gays in Jamaica, homophobia is one of the most common and popular themes of dancehall. Sometimes most of an entire night's show, presented by several deejays, will be devoted to lyrics that incite hatred and violence against gays. Mike-men routinely shout, "Everyone who hates batty boys put ya hand up in de air!" Most of the top deejays reiterate such sentiments in several songs, as in the following:

Beenie Man:
    A from me burn chi-chi man and we go burn sodomite
    And everybody bawl out say "that's right" . . .
    Cause when we burn chi-chi man nuttin' nuh wrong
        ("That's Right")

    Batty man fi dead, shoot up dem bloodclaat
        ("Batty Man fi Dead")

    I'm dreaming of a new Jamaica, come an' execute all the gays!
        ("Damn")

    Hang chi-chi gal wid a long piece of rope
        ("Han up deh")

Sizzla (when not singing "Love amongst my Brethren"):
    Nuff girl out dere . . .
    So how come some bwoy turn out batty man?
    Me say, cock the gun and kill out every one
        ("Nuff Girl out There")

    Shoot batty bwoy, my big gun boom
        ("Pump up")

Elephant Man:
    Battyman fi dead! Gimme the tech-nine, shoot dem like bird!
        ("A Nuh fi we Fault")

Bounty Killa:
    Burn a fire 'pon a puff and mister fagotty
    poop man fi drown an' dat a yard man philosophy
        ("Another Level").

T.O.K.:
    Chi-chi mon, from dem a par inna chi-chi man car
    Blaze di fire make we bun dem!
        ("Chi Chi Man")

And even the uptown heart-throb Sean Paul:

> Den yuh got some fuh-funky guy weh a try imitate ooman,
> Dem dey fassy deh we nuh want dem up inna we island . . .
> from yuh nuh like dem guy deh mek a hear shout BLAM BLAM.

As with gun-chat songs, reality often parallels the rhetorical violence. Between 1997 and 2004 alone, more than thirty gay people in Jamaica—including the country's leading gay-rights activist—were murdered, and many more were savagely beaten. A few were doused with acid and set afire by mobs shouting, "Fiya burn!" In summer 2004, Buju Banton himself was facing arrest for taking part in a group assault on six Jamaican gay men.[5]

Explaining the obsessive homophobia of the deejays and many other Jamaicans may be a task for sociologists and psychologists, although we can well imagine what Freud would say about it. Many onlookers have wondered how people historically victimized by bigotry and intolerance can show the same traits themselves. For their part, the deejays, deeply religious as they say they are, generally cite the biblical injunction against homosexuality (though they don't seem to cite the command that anyone who is rude to his parents or works on Sunday should be killed, or the Levitical instructions on selling your daughter into slavery). From another perspective, in a post–Cold-War, globalized economy, where the traditional neocolonial enemies have evaporated, gay-bashing gives Jamaican deejays a way to portray themselves as waging a new sort of righteous moral crusade—in this case, against the decadent sodomites of Babylon and their deluded defenders. Both doggerel about punanny and gay-bashing macho gun talk can thus be seen as honorable and virtuous.

In recent years, dancehall stars like Bounty Killa, Beenie Man, Sizzla, and Capleton have been finding their European and North American concerts canceled because of protests or being tolerated only if they promise not to vent their homophobia. Singers can also face legal charges in Britain and Canada, where songs that advocate killing gays violate hate-speech laws. Artists are increasingly finding themselves obliged to choose between catering either to the rudies in the yard or to the foreigners, who include not only handfuls of outspoken gays but also other open-minded people who care about things like human rights.

SOUND SYSTEMS AND SOUND CLASHES

Sound systems, as we have seen, play an important structural role in reggae culture. Typically, when one goes out on a Saturday night to a dance—be it in Kingston, New York, or Birmingham—one goes to hear a sound system rather than a live band. The system will bring its own equipment, whose key elements are a vast record collection and a towering wall of speakers, whose bass vibrates your chest and the beer in your bottle and in Jamaica can often be heard two or three towns away. More or less as in the '50s, the system also has its own personnel of "selector" (who spins the records), a mike man who hypes up the crowd between or perhaps during songs, various gofers, and possibly one or more deejays (vocalists). The mike man (MC or "mike-chatter") must have a lively stage presence, rousing the crowd with shouts of "From a bwoy nuh badda dan you, han' up in di air," or, more pithily, "Bumba-claat!" (a favorite all-purpose exclamation).

Let's hear how a visiting Jamaican American woman, who as a New York clubgoer is familiar with the latest dances, describes a Saturday night dance—in this case, a "Passa Passa" sound-system dance in Kingston's Tivoli Gardens:

> First I went shopping with my girlfriends to get the sexiest outfit that I could conjure. Then, on the way to the session, I thought that we were nearby when we heard the music very clearly, but it turned out that we were not close at all, but the music was just that LOUD. Reaching the session, we saw that it was not in a dancehall but in the middle of the road. But unlike in American block parties, the road is not blocked at all. The speaker boxes are stacked high on the sidewalk and you have the choice of either going deaf there or dancing in the road. Most, including myself, chose the latter. However, while dancing in the road you may be interrupted by a passing bus, car, or handcart, but once they have passed the pulsating music sweeps you up once again and you continue dancing. Most of the session can be compared to the "Electric Slide" song being played at an American party. Everyone knows the songs and the dances that accompany them. Whether you are in high heels or Timberlands, all across the road everyone joins in, expertly dancing the moves announced by the [deejay], like "Signal di Plane," "Summer Bounce," "Thunder Clap," or "The Blaze," among many others. It was the most exciting dance experience I have ever known![6]

In addition to providing music at dances, sound systems release records (whether legitimate or pirate compilations) and often have associations with specific producers and deejays. However, the most distinctive sort of event featuring the sounds is the sound clash. This is a musical duel between two (or possibly more) sound systems, held at a club or yard and attended by hundreds of enthusiastic "sound followers." While the sounds may play some familiar songs, on the whole the emphasis in a sound clash is on a uniquely Jamaican entity called the "dub plate."

A dub plate—also known as a "special"–is a short recording made by a deejay (or "artist") in which he sings a few lines, usually to the tune of a familiar song of his, substituting new verses that "big up" a particular sound system, which he mentions by name. The dub plates are not mass-produced or sold in stores; instead, a sound system will contract a deejay to make the dub especially for it. Cheap dub plates can be gotten from the small-time, aspiring deejays who hang out around Jamaican studios, but a big name like Bounty Killer may charge a few thousand dollars for a dub plate. (He may also take his pretty time to get around to recording it.) Audiences thrill to hear new dub plates by current stars, but they also enjoy dubs by deceased figures like Tenor Saw and Garnett Silk (d. 1994). Such recordings can be heard only at the sound clashes (or on the videotapes of them that circulate widely), as they are the exclusive property of the sounds.

Accordingly, the most popular sound systems are those, like Killamanjaro, Bass Odyssey, and Stone Love, that have been around for a few decades and have managed to accumulate hundreds of dub plates from artists so that they have a box (of dubs) that is "deep as the ocean." Jamaican pride notwithstanding, respected sounds come from all over, including David Rodigan (a white Brit), Mighty Crown Disco (from Japan), One Love (from Italy), and Massive B (from New York). In fact, even many Jamaican fans prefer the non-Jamaican sounds, as they tend to have more money and can acquire dub plates from all the top artists, sometimes arranging special duets.

A clash generally starts with rounds in which the sounds alternate in thirty-minute segments, then proceed to fifteen-minute segments, and then battle "dub fi dub" to put a "murderation" pon one another. Audience members—who tend to be mostly male—don't come to dance during the clash proper, especially since the dub plates are short and are perpetually interrupted by the MC's shouting. Instead, fans come to hear the dub plates and the lively banter of the MCs and to savor the competitive spirit of the event. If fans like a song, they may light and wave lighters and cell phones, shoot guns in the air, and shout for a "forward"—that is, for a repeat of the song. Conversely, a song deemed lame will elicit calls of "Next selectah!" or "Rinse the bloodclot tunes!" The excitement reaches a climax in the dub-fi-dub section, when the best dub plates are brought out. Generally, a panel of judges decides the winner on the basis of audience response.

Much of the fun of the clash scene comes from the rivalry, which rages not only at the clashes but also in international cyber-forums like the Internet, whose participants might as easily be Malaysian as Jamaican. To get a sense of the connoisseurship involved, let's tune in on a typical chat-room argument, in this case about the standing of Killimanjaro ("Jaro") and its MC, Rickie Trooper, vis-à-vis other sounds. (Reader beware: X-rated diction follows!)

Boomshaka: Bass Odyssey cyaan bakkle [can't battle] wid Jaro inna tune fi tune when Trooper play Tena Saw weh Odyssey a go play dem weak-ass Garnet Silk. Yes dey have Garnet pon dub, but Odyssey box is a dibby-dibby wading pool next to Jaro.

Maddog: Fly up now, John-crow! If Jaro box so deep, why Rickie playin the same dubs in every clash? And the old ones, Jaro studio couldn't cut a clean dub. Every truck and van pass you can hear it on the dubs dem—horn, tires, everyting. And besides a few Tenna Saws from '85 he cyaan go much deeper.

Boomshaka: I see you have started to disrespect. You is de same likkle yute who I had to put in his place on dancehallreggae.com. You is nothing but a cassette bwoy, you just buy tapes and listen. You don't know a ting bout yard. You don't know what tunes Jaro got, only what tunes they bring! How the hell can you expect them to carry 20+ crates of dubs and play maybe 50 songs? Tell Freddy next time two sounds buck up, just call for Saw fe Saw, I guarantee you it won't be a pretty site, cause blood will diffenately spill, an mi dun talk.

Maddog: Bwoy a get shame, change your ways! You just scout every website like a bobo duppy, saluting Trooper. Ho God, people, I believe Trooper a slide him rod inna u pum-pum. Jaro cannot go deep with sounds that cut in the '80s, and anyhow, Tenor was just a likkle above average, dem man da career take lead, skyrocket after death.

Boomshaka: Bumbaclot! You deserve to be banished to a world of AOL 3.0 with a 56K dial-up modem![7]

Whoa! We'd best exit before we're splattered with cyber-blood. Let's return to our look at dancehall and its contrasts with roots reggae.

DANCEHALL INNA FOREIGN

In many respects, dancehall, compared with the overtly international orientation of roots reggae, represented a sort of turning inward. The focus shifted from Africa and white foreign fans to the humble yard, with songs rendered in a thick patois that is often only barely intelligible to outsiders. Nevertheless, by the mid-1980s dancehall had acquired an international presence that surpassed that of Marley and Jimmy Cliff. The boom started, not surprisingly, in neighboring West Indian islands, where dancehall quickly became the youth music of choice, despite being denounced by elders and moralists as a degenerate expression of dysfunctional Jamaican ghetto culture. Dancehall soon spread to the United Kingdom, where a sizable West Indian population had existed since the 1960s. By the '80s, New York's Brooklyn and the Bronx had emerged as rival epicenters of reggae's international emergence, and by the mid-'90s, many dancehall songs were riding the crest of the U.S. and U.K. mainstream pop charts.

Dancehall's popularity in the United States rests on a number of factors apart from the sheer richness of the music. The substantial Jamaican and other West Indian communities that had evolved in New York and elsewhere by the '80s provided an initial foothold, including for the handful of dancehall studios and sound systems that appeared in this period. More important was the growing appeal of the music to African American New Yorkers and, subsequently, to Americans as a whole. Although Jamaican patwa can be initially unintelligible, many non–West Indians have managed to learn to follow it, especially after getting used to common words and phrases like "nuff a dem" (lots of), "likkle" (little), and "unu" (you all, from Igbo). Dancehall and hip-hop further share a history of West Indian participation (including Kool Herc and Africa Bambaata) and an orientation toward the lumpen ghetto milieu of marginality, machismo, guns, and drugs. They also share a convention of using records and turntables as musical instruments and of rapping, singing, or otherwise voicing over ostinatos, whether called riddims or breakbeats. By the late '80s, New York's dancehall scene featured local West Indian performers like Shinehead and Shaggy, recent immigrants like Super Cat, formidable sound systems like Bass Odyssey, and a network of clubs, record stores, and radio programs.

It was on this base that a number of crossover hits started to appear in the early '90s, often pairing Jamaican deejays like Maxi Priest and Foxy Brown with black American rappers or singers. The combo format of singer and deejay became widely popular via songs like "Murder She Wrote," as did a new hybrid of ragga-hiphop. Shabba Ranks was the first deejay to enjoy true American stardom, with his U.S.-oriented remixes and duets opening the way for a series of others. In 2004, leading the pack was Sean Paul, an uptown, fair-skinned, mixed-race Jamaican whose good looks, tuneful hits, toned-down patwa, and collaborations with Beyoncé, Snoop Dogg, and others put his music at the top of the charts, enjoyed by white preteens in Peoria as well as by B-boys in Brooklyn. For their part, Jamaicans themselves continue to debate whether such "Jamerican" artists are selling out and losing their yard credibility or whether they are the yardstick for local artists.

With dancehall, as with other musics, the foreign appeal of local—in this case, Jamaican—performers represents in some ways only an initial step in the music's globalization. The next step, which is well under way, is the music's cultivation by non-Jamaicans, in different languages. In the Americas, the most prominent example of this is *reggae en español*, or reggaetón (discussed in chapter 4), which thrives vigorously in Puerto Rico, New York, the Dominican Republic, and elsewhere. But dancehall has already become a global idiom everywhere from Malaysia to Malawi, where local artists inspired by Beenie and Bounty sing not only in English but also in local languages about local themes. Reggae has truly gone a' foreign.

BIBLIOGRAPHY

Among the many books on Jamaican music, particularly useful are Steve Barrow and Peter Dalton, *The Rough Guide to Reggae* (London: Penguin, 2001); Lloyd Bradley, *This is Reggae Music: The Story of Jamaica's Music* (New York: Grove Press: 2000); Norman Stolzoff, *Wake the Town and Tell the People: Dancehall Culture in Jamaica* (Durham, N.C.: Duke University Press, 2000); Carolyn Cooper, *Sound Clash: Jamaican Dancehall Culture at Large* (New York: Palgrave/Macmillan, 2004); Sebastian Clarke, *Jah Music:* The *Evolution of the Popular Jamaican Song* (London: Heinemann, 1980); Kenneth Bilby and Fu-Kiau kia Bunseki, *Kumina: A Kongo-Based Tradition in the New World* (Brussels: Centre d'Etude et de Documentation Africaines, 1983); and Hilary S. Carty, *Folk Dances of Jamaica: An Insight* (London: Dance Books, 1988).

RECORDS

TRADITIONAL GENRES: *Jamaican Cult Music* (Folkways FE 4461); *Folk Music of Jamaica* (Folkways FE 4453); *From the Grass Roots of Jamaica* (Dynamic 3305); *Grounation: The Mystic Revelation of Rastafari* (MRR Records); *John Crow Say: Jamaican Music of Faith, Work and Play* (Folkways FE 4228); *From Kongo to Zion: Black Music Traditions of Jamaica* (Heartbeat HB 17); *Churchical Chants of the Nyabingi* (Heartbeat HB 20); *Jamaican Ritual Music from the Mountains and the Coast* (Lyrichord LLST 7394); *Drums of Defiance: Jamaican Maroon Music* (Smithsonian/Folkways SF 40412); *The Jolly Boys* (Lyrichord LLST 7314); *Lititz Mento Band* (Haus der Kulturen der Welt SM 1512-2); *Rough Guide to Ska* (World Music Network RGNET1083CD); *Rough Guide to Reggae* (World Music Network RGNET1016CD); *Rough Guide to the Music of Jamaica* (World Music Network RGNET1056CD); *Drums of Defiance: Maroon Music from the Earliest Free Black Communities of Jamaica* (Smithsonian Folkways SFW40412 1992); *Bongo, Backra and Coolie: Jamaican Roots, Volume 2* (Smithsonian Folkways FW04232 1975); *Folk Music of Jamaica* (Smithsonian Folkways FW04453 1956); *Tougher than Tough: The Story of Jamaican Music* (Mango 162-539935-2, 1993).

8

Trinidad,
Calypso, and Carnival

Christopher Columbus's first sight of land on his third voyage was a row of three hills on the southeastern tip of a large island, which he consequently dubbed Trinidad, or "trinity." Approaching shore, the famed navigator, still in search of the Orient, was disappointed, as before, to be greeted by a delegation not of Chinese mandarins but of nearly naked albeit friendly seeming Carib Indians in canoes. Columbus tried to welcome them by having his men dance and play fife-and-drum music, but the Caribs, either feeling threatened or simply finding the music disagreeable, showered the ship with arrows and paddled off. It was an inauspicious start for musical syncretism in Trinidad and perhaps foreshadowed the fact that neither Spaniards nor Indians would play major roles in the island's subsequent musical culture.

The Spanish, indeed, took little interest in the island, and by the mid-1700s there were still few settlers on Trinidad. King Carlos III extended an invitation to Catholic French Caribbeans to resettle on the island, thereby attracting several thousand Frenchmen and their slaves from the Windward Islands, which had recently been conquered by the British. However, scarcely had the French immigrated to Trinidad to escape British Protestant rule when, in 1797, they found themselves subjects of the British, who took Trinidad, imposing an English colonial administration over what continued for a century to be a largely French and Afro-French creole population.

When the black former slaves deserted the plantations after emancipation in 1834–38, the British imported some 143,000 peasants from India to work the fields as indentured laborers. Along with them came handfuls of Portuguese, Chinese, Syrians, and even some Yoruba Africans. All of these groups gave Trinidad a rather cosmopolitan racial mixture, as is reflected in its place names, which are variously Amerindian (Chaguanas), Spanish

(San Fernando), French (Laventille), British (Belmont), East Indian (Fyz-abad), and however you choose to classify "Port of Spain."

Trinidadian national character, insofar as one can generalize, acquired a rather different hue from that of the other British colonies. The French creole cultural base, the relative prosperity, the brevity of the slave era, and the comparative mildness of British colonial rule in Trinidad seem to have favored the development of an easygoing national culture that prizes humor and fun over puritanism or pathos. If Jamaican "roots reggae" inclined toward expressions of suffering, underclass anger, and visions of messianic redemption, Trinidad's cultural heart lies more in irreverent and ribald calypsos and, above all, in Carnival, a two-month celebration of music, dance, partying, and various sorts of mass, bureaucratically managed fun.

Most of Trinidad's musical vitality and cultural dynamism has developed in spite of rather than because of British rule. Until well into the twentieth century, the colonial government, as elsewhere in the British West Indies, took little or no interest in education, preferring to spend its revenue on prisons; a 1797 law in Barbados explicitly forbade teaching slaves to read or write. The British, in their racism and Anglicizing zeal, tried further to stamp out everything they found distasteful or excessively foreign, from Chinese *whe-whe* games to neo-African religion and music.

In spite of such efforts, Trinidad remains host to a number of distinctly non-English music traditions. The music of the East Indians, who are now coming to outnumber blacks and constitute the largest demographic group, is considered in chapter 9. Spanish musical influence, deriving more from interaction with neighboring Venezuela than from early colonial rule, persists in the form of a Christmastime music called parang. Parang is traditionally performed by troupes of amateurs (*parranda* in Spanish) who, like their counterparts in Puerto Rico and elsewhere, go from house to house, partying, singing, and playing guitar- and mandolin-type instruments (here, *bandolin* and the Venezuelan *cuatro*). This music, which closely resembles the Venezuelan *joropo* (a Hispanic-derived folk-song genre), is still widely popular in areas of Trinidad. Even though neither the singers nor the listeners speak Spanish, Trinidadians throng to Yuletide functions to socialize, drink ginger beer, and dance ballroom-style to parang's syncopated rhythms, dulcet strings, and exotic-sounding Spanish texts. Indeed, far from dying out, parang has been flourishing since the 1960s, invigorated by amateur competition networks. (As we will see, there are competitions for just about every kind of music in Trinidad, making for a very lively musical culture.)

Another distinctive musical tradition is that associated with the syncretic Orisha religion, or Shango, evidently brought mostly by the 9,000 indentured Yorubans who immigrated in the mid-1800s. Like its counterparts in Cuba and elsewhere, Shango centers on ceremonies in which Yoruba deities (orishas) are honored through dance and music, the music consisting primarily of chants in Yoruba or archaic patois, accompanied by a drum trio. (Neither the songs, rhythms, nor drums seem to have much in common with those of the Yoruba-derived Cuban Santería or Brazilian Candomblé.) The British did their best to ban Orisha worship, and the threads of tradition—including, for example, knowledgeable singers and drummers—had grown weak by the 1970s. Hindu deities and East Indian worshipers had also found places in Orisha religion. Nevertheless, the religion has undergone something of a revival in recent years, although it remains a rather private phenomenon, with little presence in public culture. Elements of Orisha worship, including possession trance, are also found in the music and religious practices of Spiritual Baptists (Shouters), which resemble in some respects Afro-Protestant faiths like Jamaican Revival Zion.

Another surviving African-influenced tradition is bongo dancing, in which participants take turns dancing in the center of a ring while others sing or play drums (as in Puerto Rican bomba and Cuban rumba). Although once common at wakes, the genre is practiced only in isolated communities nowadays. Other distinctive traditions survive in Tobago, which, as its residents would attest, should not be seen as a mere miniature slice of Trinidad. In addition to creole dances like "heel and toe," these traditions include the "tambrin" band shown on the next page.

THE DEVELOPMENT OF CALYPSO AND CARNIVAL

As interesting as such folk traditions are, by far the most characteristic, prominent, and popular musical culture of the country is that of calypso and Carnival, as developed primarily by lower-class Afro-Trinidadians since the 1700s. Calypso has always had its counterparts, audiences, and performers elsewhere in the West Indies, but it is in Trinidad and Tobago that calypso and Carnival have flourished the most.

While many of the early roots of calypso—including the origin of the word—remain unclear, Trinidadian scholars have reconstructed much of the genre's history. By the 1780s, the word "*cariso*" had appeared, denoting some sort of satirical, extemporized creole song, but modern calypso emerged somewhat later as the product of a set of diverse musical influences. These included, in varying manners and degrees, the *belair* (a generic term

Tambrin band, Culloden, Tobago, 2004 (Ken Bilby)

Shango drummers at a *palais* near Port of Spain, Trinidad, playing (from left to right) omelé, iyá (or "cutter"), bo, and shaker (Jocelyne Guilbault)

for various French creole songs), the *lavway* (from "*la voix*," a masquerade procession song), neo-African genres like juba and bamboula, British ballads, Venezuelan string-band music, other West Indian creole song types, and the calinda (kalinda), which was associated with stick fighting. Stick fighting was a popular pastime among lower-class blacks in which two opponents, backed by supporters and musicians from rival plantations or neighborhoods, would fight with light, yard-long canes until blood was drawn. Each gang featured a flamboyant lead singer called the "chantwell," who would preface the fight with songs boasting of his or her team's skill and lewdly insulting the adversaries. The fight then proceeded with drum accompaniment (in a manner similar to Cuban *maní* and Brazilian *capoeira*).

By the second half of the nineteenth century, the diverse genres described earlier—along with camboulay (French, *cannes brulees*), a re-creation of a fire drill accompanied by drumming—came to be centered in pre-Lenten Carnival. Carnival had started as a dainty festival in which the French aristocrats would don frivolous masks and pay social calls. The planters allowed their slaves to celebrate in their own fashion, and by the mid-1800s, as in Cuba, lower-class (*jamette*; from the French *diamétre*) blacks had come to dominate the event, with most British and French folk retreating in fear and scorn to their homes. Jamette Carnival soon took on its own character, with its rowdy street dancing, camboulay processions, stick fights, and masquerade troupes ("mas bands") featuring revelers in snappy sailor duds, phony military regiments, and folkloric characters like ghoulish Jab-Jabs and stilt-walking Moko Jumbies.

The British authorities, ever fearful of a Haitian-type rebellion and dismayed by the brawls often provoked by the stick fights, banned camboulay in the early 1880s. In the process, they provoked bloody riots in which skilled stick fighters more than once put the lightly armed, fumble-footed policemen to run. Nevertheless, the ban on drumming was enforced, as is related in one early calypso: "Can't beat me drum in me own native land." From that time until the present, Carnival evolved as a site of contention between its lower-class Afro-Trinidadian celebrants and the bourgeois and administrative reformers who have sought somehow to control, co-opt, or cleanse it. In this vein, a local journal in 1884 denounced the "bawdy language and gestures" of dancing women in Carnival, just as newspapers do more than a century later.

CALYPSO IN COLONIALISM

By 1900, Carnival music was coalescing into two main types. One was that of the mas (masquerade) bands, in which some two or three dozen costumed revelers, led by a chantwell, would sing rowdy call-and-response chants.

Stick-fighting calinda bands and their chantwells also roamed the streets, looking for trouble. Because drums were strictly forbidden, such processions until the late 1930s often came to be accompanied by a "tamboo-bamboo" (tambor-bamboo) ensemble of bamboo tubes struck with sticks. While the biggest processions took place in Port of Spain, smaller groups cultivated Carnival contests, plays, and songs throughout the island.

Meanwhile, some of the more formalized mas bands started erecting tapia huts in which members would prepare their costumes and practice their songs, as led by the chantwells. Soon enough, such "tents" were attracting visitors and, subsequently, charging nominal admission fees, as well. As the chantwell tent songs grew more formalized and soloistic, they started to be called "calypso," which thus developed as a more elaborate, text-oriented song performed for seated audiences in large tents erected for the occasion.

The period from 1900 to 1930 saw the rapid refinement, institutionalization, and commercialization of this new form of entertainment. By the 1920s, local merchants, liquor companies, civic committees, and enterprising singers were setting up tents throughout Trinidad as commercial enterprises. Audiences paid a small admission fee to cheer or mercilessly heckle the amateur calypsonians competing for cash prizes in contests judged by local aficionados. Particularly influential in the music's development were the innovations of singer and entrepreneur Chieftain Walter Douglas, who from 1921 would set

"Ole' Mas"—Carnival in 1888 (*Illustrated London News*)

up a fancy tent in a bourgeois neighborhood and, using a genteel-sounding
Venezuelan-style string band, promoted sophisticated "oratorical" calypsos
rather than lewd, calinda-type ditties. (These calypsos were often called *sans
humanité*—loosely, "without mercy"—for the stock, semi-nonsense derivative phrase *santimanitey* that often punctuated verses.)

Calypso evolved rapidly under such conditions. String and brass instruments replaced the noisy street-band ones, and solo singing with refrain
replaced the calinda-style call-and-response format. Early calypsonians continued to use snippets from responsorial calindas, Shango songs, and assorted
creole folk songs, but most came to rely on a set of familiar, major-key stock
tunes that were essentially English in character. (Many Trinidadians prefer to
ascribe an African origin to calypso, as suggested by the West African term
"*kaiso.*") Singers adopted bombastic sobriquets and transferred the calinda
boasting tradition to the calypso stage, specializing in improvised verbal
picong duels (from the French *piquant*). French creole patois, which had
predominated until 1900, quickly died out as calypsonians like Lord Executor tried to outdo one another in their displays of pompous rhetoric. While
schoolteachers fulminated against their students' fondness for "long-winded
words and high-flown phrases," calypsonians matched their wits and vocab-
ularies, as later parodied by Mighty Sparrow in his "Well-Spoken Moppers":

> Pompomloomically speaking you're a pussyistic man,
> most elaquitably full of shitification.

The subject matter of calypsos broadened accordingly, encompassing commentary on current events, picaresque tales, and lewd double entendres, as
well as boasts and insults. Ribaldry and sarcasm remained the genre's mainstay,
and the lyrics continued to show delight in mocking pretensions, exposing
elite scandals, and ridiculing upper-class women. A favorite topic has always
been the complications caused by the hoary Trini male custom of maintaining
one or more "deputies," or mistresses, along with a wife. In this vein is the
evergreen "Shame and Scandal in the Family," first composed by Sir Lancelot
and revised in the '60s by Lord Melody. In each of this song's first three verses,
a young man asks his father for permission to marry a different woman. In
each case, the father forbids the marriage, stating that his prospective bride is
his sister, "but your mamma don't know." Finally, in the last verse, the young
man appeals to his mother, who replies, "Your father ain't your father, but
your father don't know."

For their part, calypsonians (or "kaisonians") came to enjoy considerable
notoriety, being alternately denounced and celebrated for their irreverent
music and indolent, hedonistic lifestyle. While the quintessential calypsonian

shunned work and managed to be gainfully shacked up with a supporting mistress, most found mere survival to be a challenge, since they could perform professionally only two months a year. To this day, few calypsonians have been able to support themselves solely through their art. Hence, Lord Executor, when not singing, was a petty clerk; Poser was a bus conductor; and Short Pants and Chalkdust taught school for many years. Some calypsonians, including the Mighty Sparrow himself, emigrated, returning only for Carnival season.

In the 1930s (what some call the "golden age" of calypso), Decca and RCA Victor started producing records of artists like Atilla the Hun and Roaring Lion, recorded mostly in New York. Although the records sold well in the Caribbean, the United States, and even Africa, the artists received more fame than money, since most of the profits stayed with the record companies or with entrepreneurs like bandleader-impresario Lionel Belasco. The most celebrated case involved the Andrews Sisters' early 1940s recording of Lord Invader's "Rum and Coca Cola," which sold some 5 million copies in the United States. Decca and the Andrews Sisters made the song famous; they also made the money. Lord Invader and the enterprising Belasco successfully sued the American publishers of the song, although Invader, in true calypsonian style, frittered away his settlement and died broke.

As Carnival and calypso's prominence as a vehicle for the vox populi grew, so did the controversies surrounding the music. Should the colonial authorities try vigorously to control and limit it, or should they accept it as a boost to tourism and business and a way for the lower classes to let off steam? Should ribald and politically oppositional calypsos be tolerated or repressed? Which mas processions should be supported—the unruly downtown ones or the bureaucratically controlled ones of Port of Spain's Savannah Park? How should factors of originality, poetry, melody, and presentation be weighed in judging calypso competitions? And how should the judges be selected?

Behind such administrative controversies lay the more profound struggle of Trinidadians to survive. Carnival merriment notwithstanding, many Trinidadians continued to live in abject poverty, and the colonial government remained committed more to the masses' exploitation than to their welfare. As Patrick Jones (Lord Protector) sang in 1920:

> We are ruled with the iron hand;
> Britain boasts of democracy, brotherly love, and fraternity,
> but British colonists have been ruled in perpetual misery.

Indeed, the pious British praises of human rights and freedom of speech did not apply in the colonies, where any sort of oppositional discourse, such as Marxist or black-nationalist Garveyite literature, was rigorously banned. Attempts by mine and farm workers to organize were brutally crushed, and while the British maintained a facade of parliamentary government, labor leaders like Uriah Butler were kept out of power.

Censorship of calypsos reached a peak during the 1930s. Any song criticizing the state or dealing with Afro-Trinidadian culture or religion was subject, however unpredictably, to banning. Calypsonians were required to submit their lyrics to censorship offices before singing them, and policemen were posted in tents to monitor performances. Tents hosting objectionable songs could be shut down and singers' licenses revoked. Shipments of allegedly subversive records pressed in New York were dumped in the sea, and in general calypso's role as a mouthpiece of popular sentiment was severely curbed.

Such restraints, along with the prevailing hegemony of imperial ideology, partially explain what may seem by modern standards to be the rather low sociopolitical consciousness of most calypso before the 1970s. Many calypsos were obsequiously loyalist, especially during World War II. Some praised the British for the emancipation of slaves, forgetting that the English were the most aggressive of all slave importers in the previous two centuries. Several singers righteously endorsed Britain's stated opposition to the 1936 Italian invasion of Abyssinia, not knowing that the British had secretly sanctioned the act. Few songs displayed any sense of positive racial consciousness, instead ridiculing people as "black and ugly," reinforcing negative stereotypes about Orisha worship, and presenting the ideal woman as rich, white, and stupid. As is discussed later, representations of women were especially unenlightened.

Only a handful of singers had the integrity, vision, and temerity to challenge the norm and voice genuinely progressive sentiments. Particularly prominent among these was Raymond Quevedo (Atilla the Hun, 1892–1962), who, aside from being a leading calypsonian for nearly half a century, was an indefatigable labor leader and legislator. While Atilla failed to transcend the sexism of his era, many of his songs presented the common man's point of view and, from the 1950s, explicitly called for independence.

The World War II years and the establishment of two large U.S. military bases brought an unprecedented prosperity to many Trinidadians, including calypsonians. While several thousand locals earned their first decent wages working at the bases, enthusiastic and relatively affluent GIs filled the calypso tents at Carnival time. Meanwhile, however, calypsonians watched with dismay as local women forsook their company for that of the free-spending GIs. Lord Invader's 1943 classic "Rum and Coca Cola" relates how his girlfriend, along with her mother and sisters, drove off with some soldiers:

> They bought rum and Coca Cola, way down Point Cumana,
> both mother and daughter working for the Yankee dollar.

With the end of the war and the departure of the GIs, many women had no option but to return to the sweet-talking, unemployed calypsonians. The Mighty Sparrow's immortal "Jean and Dinah" captured the mood:

> Jean and Dinah, Rosita and Clementina,
> On the corner posing, bet your life it's something exciting
> And if you catch them broke you can get 'em all for nothing
> Yankee's gone and Sparrow take over from now.[1]

This song also illustrates the primary rule of scansion for calypso, which is that you can put as many or as few syllables in a line as you want.

The 1950s were a fertile decade for calypso. The "Young Brigade" of Lord Kitchener (1922–2000) and Lord Melody was in full swing. In 1957, the Trinidad government, seeking both to promote tourism and cultivate grassroots support, established what has evolved into the National Carnival Commission, which sought to organize and promote Carnival festivities and replaced the local tent contests with a national Calypso Monarch competition. With greater freedom of expression and impending independence, some calypsos both reflected and promoted a greater sociopolitical awareness. In 1955, Atilla, for example, denounced the racism of the *Trinidad Guardian* newspaper's beauty-queen contest:

> For this *Guardian* competition
> is nothing but real discrimination.
> One thing in this world will never be seen
> is a dark-skinned girl as Carnival Queen.

More significantly, the decade—and particularly, the year 1956—saw the emergence of perhaps the two most important figures in modern Trinidadian culture. One was Eric Williams, "the Doctor," the brilliant scholar, charismatic orator, and prime minister who dominated his party (the People's National Movement, or PNM) and the nation's politics in general until his death in 1981. The other was Francisco Slinger, better known as Mighty Sparrow, who won the Calypso Monarch contest in 1956 at age twenty-one and continued for decades to be the genre's most unfailingly excellent performer. The two figures are further linked in that Williams owed more than a little of his popularity to Sparrow's eloquent support.

Mighty Sparrow was long the measure of the ideal calypsonian. Possessed of a strong, sure voice, he sang and performed well. He was prolific, managing to release an LP every year when most singers can barely muster two songs. His melodies were simple and effective while adhering to the typical sing-songy calypso style. Most important, his lyrics (some of which he acknowledged to have been written by a collaborator) were consistently clever, pithy, and catchy; many have become so familiar as to constitute a body of modern West Indian folklore in themselves. He is a master of the art of being ribald without being vulgar.

Although Sparrow is not a profound sociopolitical thinker, his 'topical commentaries often seemed to capture the mood of the nation, and he did not hesitate to criticize Eric Williams on occasion. In 1957, fresh from his first Monarch victory, he successfully organized a boycott of the Savannah Dimanche Gras competition to demand better pay for contest winners. He went on to win the Road March (the most frequently played song, chosen each year at Carnival) six times and the Monarch competition seven times before retiring from the contests in 1974. In 1992, when Carnival was first broadcast internationally via satellite, he reentered the Monarch competition and again won the prize—cash and a car. (The next year, however, he lost to Chalkdust, who almost missed the finals when his own car broke down in central Trinidad. As the show started late, he arrived just in time to perform and win the prize—a much needed new car.)

Sparrow's running *picong* duels with the older Lord Melody delighted audiences throughout the 1950s and '60s. A typical exchange went:

Sparrow:
Well, Melody, come close to me.
I will tell you plain and candidly,
don't stop and turn around and smile
because you have a face like a crocodile.

Melody:
Sparrow, you shouldn't tell me that at all,
I used to mind you when you were small.
Many nights I used to mash your head
in crossing to go to your mother's—![2]

Sparrow was still going strong until the late 1990s. When in 1993 the calypsonian Ras Shorty I's moralizing song "That Eh Enough" criticized Sparrow's still libidinous image as inappropriate to a man his age, Sparrow retorted wittily with "The More [Girlfriends] the Merrier," recalling Shorty's celebrated hedonistic days (as Lord Shorty) before his conversion to Rastafari. Despite the renown of a figure like Sparrow, in the annual calypso competition one's status is only as good as that year's song, and the playing field is level enough to include all newcomers.

MODERN CALYPSO AND CARNIVAL

With independence in 1962, calypso and Trinidadian history entered a new chapter. Inspired by the Civil Rights Movement in the United States, a vigorous local Black Power movement arose, nearly toppling the PNM government in 1970. At the same time, the increasing prominence of East Indians in the country's economic and cultural life has obliged all Trinidadians to recognize the profoundly multicultural nature of their national identity. The biggest development was the unprecedented prosperity brought by the formation of OPEC in 1973, which exponentially increased the profits from local oil reserves, and by a concurrent rise in sugar prices. Under Williams's guidance, in the course of the ten-year boom much money was wasted, and long-term planning was bungled, but most Trinidadians, whether through hard work, trickle-down economics, or civil-service sinecures, came to enjoy an essentially bourgeois standard of living. Throughout the island, the old "trash-house" shanties were replaced by modern concrete houses, often complete with TV and carport.

The era has been eventful for calypso, as well. By 1970, calypso was on the defensive against reggae and R&B, but at the same time it was revitalized by the new social and musical movements. Stylistically, the main calypso-related development was the advent of soca. In 1977, Lord Shorty (who stood six feet, four inches tall) set out to improve on calypso's customary bouncy, slightly ragged, but basically bland and generically Caribbean accompaniment patterns. He and arranger Ed Watson came up with a composite pattern they called "soca" (or "sokah," to reflect the East Indian influence), which, in a loosely standardized form, has been the norm in most calypso since. The chorus of soca artist Arrow's 1983 "Hot Hot Hot" (later covered by Buster Poindexter and, in Hindi, by Babla-Kanchan) typifies the soca beat, as schematically represented in Musical Example 17.

The terms "soca" and "calypso" are sometimes used somewhat interchangeably, but "soca" is best used specifically to distinguish dance music, as opposed to calypso proper, whose essence remains the text. Soca lyrics are usually short and inconsequential (unless one considers repeated calls to "wine on a bumsie" to be of literary significance), and the typical song consists of a

Musical Example 17. A typical soca rhythm

series of catchy vocal hooks. The usual theme of soca songs is "jam and wine," which denotes not an aperitif but "party and dance." In particular, "wining" is now the predominant West Indian up-tempo dance style, whose essence is a pneumatic pelvic pumping, ideally executed in synchronicity with an adjacent "winer," whether front-to-back, front-to-front, or back-to-back. It is fun and good exercise, as well. Soca dancing often has a collective character, as dancers respond to singers' calisthenic commands to "jump up" or "get something and wave."

Soca's popularity has sharpened the split between, on the one hand, dance music—designed for parties, mas processions, and the Road March prize— and, on the other hand, lyric-oriented calypso, a somewhat more cerebral genre confined to the tents and aimed at the Calypso Monarch trophy. In the 1994 carnival, the dichotomy was institutionalized with the establishment of separate competition categories for soca and calypso. Accordingly, the gamut of calypso controversies now includes the complaints of those who believe that mindless soca, along with imported pop, is drowning out calypso proper. The veteran kaisonian Chalkdust voiced the purist school of thought in several songs, as in his prize-winning 1993 calypso "Kaiso in the Hospital":

> The young ran amuck, they cursed in the worst way,
> drugs and sex they glorified.
> They called themselves Rock, Rap, Zouk, and Reggae,
> And Kaiso's house they occupied.[3]

Such criticisms notwithstanding, most young Trinidadians enjoy soca for what it is—namely, an exuberant, unpretentious dance music. Moreover, in reintroducing the role of dance music in Carnival and playing mas, soca filled a vacuum that has existed ever since calypso evolved as a tent-based idiom and listening-oriented steel bands replaced the processional tamboo-bamboo and biscuit-tin bands. Further, many Trinis have looked to soca as the country's hope for a music that, like dancehall, could make it onto the international market. (And many soca songs nowadays feature a gravel-voiced dancehall interlude.) So far, however, neither soca nor calypso proper has attracted more than ephemeral popularity outside the West Indian market.

Calypso's text orientation is both its strength and its weakness. The tradition of penning verses about current events makes calypso a uniquely dynamic form of grassroots folklore, closely attuned to people's daily lives, rather than a mere reiteration of sentimental cliches. However, this very specificity limits calypso's appeal to the here and now. A song about a petty corruption trial or a cuckolded minister in Port of Spain can delight local audiences at the time, but it may be forgotten within months and will mean nothing to listeners in neighboring Grenada, not to mention in the United States. Further, calypso verses are too long for pop formats, which demand short, snappy lyrics and danceable refrains.

Accordingly, the calypso recording industry has been a small-time affair, consisting until recently of a few rudimentary studios in Port of Spain and storefront labels like Strakers in Brooklyn. Distribution has been informal, at best, and as late as the '70s even Mighty Sparrow could be seen selling records out of the trunk of his car on a street corner in Port of Spain. So most albums are still slapped together as seasonal throwaway music, produced as tourist souvenirs in batches of a few thousand and often financed by the artist or by merchants whose ads plaster the backs of the CD covers. The biggest record store in Port of Spain, Rhyner's, is a modest hole in the wall, half of which is devoted to greeting cards. If Trinis buy music, it will be pirated CDs and cassettes of dancehall and R&B sold by enterprising street vendors in the "informal sector" of the economy. Such piracy has further hampered the development of a soca-calypso record industry. In the early 1990s, however, the situation improved somewhat with the construction of a first-class recording studio in Trinidad by Robert Amar and another in Barbados by the Guyanese producer Eddy Grant.

Despite such signs of progress, the mass media in most of the West Indies remain dominated by the rap, R&B, and Jamaican dancehall marketed by powerful multinationals and local pirate vendors. Calypso is mostly heard during Carnival season—after which, it's back to Beyoncé and Beenie Man. Local attitudes perpetuate such compartmentalization: Many West Indians feel saturated with calypso by the end of Carnival season. And as one Trinidadian lamented, "If my mother hears me playing a soca record after Ash Wednesday,

she shouts, 'Shut that devil's music off—it's Lent now!' " American program-
ming also dominates television, especially since local stations cannot afford
to produce the same sorts of slick shows. In the song "Satellite Robber," by
the Trinidadian calypsonian Commentator (Brian Honoré), the satellite disc
boasts:

> I'm here to rip out your heart, tear your culture apart,
> make you worship the American flag.

The next verse responds:

> I said please, Mr. Robber, I beg you remember
> I am independent since 1962.
> He said "Don't aggravate me,
> when it coming to TV, it is I who control you."

In spite of indifferent media support and the competition from rap, reggae,
R&B, and "jam-and-wine" soca, calypso remains vital. Now as before, calypso
is constantly in the news; as the recognized "people's voice," it is forever
provoking outrage and delight, eliciting public denunciations by offended
politicians and generating endless newspaper editorials and letters. The '80s
and '90s saw the emergence of talented and dynamic new artists who have
brought new levels of lyrical and musical sophistication to the art. Particularly
prominent since the 1970s are Chalkdust (Hollis Liverpool), celebrated for his
sociopolitical commentaries and his rather old-timey harangues against soca,
and David Rudder (b. 1953), an eclectic, intelligent, rock-oriented composer
and bandleader who appeared on the scene in 1986. Liverpool, who earned
a doctorate in ethnomusicology in 1993, is the author of a few books on
calypso; both he and Rudder have won the Monarch prize repeatedly. East
Indian singers like Rikki Jai and Drupatee Ramgoonai also entered the fray,
enriching the music with their own idiosyncratic Indianisms. Meanwhile, as
Jamaican dancehall becomes the favored music of Trinidadian youth, Carnival
season now includes several songs in a "ragga-soca" and "rapso" style, fusing
calypso and modern reggae. The state has also tried to revive the spontaneous
picong tradition by instituting an "ex-tempo" competition in which singers
have to improvise on themes pulled from a hat. The finalists then face each
other off, *picong*-style.

Calypso's text topics remain as varied and rich as ever. As always, their forte
is light social commentary and satire rather than, for example, the poignant
sentimentality of the bolero or the passionate intensity of "classic" reggae. In
customary fashion, many lyrics sing the praises of Carnival, steel drums, and calypso itself, sometimes berating other singers for their slackness and theatrical

gimmicks. Some songs take potshots at dancehall, which offends many because of its unmelodiousness, its frequent vulgarity, its foreign origin, and the earsplitting volume at which it was played in public minibuses until banned from them in 1994. As calypsonian Bally sang in his 1989 "Maxi Dub":

> The music live and me head on fire,
> Ah beg the driver play a little softer. . . .
> Ah wanted to cry cuz I couldn't hear soca.

Other calypso songs denounce racism, call for ethnic harmony, warn against drug abuse (e.g., Sparrow's "Coke Is Not It"), criticize the government, and lament the country's current economic decline. Despite state financing for the calypso competitions, songs do not hesitate to criticize the government, and if the government bans a song—as Basdeo Pandey's did with a Sugar Aloes song—that song's popularity is virtually guaranteed. Boasting and ribaldry persist, along with assorted miscellany. Rudder's 1993 "Dus' in deh Face" described the excitement of the pan contests at the Savannah fairgrounds, subtly using steel-band rivalry as a metaphor for the violence and crime besetting the recession-torn island. That year's calypso winner was Chalkdust, whose "Misconceptions" whimsically addressed the international satellite audience, including the verse:

> Michael Jackson, please come down here,
> there is a misconception you is fair.
> Come down and play mas with we and get back your color.

Even if such songs are forgotten by the following year, they perpetuate a unique tradition that itself remains contemporary by virtue of its very topicality.

Although the calypso and soca scenes are oriented toward solo stars, from Rudder to SuperBlue, recent years have seen the emergence of several independent soca bands, such as Xtatic, Krosfyah, and others. These bands don't fit into the Monarch competitions, but their musicianship may be higher than that of the ad hoc tent ensembles that accompany calypso singers, and they are accordingly popular.

WOMAN RISING

Trinidadian writers have commented extensively on the occasionally virulent sexism of traditional calypso.[4] From its inception, calypso has been a man's world, rooted in the macho boasting of the calinda chantwell, the ribaldry of the early tent scene, and male views on social norms in general. Among

Afro-Trinidadians, sociohistorical conditions have tended to promote temporary male–female liaisons as much as marriage and the accompanying sentiments of commitment and eternal love. Aside from the socially disruptive legacy of slavery, unemployment endemic in the later colonial period often led both men and women to avoid marital ties, which might burden either with an unproductive spouse. However, men, unlike women, enjoyed a public forum—calypso—where they could present their desires and double standards as a norm and an ideal. Hence, colonial-era calypsos often portrayed women as valuable only as meal tickets or as sexual playthings for the calypsonian stud, as in Mighty Duke's "Woop-Wap Man" ("woop, wap—next one!"). Calypsos traditionally ridiculed women as ugly, sexually infectious ("Don't Bathe in Elsie's River"), and forever trying to tie men down with obeah (black magic) or false accusations of paternity. The calypsonian Mighty Terror, for instance, sang:

> I black like jet and she just like tarbaby,
> still, Chinese children calling me daddy.

But the quintessential traditional calypsonian, even if so victimized by his faithless mate, would generally shun responsibility for the children he did sire—especially as he was more often than not unemployed and wholly dependent on whatever women he could charm. While glorifying motherhood in the abstract, calypsos showed little sympathy for the flesh-and-blood mothers struggling to raise fatherless children. (*Sans humanité* indeed!) "Sixteen Commandments," sung by Lord Shorty (before his conversion to Rastafari), is particularly explicit in its articulation of the male double standard. Warning his girlfriend to be faithful to him and not ask him for money, Shorty sings:

> If thou see me wid a nex' girl talkin', try and understand.
> Pass me straight like you ain't know me,
> let me have my woman.

Similarly, Atilla's "Women Will Rule the World" (1935) warns of women trying to improve their lot and competing with men for scarce jobs:

> I'm offering a warning to men this year:
> Of modern women beware.
> Even the young girls you cannot trust,
> for they're taking our jobs from us.
> And if you men don't assert control,
> women will rule the world.
> They say that anything that man can do
> they also can achieve too,
> and openly boast to do their part
> in literature and art.

You'll soon hear of them as candidates
for the President of the United States.
If women ever get the ascendancy,
they will show us no sympathy.
They will make us do strange things, goodness knows,
scrub floors and even wash clothes.
If these tyrants become our masters,
we'll have to push perambulators.

Goddess forbid! Indeed, poor Atilla would be spinning in his grave to see modern Trinidad with its female politicians, professors, and entrepreneurs—not to mention the female prime ministers that were elected in Great Britain and nearby Dominica.

To forestall such catastrophes, calypsos would often advise men how to deal with their women, as in "Turn Them Down," an old calypso revived by Sparrow in the 1970s:

Every now and then, cuff them down.
They'll love you long and they'll love you strong.
Black up dey eye, bruise up dey knee,
and they will love you eternally.

One antidote to such sexist manifestos would be for women to enter the calypso arena and speak for themselves—for example, as to whether they do indeed love being "cuffed down." Men traditionally have been ambivalent about the presence of women in calypso, as in the case of the New York-based entertainer Daphne Weekes (d. 2004), who encountered open hostility from other musicians for having the chutzpah to lead her own band. But although calypso may be inherently male in its emphasis on braggadocio, women have in fact established a place in it, now institutionalized in Trinidad's Woman Rising competition. Such singers as Calypso Rose and Denyse Plummer have earned their own audiences and awards, in many cases expressing support for women who have faced beatings, insults, and exploitation. Thus, Easlyn Orr sings "Woman Respect Yourself," while Singing Francine answers the "treat 'em rough" philosophy with "Run Away" (1979):

Dog does run away, child does run away,
woman does run away when man treating them bad. . . .
Woman, put two wheels on your heels.

Similarly, Lady Iere's "Love Me or Leave Me" became a slogan for abused West Indian women:

You gotta love me or leave me, or live with Miss Dorothy.
The time is too hard for me to mind a man that's bad.

In general, since the sociopolitical awakening of the 1970s, flagrantly sexist calypsos have gone out of style, and male calypsonians have often expressed more appreciative attitudes toward women. A trendsetter in this regard was Lord Kitchener's classic road march of 1973, "Flag Woman," honoring the banner-waving women who animatedly lead Carnival bands:

> Without an experienced flag woman,
> your band will have no control
> your music will have no soul.

Similarly, 1993 found Mighty Terror voicing quaint but timely sentiments in his "Tribute to All Housewives":

> Every man should assist his wife
> and let the love be lasting for life. . . .
> Don't beat you wife, take this tip from me.

By this period, the calypso judging panels would generally include at least one woman, who would presumably be less tolerant of old-style sexist cant. Female calypsonians can compete not only in the Calypso Queen competition (a smaller counterpart to the Calypso Monarch), but also in the Calypso Monarch itself. Most successful in this forum has been Denyse Plummer, a dynamic entertainer who, although most devoted to soca, has won the Calypso Monarch prize repeatedly—after having overcome public misgivings about her bourgeois white social background as well as her gender. Meanwhile, most of the self-contained soca bands feature women singers and dancers, and recent years have seen the emergence of several "soca divas" like Denise Belfon, Alison Hinds, and the Road March winners Sanelle Dempster and Faye Ann Lyon.

Sexual politics aside, calypso continues to delight in erotic puns and euphemisms, where the emphasis is on whimsical wordplay rather than sexual politics. As in other Caribbean genres, practically any ostensibly trivial or obscure song lyric can be assumed to be some sort of sexual double entendre, especially if the actual text appears to be totally innocent. A typical format is for the verses to set up a catchy refrain with a double entendre. For example, in Drupatee Ramgoonai's "Lick Down Me Nani," the verses describe an encounter between a truck and the singer's "nani" (in Hindi, "grandmother"), setting up the title line's pun, meaning either "[the truck] ran over my granny" or "lick my [pu]nanny." Or take, for example, Crazy's 1990s hit "Paul, Your Mother Come," which was banned from the airwaves. Why? Because audiences immediately recognized the refrain as a thinly disguised "Paul, your mother's cunt," and they would gleefully sing it that way at dance concerts.

Cassette piracy in Trinidad, the bane of the recording industry (Peter Manuel)

It would be a mistake to denounce such juvenilia as "sexist objectification" or a degrading insult. It's just pure whimsy, the latest in a long and hoary Caribbean tradition.

THE CARNIVAL CONTEXT

Since 1900, Trinidad Carnival has evolved into a felicitous balance of state-funded, bureaucratically organized competitions and fetes, on the one hand, and various sorts of informal merrymaking—or, to use a favorite Trinidadian word, "bacchanal"—on the other. The bacchanal comprises ad hoc partying, numerous free, open-air dance concerts, and more intimate amusements often realized nocturnally in parks, fields, and other normally public places. All these events are framed by the rhythm of the Carnival schedule itself, including the various competitions. These now include the Calypso Monarch and Calypso Queen (and junior counterparts), mas band of the year, Costume King and Queen, Road March, Panorama (the national steel-band competition), Junior Panorama, the privately funded Soca Monarch and Indian-oriented Chutney-Soca Monarch, and lesser musical categories like ex-tempo and rapso.

In a tropical country without clearly differentiated winter and summer, it is Carnival that provides the seasonal reference point for the rest of the year. Carnival is like a big ocean roller that gathers momentum and size from the Christmas season on and then breaks, foaming and crashing, over the urban streets for two riotous late-February days. The rest of the year is a period of recovery, reminiscing, and gradual preparation for the next year.

For calypsonians, preparation may commence as early as late summer, when singers start preparing their songs. Ideally, according to custom, the lyrics and melodies to these are composed by the calypsonian, who enjoys the status of a grassroots spokesperson rather than an air-headed puppet of a producer. Traditionally, a few calypsonians, like Kitchener, have been skilled composers and musicians, while most may not be. In recent decades, calypsonians have increasingly purchased songs outright from composers like Merchant; problems ensue if the same song is sold to more than one singer. Even if the singer composes his or her own lyrics and tune, he or she generally contracts an arranger like Leston Paul or Frankie McIntosh to write up a score for the ensemble that will accompany the song in the tents.

By Thanksgiving, many calypsonians have produced low-budget recordings that either are for sale or are distributed as demos to radio stations for airplay. Trinidadians by this time are eager to hear how calypsonians will sum up the political events, social issues, and scandals of the previous year. Audiences are also geared up for the proverbial bacchanal, and the new "jam-and-wine" soca tunes by stars like SuperBlue soon become familiar via airplay, record sales, and dance concerts around the country. As Carnival season gets into full swing, music thrives in the twin venues of the calypso tents and the fetes and parties featuring either live bands or deejayed sound systems.

Meanwhile, the leaders of the mas bands have decided on a theme and designed the costumes that participants will wear. By January, they are "mas-producing" them out of fabrics, wire, sequins, and other materials. Those who wish to "play mas"—that is, join a mas band—can visit the mas camp offices, view photos of the costumes, and pay a deposit for the outfit, which they will pick up on Carnival Monday. As for the foreign tourists, who number at least 100,000 every year, those who want to play mas can order the costumes on line, as all the major mas bands now boast fancy websites. (Peter Minshall's, for example, is at www.callaloo.co.tt.) Since the oil-boom years of the '70s—and with the increasing purchasing power of working women, who constitute more than 80 percent of masqueraders—"pretty mas" costumes have grown increasingly elaborate and expensive, even though they end up in the trash on Ash Wednesday (except for the shoes). But the expense of the costume (often around $120—about half a month's salary for many people) also excludes many lower-class women from the processions, such that mas has lost some of its *jamette* character.⁶

Revelers choose their mas bands according to various criteria. Those who want to be part of a heady performance-art street theater may gravitate toward Peter Minshall (discussed later), but since his costumes are often heavy and unwieldy, those who want to jam and wine their way down the street may opt for bands like Poison and Legend, with skimpier, bikini-type outfits. Those bands are also dominated by women—especially middle- and upper-class women—who can use the occasion to show off their gym-honed hard bodies. Women also thoroughly dominate other bands, like those of Harold Saldenha and Irvin McWilliams. Some revelers choose mas bands for the music, as aside from the sound-system trucks, processions may feature hot bands like Charlie's Roots or Xtatic. Other mas bands have traditional followers among certain neighborhoods or, to some extent, ethnicities and social classes. East Indians, for instance, tend to gravitate toward Peter Minshall and Poison.

Meanwhile, the mas band directors are designing and constructing two huge costumes for the Costume King and Queen competition. These extraordinary works of art are not unveiled until Dimanche Gras, at which point they are paraded on stage, each borne by a single person. After Carnival, they might be shipped around to other island festivities, but sooner or later, rather than finding a home in some huge warehouse museum, they are junked. By January, the "pan" (steel-drum) bands have also reassembled, cleaned off and retuned their instruments, and are practicing one or more current songs chosen and arranged by their leaders. Almost all of this activity, involving considerable organization, self-discipline, and expense, is undertaken by the people themselves, without any significant state assistance. The government's main role is to organize and finance some of the infrastructure for the final events.

By late January, the calypso and pan competitions are under way. In weekend concerts, competing calypsonians, from rank amateurs to big names, perform two songs apiece in "tents" (nowadays, theaters and clubs) located around the island, accompanied by the tent's house band. Only some of the singers actually have commercial records out. Along with partying Trinis, panels of judges visit the tents, confer, and, on the basis of lyric, melody, and presentation, pick twenty-four finalists who perform the weekend before Carnival. From that group, eight finalists are chosen to compete, presenting two songs each, at Port of Spain's Savannah fairgrounds on Dimanche Gras, the ("Big") Sunday before Ash Wednesday, which falls in late February or early March. The finals are witnessed either live or on TV by most of the population. The judges choose and announce a winner, or Calypso Monarch, invariably provoking both exuberant acclaim and outraged complaints from the public. In fact, the award process is increasingly regarded with cynicism as being manipulated by political and other non-aesthetic concerns, such that the emphasis in the calypso scene lies more in the tents than in the final competition.

Serious dance parties and bacchanal take place all weekend, but the formal (if that is the word) uncorking of Carnival itself begins with j'ouvert (joovay; from the French *jour overt*) at 2 A.M. on Monday. In j'ouvert, the most overt vestige of the "ole-mas," or *jamette cambouley*, revelers caked with painted mud or costumed as ghouls drink and cavort their way to dawn, accompanied by small steel bands and old-style drumming.

By mid-morning on Monday, j'ouvert's "dirty mas" revelers are mostly dispersed—or, perhaps, conked out on a sidewalk. Port of Spain's streets are now dominated by the "pretty mas" bands, whose participants, numbering in the tens of thousands, are starting to jam and wine or else "chip" (a sort of rhythmic stepping to the music) their way toward the Savannah. The processions include numerous steel bands, dance bands, and deejayed sound systems mounted on flatbed trucks, all pumping out the new soca hits at deafening volume and surrounded by throngs of dancers and revelers. As one Trinidadian put it, "What I love about Carnival is to be dancing madly in the street, to see some big minister jamming next to me and give him a big hug or pour beer on his head, whatever. Carnival is when we all really become one."

While this is going on, other officials posted at specific sites are taking note of which songs the bandleaders, disc jockeys, and steel bands—in response to audience enthusiasm—have selected as favorites. After tallying their observations, the observers announce the most frequently played song as the Road March of the year, whose composer receives a cash prize. Thus, while the Calypso Monarch is selected by judges, the winning Road March is the choice of the people themselves, although in the slightly different category of "jam-and-wine" dance music. (Kitchener and Sparrow have been the most frequent winners since the late '50s.)

For spectators, the focus of the procession is the immense mas groups, each of which is conceived and organized around some fanciful theme. Since the mid-twentieth century, winners have included such themes as "Imperial Rome," "Ye Saga of Merrie England," "Pacific Paradise," and "Bright Africa." A mas band often contains more than a thousand members, most wearing identical costumes; it also includes contestants for the Costume King and Queen prizes, who are dwarfed by the elaborate and huge costume that they arduously carry. Monday is a somewhat informal day for the mas processions, which can include both costumed and street-clothed revelers. Many people are only in "half-costume," since the outfits can be bulky, and it can be difficult to catch a maxi-taxi back home when you are dressed as a ten-foot banana. Tuesday is the proper "Day of the Bands," when only those in full costume can parade in the street, and onlookers can appreciate the extraordinary spectacle the color-coordinated bands present. Those offended by the sight of female bodies should stay at home, as the mas bands are thoroughly dominated by women, who delight in "getting on bad"—especially in front of cameras.

Since the mid-1970s, the most distinguished and controversial mas bandleader has been Peter Minshall, a Caucasian stage designer who lives and works in England, visiting his native Trinidad—like many others—only for Carnival. Minshall has a distinctive vision of mas as a work of conceptual art, a unique sort of gargantuan street theater, rather than merely a festive parade around some whimsical theme. His 1983 mas, titled "Mancrab/River," is representative. On the first day, his entourage—2,500 people strong—proceeded clad in spotless white robes, led by a pristine "washerwoman" figure. The next day, a monstrous, thirty-foot-high mechanical crab (that year's winning entry for the costume prize) killed the washerwoman, at which point all the other participants doused their white robes in colorful dyes, dramatizing man's destruction of nature. Such extravaganzas have won Minshall many fans, as well as several annual prizes. They have also sparked yet another controversy, raised by those who believe that his notions of high art and his penchant for the macabre and morbid are inconsistent with the spirit of Carnival.

Yet even Minshall's most ghoulish creations are subsumed in the larger hurly-burly of Carnival as a whole, with its overwhelmingly festive mood and its sheer plethora of events and competitions. These are generally scheduled roughly as follows, although changes sometimes occur:

Two weekends before Dimanche Gras: Calypso Queen
One weekend before Dimanche Gras: soca and calypso semi-finals,
    Panorama
The week before Dimanche Gras: Junior Calypso Monarch (schoolchildren)
Carnival weekend:
    Saturday: Kiddie Carnival, Soca Monarch
    Sunday (Dimanche Gras): Calypso Monarch, Costume King and Queen
    Monday: J'ouvert (2 A.M.); mas bands (often informal, "half-costume")
    Tuesday: "Day of the Bands" (i.e., mas bands in full costume and
        formation)
    (Ash Wednesday: lime at beach)

The Port of Spain Carnival is of course the biggest and most renowned, but smaller towns like Chaguanas, Couva, and Carapichaima stage their own regional festivities. These are much less grandiose, to be sure, but they also feature more of the traditional Carnival characters—stilt-walking Moko Jumbies, devilish Jab Molassies and Jab Jabs, Midnight Robbers, and sailors—which have tended to be eclipsed in Port of Spain by the collective and formalized "pretty mas" bands.

On the whole, there is nothing quite like Trinidad Carnival. Its popularity and importance can be gauged by the fact that the Monday and Tuesday events in Port of Spain generally draw about 700,000 participants and revelers, or about two-thirds of the entire country's population. For outsiders, it is a unique tourist attraction, while for most locals it is the focal reference point of the year, celebrating a national character based on fun, humor, and togetherness. As Mighty Sparrow sang in 1957:

> The biggest bacchanal is in Trinidad Carnival.
> Regardless of color, creed, or race,
> jump up and shake your waist.
> So jump as you mad, this is Trinidad;
> we don't care who say we bad.

STEEL BAND

Trinidad is internationally famous not only for calypso and Carnival but also as the home of the steel drum, or pan, as it is called. The invention of the steel drum is testimony to the ingenuity and creative perseverance of Afro-Trinidadians in the face of British cultural repression. As mentioned earlier, after the British banned the use of drums in Carnival mas and camboulay processions, revelers fashioned "tamboo-bamboo" ensembles by beating with sticks on bamboo tubes (and often on the heads of rival band members). The tamboo-bamboo bands combined neo–African-style call-and-response singing with lively, syncopated rhythms. In the early 1900s, innovators started to supplement the clackety-clack of the bamboo by beating on available pieces of metal, producing what one witness called "a veritable babel of sound from drums, tubs, triangles, buckets, bamboos and bottles."[6] As the vogue of "biscuit-tin bands" rapidly spread, Port of Spain residents learned that they had to chain down their garbage-can lids to prevent them from being stolen. By 1940, some of the bands had discarded the bamboo altogether in favor of louder metal objects.

Oral histories differ as to who was responsible for the next step, but around 1939 someone discovered that distinct pitches, rather than a simple, crude bang, could be sounded on an empty oil drum (of which there were plenty lying around) if the concave head was dented in a certain way. By the early

Masquerader in Brooklyn (Peter Manuel)

1940s, ingenious enthusiasts in Port of Spain's lower-income neighborhoods like Laventille were learning how to dent and burn the heads to get three or four different pitches, enabling them to play simple bugle tunes and nursery rhymes. As avid experimentation ensued, the self-taught metallurgists figured out how to generate twenty-some pitches on pans so that they could play any melody they chose. The next step was to tune the steel drums in a given band to each other and to develop different classes of pans, including "boom pans" for bass, tenor or "cello pans" for harmony, and sharp-sounding ping-pong drums for melody.

Pan fever subsequently took hold of lower-class neighborhoods like East Dry River, Watertown, and Laventille as bands practiced incessantly and jubilantly took their music to the streets at all hours of the day and night. Activity peaked during Carnival, when the steel bands were often hired to accompany sailor-mas bands. As responsorial camboulay-style singing dropped out of the picture, the bands took to playing all sorts of tunes, from folk songs and calypsos to film tunes and even classical pieces. For panmen raised in slums and lacking any formal musical training, it became a matter of pride to play pieces by Schubert and Saint-Saëns as well as Sparrow and Swallow.

The British authorities tried to ban the steel bands because of the lowlife, "saga-boy" character of many of the bandsmen, the critics' view of the music as raucous cacophony, and the rowdy fights that often occurred when two bands encountered each other in the streets. (Such feuds were even waged from hospital beds after street brawls.) Policemen would often raid innocent rehearsals and, adding insult to injury, confiscate the drums and use them as garbage cans or flower pots. But dollar-laden tourists were soon coming to see the bands, and politicians were realizing that they could gain community support by patronizing them. A vehement public debate regarding the bands raged in newspapers, Parliament, and other forums. By the mid-'40s, a decision was made to try to wean the bands from violence by accommodating and legitimizing them. So they were incorporated into Carnival and into stage and folkloric shows, and a national ensemble, Trinidad All Steel Percussion Orchestray, or TASPO, was even sent to tour England in 1951. Upright Trinidadians continued to regard panmen as hoodlums, and brawls persisted until the early '60s. As one Trinidadian remarked, "If you were in the winning Panorama band, you didn't dare show your face in town for weeks." Nevertheless, by that time the bands had largely been coaxed out of feuding, had become an integral part of Carnival, and had been taken up avidly by upper-class "college-boys" and in other West Indian islands, as well.

In the subsequent decades, pan flourished as the state promoted it as a national symbol and established the Panorama competition in 1963 and businesses patronized ensembles, who changed their names accordingly—for example, to the Amoco Renegades. Steel-band activity became increasingly focused on Carnival, when large ensembles on wheeled racks or flatbed trucks—largely replacing the old "pansides" or pan-'round-the-neck groups—could march along with the mas bands. Accordingly, the formerly diverse repertoire largely gave way to renditions of current calypsos. In the 1980s, a late-summer

Steelband Music Festival was also institutionalized to provide another venue for the music.

Steel bands have long since outgrown their underworld associations and have developed into a unique form of amateur, collective music-making. Trinidad today hosts more than a hundred bands, from serious "adult" bands to school bands and small "stage sides" that do various sorts of commercial gigs like weddings and cruise-ship concerts. Many Trinidadian youths— especially girls–play in school bands, while other bands, including top ones like the Amoco Renegades, are sponsored by businesses. Some musicians manage to earn a living playing, but most need to "scrunt"—that is, struggle to make ends meet. The bands, far from being purely grassroots entities, have to rely on some sort of institutional or commercial support, as Trinis, although fond of pan music, will seldom pay to hear it. While the steel bands to some extent have also lost their intimate links to specific neighborhoods, their membership has also grown to include women, East Indians, white Trinis, and others who were once marginal to the scene.

Scattered around the country's towns are many dozens of pan yards where instruments are stored and played. In the two months before Carnival, the pan yards come alive as musicians rehearse nightly for up to eight hours. Generally, the band either hires an arranger or has its own, who provides an arrangement of a contemporary soca or calypso hit. The arranger must choose a song that lends itself well to steel-band rendition. Lord Kitchener was one calypsonian who composed his elaborate pieces with the steel bands in mind. The arranger must make the song sound fresh and original and must know how to get a clean and clear sound out of an ensemble of essentially similar-sounding instruments. Often, several bands will be performing versions of the same song—sometimes arranged by the same person for different bands. A few top bands, like Boogsie Sharpe's Phase II Pan Groove, may introduce original compositions, especially for the Steelband Music Festival, but audiences prefer to hear the familiar current hits. Sometimes, a song will be written for a steel band and also recorded by a singer as a promotional tool. Learning a song takes a long time, as band members do not read music and must learn by rote. Even a few of the leading pan arrangers cannot read music, but they nevertheless devise brilliantly intricate and driving arrangements. Spectators and supporters also turn out for rehearsals at the best yards to listen as the arrangements evolve and to refresh themselves with beer and aloo (potato) pies sold by vendors.

In Port of Spain's Carnival, the steel bands proceed along Queen's Park with the other mobile mayhem, stopping to perform in front of the judges' bandstand in the hope of making it to the Savannah semifinals. The pans

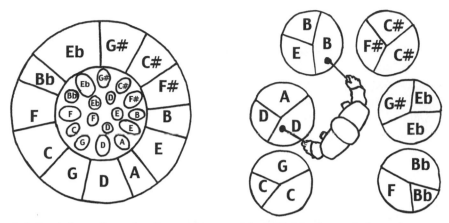

At left, pitch configuration for soprano pan (also called lead or melody pan); at right, configuration for six bass drums, with player

Bass steel drum set (Center for Traditional Music and Dance)

themselves are mounted on frames with wheels, so that the ensemble, which can number up to the decreed limit of 120 musicians, becomes like a huge ship, complete with various floats, racks, and a roof. Its prow is formed by the bass drums, some of which point outward like cannon. Mounted above the surrounding tenor, cello, and melody pans is the "engine room," a rhythm section consisting of drum kit, congas, and men beating brake drums and wheel hubs.

The focus of pan activity is the Panorama competition, whose finals take place in the Savannah stadium on the weekend preceding that of Dimanche Gras, and which the audience turns into a marathon party. If pan has lost some of its grassroots edge, top bands like Exodus and the Tropical Angel Harps generate tremendous enthusiasm among Trinidadians (especially Afro-Trinis), who love their national instrument and share the excitement generated by the music and by the intense rivalry between bands. With the Trinidad and Tobago government actively promoting steel bands and busying itself with such matters as standardizing tuning, pan music should be able to hold its own against the din of disc jockeys and dub.

CALYPSO AND CARNIVAL OUTSIDE TRINIDAD

West Indians living in countries other than Trinidad and Tobago often take justified umbrage at outsiders' tendency to identify calypso and Carnival exclusively with Trinidad. It is true that Trinidad is the primary crucible of calypso and that its Carnival is by far the biggest and most extravagant in the West Indies. But other Caribbean islands have played their own roles in calypso's evolution. First of all, such calypso as existed in the eighteenth and nineteenth centuries appears to have been part of an Afro-French creole culture spread thoughout the French Caribbean. Indeed, the first extant appearance of the word "*cariso*" refers to a singer from Martinique. Martinique was later the source of the tune of "Rum and Coca Cola," just as the Haitian folk song "Choucounne" provided the melody for "Yellow Bird." West Indian immigrants to the more affluent Trinidad have long enriched that island's music with their own traditions. And aside from the Grenada-born Sparrow, several major figures have emerged more recently in the calypso world who hail from other countries, including Arrow (Montserrat), Gabby and Red Plastic Bag (from Barbados), and Guyanese producer Eddy Grant.

Most West Indian countries also have their own versions of Carnival, of which some are recent gimmicks to attract tourists while others enjoy authentic grassroots popularity. The festivities on the island of Carriacou, as documented by Donald Hill, are typical. Old-style Carnival there commenced with informal calypso singing, family cambouly feasts, and stick fighting with calinda songs on Sunday night. Early Monday morning, a rowdy j'ouvert would take place to the accompaniment of steel bands. The rest of Monday and Shrove Tuesday would be devoted to traditional masquerade-band processions and "speech mas," in which two opposing orators (called *paywoes, shortness*, or kings), supported by local sidekicks, would hurl insults at each other and recite flowery speeches from Shakespeare (usually *Julius Caesar*) in a sort of Afro-Saxon call-and-response fashion. In recent decades, under Trinidadian influence, the calypso singing and mas processions have been organized into formal tent competitions held at schools.[7] With most of the various islands holding their own festivals, Carnival and calypso now thrive year-round, albeit in different locales, as in Nassau's Caribbean Muzik Festival, Barbados's Crop Over, and Antigua's Carnival—not to mention Toronto's Caribana festival and the late-August Carnival in Notting Hill, London. Top calypso and soca performers can try to support themselves by island-hopping after Trinidad's blowout.

Last but not least is another island: Long Island—or, more specifically, Brooklyn, which, as home to more than half a million West Indians, is the largest West Indian city outside Jamaica. Brooklyn's West Indian community has long been dynamic and distinguished, its members renowned (or by some, begrudged) for their industriousness and economic progress. The community has generated such notables as Shirley Chisolm, Sidney Poitier, Kool Herc, and, among second-generation members, rappers like Africa Bambaataa, LL Cool J, and Heavy D. Accordingly, the city has also become a center for calypso, just as it did with French Caribbean and Latin music. New York is the hub of the West Indian recording industry, and due to the city's concentrated population and the endemic piracy in the West Indies, most records sell about five times the number there as in the islands themselves. Several calypsonians, from Calypso Rose to Mighty Sparrow himself, live in New York, performing regularly at venues like S.O.B.'s for mixed Caribbean and Anglo audiences. West Indians dominate entire areas of Brooklyn and Queens, and transplanted traditions from parang to pan thrive there.

But needless to say, New York is not exactly a Caribbean city, and its West Indian culture has naturally taken on a flavor distinct from its island counterparts. For one thing, there is much more social mixing among the diverse West Indian communities than would occur in the Caribbean itself. Barbadians ("Bajans"), Guyanese, Trinis, and others do maintain their own social clubs, but, living in such close proximity, it is inevitable that they intermingle, intermarry, and develop a more unified sense of identity. At the same time, many young West Indians increasingly identify with African Americans, adopting hip-hop fashions, mannerisms, and music as their own, often to the dismay of their parents. (Conversely, quite a few African Americans with West Indian friends join steel bands and mas processions.) As a result, the typical New York West Indian may have various overlapping ethnic self-identities— for example, as Trinidadian, as West Indian, as black, and even as American.

Musical tastes reflect these intersections, as young Trini-Americans grow up enjoying rap and R&B as well as the Sparrow in their parents' record collections.

The U.S. West Indian community's main occasion to celebrate its identity is the Labor Day Carnival, in which mas groups, steel bands, and trucks with sound systems and accompanying dancers work their way down Brooklyn's Eastern Parkway. This event may have started as a miniature version of Trinidad Carnival but has long since acquired its own character. For one thing, it is hardly miniature, as it draws about 2 million people to the avenue, although most come to watch rather than to actively participate. More significant, it has much more of a pan–West Indian character than does its Trinidad counterpart, as it features processions and bands from all the various West Indian islands, some of which have no particular Carnival traditions of their own. It thus celebrates both the diversity and the unity of the West Indian community. As the ever quotable Sparrow put it in his 1969 "Mas in Brooklyn":

> You can be from St. Clair or from John John,
> in New York, all that done.
> They haven't to know who is who;
> New York equalize you.
> Bajan, Grenadian, Jamaican, *tout moun* [everybody],
> drinking dey rum, beating dey bottle and spoon,
> and no one who see me can honestly say,
> they don't like to be in Brooklyn on Labor Day.

The growth and increasing self-consciousness of the community has led, among other things, to a movement to rename Eastern Parkway "Caribbean Parkway." This request has evoked little enthusiasm from the several thousand Hasidic Jews also living on the Parkway, whose men can be seen on Labor Day wearing their black suits and derby hats in the sweltering heat, watching the raucous Carnival parade wanly from their front porches. ("You can just feel the love," as one reveler quipped.) In 1994, the Hasidic community made its own conflicting request for use of the parkway in connection with Jewish holidays. In a multicultural society, such are the issues that must continually be negotiated, in a spirit, one hopes, of compromise and mutual respect.

BIBLIOGRAPHY

Trinidadian scholars have produced several excellent books on calypso and carnival, notably Gordon Rohlehr, *Calypso and Society in Pre-Independence* Trinidad (Port of Spain: G. Rohlehr, 1990); Errol Hill, *The Trinidad Carnival: Mandate for a National*

Theatre (Austin: University of Texas Press, 1972); Keith Warner, *Kaiso, the Trinidad Calypso* (Washington, D.C.: Three Continents, 1985). See also Donald Hill, *Calypso Calaloo: Early Carnival Music in Trinidad* (Gainesville: University Press of Florida, 1993); Stephen Steumpfle, *Steelband Movement: The Forging of a National Art in Trinidad and Tobago* (Philadelphia: University of Pennsylvania Press, 1995); Peter Mason, *Bacchanal! The Carnival Culture of Trinidad* (Philadelphia: Temple University Press, 1998).

RECORDS AND FILMS

In addition to recordings by the calypso and soca artists mentioned in this chapter, see *Calypso Carnival 1936–1941* (Rounder 1105); *An Island Carnival: Music of the West Indies* (Nonesuch 72091). See also *East Indian Music in the West Indies* (Rounder, 1999); *Alan Lomax Collection: Caribbean Voyage: Trinidad: Carnival Roots: The 1962 Field Recordings* (Rounder 1725); *Caribbean Voyage and Portraits: The Growling Tiger of Calypso* (Rounder 1717); *Calypso in New York* (Smithsonian Folkways SFW40454 2000); *Calypso Awakening from the Emory Cook Collection* (Smithsonian Folkways SFW40453 2000); *Again! Lord Melody Sings Calypso: Lord Melody* (Smithsonian Folkways/Cook Records COOK00914 1957).

Films include Glenn Micallef and Larry Johnson, prod., *Mas Fever: Inside Trinidad Carnival* (Filmsound, Portland, Ore., 1989); Daniel Verba and Jean-Jacques Mrejen, prod., *Pan in A Minor: Steelbands of Trinidad* (Iskra Films, 1987).

9

East Indian Music and Big Sounds from the "Small Islands"

EAST INDIANS IN THE WEST INDIES

It is Sunday morning at the Newtown Sai Baba temple in 1994. As the neighborhood begins to awaken, the sounds of roosters crowing, songbirds chirping, and a distant Indian film song drift into the temple, where Jeevan Chowtie is preparing the room for the morning session. By 8 A.M., about two dozen Indian schoolchildren have trickled in and are seated on the floor, boys on one side and girls on the other. A ten-year-old boy tunes up a *tabla* drum pair, used in North Indian classical and light-classical music, while the other children flip through their songbooks. With Jeevan leading them on the harmonium (a rectangular, accordion-like instrument), they start singing a bhajan, or Hindu devotional song, in the Hindi language: "Ishvar Allah tero nam, sab ko sammati de bhagwan" (Whether your name is God or Allah, let everyone give respect).

The scene could be anywhere in North India, except that the temple architecture is a bit different and the children's Hindi accents are slightly off. But they are close enough, for this is not India but Guyana, home to some 400,000 East Indians. These are not Amerindians but Indians from India—the ones Christopher Columbus thought he had found in the Caribbean. Columbus was clearly confused in calling the Arawaks "Indians," but the British partially rectified the misnomer by importing to the Caribbean some 425,000 peasants from India as indentured laborers between 1838 and 1917. The Dutch brought another 35,000 to Dutch Guiana, now Suriname. While life was hard for the immigrants, most of them stayed, re-creating aspects of traditional life from the Bhojpuri region of North India whence most had come. The descendants of these immigrants now constitute the largest ethnic groups in

Trinidad and Guyana, and they make up more than a third of Suriname's population.

With Trinidad known as the land of steel band and calypso and with Guyana and Suriname little known at all, the Indo-Caribbeans have had a rather low international visibility. For that matter, even in the Caribbean they tended to remain somewhat insular and isolated on sugar plantations until recent decades. Such isolation, along with other factors, helped the Indians to retain much more of their ancestral homeland's culture than could West Indian blacks. The Indians came more recently to the Caribbean than the Africans and were not subjected to the same sorts of cultural repression. They could also look back to a mainstream North Indian Hindi-language high culture with which they could maintain some ongoing contact through books, visits, and, since the 1940s, Indian films. In recent decades, the East Indians have entered their countries' economic, political, and cultural mainstreams, and their lively musical traditions have come into the open.

Jeevan Chowtie explains to me, "Here in Guyana, it's been an uphill battle all the way. For twenty-eight years we suffered under the last government, and tens of thousands of us Indians simply left, for Queens, Toronto, wherever." Chowtie is referring to the dictatorship of Forbes Burnham and the People's National Congress (PNC), who came into power in 1964 after the U.S. CIA and the British destabilized the elected government of Cheddi Jagan, a fervently anti-imperialist East Indian leader. After Burnham's death in 1981, the PNC clung to power until 1992 when, holding free elections for the first time in thirty years, it lost to the indefatigable, seventy-six-year-old Jagan (who died in 1997).

Chowtie continues, "The country is bankrupt, but things may get better now, for us Indians and for everyone. Come to the TV station where I work, and I'll show you."

We then ride on Chowtie's motorbike through the potholed streets of Georgetown to the studio of CNS, then the country's only private television station, which opened in 1992. The studio consists of a single room cluttered with a few video machines, a camcorder, and a transmitter about the size of a refrigerator door. A rickety-looking broadcast antenna reaches fifty feet or so above the house, the upper floor of which is inhabited by the owner, an Indian entrepreneur. CNS is oriented mostly toward the country's Indian community, which, Indians feel, has been otherwise neglected by the PNC-dominated state media. At the moment, the station is broadcasting a Hindi film, and the three young women working there are merrily singing along with one of the film songs.

Hindu temple in rural Guyana, with *jhandi* flags in front (Peter Manuel)

Knowing that few Indo-Caribbeans speak Hindi, I ask one of the women how she knows the words to the song. She replies, "I love these songs; we listen to them all the time, so I know all the words, even if I don't really understand them." And indeed, Indo-Caribbean people are crazy about Hindi films and film songs; many fans are amateur or even professional crooners, who will be praised by concert emcees as "The Voice of Mukesh" (an Indian singer) or "A True Imitator" (not one of your cheap imitators). But, as I learn, Indo-Caribbeans also make their own music. In Suriname, where Indians still speak Hindi, Indian folk music thrives, and even in English-speaking Trinidad and Guyana, young and old sing Hindi-language bhajans at temples and lively songs called chowtal at the springtime Phagwa festival. In Guyana and Trinidad, as English gradually replaced Hindi, East Indians cultivated their own tradition of calypso-like, so-called local songs. In accordance with both calypso and North Indian folk customs, some of these songs could be quite ribald, as titles such as "Fowl Cock" and "Squash Long and Fine" might suggest.

But Chowtie laments, "We had a vibrant music tradition here in Guyana until the '60s, but everything stagnated under Burnham. The older musicians are dying off, and the best of the younger ones all left, whether Indians like Devindra Pooran or blacks like Eddy Grant. Trinidad is the better place for

Here and on opposite page: tassa drummers, with taziya float, at Hosay commemoration in Port of Spain, Trinidad (Peter Manuel)

Indo-Caribbean music." (Chowtie himself migrated to Queens, New York, a few years later.)

Back at my hotel, I find the Afro-Guyanese staff sitting in the lobby, glumly watching the unsubtitled Hindi film on the TV. I can't help but ask, "Do you all like this film?"

"Frankly, no," says the clerk, "but there's nothing else on until the evening." Then they can tune in to the drab and underfunded government station or watch a pirated New York station, complete with local city news and ads for Brooklyn car dealers.

Trinidad, my next stop, does indeed turn out to have a more active musical scene, for both Indians and blacks. The country as a whole is much more affluent, and although some Indians feel they have been discriminated against, Trinidad's democratic government and openly multicultural ambience have

allowed the Indians to develop quite a lively and varied musical culture. One venue for this is "Mastana Bahar," an ongoing amateur competition series in which singers and dancers compete in weekly contests that are held around the island and broadcast on radio and TV. Most of the performances consist of renditions of Hindi film songs and dances produced originally in studios in far-away Bombay. While some Indians lament that these imported songs tend to drown out the distinctively local Indo-Trinidadian traditional musics, most Indo-Trinis would counter that through Indian film music they are connecting with the much larger and richer culture of their ancestral homeland.

Indians also celebrate various annual festivals with music. In springtime, Caribbean Hindus celebrate Phagwa (or Holi) much as in India, playfully dousing one another with colored powder (or carcinogenic talc) and forming competing teams in singing exuberant chowtal songs. In a neighborhood of

Port of Spain, Shi'a Muslims commemorate Muharram—or Hosay, as they call it—by constructing elaborate taziya floats, which are paraded through the streets to the accompaniment of tassa barrel drums. The tassa playing is fast, exciting, and deafeningly loud, and is also performed at Hindu weddings and other occasions. Although largely derived from nineteenth-century Indian traditions, tassa thrives much more vigorously in Trinidad than in India, where it has essentially fizzled out.

Indo-Trinidadian Hindu weddings are particularly festive and elaborate. After a few days of preliminary rituals, the wedding culminates in a grand feast, called "tent night" or "cooking night," to which everyone in the neighborhood, regardless of race or creed, is invited. Sometimes a dance-band or deejay will be hired for such occasions, but if the host is an enthusiast of traditional music, he may contract an ensemble, consisting of a lead singer accompanied by harmonium, dholak barrel drum, and a metal rod (dantal) struck with a clapper, to perform what Indo-Caribbeans call "tan-singing" or "local-classical singing." Local-classical music is a mixture of old folk and light-classical songs from the Bhojpuri-speaking area of North India, light-classical songs on records imported from India in the 1930s, somewhat garbled elements of North Indian classical music, and some features unique to Indo-Caribbean culture. After the last ships with Indian immigrants arrived in 1917, Indo-Caribbean musicians were largely isolated from direct contact with India, so they were left to their own devices in reconstructing a professional, semi-classical traditional music. As a result, the various imported and half-remembered musical elements were jumbled up and then reassembled into an idiom that acquired its own rigor and beauty. As Trinidadian musician Mangal Patasar described the music to me, "You take a capsule from India, leave it here for one hundred years, and this is what you get." If an occasional visitor from India happened to hear local-classical music, he would invariably be flabbergasted by it, and meanwhile, on the rare occasions that a local-classical musician happened to hear classical music from India, he generally found it boring. As one told me, "Dat music ain't got no spice to it."

Although the local singers don't really know Hindi, they know the words to the Hindi songs and are generally steeped in Hindu lore. For their part, audiences don't understand Hindi, either, but the elder fans like the sound of it and prize its use as an emblem of Indianness. Basdeo "Lappo" Dindial, a Trinidadian singer, explained to me:

> I don't speak Hindi, but my mother knew it pretty well, since her parents were born in India. She taught me dozens of songs that I still sing. But we make up new songs too, gettin' the elders to help us with the Hindi; or else we take lyrics

from old poetry books and set them to melodies as we please. I studied and practiced a lot when I was young. My friends used to laugh at me, they were always drinkin' rum and knockin' bench and table all over the place, but now they see the stage I reach. I'm singin' every weekend at weddings, tryin' to keep up the tradition. Here, no matter how poor a person is, they still want to have some singin' at a wedding, even if just for a few hours. And sometimes you see a poor person, he just loves music, and you cannot charge him for it.

At a wedding where local-classical musicians are hired, two singers, who also play harmonium, will trade off singing all night, with the dholak drum (heavily amplified, like the singing) provided a bubbling, rollicking rhythmic underpinning. But since few people understand Hindi nowadays, local-classical music is declining dramatically and has all but disappeared in Guyana. Even when it is performed, by 1:00 A.M. or so, people are in a dancing mood and call out, "Give us some chutney, man!" The singers then oblige, performing chutney, meaning up-tempo songs in folk style with simple, catchy tunes. At that point, men and women commence the most uninhibited and animated dancing, continuing until mid-morning.

Chutney is a different sort of mixture of old and new, in some respects representing the process of bringing a closed family tradition into the public sphere. Chutney's roots lie in the lively songs and dances that Hindu village women would perform—with no men around—at weddings in the ancestral Bhojpuri region. In the absence of male onlookers, women could delight in making the songs and dances as comically lewd as they liked. These traditions

"Local classical" musicians (Ruplal Girdharrie and party) in Trinidad, playing dholak, two dantals, and harmonium (Peter Manuel)

were transplanted intact to the Caribbean, where until the '60s and '70s many elder women still spoke Bhojpuri (a dialect of Hindi). Around that time, chutney—as these songs came to be known–literally came out of the closet, as Indo-Trinidadians, no doubt influenced by libertine creole culture, seem to have decided that women needn't confine themselves to a stuffy back room, and that it was OK for them to sing and dance among the other wedding guests, who were mostly family and friends anyway. And just as familiarity with the old songs started to wane, recordings and radio brought lively chutney-style folksongs from nearby Suriname, where Bhojpuri was (and is) still widely spoken.

The next step happened in the mid-'80s, when many Indo-Trinis came to feel that chutney was too much fun to be confined to the occasional wedding, and entrepreneurs started holding public chutney dances at open-air clubs throughout the island, with live bands (originally featuring the traditional harmonium, dholak, dantal, and voice). In effect, folk chutney had survived just long enough to be made into a pop dance phenomenon. A tempest-in-a-teapot polemic exploded within the Indian community, as moralists denounced the ribald songs and especially the bawdy dancing of women, who were supposed to be the pristine upholders of decency, propriety, honor, modesty, and so on (while men can act any way they please).

Over the next decade, chutney definitively trumped those hoary values, despite the fulminations of the pandits. Chutney fetes have come to be held nearly every weekend in Trinidad. These generally commence as film-music concerts (more "Voice of Rafi," etc.), but after a few hours, the beer takes effect, the chutney band starts, and listeners—young and old, male and female—push aside the folding chairs, and a joyous pandemonium takes over. The dance style is unique, combining vigorous pelvic "wining" with graceful hand-and-arm gestures deriving from Indian folk dance. The result is a delight to behold, especially in its pervading sense of fun and its good, clean, wholesome, outrageous sexiness.

By the '90s the traditional harmonium-and-dholak-based group had increasingly come to be replaced by a more modern band with synthesizer and drum machine, which generally provided a soca-style rhythm. The soca beat mixes easily with the funky, heartbeat chutney rhythm (what Indians in India would call *kaherva*), and the result was soon dubbed "chutney-soca." This hybrid genre soon became a fad among Indians in Trinidad, Guyana, and the secondary diasporas in New York and Canada. Some chutney-soca retains a strong Indian flavor in its Hindi lyrics, traditional chutney-style melodies, and the thumping and pumping dholak. But English lyrics have become increasingly common, and the dholak, which is difficult to amplify, has tended to drop out, so that there is often little chutney in the chutney-soca. As with calypso, some of the vocalists sing in tune and some don't. Those who do, like Trinidad's Anand Yankaran and Rikki Jai and Suriname's Kries Ramkhelawan, are mini-stars in great demand. A few women enliven the scene and perpetuate the genre's prehistory as a women's idiom. Asha Ramcharan sings:

> When we were friendin' [courting] you were always at my side
> As soon as we get married you forget you had a bride
> Dem fellows you limin' [hanging out] with, you feel dem is your friend
> If I was a slack woman I sure take one of dem.

The flowering of the chutney scene has paralleled the increased movement of East Indians away from rural sugar plantations and into the political, economic, and cultural mainstreams of Trinidadian and Guyanese society. Economic recession in Trinidad and the enmities engendered by the racist Burnham regime in Guyana have to some extent strained relations between the Indian and black communities. But in both countries, the greater prominence and demographic growth of Indians are increasingly obliging everyone, including the traditionally more dominant Afro-Caribbeans, to acknowledge the multiracial nature of their societies. For their part, while Indians take pride in having left behind such ancestral evils as dowry, caste discrimination, and Hindu–Muslim enmity, they are proud of their ethnic ancestry. On the whole, they cherish their ties to India and in some cases look down on Afro-Caribbeans for having adopted the slave-masters' religion and lost touch with their traditional culture. Meanwhile, some Afro-Caribbeans continue to regard Indians as unpatriotic foreigners—especially, for example, when they cheer for the visiting cricket teams from India or Pakistan.

In its own way, music has mirrored the complex relations between the two groups, and it has often been the focus of debates about race relations. In the mid-'90s, when chutney-soca burst on the scene, many hailed it as a felicitous fusion of Indian and creole musics that reflected the emergence of Indians on the pop scene, their ability to celebrate Indianness and be local at the same time, and the new degree of racial cultural interaction. The musical vogue coincided with the 1996 election of an Indian prime minister, Basdeo Panday, in Trinidad. That year, a catchy chutney ("Lutela") by an elderly Indian, Sonny Mann, became a national hit and "road march" played by steel bands and took him to the finals of the Carnival season's Soca Monarch competition. (There, unfortunately, he was pelted with bottles and cans by unappreciative Afro-Trinidadians shouting, "We ain't want to hear de coolie.") The following year, a separate, privately funded Chutney-Soca Monarch competition was inaugurated, which has since become a fixture of the Carnival festivities and invariably features several Afro-Trinidadian competitors, who are no doubt attracted by the prizes and are welcomed and enjoyed by Indian audiences.

Chutney dancers in Trinidad (Peter Manuel)

For their part, calypsos traditionally tended either to portray East Indians as bizarre and exotic or, more typically, to ignore them. A celebrated case of the latter tendency was Black Stalin's 1979 "Caribbean Unity," an oft-quoted appeal to Afro-Caribbean solidarity:

> Dem is one race, from de same place,
> that made the same trip, on the same ship,
> de Caribbean man.

For obvious reasons, this message did not go over well with Indians, who are no longer content with being written out of their nations' history. However,

A temple prayer session turns into a chutney fete (Peter Manuel)

that song by Stalin (who in fact has always supported racial harmony) was quite benign compared with the venomous and divisive "attack calypsos" that have come to be aired since the mid-'90s, as both friendly interaction and competitive tension between the races have increased. As one song put it,

> Dey say it's Carnival, and it's kaiso time again
> and for the Indian man, that means plenty pain.

More specifically, it means that Indians tend to avoid the calypso tents and often complain about how their tax dollars subsidize their own vilification by singers like CroCro at the Monarch competition. (Said CroCro in a 1996 interview, "I'm not racist. Why, I had sex with an Indian woman just last week." His wife shrugged the remark off.) But it should also be noted that for each mean-spirited, clannish rant by CroCro and Sugar Aloes, there are usually a few songs that appeal for racial harmony. Some of these may be collaborative products, like the 1992 "Cry for Unity" written by the Afro-Trinidadian Ras Shorty I (formerly Lord Shorty) for Indian singer Rikki Jai, who has always tried to cross racial boundaries:

> We both come down here by boat under the hands of the master,
> I from India, you from Africa . . . .
> Between the two races since the days of slavery
> we was always enemies, is time we try unity.

Shorty's song goes on to urge Indians and blacks to "mix up cultures," and indeed, the cultures have been mixing up for a long time. In Trinidad, one can buy halal pig-tail (a sort of equivalent to kosher pork), hear a Catholic sermon by one Father Mohammad, and visit an all-purpose religious edifice known as the "San Francique Hindu Mosque." East Indian singers like Jai and Drupatee Ramgoonai have made a splash in the soca scene, introducing tassa drums and other Indianisms. Drupatee's 1989 "Indian Soca" put the case plainly:

> The music of the steel drums from Laventille
> cannot help but mix with the rhythm from Caroni [an Indian area],
> for it's a symbol of how much we've come of age, . . .
> rhythm from Africa and India,
> blend together is a perfect mixture.

Similarly, the leader of the Amoco Renegades, a top steel band, is an Indian, Jit Samaroo, and Shorty himself stated that the soca beat he invented was inspired partially by Indian tassa drumming (as heard in his late-1970s hits like "Endless Vibrations"). Meanwhile, calypsos like Sparrow's "Maharajin" and self-described chutneys by the Afro-Trini Crazy (like "Pulbasia" and "Jammania") have highlighted East Indian themes, and Indian radio and TV programs are proliferating. While some non-Indians in Trinidad, Guyana, and Suriname continue to regard such shows as ethnically divisive, a sense of cultural pluralism is becoming institutionalized in both Trinidad and Guyana. For its part, Trinidad—the proverbial land of steel band and calypso—is already being referred to more inclusively as the land of steel band, calypso, and chutney.

Chowtal: An East Indian Folk Song

Afro-Caribbean rhythms are rightly celebrated for their richness and complexity, but they are not the only source of rhythmic vitality in Caribbean music. The traditional music of India, both folk and classical, displays other sorts of rhythmic complexity and drive, relying more on linear intricacies than on African-style simultaneous layerings of interlocking patterns. One common feature of Indian music is the use of "additive" meters, often involving measures of odd-numbered beats. Chowtal, a North Indian folksong genre transplanted to the Caribbean, uses such a rhythm, which is also common in other North Indian styles and in Indo-Caribbean "local-classical" singing.

The chowtal meter can be regarded as in seven beats, divided into three plus four (hence the term "additive"). You can get the feel of it by counting "<u>one</u>-two-three-<u>one</u>-two-<u>three</u>-four" repeatedly, clapping on the underlined beats. A typical chowtal refrain is given in Musical Example 18.

e - go - ku - la   ke ja - ja-n men kan - ha - ye su - ra-na su - kh da - e

Musical Example 18. Chowtal

Chowtal is sung during Phagwa, when groups of enthusiasts (especially teenagers) form ensembles, ardently performing old and even newly composed songs. In Trinidad, where there are competition networks for just about every kind of music, chowtal groups also compete for prizes during springtime festivals.

SMALL ISLAND TRADITIONS

Although Caribbean music has tended to be dominated by the bigger islands, the smaller islands, in their musical diversity and richness, have always constituted an important part of the soundscape. They have also contributed to the big-island musics, with, for example, the calypso and soca scenes being enriched by Mighty Sparrow (born in Grenada), Arrow (of "Hot Hot Hot" fame, from Montserrat), and the "Bajan Invasion" of Barbadian soca singers—not to mention such phenomena as the honey-voiced singer Kevin Little of St. Vincent, with his 2004 hit "Turn Me On" (is it R&B? dancehall? soca?). Several small islands have their own lively calypso scenes. But the small islands should also be appreciated as repositories of their own music traditions. One might generalize that, taken individually, these music traditions might not have the richness or sophistication of big-island musics like traditional rumba or *son*. But they nevertheless have their own charm and flavor, and taken collectively they constitute a scene of great variety and interest.

Most of the islands in question are former British colonies, inhabited primarily by English-speaking descendants of enslaved West Africans and varying numbers of white people, whether long-time locals or foreign-born expatriates. In some islands, like St. Lucia and Dominica, there is a strong French Caribbean heritage, and French Caribbean creole is widely spoken. The islands range from tourist-heavy St. Thomas and Nassau to sleepy Dominica. Some, like St. Lucia, are independent countries, while others, like the Virgin Islands, are still governed by Britain or the United States. Although there is little of the desperate poverty that one sees in Haiti, some islands have lost as much as half their population as people emigrate to find work or just to broaden their horizons. In places like Carriacou, relative isolation, insularity, and underdevelopment have contributed to the survival of music traditions.

In other islands that are blessed with beaches, tourism can help sustain music and dance traditions, at least in staged forms.

Much small-island music can be grouped in a few familiar categories, especially in terms of their place on a continuum of African or European origins. On the neo-African side are the musics like Curaçao's tambú, which feature the familiar Afro-Caribbean format of drums (usually three) and call-and-response singing. Variants of this pattern may use more informal percussion instruments but retain the Afro-Caribbean emphasis on lively rhythmic ostinatos and responsorial vocals.

There are many accounts from the slavery period of such performances, several of which mention not only African-derived "goombay" drums but also stringed instruments like the "banjar" or "banye"—the ancestor of the banjo. One visitor described a call-and-response song he heard in 1790, which testified to the alienation of the slave from both his ancestral and new homelands:[1]

> If me want for go in a Ibo
>> Me can't go there
> Since dem tief me from my Guinea
>> Me can't go there
> If me want to go in a Kingstown
>> Me can't go there
> Since massa go in a England
>> Me can't go there.

Several factors militated against the survival of festive neo-African traditions in the small islands. Aside from the cessation of slave imports after 1807, the intolerant British Protestant plantation owners and missionaries tended to repress African practices and were very successful at getting slaves to internalize their masters' Eurocentric prejudices. Thus, an 1814 account from Antigua, among others, describes the contempt with which some local-born fife-and-drum-playing slaves regarded the rowdy drumming and dancing of the African-born slaves.[2] Recent decades, by contrast, have seen a revalorization of the Afro-Caribbean musical heritage, which partially offsets the marked decline of such traditions.

Small-island music traditions also include the various styles of spirituals and hymns that are sung at church services and other occasions. Although the melodies and harmonies of these musics tend to be European in style, their rhythms, like those of gospel music, may be intense and syncopated, especially in the case of Pentecostal and Spiritual Baptist traditions, which are syncretic faiths combining Protestant and African features.

Another category of music consists of the lively, percussion-dominated sounds that accompany Carnival or junkanoo traditions. Some of these festivals, like those of Antigua and Barbuda, are relatively recent inventions aimed at tourists. However, some of the masquerade themes—such as that of the "Wild Indians" bands from St. Thomas—are in their own way thoroughly traditional. Like Barbadian fife-and-drum "tuk," the Carnival ensembles may incorporate features derived from British marching bands. Several islands also have their small but colorful calypso scenes, which come alive at Carnival season, whenever that might be in the local calendar. One distinctive, albeit obscure, calypso-style tradition is the music called "benna" of Antigua, whose songs might be accompanied, as shown on page 264, by a banjo and a "bass pipe"—in this case made of PVC tubing. Nowadays, Trinidadian-style steel bands are also common in smaller islands. Steel drums also work their way into string bands, as in the case of the Harmonites String Band of St. Vincent, in which the sole string instrument, the banjo, is also supplemented by a home-made tin-can xylophone (depicted on page 264).

Particularly prominent in the small islands are the varieties of secular creole dance musics that combine syncopated rhythms with European-style melodies and dancing. Some of these can be seen as local efflorescences of string-band music, in which the melody (whether also sung or not) is provided by a fiddle,

"Wild Indian" band (nowadays also known as "Traditional Indians") during the annual Carnival procession, Charlotte Amalie, St. Thomas, U.S. Virgin Islands, 2004 (Ken Bilby)

Two members of the Rio Band performing benna, Falmouth, Antigua, 2004
(Ken Bilby)

The Harmonites String Band with a performer on tuned steel cups, Kingstown,
St. Vincent, 2004 (Ken Bilby)

Vincentian boom drum band to which a steel pan has been added, Rose Bank, St. Vincent, 2004 (Ken Bilby)

guitar, or banjo, accompanied by various instruments such as shak-shak (a shaker), some sort of scraper, a marimbula-type bass instrument, and perhaps a triangle, tambourine, or hand drum. Often, however, the melodic instrument might be an accordion, a fife, or a harmonica. The accompanying dances often stem from the country-dance/contredanse family, in which men and women typically form two lines, and partners interact and separate as in a Virginia reel. (However, this format can also be combined with neo-African drumming, as in the Haitian-Cuban *tumba francesa*.) Scottish-derived reels and jigs, along with dances like "heel and toe," can be found in such places as Tobago. Particularly common are variants of the British- and French-derived quadrille, a set dance in which, typically, a suite of five or six "figures" (dance styles, each with a distinct musical section) is executed by four couples in a circle or square. Quadrille choreography requires some training and experience, which are valued accordingly by enthusiasts. The tunes played by the accompanying ensembles are generally European in style, and perhaps in actual derivation, although the rhythms may be brisk and syncopated. Hence, in local versions of the quadrille, or the polka, waltz, reel, and mazurka, the rhythm may be so accelerated and syncopated, and the melody so obscured by the loud drumming, that they sound thoroughly Afro-Caribbean. Nevertheless, like string-band music in general, such traditions would have roots in plantation life, as slaves imitated the songs and dances of their masters or were even engaged to perform such music for their masters' entertainment.

In 1962, V. S. Naipaul wrote of one such dance tradition, with his typical mixture of condescension and insight:

> By listening beyond the drums to the accordion, one could perceive the stringed instruments of two centuries ago, and see the dances which even now were only slightly negrofied, the atmosphere became thick and repellant with slavery, making one think of long hot days on the plantation, music at night from the bright windows of the estate house.... The music and motions of privilege, forgotten elsewhere, still lived here in a ghostly, beggared elegance: to this mincing mimicry the violence and improvisation and awesome skill of African dancing had been reduced.[3]

Modern academics might tend to regard such an uncharitable description as politically incorrect, in seeing quadrille and belair dancers as deculturated mimics of the old slave masters rather than as active reinventors of a tradition. Clearly, in cultivating their own versions of creole dances and songs, West Indians were adapting the materials available to them in ways that suited their own situations and sensibilities. But the truth is that most West Indians might at least implicitly share Naipaul's disparagement, insofar as they have largely lost interest in such colonial-era dances. Except for some elders, most of today's West Indians, on the small islands as well as in Jamaica and Trinidad, are thoroughly tuned in to the cosmopolitan sounds of Sean Paul and Bob Marley, not to mention Jay-Z and Usher. Quadrille, on the whole, is for tourists, folklorists, and handfuls of elders.

But enough generalizations. Let's go island-hopping, proceeding, for lack of a better way, from north to south.

To Americans, the Bahamas, with their fine beaches and proximity to Florida, are perhaps best known as a resort area, and the local population of some 225,000 predominantly Afro-Caribbeans is outnumbered by the more than 3 million tourists who visit each year. To entertain such visitors, hotel bands play "Day-O," country and western, and whatever else is called for. At the same time, Bahamanians have also cultivated their own distinctive music traditions. Religious musics include spirituals and "anthems," which, like gospel music, may be sung in church, but they are also heard as festive, processional "rushin' songs" in the junkanoo parade. In the realm of secular music, quadrilles were traditionally danced to the accompaniment of a "rake 'n' scrape" band, featuring accordion, a saw scraped with a piece of metal, a goombay barrel drum, and possibly other instruments. The term "goombay," however, also denotes the topical songs that correspond to what others would call calypso. But the context in which the goombay drum is most often heard is the Christmastime junkanoo festival, with its rowdy street ensembles also featuring whistles, cowbells, foghorns, conches, bicycle horns, and, more recently, wind instruments like trumpets and saxes. Since the 1920s, the junkanoo tradition has been revived, regulated, and promoted by the government as a tourist attraction, but it has its own appeal to locals, who constitute both spectators and participants in the music-and-dance groups, which can include more than 1,000 people.[4]

Moving on to the Virgin Islands, to the east of Puerto Rico, one finds a music culture in many ways similar to that of the Bahamas. Historical references document the existence of a now largely extinct Afro-Caribbean dance genre accompanied by drumming and singing and called bamboula—a word that, like "calinda" (kalinda), denoted various sorts of similar genres throughout the Caribbean. Topical songs called "cariso" also flourished in St. Croix, although they are seldom heard today. Still performed in St. Croix, whether for tourists or local entertainment, are quadrilles and other European-derived dance forms, as accompanied by a "fungi band" or "scratch band"—so named for the güiro-type gourd scraper that plays alongside fiddle, accordion, other percussion instruments and, nowadays, electric guitar. Quadrilles and similar dances also survive in Montserrat, where they are part of a "jumbie dance"— "jumbie" being a West African–derived word here denoting both a drum and a spirit. The northern and central Caribbean is subject to periodic devastating hurricanes; Montserrat has also been cursed by volcanic eruptions since 1995, which have led to the emigration of all but around 3,000 stalwarts.

In the islands of Dominica and St. Lucia, English colonial culture was imposed—in some respects, only superficially—on a more resilient layer of French Caribbean creole culture and language. Although these islands are small, their rugged terrain traditionally impeded transportation and promoted the cultural isolation of individual communities. In Dominica, as in some other French Caribbean islands discussed in chapter 6, one might still encounter drum-based Afro-Caribbean ensembles accompanying dances called bélé or belair (presumably from "belle air," or pretty song). Both church and state militated against Afro-Dominican culture until independence in 1965 led to a reappraisal of such traditions and a somewhat ephemeral vogue of *"cadence-lypso,"* a local mixture of Haitian *cadense* and calypso. In both Dominica and St. Lucia, as elsewhere, local versions of the quadrille (kwadril) have come to be seen by many people as relics of the colonial era. Since the early 1800s, performances of quadrilles and other dance genres in St. Lucia have taken place especially in the context of weekly meetings by two rival social-support societies, the La Rose and La Marguerite societies, which have branches in every town.

The French creole cultural layer found in islands like St. Lucia and Trinidad is absent in Barbados, where four and a half centuries of uninterrupted British rule led to an even more thorough suppression of neo-African drumming and dance traditions. Hence, the drums used in the percussion-and-flute bands called tuk, heard nowadays at festivals, derive more from British regimental bands of the colonial era. But regardless of whether they can be traced to Africa, percussion traditions flourish both in Barbados and nearby St. Vincent, as in the "boom-drum" band shown on page 265. Although the 1960s–70s in Barbados saw the flourishing of calypso-like songs called "spouge," more conspicuous in the 1970s and '80s was the emergence of a lively local calypso and soca scene. This is especially centered on the summertime Crop Over festival, which attracts both tourists and performers from Trinidad and elsewhere.

Moving southward to Grenada, we find a scene that is by now familiar: historical references to extinct belair and kalinda dances, a defunct quadrille tradition, and a reinvented summertime Carnival, with calypso and masquerade bands. However, we also encounter a neo-African tradition shared with Trinidad: the Shango religion, deriving from the practices of Yoruba indentured workers who immigrated from West Africa in the mid-1800s.

Traditional musics are somewhat more vital on the smaller and (even) less developed island of Carriocou (population around 5,000). Particularly distinctive, and still performed, is a neo-African tradition called "big drum." This genre features an ensemble of three hand-played barrel drums (which are not unusually big) and shak-shaks, in front of which a few people dance while others provide responsorial singing in French Creole. Big-drum rhythms are numerous, exciting, and varied. The names of the drums—boula and kata, creolized as "cutter"—recur elsewhere in the French Caribbean cultural sphere and are of African origin. Interestingly, several of the rhythms bear names that, according to local belief, reflect the specific African nations whence they originate; these names include Igbo, Manding, Kongo, Arada, Moko, and Cromanti. The last term, which also denotes Afro-Caribbean religious or musical practices in Suriname and Jamaica, refers to the primarily Akan slaves who were shipped by the British through the Dutch fort of Cormantine in West Africa.

Meanwhile, in Carriacou, as in other islands, string bands once were quite important at lifecycle events, and they still play at wedding parties and gravestone-raising ceremonies. Members of string bands also have a new social role: Via the freshly minted lyrics to their songs, they publicize to the rest of the community (especially during Parang season, for example) the misbehavior of other Carriacouans. In doing so, they reassert traditional social standards and expectations common to the extended community.[5]

We can allow our southwesterly momentum to carry us on to the South American mainland, to the former British colony of Guyana, which is an essentially West Indian rather than a Latin American nation. In its mixed East Indian and creole demography, it bears some affinities with Trinidad, without that country's French connection and oil wealth. As we discussed the East Indian music scene earlier in this chapter, here we should mention the lively tradition of que-que, a song and dance form still performed by many Afro-Guyanese at weddings. Que-que can occur at several points in the wedding festivities, such as the prenuptial night, when the groom's party arrives at the bride's house to discover that she has been "hidden" by her friends, whether in the crowd, in someone else's clothing, or in a nearby tree. In que-que, male and female dancers form two lines, while others sing responsorially, with rhythm being supplied by clapping and the stamping of the dancers feet. The role of the lead singer is taken by anyone with the energy and creativity to make up lyrics; the que-que can go on for hours, with men and women taking turns singing lead. As in other wedding songs throughout the world, the ribaldry of the songs can serve to prepare the bride for the wedding night and make light of the impending consummation. Hence, a song might go:

Coolie man ting ting
   long e so long e so
white man ting ting
   lillie so lillie so
Chinee man ting ting
   lillie so lillie so
[groom's name] ting ting
   biggie so biggie so.

One can see why children are generally not supposed to be present at such que-que sessions. Another part of Guyana's creole music heritage is the repertoire of folksongs associated with "pork-knockers"—the local term for the hardy, independent gold prospectors who spend most of the year sloshing about in the muddy streams of the country's rain forest.

INDO-CARIBBEAN BIBLIOGRAPHY

Regarding Indo-Caribbean music, see Peter Manuel, *East Indian Music in the West Indies: Tan-singing, Chutney, and the Making of Indo-Caribbean Culture* (Philadelphia: Temple University Press, 2000), and Helen Myers, *Music of Hindu Trinidad: Songs from the Indian Diaspora* (Chicago: University of Chicago Press, 1999). For a thorough ethnography of Indo-Trinidadian society with reference to music, see Steven Vertovec, *Hindu Trinidad: Religion, Ethnicity, and Socio-economic Change* (London: Warwick University Press, 1992).

INDO-CARIBBEAN RECORDS AND FILM

East Indian Music in the West Indies (Rounder, 1999); *Tan-Singing of Trinidad and Guyana: Indo-Caribbean "Local-Classical" Music*, prod. Peter Manuel (video documentary, 2000). See also the CDs in the books by Manuel and Myers cited earlier.

SMALL ISLAND BIBLIOGRAPHY

See relevant entries in Dale Olsen and Daniel Sheehy, eds., *The Garland Encyclopedia of World Music: South America, Mexico, Central America, and the Caribbean* (New York: Garland Publishing, 1998); Lorna McDaniel, *The Big Drum Ritual of Carriacou: Praisesongs in Rememory of Flight* (Gainesville: University Press of Florida, 1998).

SMALL ISLAND RECORDINGS

The Big Drum and other Ritual and Social Music of Carriacou (Folkways FE 34002); *Alan Lomax Collection: Caribbean Voyage: Dominica—Creole Crossroads* (Rounder 1724); *Alan Lomax Collection: Caribbean Voyage: Carriacou Calaloo* (Rounder 1722); *Alan Lomax Collection: Caribbean Voyage: Brown Girl in the Ring* (Rounder 1716); *Caribbean Voyage: Grenada: Creole and Yoruba Voices* (Rounder 1728); *Music of the Bahamas, Volume 2: Anthems, Work Songs and Ballads* (Smithsonian Folkways FW03845 1959); *Music of St. Lucia* (Cook Records/Smithsonian Folkways COOK00103 1953); *Caribbean Folk Music, Volume 1* (Smithsonian Folkways FW04533 1960); *Bamboo-Tamboo, Bongo and Belair* (Cook Records/Smithsonian Folkways COOK05017 1956); *B.W.I. (British West Indies) Songs* (Smithsonian Folkways FW08809 1957).

10

Five Themes in the Study
of Caribbean Music

UNITY AND DIVERSITY IN A CONTINENT OF ISLANDS

In the opening chapter of this book, we briefly looked at some aspects of unity and diversity in Caribbean culture and music. Having surveyed the region's individual music styles, we may now be better poised to tackle some fundamental questions: To what extent does the Caribbean constitute a unified musical area? Is Caribbean music just a colorful collage of diverse genres, without any pan-regional continuity? In what sorts of ways has music been able to transcend linguistic boundaries?

The Caribbean has always been culturally and politically divided by geography, language, political dominion, and ethnicity. The linguistic and colonial boundaries are the most obvious, and to some extent one can divide the area into three major cultural zones—that is, Spanish, English, and French. However, even these subregions are in some respects internally fragmented in terms of rivalries as well as musical traditions. Residents of the nearby French islands of Martinique and Guadeloupe manage to look down on each other, and the calypso line "Small island, go back where you really come from" long expressed Trinidad's attitude toward its neighbors. The end of colonialism has only exacerbated such fragmentation. The pan–West Indian federation fell apart in 1962, and a few years later, tiny Anguilla seceded from St. Kitts-Nevis, even though it had no telephones, power, or paved roads. (As calypsonian Wrangler Wynne sang, "I caught a Barbadian in my room last night, he said he was lookin' for the Federation site.") In what ways, then, have musical tastes and traditions reflected such divisions, and in what ways has music transcended them?

The parallels between musical and linguistic boundaries are obvious. A Martinican feels closer to France than to nearby Barbados. Similarly, despite

Cuba's proximity to Jamaica, its similar history, and its overwhelming musical influence on the Spanish Caribbean, Cuban music does not seem to have much impact on Jamaican popular music. Linguistic fragmentation reaches an extreme in the southern Caribbean Basin, where the national languages of the adjacent Venezuela, Guyana, Suriname, French Guiana, and Brazil, are, respectively, Spanish, English, Dutch, French, and Portuguese.

However, such disparities represent only part of the picture. For one thing, as we noted in chapter 1, the entire region shares a set of basic sociomusical attributes, including the presence of an Afro-Caribbean cultural common denominator; a history of musical syncretization; the strength of oral traditions; and the emergence of lower-class, African-influenced work songs, religious musics, Carnival traditions, and creole, duple-metered dance-music genres. Further, even the boundaries between the Spanish, French, and English zones have often been fluid and permeable. The French creole zone formerly extended to eastern Cuba, Trinidad, and elsewhere in the present Anglophone realm (including New Orleans), and in terms of language and musical tastes, Dominica and St. Lucia still straddle the two.

Internal migrations have also left musical traces that traverse linguistic barriers. Haitian culture and music pervade eastern Cuba, just as Cuban dance music heavily influenced the 1950s Haitian konpa. West Indian migrants to southern Puerto Rico appear to have contributed to the emergence of plena, and the Trinidad calypso was enriched by melodies brought from throughout the region. The Afro-Curaçaoan tambú, as brought to Puerto Rico by immigrants, appears to have been the source of the bomba rhythm called *holandés*, while the tambú of modern Curaçao bears obvious influence of the Cuban rumba, presumably deriving from the guest workers who resided in Cuba. Descendants of Afro-American migrants from the southern United States preserve their own traditions in the Dominican peninsula of Samaná, and laborers from just about everywhere migrated to Panama to work on the canal. Internal migrations have continued in recent decades as Haitians seek work in the Dominican Republic, Dominicans flock to Puerto Rico, and small-island West Indians migrate to prosperous Trinidad (while everyone migrates to New York). Similarly, despite strained relations between Haitians and Dominicans (including disputes about the origin of the *méringue*/merengue), the two nations' musical histories are inseparable. As we saw in chapter 6, the mid-twentieth century Haitian konpa emerged to some extent as a local variant of the Dominican merengue, while modern Dominican bandleaders like Wilfrido Vargas have mercilessly plagiarized Haitian hits.

Since the 1950s, the conflicting trends toward unity and diversity have acquired a new dimension with the spread of the mass media. It may seem contradictory to speak of simultaneous homogenization and diversification, but that is in many ways what has happened, especially as the sheer amount of musical production and recording increases. One common denominator has been popular music from the United States, which now pervades the entire region. Rap, rock, and R&B have their own undeniable appeal and vitality, and when backed by powerful multinational record companies, they can tend to put local musics on the defensive throughout the Caribbean. In many countries, local broadcast media are so poorly funded that they can barely compete with the United States. In some smaller countries, there is hardly any local TV at all. Instead, everyone watches pirated satellite transmissions from the United States, complete with New York City news and ads for products that are unavailable as well as unaffordable. So it is not surprising that rap and R&B have a strong presence in West Indian airwaves, constituting a new sort of musical lingua franca. The presence of these cosmopolitan musics may at once enrich local music scenes by broadening horizons and impoverish them by displacing and devaluing local musics.

A new and distinctly Caribbean sort of pan-regional common denominator has been dancehall reggae and its Spanish-language variant, reggaetón. The international popularity of dancehall, indeed, has transcended language barriers and provided a kind of cultural unity and contact that is unprecedented in the Caribbean. In general, the mass media, together with interaction of migrant communities in New York and elsewhere, facilitate all sorts of musical cross-fertilization and fusions, from Garifuna punta-rock and Spanish-language soca to Fulanito's fusion of merengue, rap, and house. Many of these hybrids are just ephemeral gimmicks and fads, but others may be more than that. Indeed, in an age of multiple identities and crisscrossing media networks, some of the most vital and dynamic artistic creations may be coming from the borders and interstices rather than the stylistic hinterlands. The borders can of course be virtual rather than geographical, for this is the era of the remix, in which fusions of languages, styles, and genres can operate both as statements of social solidarity and as postmodern pastiches.

RACE AND ETHNICITY

The history, styles, and meanings of Caribbean music are intimately linked to issues of race in several ways. Musical genres are often associated with or claimed (plausibly or not) by specific ethnic groups; alternately, they may be celebrated as national patrimonies whose appeal transcends such boundaries. Throughout the region, song texts chronicle and articulate popular attitudes regarding race. Perhaps most significant are the ways in which music not only passively reflects race relations but actively influences them. In some cases, it serves as a powerful symbol of racial syncretism and harmony, often situating local versions of Afro-Caribbean music in the mainstream of national culture.

It is impossible to generalize about race relations and attitudes in the Caribbean, except to say that they are complex, diverse, and often different from those in the United States. Thus, for example, throughout the West Indies black people may historically have internalized colonial prejudices, but because they generally constitute demographic majorities, unlike many North American blacks, they are less likely to regard themselves as members of an alienated and marginalized minority. Race relations in the Spanish-speaking Caribbean are generally more fluid and flexible than in the English-speaking world. For many Puerto Ricans, this tradition of tolerance and mixing has been a source of nationalistic pride vis-à-vis the United States. Certainly, North American and English racial ideology, which traditionally recognizes only black and white, is relatively unusual in the Spanish and French Caribbean, especially since so many people are of mixed ancestry. Instead, people may be highly conscious of shades of coloring. Even within Afro-Caribbean communities, social preferences for lighter skin, thin noses, and straight ("good") hair remain widespread, although they have been much challenged—including by music—in recent decades. For North Americans, understanding such attitudes is complicated by the entirely different norms of discourse about race. Especially in the Hispanic Caribbean, people simply do not talk about race in the same ways that Americans do.

In some cases, racial attitudes are expressed openly in song, as in the '50s chachachá "Negra bembon," in which a black man chides a *mulata* for thinking herself superior. At the same time, one must be careful in trying to draw conclusions from song texts. For example, in Latin music, innumerable songs portray the ideal woman as a *mulata*. This convention could be interpreted as an indication of racial openness on the part of the singer, or a black preference for lighter skin, or, perhaps most often, a white stereotype of *mulatas* as hot and sexy—a stereotype that at once exoticizes mixed-race women and devalues the sexuality of others.

In general, the styles, associations, and breadth of individual music genres tell us much about the racial and cultural composition of Caribbean societies as a whole. Most Caribbean musical cultures exhibit a continuum of genres, ranging from the African-derived to the European-derived. The proportions vary considerably from island to island, however. An obvious contrast is between some smaller West Indian countries, where neo-African cult musics are relatively weak and marginal, and Cuba and Haiti, where they are extremely widespread. Even in Trinidad, for example, Shango worship has remained a private subculture to such an extent that calypsonians have traditionally portrayed it as an exotic and bizarre cult, to be feared or ridiculed. By contrast, innumerable Cuban popular songs refer with easy familiarity to the orishas (spirits) whose religion pervades lower-class Afro-Cuban life. Similarly, one can trace a direct evolution from Congolese secular dances through the traditional rumba and on to modern Cuban dance music and salsa, as reflected, for example, in modern salsa versions of old *sones* like "Kikiribú mandinga" (That's the End of That!), with its combination of African words and colloquial Spanish. By contrast, the weakness of such threads of continuity in the West Indies led Trinidad's Prime Minister Eric Williams to speak, however exaggeratedly, of Afro-Trinidadians as a "deracinated" people with "nothing indigenous."

Throughout much of the Caribbean, the emergence of creole popular musics has involved a process of accepting and legitimizing local forms of Afro-Caribbean music. This process occurred in different forms and in different stages throughout the Caribbean. It happened especially late in the British West Indies, where colonial masters had so successfully instilled ideas of black racial inferiority among their Afro-Caribbean subjects. Hence, many colonial-era calypsos mocked people with negroid features, and the waves of the French and Spanish Caribbean *negritud* movement seemed to bypass the English-speaking islands. It was not until the 1970s that a black pride movement—in the idiosyncratic form of Rastafari—forced a reassessment of such colonial prejudices. Since then, roots reggae songs have explicitly and defiantly celebrated Africa and blackness, and self-denigrating racist calypsos have gone out of style. In subsequent decades, dancehall songs have voiced popular Jamaican attitudes with particular frankness. After the singer Buju Banton was criticized for his "Love me Browning," which eulogized fair-skinned girls, he released his own rejoinder, "Love Black Woman."

In Cuba and Puerto Rico, the local version of the *negritud* movement generated a degree of white bourgeois interest, however qualified and obscurantist, in local black music and culture. In *negrista* poetry, this often took the form of white poets writing verse in colloquial *bozal* (fresh-off-the-boat slave) speech and "oogah-boogah"–type, African-sounding mumbo-jumbo. In early–twentieth-century Cuba, white composers wrote many theater songs that eulogized blackness in a somewhat sentimental, exoticizing fashion. In Puerto Rico, where white literati had traditionally ignored black traditions, the essayist Tomás Blanco took a step forward in a 1935 article declaring his island's culture to be mulatto, as best embodied in the plena. Still, this formulation neglected bomba, which is thoroughly Afro-Puerto Rican rather than mulatto. In the '40s and '50s, the Afro-Cuban bandleader Arsenio Rodríguez could draw on his own family heritage to present a more authentic black perspective, as in "Bruca Maniguá," with its mixture of Spanish and Congolese words:

Yo son Carabalí, negro de nación
sin la libetá, no puedo viví
Mundele caba con mi corazón
tanto matrata, cupo van filirí
chechere bruca maniguá, ae!

I'm a Carabali, a black man from Africa
Without freedom I can't live
The white man is breaking my heart
From so much abuse my body is dead
Powerful witch from the bush!

In the same period, Afro-Puerto Rican singer Ruth Fernández liked to remind listeners of the island's African heritage in the song "¿Tu abuela, dónde está?" (Where's Your Grandmother?), addressed to a negrophobic man who denies his mixed racial ancestry:

You like the foxtrot, and me, "Bruca Maniguá"
If you're so proud of looking white, "¿Tu abuela, dónde está?"
You're a polished *blanquito* [a pass-for-white snob] and among high society,
you don't want anyone to see your mother's mother
But I know her well, her name's Siña Tatá
You hide her in the kitchen, because she's a genuine negress
Here, whoever doesn't have Dinga [blood] has Mandinga.

While some Dominicans have tried to deny the African-derived elements of merengue, in most countries, the Afro-Caribbean elements of modern popular musics are now recognized and celebrated. Reggae, the Cuban *son*, the plenas and bombas of Puerto Rican bandleader Rafael Cortijo, and even the imagery in Tego Calderón's reggaetón videos are all so overtly Afro-Caribbean that their popularity has at once reflected and helped create a wholesale mainstreaming of black identity.

However, developing an inclusive sense of national identity involves more than a simple, unidirectional acceptance of black culture. It may also demand a new sort of openness on the part of Afro-Caribbeans. The Trinidadian Denyse Plummer, as a fair-skinned teenager of biracial parents, sought to blend in with the predominantly white community she was raised in, and when she later started singing calypso, she was heckled and pelted by black audiences who resented her for being whitish, bourgeois, and female. But both through her prodigious talent and through the advent of a less proprietary public sense of popular culture, by the '80s she was well accepted by Afro-Trini audiences and went on to win the Calypso Monarch prize repeatedly. Similarly, while the Rasta aspect of roots reggae celebrated Africa and black nationalism, dancehall culture has become a remarkably open arena in which the ethnicity of Super Cat (an Indo-Jamaican) or David Rodigan (a white Brit) is essentially a non-issue.

The modern tendency to celebrate Afro-Caribbean culture as national culture is naturally complicated by the presence of other ethnic groups. Even leaving aside Cuba and Puerto Rico, with their substantial white populations, many West Indian islands have significant East Indian, Chinese, Syrian, and European communities. As we saw in chapter 9, the identity question is particularly marked in Trinidad and Guyana, where East Indians outnumber blacks. The oft-heard saying, "All ah' we is one"—which could be taken to imply that everyone should conform to a creole mainstream—is giving way to a more explicit multiculturalism. Although ethnic stereotypes still abound, and communities are often polarized by politics, the norm remains one of interracial courtesy and tolerance, not Balkan-style fratricide. And typically, the contradictions raised by Afrocentricism are expressed not in violence but in whimsical songs, like the calypso "Split Me in Two," by Mighty Dougla. Dougla, whose sobriquet denotes an Indian-African mulatto, contemplates his fate under an imaginary law repatriating all Trinidadians to their ancestral homelands:

Can somebody just tell me
where they sending poor me?
I am neither one nor the other,
six of one, half dozen of the other.
If they serious about sending back people for true,
they got to split me in two.

Such complexities and contradictions are reflected in the ethnic associations of musical styles in general. Many music genres remain identified with particular communities, with tastes and affiliations serving as boundary markers. For example, one Indo-Guyanese youth told me, "I like all kinds of Indian music, and nothing else." However, what is perhaps more marked is the tendency for Afro-Caribbean popular musics—son, reggae, soca, and konpa—to become integrating symbols, uniting audiences of all communities. In such cases, music serves less as a flame beneath a melting pot than as a dressing poured over a mixed salad, integrating its diverse elements into a coherent whole.

Meanwhile, the entertainment industry does not hesitate to foreground—or, in some cases, obscure—a performer's ethnic identity for its own commercial purposes. Since the 1990s, in mainstream U.S. pop culture, being Latino has become fashionable—in certain contexts and to certain degrees. Although Jennifer Lopez's music has no particular Latin stylistic flavor, her Puerto Rican ancestry is certainly part of her image, and, like Christina Aguilera, she does sing in Spanish as well as in English. Similarly, Ricky Martin's music, whether sung in English or Spanish, falls into the pop rather than Latin category, and he is successfully promoted to the Anglophone market as a sexy Latino (Latin, but not too Latin). For his part, Marc Anthony more overtly embodies "crossover" marketing; much of his repertoire is mainstream English-language pop, but he also sings straight-ahead salsa, draping himself in the Puerto Rican flag in his Latino-oriented concerts. And although he complains about the term "crossover," there may be no better term to describe his dual target audiences and his release of songs like the *son–montuno*–flavored "I Need to Know/Dímelo" in both Spanish and English versions.[1]

MUSIC, SEX, AND SEXISM

In the Caribbean as throughout the world, love and male–female relationships have always been favorite song topics. Throughout the region, music relates the perennial themes of love, betrayal, and loss. Caribbean men, especially in the Spanish-speaking areas, often use songs to convey their feelings, singing softly in a lover's ear, playing a romantic record over and over for a beloved woman, or even giving a sweetheart a chosen recording. In a lighter vein, songs throughout the region display an uninhibited delight in sexuality, typically expressed in whimsical, thinly disguised puns and double entendres. Beyond this level, however, the particular sentiments expressed in Caribbean music reflect the attitudes and values in the region, many of which, rather than being universal, are products of specific sociohistorical conditions.

It is difficult to generalize about gender relations in the Caribbean, as in most complex societies. Throughout the region, for example, one finds nuclear families as well as strong extended family structures. Kinship networks help provide stability and cohesion to families in situations where the men are absent or peripheral, for whatever reason. In the twentieth century, it has become quite common for men to have only loose ties to their children and partners. To a considerable extent, this condition is a legacy of slavery, which undermined the role of the male provider and, more significant, destroyed traditional African kinship structures, which had to be rebuilt afresh after emancipation.

With modernization, familial ties have been further strained by urbanization and greater mobility, which disrupted village kinship networks, and above all by poverty and unemployment. As traditional men's occupations like cutting sugarcane have been mechanized, the role of the male breadwinner has been increasingly weakened. In some cases, women stand better chances than men do of finding jobs, whether as domestics or as workers in factories whose managers prefer women because they are less likely than men to organize. Such conditions can put a tremendous strain on family cohesion. The devoted but unemployed father unable to feed his children can suffer unbearable grief and guilt, as chronicled in Zeigfield's 1938 calypso "Depression":

> Five children and a wife and myself to mind,
> but to me the world is so unkind.
> No work, no food, no clothes to wear.
> If things go on, I'll die in despair.

Such a father, however well-meaning, may even be ejected by a wife who, out of duress, finds a better provider or who is herself employed but unable to feed a dependent man. Alternately, the man may simply avoid responsibility, going from one mate to another, ignoring whatever children he sires, and hoping ideally to shack up with some woman whom he can charm into supporting him. Thus, throughout the Caribbean, as elsewhere, many lower-class men and even women have tended to avoid marital or even emotional ties that may become burdensome and frustrating. When relationships become mediated primarily by money, some employed women shun male hangers-on, and unemployed women accept men's advances only if they get something tangible in return. As Growling Tiger's calypso "Money Is King" (1935) relates:

> If you have money and things going nice,
> any woman will call you honey and spice.
> If you can't give her a dress or a new pair of shoe,
> she'll say she have no uses for you.

At worst, the women struggle to support the children, and the underemployed and demoralized men hang out in bars, listening to songs that pump up their egos and soothe their frustrations.

Music is part of this condition, but on the whole it reflects not universal feelings but predominantly male viewpoints, in accordance with male domination of most aspects of the music world and of public culture in general. Many modern Caribbean songs articulate the most self-indulgent forms of male boasting and its flip side, self-pity. Such songs may be extremely influential in presenting a certain male ideal, that of the swaggering macho stud who attracts women by his charm alone and promises nothing more than a good time. Some songs offer specific advice to other men, like the several old calypsos warning against marriage (for example, Atilla's "I'll Never Burden Myself with a Wife"). In genres as disparate as calypso, bolero, and reggae one finds denunciations of women for their alleged faithlessness, moral degeneracy, and ugliness.[2] While men boast of their sexual conquests and demand that women submit to them,[3] they denounce promiscuous women and rail against supposedly false accusations of paternity.[4] Men's irresponsibility is celebrated, and women are repeatedly portrayed as valuable only for sex.[5] Jamaican dance-hall deejays often clarify that they offer women only sex, rather than commitment, while at the same time deriding as prostitutes women who demand some material compensation for their favors.[6] Traditional calypsos, plenas, and other songs have portrayed women as trying to tie men down with black magic (obeah, *brujería*).[7] A few songs have urged men to keep their women in line and even to gain their love by beating them.[8] Many songs have articulated a paradigmatic dichotomy between the respectable yet devalued wife and the sexy and seductive mistress—in West Indian parlance, the wifey vs. the matey or deputy, or in Spanish, the *señora* vs. the *mujer de la calle* (woman of the street, quintessentially a mulata).[9]

Portrayals of women in Caribbean music vary according to individual genres and their social backgrounds. Overtly sexist songs are relatively unusual in the Spanish Caribbean, perhaps due to the persistence of Hispanic ideals of family honor—ideals that many West Indian women might find repressive in their own way. The norm in most Latin music, whether sentimental boleros or upbeat salsa songs, is a genteel sentimentality, often idealizing women, however unrealistically. There are, however, plenty of boleros and bachatas that denounce women as *mentirosas, traidoras,* and *abusadoras* (liars, cheats, and abusers).

Such song lyrics may seem sexist to some. But interpreting their social significance may be far from simple and may involve recognizing the contradictory relationships between expressive discourses like popular song and actual gender relations and attitudes. Most Caribbean popular music is dance music, in which the literal meaning of the text may be less important than the purely musical aspects. Accordingly, many listeners are easily able to ignore or shrug off the verses' problematic aspects, especially in the ideal listening context of the dance floor. One female West Indian college student told me, "I like dancehall, and I don't mind the sexist songs; I just don't take the words seriously." Another concurred: "I like this music because of how it sounds, not because I agree with the message it sends." Even in word-oriented dancehall, the text may be valued less for its message than for the way its rich alliterations, internal rhymes, and rhythmic delivery contribute to the kinetic drive of the music. The danger, however, is that among some listeners, the sexism and homophobia of the lyrics may be so rampant and ingrained that they are taken for granted.

As for the many bachatas and boleros in which broken-hearted men bitterly denounce women as liars and traitors, the innumerable female fans of such songs, rather than taking offense, may appreciate the vulnerability the male singer expresses and, in listening, can easily identify with the abstract emotions of longing and heartbreak he voices. The listener's ability to relate in this "transvestite" manner may be conditioned by the way and the extent to which a song is identified with a particular gender, depending on grammar, the sex of the singer, and other factors. Sentimental love songs are particularly likely not to be strongly gendered in their text content, such that listeners can easily transcend the overt and superficial gendering that is present. By contrast, a female listener might well have difficulty assuming the subject position in Beenie Man's "Yaw Yaw," in which the deejay boasts of having impregnated several women and sings admiringly of a friend who has twelve children who are still teething.[10]

One factor that is changing the gender dynamics of Caribbean music is the increasing ability of women to voice their own viewpoints. Women have always played important roles in performing certain kinds of Caribbean music, from domestic lullabies to church hymns, but in the Caribbean, as elsewhere, the worlds of professional folk music and commercial popular music have traditionally been dominated by men. Women have entered these genres, but they often have to contend with predominantly male personnel and male-oriented performance norms (and the producers' habit of putting a bikini-clad bimbo on album covers). Moreover, in patriarchal societies, any woman who expresses her sensuality in public runs the risk of being perceived as a sex object by men, especially in a genre so oriented toward "slackness" as Jamaican dancehall. Thus, for example, the flamboyantly sexy dancehall performers Patra and Lady Saw are seen by some West Indian women as embarrassments who reduce women to the status of bimbos and sex toys and cater to the male deejays' degrading stereotypes. Other West Indian women, however, resent the traditional double standard that allows men but not women to flaunt their sexuality, and they enjoy how the new breed of liberated women like Lady Saw, rather than being passive sex objects, can present themselves as fully in control of their exuberant sexuality. They ask, "If men can act that way, why can't we?" One female West Indian student told me, "My sisters and I were raised in a fundamentalist Christian family, and we were taught to be ashamed even to see our own naked bodies in the mirror. But Lady Saw and Patra changed all that for me!"

Other female performers, from salsa's Celia Cruz to reggae's Tanya Stephens, manage to find ways to constitute female role models without portraying themselves as boy-toys. Latin women have been able to find particular inspiration in songs like La India's "Ese hombre" (That Man) and Olga Tañón's merengue "Es Mentiroso" (He's a Liar), which turn the tables on men by denouncing duplicitous and philandering former partners. Merengue singer Lidia de la Rosa resignified the evergreen "La Chiflera," with its denunciation of duplicitous women, by adding her own verses, "If the man is going to have a good time, the woman will, too."[11]

In many cases, however, female performers have relied on male producers and composers. The all-female merengue group Las Chicas del Can showed that women could play and sing just like men, and their songs included some witty feminist manifestos, such as that presenting a woman getting back at her cheating man by doing the same ("It wasn't one man, nor two, it was three"). Some people, however, felt that the band's ability to serve as female role models was compromised by the fact that Las Chicas, from its compositions to its skimpy "jiggle-show" outfits, was overwhelmingly the creation of a male producer, Wilfrido Vargas. To what extent, and in what way, does the gender of the author matter? Does it matter that Cuban singer La Lupe's moving and poignant neo-feminist song "La Tirana" was written by a man (Tite Curet Alonso)? Or, for that matter, that Aretha Franklin's liberated–soul-sister anthem "Respect" was also written by a man and earlier recorded by Otis Redding?

In many cases, more important than a song's lyrics are the dynamics of how the song is used, especially in terms of what is happening on the dance floor. Whether in a reggae club or Trinidad's Carnival procession, it often seems that, regardless of the song lyrics, women are ruling the scene, flaunting their sensuality in a way that is more for their own enjoyment than aimed to entice men. Hence, while a dour critic might regard the words of the merengue "La Tanga" (The Thong) as "objectifying," when that song is performed in clubs women love to jump to the stage and strut their stuff to wild applause. Similarly, a Jamaican college student emphasized to me how the sexy, hedonistic lyrics of dancehall songs are perfectly suited to the party and club milieu. She wrote, "As couples gyrate against a wall to lyrics like 'Wine pon me Gal' and 'Flex Girl Time to Have Sex,' the content of the song is not offensive, but necessary. If dancehall performers began to base the contents of their songs on world peace, family life, or even the sweetness of falling in love, the music would lose its edge and popularity."

A disparaging voice might argue that the celebration of sexuality for its own sake can serve to reduce individuals to bodies and body parts and encourage the sexual exploitation of women and the failure of men to take responsibility for the children they sire. These are not merely narrow, puritanical concerns in societies or subcultures where the weakness of the institution of the family places great burdens on women and children. At the same time, it could well be argued that the dance floor is the one arena in which sensuality can be celebrated in a controlled and even artistically creative context. It is clear that millions of women in the Caribbean and elsewhere experience popular music as a liberating and even exhilarating force precisely because it allows them to experience and, through dancing, express their own sexuality, free from the traditional constraints of family, religion, and patriarchy in general. In that sense, the open eroticism of much Caribbean dance music, however rampant with objectification and hedonism, may constitute an essential and arguably liberating aspect.

CARIBBEAN MUSIC INTERNATIONAL

Liberty Avenue in Queens and Brooklyn's Nostrand Avenue typify the new kind of polyglot Caribbean migrant neighborhoods that have emerged in New York City and elsewhere. West Indian snack bars offering calaloo and roti adjoin Chinese-Cuban eateries, while groceries hawk coconuts, curry powder, fresh fish from Guyana, cassava, and day-old Caribbean newspapers. On the sidewalk, one hears a Babel-like chatter of Spanish, Jamaican patwa, Haitian creole, Afro-American jive, and even standard English (though usually with a Caribbean lilt). Meanwhile, ghetto-blasters, car stereos, and storefront cassette players boom out the throbbing rhythms of merengue, salsa, soca, and reggae, which intertwine like some perpetually changing postmodern polyrhythm.

New York has become a Caribbean city, especially since the 1980s, when its Caribbean population reached a sort of critical mass of more than 2 million. As of 2005, more than a third of the city's 8 million residents are Caribbean immigrants or their children. New York is now the biggest Caribbean city and the second biggest Jamaican, Haitian, and Guyanese city. There are more people from Nevis in New York than there are in Nevis itself. Dominicans, numbering more than 800,000, have become the dominant community in Washington Heights ("Quisqueya Heights") and parts of Queens and Brooklyn, as have Puerto Ricans in Spanish Harlem and the Lower East Side ("Loisaida") of Manhattan, and English-speaking West Indians elsewhere in Brooklyn and Queens. While other North American cities like Cleveland and Detroit have degenerated into depopulated rotting shells, New York's economy has been revitalized by Caribbeans who bring their traditions of initiative and self-reliance. As the saying goes, when a West Indian gets ten cents above a beggar, he opens a business—and adds color and vitality to the city's street life and culture.

The vicissitudes of the immigrant experience—especially to New York—have been voiced, whether poignantly or humorously, in dozens of plenas, *aguinaldos*, merengues, calypsos, and dancehall songs. Taken retrospectively, many of these can be seen to articulate a loosely sequential set of stages, or what Juan Flores, in reference to Newyorican identity, calls "moments,"[12] in terms of their attitudes toward New York vis-à-vis the island former homeland. The starting point for these is the immediate reality of the forsaken homeland and the difficult and often hostile new urban environment. In this initial stage, the immigrant community is an isolated "island in the city," whence the singer longs to return home: "Yo me vuelvo a mi bohío" (I'm going back to my hut). The harshness of the dislocation engenders Flores's second "moment," an enhanced and often idealized appreciation of the Caribbean homeland, which is eulogized as a place of physical and emotional warmth, in contrast to cold and unfriendly New York. As Flores points out, this new appreciation of the homeland, although nostalgic and utopian, can extend to its Afro-Caribbean aspects. It can also constitute a necessary step toward the next "moment" or state of mind, in which immigrants—or, more typically, their children—transcend sentiments of despair and loss, embrace their new homeland, and assert the legitimacy of their own culture therein. Thus, in the '70s, New York *salseros* saw themselves not as some voiceless, disempowered minority, but as the musical messengers of a new sense of Latino pride which, like salsa, emerged in New York, while drawing from island tradition. Hence, Bobby Rodriguez could sing:

> I bring you a message . . . . It's the *clave* of the *guaguancó* rhythm
> the modern sound from the enchanted isle (Puerto Rico)
> I sing to my Puerto Rico and to Los Angeles as well
> to Venezuela and Santo Domingo.[13]

This dynamic and transplanted modernization of island-based music paves the way for the culminating "moment," in which Caribbean-Americans actively and selectively embrace other aspects of mainland (perhaps especially Afro-American) culture, along with other Caribbean cultures. This process is nowhere more apparent than in music, when local performers freely combine salsa, merengue, and reggae with rap and R&B, and with each other. And as Flores stresses, such hybrids should no longer be seen as a case of Caribbean Americans passively assimilating to the hegemonic mainland culture, but rather as dynamic artistic collaborations enacted from a position of cultural strength and confidence.

Many Caribbean immigrants keep closely in touch with their homelands by way of cut-rate phone cards, satellite TV, faxes and modems, camera phones, and frequent visits. With their dual senses of loyalty and their networks of families and friends in both places, they constitute transnational communities that are economically, emotionally, and culturally as much "there" as they are "here." For others, "home" is a distant island that they may have never seen, barely remember, or remember in a way that hasn't existed for decades. Homeland ties may be particularly poignant for undocumented workers who are unable to return home, except to leave the United States for good. For all of them, music and food can assume new significance as symbols of identity; curry goat and reggae music can represent Jamaica, just as roti and calypso signify Trinidad. Caribbean migrants and their descendants develop complex and multiple senses of identity, so that a second-generation Jamaican may see himself or herself in various contexts as Jamaican, West Indian, Afro-Caribbean, Afro-American, Brooklynite, or just plain American. Most Caribbeans, rather than wishing to assimilate totally, want to retain some sense of their origins, and their musical tastes generally reflect these cosmopolitan and overlapping senses of identity.

Emigration has mixed effects on musical culture in the homelands. Emigrants can enrich island culture by sending money home and by serving as conduits for new trends and ideas. Haitians in the United States, for example, send considerable money back home to support Rara festivals. At the same time, the tendency for the best and brightest to emigrate can deplete the ranks of talented musicians on the islands. Lesser folk-music genres that fail to thrive in emigrant communities can decline altogether. For example, folksong traditions formerly maintained in lively "tea meetings" on islands like Nevis and St. Vincent have been eclipsed markedly because most of the creative performers have left.[14] Islanders left behind express their demoralization in songs like the early 1990s calypso from Dominica "Dominicans Come Home."

Such instances of cultural impoverishment are to some extent counterbalanced by the thriving of Caribbean culture abroad. As we have seen, New York, with its media infrastructure and concentrated Caribbean enclaves, has been a center for Caribbean music for many decades. From the 1920s, most of the leading Puerto Rican composers and performers, from Manuel "Canario" Jiménez to Rafael Hernández, came to live in the city, and much of the evolution of Latin dance music took place here. The mambo evolved mostly in clubs like the Palladium, and salsa emerged as a barrio reinterpretation and resignification of Cuban dance music in the late 1960s. New York continues to be the center of the recording industries for Haitian and West Indian music, and record piracy throughout the Caribbean makes it the biggest record market. Other cities, like Toronto, Birmingham, and Paris, have played similar roles in the development of modern Caribbean music, collectively hosting more clubs, record producers, and top groups than the islands themselves.

Of course, the international presence of Caribbean music has never been limited to immigrant communities. In the nineteenth century, the habanera charmed European salon dancers, and Jamaican regiments brought by the British to their West African colonies introduced not only European brass band music but also their own syncretic "goombay." Since then, Caribbean commercial popular-music styles have found their own international audiences, often in accordance with the eccentricities of the global music industries. In some cases these may be motivated by the sheer power of the music. In the 1950s in the United States, the mambo was, by any standards, some of the hottest dance music around. In other cases, Yankee demand for some sort of superficially exotic, sensuous, and tropical beat has generated ephemeral fads of various bowdlerized versions of Caribbean music. Hence, the first LP in the world to sell a million copies was not by Elvis, or the Beatles, but Harry Belafonte's 1956 *Calypso*, which spawned a brief but furious fad of ersatz calypsos and shaped the repertoire of West Indian tourist music for generations. As Belafonte often pointed out, most of the songs on the LP, like "Day-O," were not calypsos at all, but the vogue led to corny "calypsos" subsequently being recorded by such aspiring entertainers as Louis Farrakhan, Maya Angelou, Robert Mitchum, Alan Arkin, Jack Lemmon, and Rita Hayworth. (Said Trinidadian scholar Keith Warner of Hayworth's "calypso" dancing in the film *Fire Down Below*, "It just looked to us like another white person who can't dance.")

Some of the most significant disseminations of Caribbean music have largely bypassed the developed West, with the mass media allowing Caribbean musics to spread way beyond the reach of Caribbean musicians themselves. Thus, for example, Cuban dance music became a dominant urban popular music in Africa during the mid-twentieth century, providing, among other things, a model for the composition and performance of horn-based dance musics, which later evolved into the more distinctively local genres like Congolese soukous. Since the 1970s, roots reggae came to enjoy phenomenal popularity in African countries like Gambia, whether in the form of old Bob Marley records or new songs in local languages by performers like Alpha

Blondy (Ivory Coast) and Lucky Dube (South Africa). With the added input of dynamic groups like Steel Pulse in Great Britain, roots reggae in many respects came to flourish outside the Caribbean more than in its homeland, Jamaica. For that matter, dancehall has also become a global style, easily adapted to local languages everywhere from Malawi to New Zealand. Similarly, zouk—or "Cabo zouk"—sung in Cape Verdean creole has become the dominant dance music in Cape Verde and its diasporic communities in Europe and New England.

In general, musics like salsa, reggae, and zouk have taken on lives of their own outside the Caribbean, becoming truly international. This process, however, does not signify a global cooptation of Caribbean music, for the region itself and its émigré musicians continue to be sources for the most dynamic innovations. For the most creative artists, Caribbean music now involves combining international sounds and Caribbean cross-fertilizations while often reaching deep into local traditions for inspiration.

MUSIC AND POLITICS

The Caribbean has long served as a vacation retreat for many foreigners; Caribbean people themselves, however, have historically had to contend with toil, relative poverty, and repressive and corrupt governments that have often been imposed by outside forces. One function of music in the Caribbean, as elsewhere, has always been to provide some sort of escape from such adversity. In dancing and singing, people can temporarily forget their woes, reaffirm community ties and values, and cultivate their own artistic creativity. But it has also been the nature of music and verse to express the full range of human emotions, including those related to sociopolitical conditions. Through music, men and women can voice aspirations and ideals, strengthen group solidarity, and transcend adversity by confronting it and transmuting it into song. Accordingly, music in the Caribbean has often been explicitly linked to sociopolitical struggles.

Local music genres, whether overtly political or not, can be important symbols of nationalistic pride and identity. In the nineteenth century, both Cuban habaneras and Puerto Rican danzas, aside from being fashionable dances, were celebrated as symbols of bourgeois and petty bourgeois opposition to Spanish rule. The unofficial Puerto Rican anthem, "La Borinqueña," is a gentle danza rather than a military march. Many other songs and *décimas* of this period also explicitly celebrated the independence struggle and, later, nationalistic opposition to Yankee domination. Populist dictators like Trujillo have also promoted local musics for their own propaganda purposes.

Some musicians themselves have entered the realm of politics. Harry Belafonte, however maligned for his commercialization of calypso, was a fervent champion of progressive causes and a critic of racism and American imperialism. Merengue innovator Johnny Ventura was an outspoken opponent of the Balaguer dictatorship in the Dominican Republic and held important political offices, while salsa artists Ruben Blades and Willie Colon both ran energetically, if unsuccessfully, for political office. While Colon has composed songs dealing with everything from military despots to AIDS, he said during his 1994 campaign for the U.S. Congress, "Sometimes writing a song is not enough."

In the twentieth century, one of the greatest challenges for Caribbean countries has been to ameliorate poverty by gaining control over their own natural resources and by creating social justice. North American imperialism has in many cases impeded such progress. Virtually whenever a Caribbean state has attempted significant reform—redistribution of wealth, land reform, or nationalization of resources—the United States has intervened, often by overthrowing governments in the name of "safeguarding American interests" and "fighting communism." Aside from the numerous regional military occupations in the early twentieth century,[15] the CIA destabilized elected governments in Guatemala (1954) and Guyana (1962–64), effectively replacing them with corrupt and brutal dictatorships. In 1964, the U.S. Marines invaded the Dominican Republic to restore the Trujillo elite to power. In the 1970s, U.S. hostility helped undermine the reformist People's National Party (PNP) government in Jamaica, leading to its defeat in 1980 by the more pliant Jamaican Labour Party. In 1991, U.S.-trained Haitian generals on the CIA payroll ousted elected Prime Minister Jean-Bertrand Aristide and instituted a reign of terror. While American intervention in 1994 nominally restored Aristide to office, it has served to sustain the infrastructure of military and paramilitary repression, and in 2004 Aristide was again pressured by the United States—albeit in complex circumstances—to abdicate. Since 1959, the Cuban people have had to endure all manner of Yankee hostility, including armed invasion in 1962, ongoing CIA-backed sabotage and terrorism,[16] and a crippling embargo.

During this period, much of the Caribbean music industry has been dominated by North American–owned multinationals with a vested interest in maintaining the status quo. There has also been a marked tendency—and often explicit pressure from producers—for musicians in the industry to avoid controversial song lyrics and stick to stock romantic or sexual themes. Nevertheless, different forms of Caribbean music have, in their own way, confronted social reality and reflected, however idiosyncratically, the demand for social justice. Such uses of music were particularly prominent in the 1960s and '70s, which were a period of sociopolitical ferment, mobilization, and optimism throughout the region, as in much of the world. The Cuban Revolution was thriving, the Dominican dictator Rafael Trujillo was dead at last, and the newly independent West Indian states thought that they could for the first time control their own national destinies. As Bob Marley sang (ambiguously, to be sure): "If you are the big tree, we are the small axe, ready to cut you down." In the United States, this was the era of the youth counterculture and the Black Power movement, whose influence spilled over into the Caribbean. And last, even if the Soviet bloc itself did not constitute an attractive model, at least its existence and the aid it could provide implied the possibility of an alternative to Yankee domination and cultural "Coca-Colonization."

The *nueva canción* of Cuba and, to a lesser extent, of Puerto Rico and the Dominican Republic was one form of music explicitly linked to the optimism and idealism of the era. Other genres have mirrored the spirit of the age in their own ways. Salsa of the 1970s emerged as the youthful voice of the barrio, self-consciously assertive and optimistic, chronicling the vicissitudes of lower-class urban life with a dynamic exuberance. In Jamaica, the sociopolitical ferment of urban youth found expression in roots reggae, which was linked not only to Rastafari but also to the activism and idealism of the 1970s PNP government. Calypsos by Black Stalin, Chalkdust, and others also reflected the influence of the Black Power movement and the broader political consciousness of the period.

In subsequent years, however, political developments frustrated most of the aspirations of the 1960s and '70s, leading to the decline of the utopian idealism expressed in that period's music. By the 1980s, the American youth counterculture had declined, and the Civil Rights Movement, having achieved some important goals, dissipated in the face of more intractable problems of economic equity. In the Latino community, the Young Lords self-destructed, and salsa lyrics withdrew from barrio assertiveness to the safe common-denominator topics of romance and melodrama. The years around 1990 found the Cuban Revolution in crisis, the Trujillo–Balaguer elite back in power, and the Puerto Rican independence movement marginalized for good. The *nueva trova* movement seemed to sputter out accordingly. In Jamaica, the PNP experiment collapsed under hostility from the United States and the International Monetary Fund, leading to a return to the status quo of multinational exploitation and laissez-faire capitalism. Accordingly, roots reggae's militancy has largely given way to the boasting and slackness of dancehall, and Bob Marley's "Redemption Song" has given way to Mad Cobra's "Flex, Time to Have Sex."

In retrospect, the 1960s and '70s, with their exuberant optimism and idealism, seem like a passing revolutionary historical moment, at once admirably idealistic and naively utopian. In the globalized "New World Order," with its absence of clear imperialist antagonists, singing of revolution and redemption has become like spitting into the wind, and popular music seems to have retreated into sensuality, sentimentality, and lumpen nihilism. Perhaps it may be inappropriate to expect dance music to do more than entertain, although the music of Ruben Blades and Juan Luis Guerra, and songs like Buju Banton's "Untold Stories," suggest ways of transcending the norms of commercial entertainment. And there is something to be said for dancing through adversity, in a way that combines both escapism and affirmation of life, community, and hope.

Notes

CHAPTER ONE

1. The Inquisition, although hardly an indication of cultural tolerance, was a religious campaign rather than a racial one and was aimed at Jews and Moors, not blacks.

2. In Trinidad and Guyana, a "creole" generally implies a black or mulatto person, as opposed to an East Indian, and "creolization" thus has a different meaning, referring, for example, to the phenomenon of an East Indian adopting Afro-Trinidadian manners.

3. In Roger Abrahams and John Szwed, eds., *After Africa: Extracts from British Travel Accounts and Journals of the Seventeenth, Eighteenth, and Nineteenth Centuries concerning the Slaves, the Manners, and Customs in the British West Indies* (New Haven, Conn.: Yale University Press, 1983), 301.

4. Derek Walcott, "The Muse of History," in *Is Massa Day Dead? Black Moods in the Caribbean*, ed. Orde Coombs (Garden City, N.Y.: Anchor Books, 1974).

CHAPTER TWO

1. *Guaguancó* is pronounced "wa-wan-có." Perhaps this is a good place for a word on Spanish pronunciation in general, with which all North Americans should be familiar. Briefly, *j* is an aspirated *h*; *ll* is like *y*; *h* is silent; *z* is like *s*; *gue* is like *gay*; *güe* is like *gway* (or *way*); and *qui* is like *key*. Hence, *jolla* is pronounced *hoya*; *hija* is pronounced *ee-ha*; *quinto* is pronounced *keen-toe*; and *son* falls somewhere between *sun* and *sone*.

2. Note that this *décima* uses the word "American" to refer to the United States. Today, many Cubans, Puerto Ricans, and other Caribbean peoples (who are also "Americans") would resent such a usage, preferring the term "North American." In deference to this school of thought, I favor that usage in this book.

3. Alejo Carpentier, *La música en Cuba* (Mexico City: Fonda de Cultura Económica, 1946), 104–105, and in the translation of this work, *Music in Cuba*, trans. Alan West-Duran, ed. Timothy Brennan (Minneapolis: University of Minnesota Press, 2001), 130.

4. "Yo nací de Africa, tal vez soy del Congo, tal vez soy del Ampanga .... Yo no soy Rodríguez, yo no soy Fernández .... Tal vez soy Amoto, tal vez soy Momomba."

5. In Steven Loza, *Tito Puente and the Making of Latin Music* (Urbana: University of Illinois Press, 1999), 68.

6. "La esencia del guaguanco" was originally released on *La Perfecta Combinación* (Fania 4XT-SLPC-380). It was composed by Tite Curet Alonso.

7. Sue Steward, ¡*Música! The Rhythm of Latin America: Salsa, Rumba, Merengue, and More* (San Francisco: Chronicle Books, 1999), 79.

8. Pablo Menéndez, as quoted in Mark Kurlansky, *A Continent of Islands* (New York: Addison-Wesley, 1992), 113.

9. Silvio Rodríguez, "Pequeña serenata diurna" (Little Daytime Serenade): "Vivo en un país libre / cual solamente puede ser libre / en esta tierra, en este instante / y soy feliz porque soy gigante . . . . Soy feliz, soy un hombre feliz / y quiero que me perdonen / por este día / los muertos / de mi felicidad."

10. Congressman Robert Torricelli, sponsor of the early 1990s law tightening the embargo, stated, "I want to wreak havoc on that island." See, for example, www.greenleft.org.au/back/2001/455/455p21.htm.

11. In Eugene Robinson, *Last Dance in Havana* (New York: Free Press, 2004), 121.

CHAPTER THREE

1. Chuitín and Chuito, "Quién manda en la casa," on *Un jíbaro terminao*, vol. 2 (Ansonia SALP 1519).

2. Baltazar Carrero, "El jíbaro de rincón," on *Tierra adentro* (Ansonia SALP 1537).

3. Ramito, "Puerto Rico cambiado," on *Parrandeando* (Ansonia SALP 1492).

4. James McCoy, "The Bomba and Aguinaldo of Puerto Rico as They Have Evolved from Indigenous, African, and European Cultures" (Ph.D. diss., Florida State University, Tallahassee, 1968), 167. A typical bomba text is: "The policeman's wife ran off with the fireman / to see if he could put out the fire" (La mujer del policía se fue con el bombero / porque ella quería saber cómo se apagaba el fuego): Mohammed Dua, *Nueva colección de bombas Puertorriqueñas* (San Juan: self-published, 1990). For more discussion of modern bomba, see Hal Barton, "A Challenge for Puerto Rican Music: How to Build a *Soberao* for Bomba," *Centro de estudios puertorriqueños Bulletin* 16, no. 1 (2004): 69–89.

5. "Mamita llegó e Obispo / llegó el Obispo de Roma / mamita, si tú lo vieras. ¡Qué cosa linda, qué cosa mona! . . . El Obispo no toma ron / que le gusta la cañita / Mamita, so tú lo vieras, ¡qué cosa linda cuando se pica!"

6. As quoted in Juan Flores, *Divided Borders: Essays on Puerto Rican Identity* (Houston: Arte Publico Press, 1993), 104.

7. Rafael Hernández, "Yo vuelvo a mi bohío."

8. El Gallito de Manatí, "Culpando el subway," on *Tierra adentro* (Ansonia SALP 1537).

9. Baltazar Carrero, "Un jíbaro en Nueva York," on *Tierra adentro* (Ansonia SALP 1537).

10. "No sufren por nada / aunque estén ausente / si brille en sus mentes / su tierra adorada / siempre recordara / una vida entera. / Si un día cualquiera / verás tu regreso, / vente con un beso; / tu patria te espera / en la Navidad, Borinquen" (*aguinaldo orocoveño*).

11. Jorge Javariz, as quoted in Ruth Glasser, "The Backstage View: Musicians Piece Together a Living," *Centro de estudios puertorriqueños Bulletin* (Spring 1991): 25.

12. "Yo tuve un sueño feliz, quise hacerlo una canción, y mi guitarra cogí, puse todo el corazón, concentré pensando en ti . . . . Era en una playa de mi tierra tan querida . . . "

13. In John Storm Roberts, *The Latin Tinge: The Impact of Latin American Music on the United States*, 2nd ed. (New York: Oxford University Press, 1999), 87.

14. Ibid., 86; Glasser, "The Backstage View."

15. Flores, *Divided Borders*, 104.

CHAPTER FOUR

1. In fact, some of Pacheco's early hits, despite LP titles like *Pacheco y su Nuevo Tumbao* (Pacheco and His New Beat), were simply well-executed covers of forgotten and by then unavailable recordings by the Cuban bands of Felix Chappotin and Benny Moré.

2. Sergio George, interview with Vernon Boggs, *Latin Beat*, vol. 3, no. 1, February 1993.

3. A reference to the Cuban nationalist José Martí, who wrote of the United States in an 1895 letter: "I have lived inside the monster and know its entrails."

4. Willie Colon, "Calle lune calle sol," on *Lo mato* (Fania SLP 00044) (copyright by José Flores, Sonido Inc.).

5. From Willie Colon's 1967 "El malo": "El malo de aquí soy yo, porque tengo corazón."

6. The second line of "Juanito Alimaña" refers to Rafael Hernández's 1930s "Lamento Borincano," with its portrayal of the optimistic *jíbaro*: "Sale loco de contento con su cargamento por la ciudad" (He leaves, full of joy, for work in the city).

7. Salsa's rise in Venezuela is documented in Lise Waxer, "Llegó la salsa: The Rise of Salsa in Venezuela and Colombia," in *Situating Salsa: Global Markets and Local Meaning in Latin Popular Music*, ed. Lise Waxer (New York: Routledge, 2002).

8. Ruben Blades, as quoted in Jeremy Marre and Hannah Charleton, *Beats of the Heart: Popular Music of the World* (New York: Pantheon, 1985), 80.

9. Ruben Blades, as quoted in "Singer, Actor, Politico," *Time*, 29 January 1990, 50.

10. Ibid., 52.

11. Eddie Palmieri, "Ven ven," originally on *Cheo y Quintana* (Barbera LP B205 SENI 0798).

12. The cover bands, which are thus generally unable to get original scores for the hits they play, have to have someone transcribe the songs, including the complex horn parts, from records. Chris Washburne, who plays for both original and cover bands, told the author, "Sometimes I'll be playing in a cover band, doing a song that I also play in its original version. It can really throw me off when I'll be playing my part, more or less on automatic pilot, and then all of a sudden there's a change, because the guy who transcribed it from the record got the part wrong."

13. As of 2005, some websites promoting "on two" dancing include www.salsanewyork.com and www.salsaweb.com. See Sydney Hutchinson, "Mambo on 2: The Birth of a New Form of Dance in New York City," *Centro de estudios puertorriqueños Bulletin* 16, no. 2 (2004): 109–37.

14. Jorge Manuel López, interview, *El Diario*, 24 September 1993, 32.

15. Pablo Guzmán, "¡Siempre Salsa!" *Village Voice*, 25 June 1979, 92.

16. Vico C, "Bomba para afincar," on *Hispanic Soul* (Prime CD 1014): "Puerto Rico tiene bomba para brincar, Venezuela tiene bomba para pegar, Colombia tiene bomba para gozar."

17. Latin Empire, interview with Juan Flores, "Latin Empire: Puerto Rap," *Centro de estudios puertorriqueños Bulletin* (Spring 1991): 81. A number of black English-language rappers (including Dres of Black Sheep and former Fat Boy Prince Markie Dee) are Latino.

18. Edgardo Díaz, "Pablo Milanés: Un canto sin dirección," *El Mundo* (San Juan), 2 February 1985, 52.

CHAPTER FIVE

1. See Martha Ellen Davis's discussion of these traditions in *The Garland Encyclopedia of World Music: South America, Mexico, Central America, and the Caribbean* (New York: Garland Publishing, 1998), 850–57.

2. Paul Austerlitz, *Dominican Merengue in Regional, National, and International Perspectives* (Philadelphia: Temple University Press, 1997), is a principal source for information on merengue in this chapter.

3. "Tropicó, mira tu chivo, después de muerto, cantando" (Manuel del Cabral).

4. After all, the Nobel Prize was given to Vietnam War architect Henry Kissinger.

5. "Puerto Rico queda cerca, pero móntate en avión, y si consigues la visa, no hay problemas en inmigración; pero no te vayas en yola, no te llenes de ilusiones, porque en el Canal de la Mona, te comen los tiburones" (Wilfrido Vargas).

6. Willie Rodríguez, as cited in Deborah Pacini, *Bachata: A Social History of a Dominican Popular Music* (Philadelphia: Temple University Press, 1995).

7. For example, journalist Alex Soto, *Listin*, 6 October 1993.

8. Daisane McLane, "Uptown and Downhome," *Village Voice Rock 'n' Roll Quarterly*, Winter 1991, 15.

9. All bachata texts cited in this section are from Pacini, *Bachata*.

10. This song is adapted from a Congolese soukous tune by Lea Lignazi, "Dede Priscilla," on *Sound d'Afrique II "Soukous"* (Island ISSP 4008).

11. Hector Guttierez, *Latin Beat*, vol. 3, no. 2, March 1993, 37.

12. I am indebted to Sydney Hutchinson for this information on current *merengue típico*.

CHAPTER SIX

1. In Haiti, "Vodou" is most often used to refer to a specific rite in the Rada denomination of spirits. Recently, writers have used the term to refer to all Rada religious rituals. Although Haitians do not have a single term to refer to all religious rituals associated with African ancestral spirits, I use the term "Vodou" to refer to spiritual practices in general. My purpose is to contrast the practice of Vodou with the stereotypical depiction of Haitian spirituality known as "voodoo."

2. The word "Rara" should be pronounced by rolling the sound *r* in the back of the throat, as in French.

3. Gage Averill, *A Day for the Hunter, a Day for the Prey: Music and Power in Haiti* (Chicago: University of Chicago Press, 1997), is the principal source of information on Haitian popular music in this chapter.

4. The contredanse, which was among the most popular dances at *bals*, or dances of the colonial elite, was eventually adopted by the rural Haitian population and is still performed today at outdoor festivals known as *fèt champèt*.

5. Tabou Combo, "Konpa ce pam," on *Aux Antilles* (Zafem Records TC 8056CD).

6. Jocelyne Guilbault, *Zouk: World Music in the West Indies* (Chicago: University of Chicago Press, 1993), is the principal source of information on zouk in this chapter.

7. Dominique Cyrille, "Sa Ki Ta Nou (This Belongs to Us): Creole Dances of the French Caribbean," in *Caribbean Dance from Abakuá to Zouk: How Movement Shapes Identity*, ed. Susanna Sloat (Gainesville: University Press of Florida), 244.

8. Guilbault, *Zouk*, 32.

9. Ibid., 216.

10. Julian Gerstin, "Interaction and Improvisation between Dancers and Drummers in Martinican Bèlè," *Black Music Research* 18, nos. 1–2 (1998): 126.

11. Despite their slightly different versions of French-based creole, the languages of Martinique, Guadeloupe, Dominica, and St. Lucia will be referred to as Kwéyòl.

12. Guilbault, *Zouk*, 144.

CHAPTER SEVEN

1. Partly because Kumina *is* one of Jamaica's most African musics, popular books and films on Jamaican music continue to make the error of equating it with Maroon music. For instance, the recent film *Before Reggae Hit the Town*, dir. Mark Gorney (University of California Extension Center for Media and Independent Learning, 1990), includes a scene of Kumina drumming and dancing and represents it as "Maroon music." In fact, the main music-and-dance tradition of the Maroons, called "kromanti play," is separate from Kumina, going back to the eighteenth century and featuring entirely different kinds of drums and musical genres. Kumina, in contrast, is derived largely from traditions introduced to Jamaica during the nineteenth century by African contract laborers, primarily from the Congo region. Unlike Kumina, Maroon kromanti play has had almost no influence on Jamaican popular music, since it has traditionally been considered secret and until recently was never played outside Maroon communities. Maroon music has been able to exert a slight influence on outside styles only by way of the Kumina tradition, to which it has lent a number of songs learned by Kumina musicians from Maroons visiting their ceremonies.

For more on the influence of the Kumina religion and its music on the Howellite Rastafarians, see Kenneth Bilby and Elliott Leib, "Kumina, the Howellite Church and the Emergence of Rastafarian Traditional Music in Jamaica," *Jamaica Journal* 19, 3 (1985): 22–28.

2. Shabba's quote is from "Gun Pon Me," as cited in Carolyn Cooper, *Sound Clash: Jamaican Dancehall Culture at Large* (New York: Palgrave/Macmillan, 2004), 154. Burrell is quoted in *XLR8R*, no. 82 (November 2004): 50.

3. Half Pint, as quoted in Brian Jahn and Tom Weber, *Reggae Island: Jamaican Music in the Digital Age* (Kingston: Kingston Publishers, 1998), 108.

4. See Cooper, *Sound Clash,* chap. 2.

5. In 2004, Human Rights Watch issued a scathing report, "Hated to Death," on the persecution of gays in Jamaica (at www.hrw.org). Homophobia flourishes on institutional as well as grassroots levels; gay sex is punishable by up to ten years in prison, and the 2001 theme song of the Jamaican Labour Party was T.O.K.'s gay-bashing "Chi Chi Man." Note, however, that calls to "burn a fire 'pon" someone can be taken either literally or as referring metaphorically to a process of purification. Beenie Man, for his part, issued a vague apology for his homophobic lyrics in 2004, but deejays like Sizzla, despite being banned from entering the United Kingdom, have remained defiantly unrepentant. In February 2005, a deal was brokered between British gay-rights organizations and leading dancehall record companies and promoters, under which the latter agreed to curb releases of gay-bashing songs, while gay activists suspended their campaigns against homophobic singers; see "Ceasefire Brokered in Reggae Lyrics War," *The Guardian,* 5 February 2005.

6. From a concert report written for the author by Dainia Lawes, a student at John Jay College, New York, in 2004.

7. This dialogue is freely adapted from postings at www.reggaeweb.com.

CHAPTER EIGHT

1. "Jean and Dinah" (words and music by Don Raye and Mighty Sparrow), © 1957 MCA Music Publishing, a Division of MCA, Inc. Copyright Renewed. International Copyright Secured. All Rights Reserved. Used by Permission.

2. Mighty Sparrow and Lord Melody "Picong" (1957), on *Calypso Kings and Pink Gin* (Cook 1185).

3. Chalkdust, "Kaiso in the Hospital," on *Chalkdust–Visions* (Straker GS2365).

4. See Gordon Rohlehr, *Calypso and Society in Pre-Independence Trinidad* (Tunapuna, Trinidad: self-published, 1990), chap. 5; Keith Warner, *Kaiso! The Trinidad Calypso* (Washington, D.C.: Three Continents, 1985), chap. 4.

5. Hope Smith discusses these and other aspects of modern carnival and calypso in Ph.D. dissertation, "Gender Misbehaving: Women in Trinidadian Popular Music" (University of Texas, Austin, 2001).

6. In Stephen Steumpfle, *Steelband Movement: The Forging of a National Art in Trinidad and Tobago* (Philadelphia: University of Pennsylvania Press, 1995) 27.

7. See Donald Hill, *The Big Drum and Other Ritual and Social Music of Carriacou* (Folkways FE 34002).

CHAPTER NINE

1. In Roger Abrahams and John Szwed, eds., *After Africa: Extracts from British Travel Accounts and Journals of the Seventeenth, Eighteenth, and Nineteenth Centuries Concerning the Slaves, the Manners, and Customs in the British West Indies* (New Haven, Conn.: Yale University Press, 1983), 290.

2. In Lorna McDaniel, *The Big Drum Ritual of Carriacou: Praisesongs in Rememory of Flight* (Gainesville: University Press of Florida, 1998), 89–90. See also the similar 1831 account cited in Richard Burton, *Afro-Creole: Power, Opposition, and Play in the Caribbean* (Ithaca, N.Y.: Cornell University Press, 1997), 67.

3. Naipaul, *The Middle Passage* (London: Penguin, 1962), 231.

4. Much of the information on small island music comes from entries in Dale Olsen and Daniel Sheehy, eds., *The Garland Encyclopedia of World Music: South America, Mexico, Central America, and the Caribbean* (New York: Garland Publishing, 1998). Other informative sources, aside from those cited at the end of chapter 9, include John Szwed and Morton Marks, "The Afro-American Transformation of European Set Dances and Dance Suites," in *Dance Research Journal* 20, no. 1 (1988); Donald Hill, liner notes, *The Big Drum and other Ritual and Social Music of Carriacou* (Folkways FE 34002).

5. Thanks are due to Rebecca Miller for this information.

CHAPTER TEN

1. Marc Anthony (born Marco Antonio) has stated, "This crossover thing really displaces me. Like I'm coming in and invading America with my music. I was born and raised in New York, man" (as quoted in Licia Fiol Matta, "Pop *Latinidad*: Puerto Ricans in the Latin Explosion," *Centro de estudios puertorriqueños Bulletin* 14, no. 1 [2004]: 40).

2. For example, Mighty Sparrow's 1950s calypso "Jean Marabunta" (see Keith Warner, *Kaiso! The Trinidad Calypso* [Washington, D.C.: Three Continents, 1985], 100); Rafael Cortijo, "Severa" (1950s Puerto Rican *guaracha*).

3. For example, Buju Banton, "Have to Get Your Body Tonight" (" . . . even by gunpoint"), or Bounty Killa's "Stucky" (1980s dancehall).

4. For example, in El Gran Combo's "Me dicen papá" (1970s Puerto Rican salsa), the singer complains about all the multiracial children who call him "Papa" and whom he must support, noting that some of them resemble his friends who hang around, and one of them looks like the bolero singer and famed ladies' man Daniel Santos. Other songs in this vein include Mighty Terror's "Chinese Children" and Sparrow's "Child Father" (calypsos; see Warner, *Kaiso!* 97–98); and Bounty Killa's "Living Dangerously" (dancehall).

5. For example, Atilla's "I'll Never Burden Myself with a Wife" (1930s calypso).

6. For example, Beenie Man, "Old Dog" and "Nuff Gal" (1990s dancehall); Coupé Cloué, "Fem colloquint"; and Miami Top Vice (T-Vice), "Yo tout pou Zin" (Haitian konpa). In "Old Dog," Beenie Man states that it is simply his nature to need many women, often two or three at a time, and that he even intends to seduce his mother-in-law.

7. For example, Cortijo's "Huy que pote" (1950s Puerto Rican plena) and the colonial-era calypsos cited in Gordon Rohlehr, *Calypso and Society in Pre-Independence Trinidad* (Port of Spain: G. Rohlehr, 1990), 258–63.

8. For example, Mighty Sparrow, "Turn Them Down" (calypso); Hector Lavoe, "Bandolera"; Johnny Pacheco, "Préstame los guantes" (salsa); Daniel Santos, "Yo la mato" (bolero); and Johnny Ventura, "Dále un palo" (merengue).

9. For example, the recent Dominican merengue "La Grua (The Tow Truck)," which depicts the possessive wife dragging her husband away from his girlfriends at the dance club.

10. During an interview with one of my students, Sabrina Hannam, Beenie Man stated that he was in fact a monogamous, devoutly religious family man, and that the

playboy image was merely a commercial pose. He further asserted that he sang because God told him to, although, as she observed, "God did not specify what type of song should be sung."

11. "Si el hombre se divierta, la mujer también vacila" (pointed out to the author by Sydney Hutchinson).

12. Juan Flores, " 'Qué assimilated brother, yo soy asimilao': The Structuring of Puerto Rican Identity in the U.S.," in idem, *Divided Borders: Essays on Puerto Rican Identity* (Houston: Arte Público Press, 1993), 182–95.

13. "El Mensaje" (1975): "Te traigo un mensaje. . . . Es que tengo la clave de este ritmo guaguancó, sonido moderno de la isla del encanto, Yo le canto a mi Puerto Rico y a Los Angeles también, a Venezuela y Santo Domingo."

14. Roger Abrahams, *The Man-of-Words in the West Indies* (Baltimore: Johns Hopkins University Press, 1983), 12, 16.

15. These include occupations of the following countries: Nicaragua (1910, 1912–33), Honduras (1903, 1907, 1911–12, 1919, 1924–25), Cuba (1906–09, 1912, 1917–20, 1933–34), Mexico (1913–17, 1918–19), Panama (1921, 1925, 1989), the Dominican Republic (1916–24), and Haiti (1915–34).

16. In 1976, for example, the CIA-trained terrorist Orlando Bosch blew up a Cuban civilian airliner, killing all seventy-three people aboard. Bosch has lived in Miami since 1990, when President G. H. W. Bush intervened to terminate his short U.S. prison sentence. See, for example, Ann Louise Bardach, *Cuba Confidential: Love and Vengeance in Miami and Havana* (New York: Vintage, 2002), chap. 7.

Glossary

abakuá. An urban Afro-Cuban secret society derived from the Efik people of Calabar.

abeng. A cow's horn blown as a trumpet in Haiti, Jamaica, and elsewhere.

afranchi. Creole mulatto class in Haiti.

aguinaldo. (1) A kind of Puerto Rican *jíbaro* (peasant) music performed especially during the Christmas season. (2) A small Christmas gift.

arará. A Dahomeyan-derived Afro-Cuban sect.

areito. An Arawak socioreligious ritual with music and dance.

bachata. A romantic, guitar-based bolero style of the Dominican Republic.

balada (ballad). A sentimental Spanish-language song in mainstream, commercial pop style.

bamboula. A colonial-era name for several kinds of Afro-Caribbean dance and song forms.

bandu. The deeper voiced of the two drums normally played in traditional Jamaican kumina music on which an unvarying supporting rhythm is played.

bandurria. A Spanish-derived, mandolin-like instrument used in Cuban peasant music (especially *punto*).

bann rara. A Haitian rara band.

barriles de bomba. Bomba barrel drums.

batá. A double-headed, hourglass-shaped drum played in a trio, used in Afro-Cuban Santería music.

bélé/belair. A term for a variety of French Caribbean Afro-creole voice-and-percussion song and dance forms; in Trinidad, a creole song constituting a predecessor to calypso.

bembé. (1) In Cuba, a type of Santería party, using eponymous drums and rhythms, wherein possession may occur, despite the prevailing festive air. (2) The staved barrel drums used in the *bembè* party. (3) In some circles, a term used loosely to describe any Santería ceremony with music and dance.

benna. A creole folksong genre of Antigua.

benta. A monochord, found in Jamaica, Curaçao, and elsewhere, consisting of a long bamboo stick out of which a strip has been cut, which is struck with a stick while the strip is stopped with a gourd.

bhajan. A generic term for a Hindu devotional song, such as those sung in India and in Indo-Caribbean society.

biguine. A creole early- and mid-twentieth-century dance-music genre of Martinique and Guadeloupe.

bogle. A Jamaican popular dance style of the 1990s, named after its creator.

bolero. A romantic, danceable song in slow quadratic meter, popular through-out the Spanish Caribbean, with a characteristic bass pattern (when bass is present) of a half-note followed by two quarter-notes.

bomba. An Afro–Puerto Rican dance and music genre using barrel drums of the same name.

bombo. A Spanish drum used in military bands and in Cuban conga/*comparsa* processions.

bongó (bongo). (1) A pair of small, joined hand drums. (2) An archaic Afro-Trinidadian social-dance genre, traditionally performed at wakes.

botánica. A store selling articles pertaining to Afro-Caribbean religions, es-pecially Santería and folk Catholicism.

boulá (bulá). A name for a drum used in Haitian Vodou music, Cuban *tumba francesa,* and Carriacou "big drum" music.

bubbling. (1) A Jamaican generic term for dancing. (2) In some circles (e.g., in Suriname), a term for Jamaican dancehall music.

buru (burru). A specific style of neo-African Jamaican music, played pri-marily in the parishes of Clarendon and St. Catherine, that uses three drums and a variety of percussion instruments. The term is also used more broadly in Jamaica to refer to any music of obviously African origin.

cabildo. Town hall, chapter; in Cuba, an Afro-Cuban mutual-aid society.

cadens. See *kadans.*

cajón. Spanish; literally, "box." The wooden box sometimes used as a drum in Cuban *rumba columbia.*

calinda (kalinda). A colonial-era name for several kinds of Afro-Caribbean dance and song forms. In Trinidad, calinda was especially used to accom-pany stick fighting.

camboulay (canboulay). A nineteenth-century Afro-Trinidadian festival with drumming and dancing, derived from a plantation fire drill (from the French *cannes brulees*).

canción. Literally, "song," especially a through-composed, sentimental, slow song (cf. *balada*), not associated with dance.

canto. Spanish; literally, "chant." The first section of a rumba (synonym, *largo*).

catá (katá). A term for a drum in Cuban *tumba francesa* music and in Carriacouan "big drum" music (cf. the "cutter" lead drum in Afro-Trinidadian music and tassa drumming).

cascara. "Shell," also the term for the hollowed stick or log that is struck with two sticks in rumba and other Afro-Cuban genres.

chacha. Uncovered baskets shaken like rattles in Santiago de Cuba *comparsa*.

chachachá. A Cuban popular dance and music genre in medium tempo that flourished in the 1950s.

cha madigra. In Haitian Carnival, mobile floats carrying bands.

changüí. A creole music genre of eastern Cuba.

charanga. A Cuban dance ensemble consisting of flute, two violins, piano, bass, and percussion (originally called *charanga francesa*).

chowtal. A responsorial folksong form performed by Hindu Indo-Caribbeans during the vernal Phagwa or Holi festival, derived from the Bhojpuri region of North India.

chutney. (1) An East Indian spiced condiment. (2) A light, fast Indo-Caribbean song and dance in modernized Indian folk style.

Cibao, El. Densely populated valley of central-northern Dominican Republic.

cinquillo. A Cuban term for the rhythmic ostinato pervading danzón and related genres (in note values, long–short–long–short–long, or 8th–16th–8th–16th–8th, or x–xx–xx–).

clave. (1) Spanish, feminine; literally, "key" (especially used metaphorically), and the wooden pegs used in ships. (2) One of a pair of hard wooden sticks, struck together. (3) The characteristic ostinato played on *clave* sticks. (4) In "coros de clave," a nineteenth- and early-twentieth-century urban genre of Cuba, in 6/8 meter, sung by strolling choruses (from José Anselmo Clavé). (5) Spanish, masculine: "clavichord."

cocolo. Slang, originally a derogatory Spanish Caribbean term for black people or fans of Afro-Latin dance music; loosely, "coconut-head."

colmado. In the Dominican Republic, a neighborhood store.

columbia. One of the three main types of Cuban rumba, danced by a solo male, in what could be regarded as 12/8 meter.

comparsa. A street procession associated with Cuban Carnival, incorporating music and ambulatory dance (especially conga).

compas. See *konpa dirèk*.

conga. (1) A single-headed, Congolese-derived drum used in Cuban dance music. (2) A song and processional dance genre, characteristically used in *comparsa* processions. (3) A group that performs such a genre.

conjunto. In Afro-Latin music, a standard dance ensemble consisting of a rhythm section, two to four horns, and vocals.

contradanza. (1) A nineteenth-century Cuban salon and popular dance and music genre, known more commonly abroad as habanera, especially if sung. (2) A Spanish salon dance and music genre of the eighteenth and early nineteenth centuries.

contredanse. A French and Franco-Haitian salon and popular dance and music genre dating from the late eighteenth century.

controversia. (1) Spanish: literally, "debate, argument." (2) A Cuban and Puerto Rican campesino music genre in the form of a duel between two singers.

coro. In salsa, *son*, and other Latin musics, the "chorus" or refrain, which also functions as a hook.

cuatro. (1) Spanish; literally, "four." (2) A Puerto Rican guitar-like instrument with five doubled strings used in *jíbaro* (peasant) music. (3) A ukulele-like instrument used in Venezuela, in Suriname, and in Trinidadian parang.

cuchifrito. A kind of fried snack.

cumbia. A popular music genre of Colombia and, subsequently, Central America and elsewhere.

dancehall. A style of Jamaican popular music that arose out of reggae in the 1980s and currently remains the dominant popular style.

dantal (dand-tal, dhantal). In Indo-Caribbean and Bhojpuri Indian music, two steel rods (one long and straight, the other short and U-shaped) struck together rhythmically.

danza. (1) A popular and salon dance and music genre of Puerto Rico. (2) A roughly synonymous term for the nineteenth-century Cuban contradanza (distinguished irregularly by certain writers).

danzón. A Cuban salon music genre popular from the late nineteenth century to the mid-twentieth century.

décima. A Spanish-derived text form of ten octosyllabic lines, usually with the *espinela* rhyme scheme *abbaaccddc*.

deshoukaj. Haitian creole; literally, "uprooting." Refers to the popular attempts to destroy vestiges of the Jean-Claude Duvalier dictatorship in Haiti in the late 1980s.

dholak. The standard barrel drum used in North India and to accompany various kinds of music in Indo-Caribbean society.

dub. (1) A substyle of reggae remixes that flourished during the 1970s and early '80s, characterized by special studio effects such as fades, echo, reverb, and shifting of recorded tracks. (2) In some circles, a synonym for dancehall music.

dub plate. In dancehall, a recording (usually a 45 r.p.m. vinyl record) custom made for a sound system, in which the deejay, typically singing to the tune of an existing hit of his or hers, sings new lyrics praising the sound system.

dub poetry. A Jamaican genre of poetry (also disseminated in printed form) usually performed with reggae-style accompaniment, using Jamaican creole language and uncompromising political lyrics.

estribillo. Spanish; chorus, refrain.

etu. A Yoruba-influenced genre of neo-African music played in Western Jamaica.

fiesta patronal. In Puerto Rico and elsewhere, the festival in which a town honors its patron saint.

funde. (1) The "time-keeping" drum in traditional Rastafarian *nyabinghi* music. (2) The name of one of the three drums used in traditional buru music.

fusilamiento. Spanish; literally, "firing." In Dominican music, the adaptation of a pre-existing song to merengue format.

galleta. A military-style bass drum used in Cuban conga processions.

goombay (gumbé). A common colonial-era term denoting various kinds of Afro–West Indian drums, dances, and festivals; more specific meanings include: (1) An African-derived Jamaican religion and the neo-African music associated with it. (2) The square-frame drum used in this music, which is also used by Maroons in some communities. (3) A pre-Lenten masquerade festival in Bermuda.

guaguancó. The most popular kind of Cuban traditional rumba.

guajeo. In Cuban dance music, a melodic ostinato, especially as played by the *tres* in a *son*.

guajira. (1) A female peasant of Cuba. (2) A kind of folk and popular music associated with or eulogizing Cuban rural life (from *música guajira*). (3) In Spain, a *cante* or song type of flamenco loosely derived from Cuban peasant music.

guajiro. A Cuban peasant.

guaracha. (1) In nineteenth- and early-twentieth-century Cuba, a light, often satirical or bawdy theater song, typically alternating verse and chorus (in contrast to the *son*'s *largo–montuno* form). (2) Subsequently, in Cuba and Puerto Rico, a term (roughly synonymous with *son*) for a light, up-tempo song.

güira. A Dominican scraper, typically made of a serrated metal cylinder, scratched with a few metal prongs attached to a handle.

güiro. A gourd scraper, used especially in Cuban popular music.

habanera. (1) Alternative term for the nineteenth-century Cuban contradanza (from *contradanza habanera*, or Havana-style contradanza). (2) A slow, languid, sentimental song, especially as flourishing in early-twentieth-century Cuba.

harmonium. A hand-pumped, accordion-like keyboard instrument popular in India and in Indo-Caribbean music.

holandés. A rhythm used in Puerto Rican bomba.

iyesá. An Afro-Cuban, Yoruba-derived religious sect whose *cabildo* still exists in Matanzas.

Jab-Jab. A ghoulishly costumed stock character in Trinidad Carnival.

jíbaro. A Puerto Rican peasant, implicitly white or mulatto.

joropo. A Venezuelan folksong genre in fast 6/8 meter.

junkanoo (John Canoe). In Jamaica and other West Indian islands, a festival with music, often performed in street processions.

kadans ranpa. Haitian creole; literally, "rampart rhythm." A Haitian dance rhythm popularized by Weber Sicot in the 1950s.

kete. The ensemble of three drums used in traditional Rastafarian music, consisting of repeater, *funde*, and bass; also sometimes used to refer to the repeater drum alone.

konpa dirèk (*compas direct*). A Haitian dance rhythm popularized by Nemours Jean-Baptiste in the 1950s.

Kromanti Play. Traditional religion of the Maroons living in the Blue Mountains of eastern Jamaica.

Kumina. (1) An African-derived religion in eastern Jamaica and the neo-African music associated with it. (2) (Lowercase) The name of a new, secular, urban style of drumming that developed in Kingston and contributed to the development of *nyabinghi* drumming.

kyas (also, *playing kyas*). The higher-pitched of the two drums normally used in kumina music, which plays the more complex rhythmic patterns.

largo. The initial section of a Cuban rumba (following the short introductory *diana*), where the lead vocalist sings an extended text (synonym, *canto*; in salsa, also called *guia* or *tema*).

Latin jazz. A predominantly instrumental, latter-twentieth-century genre featuring jazz-oriented solos over Afro-Cuban rhythms, intended primarily for listening rather than for dance.

lucumí. An Afro-Cuban of Yoruba descent.

lwa (loa). A spirit in Haitian Vodou.

malimba. Haitian term for *marimbula*.

mambo. (1) An up-tempo, predominantly instrumental, big-band dance-music genre featuring antiphonal sectional arrangements for contrasting brass instruments, flourishing especially in the 1950s. (2) An instrumental interlude in the *montuno* section of a salsa or Cuban-style dance-music song (especially, one in which the chord progression departs from that of the *montuno*). (3) The vamp-like, harmonically static coda of a late-1930s and 1940s danzón. (4) A devotional song in the Afro-Cuban, Congolese-derived *Palo* religion. (5) The ostinato-based second section of a merengue often featuring call-and-response vocals (synonym, "jaleo"). (6) Among "on two" salsa dancers, a term for their style of dance, also loosely used to designate the music—for example, "on two mambo dance."

manman. The largest drum in the Haitian Vodou ensemble.

marimba. (1) In the Dominican Republic, the African-derived lamellophone, in Cuba, called marimbula. (2) Elsewhere, a xylophone with wooden keys.

marimbula. In Cuba, a lamellophone, used as a bass instrument, consisting of plucked metal keys mounted on a wooden box.

Maroon. A runaway slave or a descendant thereof (in Haitian creole, *mawon*).

masón. A dance genre in Cuban *tumba francesa* in which men and women form opposing lines and perform choreographic figures, derived from the contredanse.

mbira. One African name for a family of hand-held melodic instruments, each featuring plucked metal keys mounted on a small wooden box, with or without a gourd amplifier.

mento. A Jamaican creole folksong genre played on a variety of instruments, most typically featuring guitar, banjo, fife (or fiddle), and rhumba box (bass lamellophone).

mereng (*méringue*). A popular creole music and dance genre of Haiti, especially as flourishing in the nineteenth century and the first half of the twentieth century.

merengue. A popular creole music and dance genre of the Dominican Republic.

mini-djaz. A Haitian popular dance music of the 1960 and 1970s, especially as played by electric-guitar–based combos, perhaps with trumpets.

Moko Jumbie. A traditional stilted, costumed stock character in Trinidad Carnival, also formerly common in other Afro-Caribbean festivals.

moña. An instrumental interlude during a salsa *montuno*, similar to the second definition given for mambo, except that a moña, unlike a mambo, occurs over the same chordal ostinato used in the rest of the *montuno*.

montuno. The final, and usually longest, part of a rumba, *son*, or salsa song, employing call-and-response vocals over a rhythmic and harmonic ostinato.

ñañigo. A member of a Calabari-derived Afro-Cuban *abakuá* society.

negritud. An early-twentieth-century literary and cultural movement of the Spanish and French Caribbean, celebrating Afro-Caribbean heritage.

ngoma. (1) In Cuba, a Congolese-derived cylindrical drum. (2) In Africa, a Bantu term for a variety of regional drums and music and dance genres.

nouvel jenerasyon. Haitian creole; literally, "new generation." Haitian pop music of the 1980s and 1990s.

nueva canción. Spanish; literally, "new song." The Latin American variety of singer-songwriter music, explicitly or implicitly identifed with progressive politics and cultural policies.

nueva trova. A Cuban efflorescence of *nueva canción*.

nyabinghi. (1) A traditional, drum-based Rastafarian musical style. (2) Formal Rastafarian gatherings or ceremonies.

obeah. A body of African-derived beliefs and practices relating to medicine, ritual, and, especially, magic.

orisha. A deity or spirit in Yoruba and Afro-Caribbean Yoruba-derived religions.

orquesta típica. In the second half of the nineteenth century, a Cuban horn-dominated ensemble primarily playing danzón and contradanza, consisting of cornet, trombone, *figle, bombardino* (saxhorn), two clarinets, two or more violins, contrabass, *timbales*, and güiro.

oru del igbodú. The initial, semiprivate part of a Santería ceremony during which a suite of drum "salutes" to the orishas is performed before an altar.

palitos. Spanish; literally, "little sticks," such as those used to play rhythmic ostinatos on the side of a drum or a log (or *cascara*) in traditional rumba and other Afro-Cuban genres.

palo. Spanish; literally, "stick." (1) A Congolese-derived Afro-Cuban religion. (2) Drums used in Afro-Dominican music and, by extension, the music itself (e.g., "*música de palo(s)*").

pandereta (pandero). A jingle-less tambourine (frame drum) used in Puerto Rico and elsewhere.

parang. A Trinidadian Christmas-season song and dance genre of Venezuelan derivation (from the Spanish *parranda*, "spree, party").

paseo. Promenade. In traditional bomba, merengue, and contradanza, an initial ambulatory choreographic figure.

perico ripiao. Spanish; literally, "ripped parrot." The traditional style of Cibao merengue, played on a ensemble of accordion, *tambora*, güira, and optional saxophone and marimba.

picong. A musical verbal duel between two calypso singers (from the French *piquant*, "spicy").

piquete. In bomba dancing, a move or pattern.

playing kyas. See *kyas.*

plena. A creole song form of Puerto Rico that exists in both acoustic and dance-band versions.

Poco. Shorter, more common term for Pocomania.

Pocomania (Pukkumina). A blanket term for the Afro-Protestant religions that developed in Jamaica during the nineteenth century, as well as for the music associated with them; also sometimes used to refer to a specific, more African branch of the larger category of religions known as Revival.

polyrhythm (polymeter). A composite rhythmic structure combining two or more regular meters (most typically, a repeating 12/8 pattern internally subdivided into duple and triple pulses).

ponche. (1) Spanish; literally, "punch." (2) In salsa, a rhythmic break (set to the second and third beats of the "three" part of the "two–three" *clave* pattern). (3) In bomba dancing, an abrupt, jerky move that initiates the rendering of other moves (*piquetes*) and the interaction with the drummer.

pork-knocker. A Guyanese gold prospector.

punta. A folk music and dance genre of the Garifuna (Black Caribs) of coastal Honduras and Belize.

punto. In Cuba, the musical rendering of a *décima.*

quadrille (kwadril). In the British and French Caribbean, a dance, with accompanying music, generally involving a series of choreographic figures performed by men and women arranged in squares or a circle.

que-que. An Afro-Guyanese song and dance form, with call-and-response singing, typically performed at weddings.

quinto. Spanish; literally, "fifth." The higher-pitched conga in Cuban rumba.

ragga. (1) In some contexts and regions, Jamaican dancehall music. (2) Dancehall using a synthesized rather than acoustic soundtrack.

raggamuffin. (1) A substyle of Jamaican dancehall music that developed in the late 1980s. (2) Since at least the 1970s in Jamaica, a poor young resident of the ghetto.

ranchera. A popular sentimental song genre of northern Mexico and Tex-Mex music.

Rara. Haitian street celebrations, with music provided by *bann rara* (Rara bands).

Rastafari (Rastafarianism). A politico-religious movement that developed in Jamaica in the 1930s and has since grown to become a world religion. Its original prophets proclaimed the divinity of Emperor Haile Selassie (Ras

Tafari) of Ethiopia and predicted the imminent repatriation of the faithful to Africa.

reggae. A specific genre of Jamaican popular music that developed around 1968 and remained the dominant form until the early or mid-1980s. Since the late 1960s, however, the term has often been used to refer to all styles of Jamaican popular music, including dancehall.

reggaetón. A genre of Hispanic Caribbean (especially Puerto Rican) popular music. It is regarded as a Spanish-language counterpart of dancehall, although it has its own distinctive style and rhythm.

repeater. The highest-pitched of the Rastafarian drums used in traditional *nyabinghi* music, which plays the more complex rhythmic patterns.

Revival. A blanket term for the indigenous Afro-Protestant religions that developed in Jamaica during the nineteenth century, as well as the music associated with them (see also Poco, Pocomania).

rhumba box. A Jamaican bass instrument with plucked metal lamellae; equivalent to Cuban *marimbula* and Dominican *marimba*.

riddim. A Jamaican term (derived from "rhythm") used to refer to the underlying recorded rhythm tracks that are often recycled to create new songs or to back deejay lyrics in Jamaican popular music. A "riddim" is usually defined by a bass melody and the basic accompanying drum patterns.

rockero (roquero). In Puerto Rico and elsewhere, one who likes rock music (as opposed, for example, to *cocolos*, who prefer Latin music).

rock steady. A Jamaican popular music style that supplanted ska and was dominant around 1966–68.

rumba. (1) An Afro-Cuban secular dance and music genre, with voice and percussion (congas, *palitos*, and *clave*). (2) In informal and imprecise usage, a *son* or other popular song evocative of a traditional rumba.

salsa dura (also *salsa caliente*). "Strong," "hot," hard-driving salsa music, as opposed to *salsa romántica*.

salsa romántica (also *salsa sensual*). "Romantic," "sensual," sentimental salsa, as emerged in the 1980s, with a softer, less percussive sound and exclusively romantic lyrics.

sans humanité. French; literally, "without mercy." A standard and essentially meaningless rhetorical phrase (corrupted to *santimanitey*) inserted at the end of early-twentieth-century calypso verses (later replaced by "in this colony" and, after 1962, "in this country").

Santería. A Yoruba-derived Afro-Cuban religion, also called Regla de Ocha.

segon. An accompanying drum in Haitian Vodou music.

seis. Spanish; literally, "six." The most important subgenre of Puerto Rican peasant (*jíbaro*) music; also a kind of simple dance done by altar boys in the cathedral of Seville, Spain.

shak-shak. In the West Indies, a shaker or maracas.

ska. A Jamaican popular music that emerged in the early 1960s derived in part from American rhythm and blues.

soberao. In bomba dancing, the ring of people around the dancer.

son. The most popular Cuban music and dance genre of the twentieth century.

songo. A modern Afro-Cuban dance-music rhythm popularized in the 1970s by Los Van Van.

soukous. A popular Congolese dance-music genre.

spouge. A creole Barbadian song form, or the distinctive rhythm used therein.

subidor. In Puerto Rican bomba, the lead drum.

tabla. A North Indian drum pair used in classical and light-classical music.

tambora. Spanish, "drum." The double-headed drum used in Dominican merengue.

tambú. (1) A genre of neo-African music played in western Jamaica that is rhythmically similar to kumina music. (2) A Maroon genre of drumming and song within kromanti play that has been influenced by kumina music. (3) In Curaçao, a traditional voice-and-percussion genre that shares some features with Cuban rumba.

tan. In North Indian classical music, a fast melodic run.

tan singing. Indo-Caribbean "local classical" music.

tassa. A shallow kettle drum and the ensemble that it leads (also containing *dhol* barrel drums), derived from India, currently used in Trinidad to entertain at Hindu weddings and enliven the Shi'a Moharrum or Hossay commemoration.

tcha-tcha. The Haitian term for maracas (small gourd rattles).

telenovela. Spanish; literally, "television soap opera."

tigueraje. Spanish; literally, "tigerness." Dominican slang for feistiness, vigor.

timba. (1) Cuban dance music that emerged in the 1990s and typically features aggressive, jazz-informed horn riffs, shouted multiple *coros*, and lyrics commenting wryly on contemporary street life. (2) In traditional Cuban parlance, (a) sexuality (e.g., "*tener timba*"); (b) a group of gamblers; (c) rowdiness, noise, excitement ("*hay mucha timba allá*").

timbales. In Latin music, a pair of metal drums, usually mounted on a stand, with a cowbell.

típico. (1) Traditional. (2) Typical (especially, typical of a given country or region).

toasting. A type of indigenous Jamaican rapping by deejays that came to dominate Jamaican popular music during the dancehall era of the 1980s.

toque de santo. A Santería ceremony with music and dance.

tres. Spanish; literally, "three." A Cuban guitar-like instrument with three doubled courses, usually tuned D–G–B.

tuk. Barbadian ensemble featuring snare and bass drums and flute.

tumba francesa. (1) A Haitian-derived mutual-aid and social-recreation society of eastern Cuba. (2) The characteristic music and dance form of such societies.

tumbador. The lower-piched congas used in rumba.

twoubadou. Haitian creole, "troubador." A Haitian singer of topical or popular songs, usually accompanied by guitar, maracas (*tcha-tcha*), *malimba*, and *tanbou* drum.

vaksin. A bamboo trumpet used in Haitian Rara and Dominican *gagá* bands.

vallenato (*música vallenata*). An accordion- and vocal-dominated folk and popular music genre of northeastern Colombia.

vejigante. In the Fiesta de Santiago Apóstol of Loíza, Puerto Rico, a ghoulishly costumed stock character (from the Spanish *vejiga*, "bladder").

velación. In the Dominican Republic, a nightlong ceremony and social dance with Afro-Dominican music.

Vodou (Voodoo, Vodun, Voudoun). The Afro-Haitian religion, primarily of Dahomeyan and Congolese derivation.

yambú. One of the three extant forms of Afro-Cuban traditional rumba, with a rhythm and dance style similar to that of the *guaguancó* but somewhat slower.

yanvalou. A polyrhythmic Haitian Vodou rhythm.

yeye. The 1960s Haitian term for rock music (from the Beatles' "She loves you, yeah, yeah, yeah").

yuba. (1) A *tumba frances*a dance during part of which a man dances in front of a drum laid horizontally on the floor. (2) A term for other archaic, now extinct Afro-Caribbean dances.

zapateo. A Spanish-derived, nearly extinct Cuban folk dance that features heel stomping (cf. Spanish *zapateado*).

zarabanda (sarabanda, sarabande). (1) A Congolese spirit worshiped in Cuba. (2) An Afro-Latin music and dance genre, perhaps originating in New Spain (Mexico), that flourished in Spain in the decades around 1600. (3) A seventeenth-century Baroque classical stylization of the Afro-Latin music and dance genre that flourished in Spain around 1600.

zarzuela. Spanish and Spanish Caribbean light opera.

zouk. A popular dance music of Martinique and Guadeloupe.

Index

311

PETER MANUEL is professor of music at John Jay College and the CUNY Graduate Center. He is the author of five books and many articles on musics of India, the Caribbean, Spain, and elsewhere. He also plays sitar, jazz piano, and flamenco guitar.

KENNETH BILBY is a research associate in the Department of Anthropology, Smithsonian Institution.

MICHAEL LARGEY is associate professor of music at Michigan State University, East Lansing.